SHAKESPEARE IN UKRAINE

Mirror, Prism, Megaphone

Shakespeare in Ukraine

Mirror, Prism, Megaphone

IRENA R. MAKARYK

UNIVERSITY OF TORONTO PRESS
Toronto Buffalo London

ISBN 978-1-4875-6597-8 (cloth)   ISBN 978-1-4875-6599-2 (EPUB)
ISBN 978-1-4875-6598-5 (uPDF)

Library and Archives Canada Cataloguing in Publication

Title: Shakespeare in Ukraine : mirror, prism, megaphone / Irena R. Makaryk.
Names: Makaryk, Irene Rima, author
Description: Includes bibliographical references and index.
Identifiers: Canadiana (print) 20250176645 | Canadiana (ebook) 20250178966 |
ISBN 9781487565978 (cloth) | ISBN 9781487565992 (EPUB) |
ISBN 9781487565985 (PDF)
Subjects: LCSH: Shakespeare, William, 1564-1616—Appreciation—Ukraine. |
LCSH: Shakespeare, William, 1564-1616—Stage history—Ukraine. |
LCSH: Shakespeare, William, 1564-1616—In literature. |
LCSH: Theater and society—Ukraine.
Classification: LCC PR2971.U5 M35 2025 | DDC 822.3/3—dc23

Cover design: Mary Beth MacLean
Cover image: Daria Hrachova as Titania, *A Midsummer Night's Dream*,
directed by Andrii Bilous. Photo by Sofiia Sanina.
With the kind permission of the Kyiv Molodyi Theatre.

We wish to acknowledge the land on which the University of Toronto Press
operates. This land is the traditional territory of the Wendat, the Anishnaabeg, the
Haudenosaunee, the Métis, and the Mississaugas of the Credit First Nation.

This publication was made possible in part by the financial support of the Canadian
Foundation for Ukrainian Studies.

University of Toronto Press acknowledges the financial support of the Government of
Canada, the Canada Council for the Arts, and the Ontario Arts Council, an agency of
the Government of Ontario, for its publishing activities.

Canada Council
for the Arts

Conseil des Arts
du Canada

Funded by the   Financé par le
Government   gouvernement
of Canada   du Canada

Canada

Канадська
фундація
українських
студій

Canadian Foundation
for Ukrainian Studies

Fondation canadienne
des etudes ukrainiennes

Contents

List of Illustrations

Acknowledgments

An academic career of well over forty years inevitably involves accumulation: of mentors, colleagues, friendships, students, ideas, and memories – to say nothing of books and things. As Shakespeare well knew, at truly important moments in life, words fail. "Thanks" seems to be a very small word indeed for all the good fortune I have experienced during these years, but this word will nonetheless have to stand as the simple theme of this Acknowledgments page.

While writing my dissertation on Shakespeare's comedies under the supervision of the witty and wise Sheldon Zitner at the University of Toronto, I began work on my first article ("Soviet Views of Shakespeare's Comedies," 1982[1]) that also served as the subject of my job talk for a position at the University of Ottawa. Since then, I have sporadically returned to examining Shakespeare performance and reception in Ukraine while also reaching out to other areas of Shakespeare reception (Canada, Afghanistan, Russia) and to various aspects of theatre history (Paris, New York, the Arctic). The thread that ties together these various publications and research interests has been the inestimable value of culture, especially as solace and inspiration during periods of great social and political upheaval.

I was teaching a graduate course on "Shakespeare and War" in 2022 when Russia began its full-scale invasion and war on Ukraine. What had hitherto been, for me, history and theory, suddenly became awful reality. Yet, ironically, this terrible moment strengthened ties among Shakespearean colleagues. Indeed, the worldwide Shakespearean network has been an invaluable source of support to Ukrainian scholars who continue to teach Shakespeare in bunkers, basements, and hallways; they amazingly also still publish, supervise graduate student projects, and organize online conferences and events.

My generation, like that of thousands of Ukrainian descent, has led a double life. Born in Canada to displaced persons fleeing both Nazi and Soviet forces, we attended public school in the daytime and Ukrainian school in the evening; high school was followed by a Saturday morning program of Ukrainian studies in history, literature, culture, geography, grammar, and religion. The program culminated in *matura*, an oral examination carried out by a panel of teachers and chaired by a neutral outsider, a professor from an Ontario university. This exigent academic program was fashioned by remarkable, accomplished teachers, many with PhDs, who were determined to ensure that Ukraine's complex history and rich culture would be understood, passed on, and not be erased from memory. Among the luminaries-refugees who taught at my Saturday morning school was the renowned archaeologist Yaroslav Pasternak, professor at Lviv University, who had taken part in over sixty archaeological digs including that of the ancient princely city of Halych.

The essays in this volume are thus, in some part, a result of that education. As I hope they show, Shakespeare's works have served in many capacities and in various troubled periods of Ukraine's history. The following chapters are presented in historical chronological order rather than the order in which they were originally written and published. I am deeply grateful to the various editors and publishers of journals and of collections, all noted below, for permission to reprint these articles and book chapters. Each chapter has been revised, in varying degrees, and updated to include more recent sources. Some repetition of historical facts, a result of the essays' original stand-alone status, has been retained in cases where such an excision might materially affect the argument.

Serving as an introduction, Chapter One begins with the present moment and then turns back to the nineteenth century, sketching out the long, arduous path to acquiring the right to read, study, and perform Shakespeare in Ukrainian. Chapter Two, "Calibans All: Shakespeare at the Intersection of Colonialisms," first appeared in *Multicultural Shakespeare: Translation, Appropriation, Performance* (2004).[2] Chapter Three, "'North by North West': Shevchenko and Shakespeare," a conference paper, was published in *Slavic Drama: A Question of Innovation, Proceedings* (1991).[3] Chapter Four, "Ophelia as Poet: Lesya Ukrainka and the Woman as Artist," first appeared in *Canadian Review of Comparative Literature / Revue Canadienne de Littérature Comparée* (1993).[4] Chapter Five, "Periphery against Centre: *Hamlet* in Early Soviet Ukrainian Poetry," was first published in *Living Record: Essays in Memory of Constantine Bida* (1991).[5] The work of the theatrical giant, Les Kurbas, has been the subject of many of my articles as well as a book-length study, *Shakespeare in the Undiscovered Bourn* (2004).[6] Here, I have included just two articles focusing on Kurbas's productions of *Macbeth* and its reception: Chapter Six; "Shakespeare Right and Wrong," was published in *Theatre Journal* (1998), and Chapter Seven, "The Perfect Production: Les Kurbas's Analysis of the Early Soviet Audience," in *Gramma: Journal of Theory and Criticism* (2007).[7] Chapter Eight, "*Hamlet*, 1943," an extensively revised paper, was originally titled "Wartime Shakespeare" and published in *Shakespeare in the Worlds of Communism and Socialism* (2006).[8] The topic of Shakespeare during in the Stalinist period of the 1930s and 1940s forms the subject of Chapter Nine, "In a Crooked Mirror: *Hamlet* as Intertext in the USSR 1934–43." An earlier version, "Shakespeare Inside Out: *Hamlet* as Intertext in the USSR 1934–43," was published in *Shakespeare in Cold War Europe: Conflict, Commemoration, Celebration* (2016).[9] Chapter Nine also incorporates sections from "Stalin and Shakespeare," published in *International Shakespeare Yearbook* (2021).[10] Chapter Ten, "Commemoration as Amplification: The 'Universal' versus the National Bard," appeared as "Divergence and Convergence: The 'Universal' versus the National Bard," in *Memorialising Shakespeare. Commemoration and Collective Identity* (2022).[11] As Chapter Eleven reveals, Les Kurbas's theatrical work continues to influence and astonish, even in this century. This chapter looks at Kurbas's use of the cabaret tradition in his 1924 *Macbeth*. "Antic Dispositions: Shakespeare, War and Cabaret" was published in *Shakespeare Survey* (2019).[12] The chapter has been expanded to reflect Shakespeare's function and status within the charged circumstances of Russia's current war on Ukraine. The volume closes with an "Afterword: Shakespeare at War Today" and gives the final word to Professor Nataliya Torkut, Director of the Shakespeare Centre in Zaporizhzhia, Ukraine. The text of the formal toast, "To the Immortal Memory of William Shakespeare," she delivered on 23 April 2023 in Stratford-upon-Avon is reprinted here with her permission.

Early versions of many of the chapters in this book saw first light at research seminars, panels, and presentations at specialized conferences. I am particularly grateful to colleagues who offered thoughtful comments to my work presented at the following meetings and conferences: Canadian Association of Slavists' Annual Conference (Halifax, 1981); "Slavic Drama: The Question of Innovation" (University of Ottawa, 1991); "Shakespeare and Communisms" (Penn State, 1994); "Nationalist and Intercultural Aspects of Shakespeare Reception," Seminar, Shakespeare Association of America (Philadelphia, 1994); "Shakespeare and the World of Communism" (Folger Shakespeare Library, 1996); "The Uses of Shakespeare," Seminar, International Shakespeare Association Meeting (Los Angeles, 1996); "Shakespeare and Theatrical Modernism"

(McGill University, 1997); "Theatre and Nation," Waterloo Elizabethan Conference 16 (1997); "Nineteenth Century Shakespeare," Seminar, Shakespeare Association of America (Montreal, 2000); World Congress of the International Council on Central and East European Studies (Berlin, 2005); "Ukrainian Modern Art: Modernity, Identity, Tradition," Symposium (University of Toronto, 2007); "Ukrainian Modernism" Symposium (Harvard University, 2007); Shevchenko Scientific Society, Canada (Toronto 2010); Shevchenko Society of America (New York, 2011); "History, Memory, Performance" Conference (University of Ottawa, 2012); "Cold War Shakespeare," Panel, Shakespeare 450. Société Française Shakespeare (Paris, France, 2014); "Modernism Symposium," Ukrainian Museum (New York, 2015); University of York Shakespeare Festival (York, UK, 2015); "Celebrating National Bards Symposium" (Penn State, 2016); and at the various meetings of the International Shakespeare Conference at Stratford-upon-Avon (2008, 2010, 2012, 2018).

Yet a few other words of thanks must be recorded. First, expressions of deep gratitude to the University of Ottawa, where I have spent the past forty-four years and where I have received consistent support and encouragement in all my endeavours. Special thanks to the Canadian Foundation for Ukrainian Studies for financially supporting the publication of this volume with the University of Toronto Press. I have had a long and fruitful professional relationship with the Press's various editors and designers, especially with Suzanne Rancourt, Editorial Director, Humanities, who has been involved directly or indirectly with many of my publications, with Richard Ratzlaff with whom I worked on books before 2018, and with Stephen Shapiro, Acquisitions Editor for this volume and for my previous book, *April in Paris*. Notably, the University of Toronto Press was one of the first major academic publishers in the world to take on a series in Ukrainian studies. The Press continues to maintain that ever more significant role today. Much gratitude for the work of all the anonymous reviewers who, over the years and including in this instance, have taken the time to carefully read and make valuable suggestions and comments to my manuscripts.

A few other words of thanks are in order: Larysa Bilous for preparing the Index and for reviewing my transliterations; Henri Feist, one my former students at the University of Ottawa, for assistance in converting four of my older papers from pdf to a workable Word format and saving me from much technological anguish and gnashing of teeth; Anna Vozna, PhD candidate in Political Science, for retyping the Cyrillic passages in Chapter Four and thus freeing me up from the laborious task of two-finger typing of Ukrainian text; Larissa Zajac, for her cheerful support of all my projects; historians Natalia Zajac, and her husband,

Ethan Menchinger, for the important precisions they suggested to my Introduction. Most of all, thanks without end to my yoke-mate, fellow sharer in the world's pleasures and troubles, the first reader of my work, and my unfailing supporter, my husband, Yaroslaw Zajac.

This book is dedicated to all those in Ukraine who, despite the horrors of war, nonetheless continue to write, perform, and create. They are the defenders and keepers of the spark of the human spirit; they are those who inspire *us*.

A Note on Transliteration

Throughout the text, the spelling of Ukrainian and Russian names has been simplified for ease of reading. Thus, "Starytsky" rather than "Staryts'kyi," "Zelensky" rather than "Zelens'kyy"; however, when known, I have used the spelling of the names of the creators that they themselves use in English (e.g., Nataliya Torkut, not "Nataliia"), even at the risk of some inconsistency. The endnotes, however, follow a modified Library of Congress System of transliteration including hard and soft signs but no ligatures.

SHAKESPEARE IN UKRAINE

Mirror, Prism, Megaphone

1

Introduction – Shakespeare in Ukraine: Mirror, Prism, Megaphone

Just days after Russia's sudden invasion of Ukraine on 24 February 2022, Ukrainian president Volodymyr Zelensky solemnly addressed the British Parliament. Invoking Shakespeare's *Hamlet*, he forcefully asserted Ukraine's response to the Danish Prince's existential question: "to be."[1] No allusion could be briefer nor more easily understood. As one of the most translated phrases in literature, these two simple words nonetheless carried complex depths of meaning: the gravity of the threat to Ukraine's existence and the equally firm determination to defend Ukraine's sovereignty in the face of unprovoked aggression. In effect, this concise allusion acted as a metaphorical megaphone, asserting Ukraine's right to exist and, as importantly, Ukrainians' identification with Western cultural markers and values. Hamlet's "to be" not only linked Ukraine to Britain but beyond, to international like-minded states around the globe.

The President's turn to Shakespeare in the early days of the war was not the only one. Another Shakespearean moment spontaneously arose shortly after the President's public address, also only days after the war began. In Ivano-Frankivsk on 7 March 2022, citizens huddled together for a performance of *Hamlet* in the basement of the Ivan Franko National Academic Music and Drama Theatre, the only reasonably safe venue that could serve as a bomb shelter in that city, Directed by Rostyslav Derzhypilsky, the quickly arranged performance was a revival of an earlier production created in the same space. Now it was being performed while taking on the additional function of sheltering its audience from air strikes. British scholar Michael Dobson, an eyewitness of the 2018 production, described the venue as "a cavernous concrete basement, only partly full of heating ducts and obsolete electrical equipment…pointedly built on top of a German war cemetery" that provided "the opportunity to set the most famous gravediggers in world drama to work in close proximity to some real graves." To reach this "shadowy modern crypt," spectators "were led through dark passages and down rusting stairs…by hooded figures carrying candles." Once there, the spectators saw

> among the broken floor tiles and rusting cables the principal characters in Shakespeare's play were laid out on biers as if dead….Selectively revived in turns by a sort of black mass…the cast of *Hamlet* were compelled once more to enact the fatal events which had convened this feast in Death's eternal cell, in a mode that combined the nakedly and convincingly traumatic with a Goth-influenced rock soundtrack and some exquisite passages of wordless dance. In a frightening, potentially endless postmodern limbo, its prince, denied the certainty even of his own mortality, had gone to sleep only to dream, and they weren't nice dreams. The whole play…[was] as fiercely capable as ever of shaking our disposition with thoughts beyond the reaches of our souls.[2]

Utilizing this same evocative, haunting, space in 2022, Derzhypilsky chose not to stage a reassuring, amusing entertainment for his anxious spectators but, instead, to reprise his thought provoking, edgy production of *Hamlet*. This time, however, the Danish Prince, played by Oleksiy Hnatkovsky, came on stage draped in the Ukrainian flag, a poignant rallying gesture visually signalling the existence of Ukraine, its bonds with the "universal" Bard, and with the West. Shakespeare's play mirrored Ukraine's existential question. Pointedly recalling another international moment of historical crisis, Derzhypilsky and his actors publicly dedicated their production to the people of the United Kingdom for both unhesitatingly supporting Ukraine and in recognition of what British civilians themselves had endured during the Blitz of the Second World War. A distillation of memory, identity, and trauma, *Hamlet* thus also simultaneously served as a wellspring of human connection and empathy.

Canadian scholar Annie Brisset has reminded us that theatre, the most social of the arts, "grows directly out of a society, its collective imagination and symbolic representations, and its system of ideas and values." Unlike other literary genres, theatre must stay "close to the collectivity," especially in periods in which the collectivity feels imperilled.[3] For these reasons, theatre makes a particularly effective genre by which to examine assumptions about cultural identity, memory, and value. Shakespeare, the playwright most often considered "beyond nationality," and the property of many cultures and nations, presents a useful prism through which to view Ukraine's cultural history. Conversely, Ukraine is able to speak to the rest of the world through the amplified voice of Shakespeare whose works that have become, in effect, a shared, understood language, a kind of cultural Esperanto.

The trans-historical and trans-geographical connections encapsulated by the two moments at the very start of the Russian war on Ukraine potently reveal Shakespeare's significance to the cultural history of Ukraine. In part, this importance lies in the fact that access to his works was long forbidden. Although Ukrainians first encountered Shakespeare in the late eighteenth century, they were only permitted to read or see his works in a foreign language. Divided between the Austro-Hungarian and the Russian empires in the eighteenth century, Ukraine was subject to the assimilatory practices and censorship of the officialdom of both major powers. German-language and Polish touring companies brought productions of Shakespeare's tragedies to Lviv, the most important city of Right-Bank Ukraine (that is, on the Right or West side of the Dnipro River). Right-Bank Ukraine included Galicia, Bukovina, Podolia, and a part of Volyn (most of it ceded to Russia after 1793) and now all in Western Ukraine. In Eastern or Left-Bank Ukraine, in the major city of Kharkiv, a spectator attending the theatre could see Russian-language stage productions. Left-Bank Ukraine included the regions of what today are Chernihiv, Poltava, Sumy, as well as eastern parts of the Kyiv and Cherkasy regions.

During the second half of the seventeenth century, Left-Bank Ukraine gradually fell under Muscovite control and, in the following century, eventually under its domination. The complicated geopolitical history of this period has been analysed by many historians, including, most recently, by internationally renowned historian Serhii Plokhy in his concise history of Ukraine.[4] Two events, in particular, left a lasting wound. One was a social transformation, the culmination of a process initiated much earlier: the enserfment of hundreds of thousands of peasants living on gentry estates. Another was the political and physical destruction of the Hetmanate state and, in 1775, of its main fortress, the Zaporozhian Sich (razed to the ground), on the direct orders of Catherine II (1762–96).[5] The Hetmanate had been an early democratic-like state located in an autonomous region in south-eastern Ukraine near what today is (was) the Kakhovka Reservoir. (The Reservoir was blown up by the Russians during the war in 2022, resulting in massive ecological damage through flooding of the lower part of the river.) At the Zaporozhian Sich, all decisions including the election of its leader, the Hetman, were made by its highest authority, the assembly, whose members included many different ethnicities, among them, Ukrainians, Moldavians, Tatars, Poles, Lithuanians, Jews, and Russians. Many were outlaws, runaway serfs, and slaves seeking freedom, but there were also peasants, merchants, and members of the minor nobility. A military and political organization, the Zaporozhian Cossacks was created to defend its settlers from raiding incursions by the Ottoman Turks, as well as to continue to battle for their continued independence from the many outlying, encircling, political entities. Once destroyed, this region was promptly annexed to Russia. Today, Zaporizhzhia retains a special, even mythological, potency for many Ukrainians for which it represents a centuries-old tradition of freedom, democracy, and desire for independence. It is perhaps not surprising that, in 2009, the Ukrainian Shakespeare Centre was created and took firm root in Zaporizhzhia.

Beyond eighteenth century territorial incursions and annexations, Russian control over Ukraine extended to cultural and linguistic domains. While audiences could enjoy Shakespeare in Russian, they were prevented from doing so in their native language by censorship and through a series of tsarist decrees and memoranda. At the height of the prohibitions, during the reign of Alexander II (1855–81) a secretly distributed Circular written by Pyotr Valuev, Minister of the Interior, infamously declared that "no separate Little Russian [i.e., Ukrainian] language ever existed, does exist, or ever could exist." A little over a decade later, the 1876 Ems Ukaz (decree), signed by the tsar, banned the importation and publication of all books in and translations into Ukrainian, including the Bible and Shakespeare. In 1881, the teaching of the Ukrainian language in public schools and its use in church sermons was prohibited. All theatre performances were banned. Librarians were instructed to remove all Ukrainian books in print from their shelves. Even Ukrainian folksongs, when publicly performed, had to be sung in Russian or in another foreign language[6]

Other restrictions remained in place up to 1917 and were never officially rescinded. These included limitations on subject matter and genre: domestic and folkloric themes only, but no satire, history, romantic verse plays, or plays of urban life. Upper and middle-class characters were required to speak Russian, peasants and children, Ukrainian. Further, Ukrainian plays were allowed only if a Russian play was staged first on the same night and consisted of the same number of acts. Such constraints encouraged both national stereotypes (the Ukrainian equivalent of the stage Irishman), and generic ones: sentimental and melodramatic plays with obligatory musical and dance numbers featuring large choirs dressed in authentic embroidered shirts.[7]

Authorization to play Shakespeare never came. Tsarist censors refused permission to stage *Hamlet* because, they argued, a Ukrainian production might evoke laughter in its presumption to treat a world classic in a "peasant" language.[8] Ukrainian Shakespeare could only be performed privately, at the home of trusted friends. Thus, Shakespeare acquired a special cachet, and his works became associated with the desire for independent cultural self-expression. Full liberty for the Ukrainian theatre, however brief, was to come, paradoxically, only with the chaos of world war, revolution, and civil war.

Chapter Two of this volume, "Calibans All: Shakespeare at the Intersection of Colonialisms," initiates the story of Ukrainian engagement with Shakespeare by focusing on the arrival of Ira Aldridge in the Russian empire. Shakespeare's works as performed by this magnificent Black American actor served as mirrors of colonialisms, and, at the same time, as cultural mediators through which a remarkable friendship developed between Aldridge (1807–67) and social revolutionary, poet, writer, and artist Taras Shevchenko (1814–61). A great admirer of Shakespeare whom he read in Russian (in the absence of Ukrainian translations) and also possibly in the French that he studied at the Academy of Arts, Shevchenko would have known the Bard's works as melodramatic theatrical pieces; they were also generally portrayed in such a manner on Russian stages. Shevchenko's short-lived experiments with creating drama revealed his embrace of a melodramatic aesthetic that he would have assumed was also espoused by Shakespeare. Shevchenko's dramas and their connection to a "Shakespearean" aesthetic are examined in Chapter Three, 'North by North West': Shevchenko and Shakespeare."

Touring extensively in the Russian empire, Aldridge created a sensation between 1861 and 1866 when he performed in various Ukrainian cities. Igniting a passion for Shakespeare, Aldridge provided a model and the inspiration for continuing the struggle to establish a distinctly Ukrainian theatre. As Aldridge's fame spread, a young man named Ivan Tobilevych (1845–1907) determinedly walked sixty kilometres to see Aldridge perform.[9] Later himself becoming an actor, playwright, and a founder of the Ukrainian Theatre of Koryfeiv (Theatre of Coryphaei; that is, Theatre of Star Actors), Tobilevych (stage name: Ivan Karpenko-Kary) fondly recalled that his passionate love for the stage had stemmed from Aldridge's powerful performances.[10]

Despite an intense desire, an independent Ukrainian theatre was only created in the twentieth century. Following the 1905 Revolution, when the Ems Ukaz was rescinded, the first stationary theatres were finally permitted to be created. In 1907, Tobilevych's brother, Mykola Sadovsky (stage name; 1856–1933), was able to establish the first stationary Ukrainian theatre. (Earlier, some limited touring had been possible but performance in Kyiv was prohibited.) This was an event of extraordinary national-cultural import – as significant as the creation of the Abbey Theatre for the Irish. Reflecting the long, arduous route to cultural enfranchisement under imperialist conditions, Sadovsky, actor, director, and theatre entrepreneur, adopted a crown of thorns as his troupe's

Figure 1.1. *Hamlet: A Tragedy in Five Acts* by W. Shakespeare. Translated into Ukrainian by M. Starytsky, 1882.

emblem. The third brother in this remarkable theatrical family, actor Panas Saksahansky (stage name; 1859–1940), was also a deep admirer of Shakespeare and went on to translate and direct a successful Ukrainian production of *Othello* in 1926.[11]

Translations of Shakespeare into Ukrainian formed the necessary, foundational step in conceiving of a production. The first amateur performance of excerpts from *Hamlet* in Ukrainian took place in private in Kyiv while Ukraine was still under imperial rule. Translated, directed by, and starring Mykhailo Starytsky (1840–1904) in the title role, the play was accompanied by music especially written for the occasion by the brilliant Ukrainian composer Mykola Lysenko (1842–1912). Despite censorship regulations, Starytsky dared to publish the full text of his translation, an event which raised a storm of controversy. Following Starytsky, writers Panas Myrny (*King Lear*, 1897; 1849–1920), and Lesya Ukrainka (*Macbeth*, excerpt, 1897) undertook to translate Shakespeare. Other translators included prominent figures of the Ukrainian theatre such as Marko Kropyvnytsky (*Othello*, 1906; 1840–1910) and the aforementioned Panas Saksahansky (*Othello*, 1925).

Poet and dramatist Lesya Ukrainka (pen name of Larysa Kosach-Kvitka; 1871–1913) frequently alluded to the works of Shakespeare, particularly in her poetry, as is discussed in Chapter Four, "Ophelia as Poet: Lesya Ukrainka and the Woman as Artist." Born in Western Ukraine to a family of deep intellectual interests (her mother was also a writer), Ukrainka travelled extensively throughout Europe and the Middle East because of her health. She brought to Ukrainian literature a vast knowledge of various traditions, both ancient and contemporary, and created a conspectus of essential works that she believed must be translated so that Ukrainians could aspire to become equal partners at the European high cultural table. Among these essentials were the works of Shakespeare.

The most influential and enthusiastic promoters of Shakespeare in the late nineteenth and early twentieth centuries were Panteleimon Kulish (1819–97) and Ivan Franko (1856–1916). Kulish, himself a major writer of historical fiction, was also a prolific translator of Shakespeare. His translations, published in Western Ukraine, included *Othello*, *Troilus and Cressida*, and *Comedy of Errors* (1882); *Hamlet* (1889); *Coriolanus*, *Macbeth*, *The Taming of the Shrew*, *Julius Caesar* (1900); *Antony and Cleopatra*, *Much Ado About Nothing*, *Romeo and Juliet* (1901); and *King Lear*, *Measure for Measure* (1902), Proclaiming Shakespeare a "Homer of the New World," Kulish expressed his admiration in his poetic manifesto, "To Shakespeare," in which he also underscored the importance of the Bard for Ukrainian culture especially as a means by which Ukrainians could signal their Europeanness. The introductions to Kulish's translations were provided by the equally prolific poet, scholar, novelist, and literary editor Ivan Franko, the founder of Shakespeare scholarly studies in Western Ukraine, where, under Austro-Hungarian rule, censorship laws were more relaxed. In addition to publishing twelve research papers on Shakespearean topics, Franko also translated *The Merchant of Venice* and a dozen of the Sonnets – the first Ukrainian translations of Shakespeare's poems.

Franko also maintained close contact with Mykola Storozhenko (1836–1906), the first professional Shakespearean in the Russian empire and an elected member of the New Shakespeare Society in Britain. Franko edited and published Storozhenko's study of Western European literature to up to the end of the eighteenth century, a work that could only be published in Lviv because it was written in Ukrainian. Born in Irzhavets (Poltava Gubernia) in Ukraine, Storozhenko studied in Moscow and spent two years in Britain, perhaps at Oxford University. From 1872 a professor and chairholder of the newly formed faculty of world literature at Moscow University, Storozhenko lectured and published widely on his beloved Shakespeare, on many other early modern English dramatists, as well as on Shevchenko (his other great interest) but, of necessity, in Russian.[12]

Like the erudite Storozhenko, all intellectuals living in the Russian empire were unable to publish work in Ukrainian until the relaxation of censorship following the 1905 Revolution.[13] The brief spell of liberalization that followed bred an optimism that grew when news of the overthrow of the tsarist regime reached Kyiv on 13 March 1917. A few days later, the Central Rada (Council) was established. In April, the National Congress in Kyiv elected historian Mykhailo Hrushevsky as president. A series of Universals (Edicts) were issued by the Ukrainian parliament, including the First Universal (23 June 1917) declaring universal suffrage, law and order; the Third (20 November 1917), proclaiming the Ukrainian National or People's Republic (UNR); and the Fourth, which declared Ukraine's independence and proclaimed the UNR with the Rada as its representative body. Kyiv was created the capital of the Ukrainian state. A period of cultural renaissance immediately followed with the rapid creation of a Ukrainian university, Academy of Sciences, National Theatre, National Library, and many other institutions. Theatres sprang up like mushrooms. The following year, by the Act of Union of all Ukrainian lands (22 January 1919), the Western Ukrainian National Republic (formerly under Austro-Hungary) joined the UNR. These proclamations of independence coincided with social, national, and aesthetic revolutions; together, they created an electric surge of creativity in all areas of cultural endeavour.[14]

Thus, despite the upheaval of world war, revolutions, civil war, anarchy, and many changes of government, euphoria dominated both in the world of culture as well as state-building. At last, artists could have direct, unmediated access to the texts, genres, and subjects which hitherto had been prohibited and which, in turn, they hoped, would inspire the creation of a new art, new modes of expression, and representation. The burning question was how to escape provincialism without falling into the trap of neo-colonialism of another sort – the classic situation of colonized countries. Very much aware of this snare, writers such as novelist and polemicist Mykola Khvylovy (1893–1933) explained that Ukraine's preferred orientation was to the West, not to the North and East: "Europe is the experience of many ages….It is the Europe of a great civilization, the Europe of Goethe, Darwin, Byron, Newton, Marx and so on." To reject the models of Russia for those of Europe was "not with the goal of yoking our art to some other wagon bringing up the rear, but with the aim of reviving it after the asphyxiating atmosphere of backwardness."[15] The euphoria did not last. By June 1920, the Bolsheviks retook Kyiv and in November 1922, the USSR was created with most of Ukraine incorporated into the new political entity.[16]

Chapter Five, "Periphery Against Centre: *Hamlet* in Early Soviet Ukrainian Poetry," examines the use Ukrainian poets made of themes from *Hamlet* in the early Soviet period. In the 1920s and early 1930s, the poetic works of Maksym Rylsky (1895–1964), Mykola Bazhan (1904–83), and Yevhen Pluzhnyk (1898–1936) employed images and allusions to Shakespeare's work that alluded to ties with and affinity for the West; these allusions also implied an oblique challenge to the prevailing conservative aesthetic and, especially, to the political system. Themes from *Hamlet* became a means of interrogating both literary and political canonicity. Notably, the bulk of new translations of Shakespeare's plays appeared during the short period of active Ukrainianization (1923–9) when the Bolshevik government temporarily supported various cultural initiatives in order to gain support for the newly created Ukrainian Socialist Soviet Republic.

The first stage production of a Shakespeare play, *Macbeth* in 1920, was openly announced as a great historical moment for Ukrainian culture, in effect, a proclamation of Ukrainian cultural sovereignty. Directed by the charismatic Les Kurbas (1887–1937), a committed modernist educated in Vienna and Lviv, it was only one of his many proposed Shakespeare projects. Indeed, he had the ambition to stage the whole canon and to astonish the world, not just Ukrainian or Eastern European audiences, with his theatrical experiments. Staging and reworking *Macbeth* became a process of rethinking theatre itself. His 1924 *Macbeth* was, in its time, arguably the most radical Shakespeare production not only in the USSR but in all of Europe. It remains a seminal production that is mined a number of times in this volume. Kurbas himself described the need to stage Shakespeare through the "prism of the contemporary world view" rather than to attempt the unnecessary and impossible task of reconstructing a "museum" Shakespeare.[17] His productions laid the foundations for Ukrainian theatre and film, influencing hundreds of performers, directors, designers, and scholars, both then and now. Kurbas remains the single most influential figure of Ukrainian theatre to this day. Aspects of this pivotal figure's Shakespeare productions are discussed in Chapter Six, "Shakespeare Right or Wrong?" The following Chapter, Seven, "The Perfect Production: Les Kurbas's Analysis of the Early Soviet Audience," focuses on the innovative, extensive surveys of the audiences of his 1924 *Macbeth* as carried out by Kurbas's Berezil Artistic Theatre Association. This chapter analyses how Kurbas understood the architectonics of Shakespeare's plays and their effect on audiences. Through concerted, detailed, and multiple analyses of audience responses, Kurbas hoped to create the perfect production and thus replicate the success that classical works continue to have in shaping our emotions and our intellectual responses.

The political quicksand of the 1920s ensured that Kurbas's modernist productions were not permitted to flourish much beyond that decade. In 1926, that proponent of ethnographic theatre, Panas Saksahansky, staged a counter to Kurbas's experiments. *Othello* was performed in Katerynoslav (renamed Dnipropetrovsk in 1926 and Dnipro in 2016) at the Maria Zankovetska Theatre. This melodramatic production became the embodiment of domesticated Shakespeare. In Saksahansky's interpretation, Othello was an idealized figure and a victim, not of jealousy or doubt, but of his belief in the nobility and goodness of other people. Saksahansky's approach to Shakespeare led the way to the future (as well as back to the past, the nineteenth century): the tendency to domestication, folklorization, and melodramatization that became dominant in the Soviet Ukrainian theatre of the late 1920s, 1930s, and beyond.

Chapter Eight, "In a Crooked Mirror: *Hamlet* as Intertext in the USSR 1934–1943," looks at the work of propagandist Oleksandr Korniychuk (1905–72) and his reworking of *Hamlet* and other Shakespeare plays Supported by Stalin. Korniychuk aimed to challenge and supplant the Bard by re-codifying his works and revealing their gaps and omissions. His goal was to become a Soviet classic, to create Soviet literary models for emulation, and thus to out-Shakespeare Shakespeare. Lionized in his day, Korniychuk's fortunes have dramatically fallen along with the fall of the USSR.

The looming presence that dictated all cultural policies in the Soviet Union from the late 1920s to his death in 1953 was Joseph Stalin. His microscopic engagement with all cultural matter stemmed from his firm belief in the deep influence and power of culture to shape our understanding. Stalin's active involvement in cultural matters also contextualizes the repression, imprisonment, and executions of the Great Terror (Great Purges) of the late 1930s. Among the many victims were Ukrainian Shakespeare translators and directors including Mike Yohansen, Hnat Khotkevych, and Les Kurbas. In the terrible years of the Holodomor (the man-made Famine, 1932–3) and the Great Terror (1937–8), Ukrainians nonetheless tried to continue to promote and develop Ukrainian culture, often at their own peril. Their work included Shakespeare translations. Leonid Hrebinka translated *Hamlet* (1939); Maksym Rylsky, *Twelfth Night* (1939) and *King Lear* (1941); Viktor Ver, *Hamlet* (1941); Mykola Ivanov, *The Merchant of Venice* (1942); and Mykhailo Rudnytsky, mentioned earlier, *Hamlet* (1943).

Chapter Nine, "*Hamlet*, 1943," analyses the first production of this play in Ukraine under the horrific circumstances of Nazi occupation and not long after the short-lived Act of Proclamation of Ukrainian Statehood, issued in Western Ukraine on 22 June 1941. I began research on this topic in 1995 when the Ukrainian archives were just beginning to open under the promising circumstances. In a 1991 referendum, 92 per cent of Ukraine's citizens voted for independence. The 1943 *Hamlet*, translated by Mykhailo Rudnytsky (1889–1975), had been performed by some of the former members of Kurbas's troupe who had managed to survive the political "cleansing" of Stalin's regime. After returning from a labour camp on the Solovetsky Islands in Russia's far north, theatre director and actor Yosyp Hirniak (1895–1989) decided to realize the dream of his friend and colleague, Les Kurbas. For director Hirniak and his lead actor, Volodymyr Blavatsky (1900–53), this production was both a declaration of war against art as propaganda, and an assertion of Ukrainian cultural identity and independence. Hamlet's hesitation was interpreted as an allusion to the state of Ukraine squeezed between two possible, equally terrible, fates: falling to the Nazis or to the Bolsheviks. Never mentioned in Soviet theatre encyclopaedias nor in Soviet Shakespeare scholarship, most recently in Ukraine this production has become a focus of scholarly attention. New details about its translator, Rudnytsky, have appeared in a fascinating, deeply researched, part memoir, part history, of Lviv during the Second World War by scholar and Polish diplomat Ola Hnatiuk.[18] An excellent online exhibition, launched in 2024 with a mini-conference, has brought together and now makes generally available much primary evidence, including photos of the translators, actors, and images of Lviv in wartime.[19]

After the death of Stalin (1953), who had tacitly questioned the need for *Hamlet*, the play once again appeared on the stages of Ukraine, as well as in Russia. Borys Nord produced the play at Kharkiv's Shevchenko Theatre (1956), while Borys Tiahno staged it at the Maria Zankovetska Theatre in Lviv (1956). Nord's production cast Yaroslav Helias as the Danish Prince actively struggling against the world's evil; it is said that Nord was influenced by Peter Brook's tour of *Hamlet* in the USSR.[20] Tiahno's Western Ukrainian production, on the other hand, had Oleksandr Hai as Hamlet continuing the long philosophical tradition of attempting to preserve his moral character within the circumstances of a corrupt and stultifying Denmark. Tiahno's version had especial resonance for the younger generation of the creative intelligentsia, who, since the mid-1950s, had courageously opposed the repressive regime by actively promoting the preservation of Ukrainian culture and identity.

Chapter Ten, "Commemoration as Amplification: The 'Universal' versus the National Bard," analyses aspects of the complex and sometimes intersecting Soviet strategies of rituals of commemoration, containment, and celebration of two types of bards: the "universal," Shakespeare, and the "national," Taras Shevchenko, each of whom posed particular challenges to the authorities and ideologies of the multinational Soviet state. Adding a third figure, Alexander Pushkin to the mix, this triangulation of Shakespeare-Shevchenko-Pushkin helps clarify the functions of Soviet commemorations of cultural icons and their use as ideological weapons.

After Ukraine gained independence in 1991, theatre productions, translations, and scholarly endeavours were freed from censorship and ideological circumscription. As in the 1920s, experimentation reigned throughout most of Ukraine's stages. Interest in Shakespeare was further stimulated by the postmodern writer and translator Yuri Andrukhovych, who, combining radical modernization with domestication, published new translations of *Hamlet* (2000), *Romeo and Juliet* (2015), and *Twelfth Night* (2017). At the Kyiv Molodyy Teatr (Young Theatre, its name an echo of Kurbas's first company) in 2000, Stanislav Moiseyev directed a production of *Hamlet* focused on King Claudius's corrupt court and its ability to sway and easily manipulate the Danes. Valeriy Legin's Hamlet, a man of action, dared to resist authorities. One of the more provocative productions was Andriy Zholdak's postmodern *Hamlet. Dreams* (Kharkiv Shevchenko Academic Theatre, 2002). Shakespeare's text, heard from behind the proscenium frame rather than spoken by the actors, was enveloped by a rich soundscape that included spiritual and popular melodies, the mechanical hum of a train, sounds from the natural world (such as the surf, the thud of horses' hooves), and punctured by recognizable music from the Third Reich. Andriy Kravchuk's solitary Hamlet wandered through the oneiric scenes entirely nude, his nakedness symbolizing the nakedness of the human soul. A great-grandson of the playwright Ivan Tobilevych (Karpenko-Kary), Zholdak also conceived of and directed *Romeo and Juliet. A Fragment* (2005), another controversial adaptation but also both an homage to beauty and an exploration of the depths of absolute passion.

Vladyslav Troitsky's *A Prologue to Macbeth* (2004, The Dakh Theatre, Kyiv) formed the first part of his Shakespeare-based trilogy *Mystical Ukraine* and was one of the first post-independence attempts "to employ Shakespeare's dramatic legacy as a mirror to reflect Ukrainian contexts."[21] Troitsky's seventy minute adaptation with its ritualistic Ukrainian cultural elements retained only key events from Shakespeare's play but added others, while focusing on archetypal themes of love, betrayal, treachery, and the tragedy of infertility. Employing a soundtrack of folk songs performed by the DakhaBrakha ethno chaos band, the adaptation displayed a pre-historic, animistic, vicious society.

Dmytro Bohomazov, founder of Free Stage Theatre in Kyiv (2001), and principal director of the Ivan Franko National Academic Drama Theatre in Kyiv (from 2017), directed a number of experimental versions of Shakespeare's plays: *Twelfth Night* (1995, 2017), *A Midsummer Night's Dream* (2003), *Othello* (2004), *Hamlet* (2009), and *Coriolanus* (2018). Bohomazov's 2008 adaptation of *Richard III*, ironically titled *Sweet Dreams, Richard*, was a fifty-minute electro-acoustic multimedia production centred on Richard's nightmare when the ghosts of those he has murdered come back to haunt him, curse him, and predict his imminent death at the battle of Bosworth Field. Chanting in English, the ghosts were part of a visual and acoustic phantasmagoria. Employing sophisticated audio techniques and equipment, video projections, contemporary choreography, and a variety of other performance strategies, the production also drew from some of the staple images and devices of horror films. Like Troitsky's versions of *Macbeth*, Bohomazov's adaptation offered a dark, posthumanist view of the world.

In 2021, Alex Borovensky, founder of the ProEnglish Theatre in Kyiv, created *Forgetting Othello*, an adaptation of Shakespeare's play using docudrama techniques: monologues taken from the personal experiences of refugees from Africa and the Near East. Once again, Shakespeare's text was employed as a prism through which a fruitful exploration of contemporary issues – power, gender, and identity – were explored. The rousing motto, "To Act is to Breathe. To Act in English is to Breathe Fire," was taken up by Borovensky's ProDrama School, an offshoot of his theatre.[22]

Chapter Eleven, "Antic Dispositions: Shakespeare, War, and Cabaret," takes us to the Russian invasion of Donbas in 2014 and, further on, to the full-scale war begun in 2022. Focusing on the characteristics of Shakespeare cabaret from Les Kurbas's work in the early twentieth century to the Freak Cabaret of the Dakh Daughters in the twenty-first century, this chapter considers the role of theatre in wartime. What approach may best embody war's terrible spectrum, from barbarism to moments of great humanity and tenderness? War invites questions about essential values, connections, and cultural, political, and emotional spaces. The chapter invites us to consider where and how Shakespeare fits into the landscape of drones, air raid sirens, and missiles.

One answer has been provided by Rostyslav Derzhypilsky, a charismatic and hyper-energizing force in Ukrainian theatre, mentioned at the beginning of this chapter as having staged *Hamlet* at the start of the Russian war in 2022 and one of the most renowned contemporary experimental directors in Ukraine. His productions have garnered many awards, including for the aforementioned nightmarish

2018 *Hamlet* that achieved top standing at the All-Ukrainian Festival "Hra" (Play/Game) that year. Derzhypilsky was one of the catalysts for what seemed to be an impossible wartime project: the first Ukrainian Shakespeare Festival held from 17–22 June 2024 in Ivano-Frankivsk. Insisting that this is a "perfect time" to create international platforms, Derzhypilsky emphasized Shakespeare's strong historical connections to Ukraine in wartime. Invoking Les Kurbas's 1920 *Macbeth* and Yosyp Hirniak's 1943 *Hamlet*, Derzhypilsky considers Shakespeare as amplifying, strengthening Ukrainian voices in their existential struggle to exist;[23] cultural work is considered a necessity in wartime. The Festival's website insists that such an event "is not an 'a holiday of art' or 'entertainment during the war'. Rather, it avers that the aim is to 'be an instrument of social and political change, a tool of public diplomacy and a platform for dialogue with the democratic world."[24] Bringing together productions from Ukraine, Moldova and Italy, as well as public lectures, discussions, round tables, and master classes, the Festival presented an ambitious program of events created in circumstances of great duress.

Appropriately, Shakespeare's great tragedy of a warrior, *Coriolanus*, opened the Festival. On the occasion of the launch of this first Ukrainian Shakespeare Festival, Martin Harris, the British High Commissioner of the United Kingdom to Ukraine, remarked:

> Ukrainian culture, as part of the world cultural heritage, once again finds itself under attack from Russia. The war against Ukraine can be seen through the prism of Hamlet's "to be or not to be". With its aggression, Russia seems to say to Ukraine "not to be", denying its right to be itself. Despite these brutal attempts, Ukraine responds with a resolute "to be". To be for Ukrainian language, theater, peace. To be for the Ukrainian Shakespeare Festival.[25]

British Shakespeare scholar Nicoleta Cinpoeş, one of the international attendees and an early enthusiastic proponent of the Festival, observed that "[i]n Ukraine, actors and artists are considered as part of the frontline – that is acknowledged by the government, because they are responsible for caring for the home-front communities and preserving the heritage of the country for the future."[26] In another instance of connections and cultural diplomacy, on 26 June 2023, Maya Harbuziuk, Dean of the Faculty of Culture and Arts at the Ivan Franko National University in Lviv, presented the Speaker of the British House of Commons with a puppet of Hamlet as a symbolic gift from the Lviv theatre community, an item which was placed beside the pilot's helmet earlier given by President Zelensky on which is written, "We have freedom – give us wings to protect it."

The First Ukrainian Shakespeare Festival is not a solitary event but rather part of an efflorescence of cultural activities in Ukraine and beyond, ironically instigated by the war and by Ukrainians' desire to share their cultural heritage as well as to focus attention on Ukraine's plight. The "Afterword: Shakespeare at War Today," examines some of these events and productions and concludes with "A Toast to the Immortal Memory of William Shakespeare," by Nataliya Torkut, director of the Shakespeare Centre, in Zaporizhzhia, Ukraine, who, with her students, family, and countrymen, is living these questions. The Ukrainian Shakespeare Centre continues the scholarly work initiated in the nineteenth century by Ivan Franko and, in the twentieth, by Oleksandr Biletsky, Iryna Vanina, Maria Shapovalova, and, now, many, many others. The Centre is involved in a variety of different activities some of them described in this final section, including the publication of two scholarly journals, a month-long annual celebration of Shakespeare, and a state-wide student competition that brings in creative and scholarly projects from all corners of Ukraine. Remarkably, it has continued this wide spectrum of activities despite the war. Shakespeare, prevented from rooting himself in Ukrainian soil before the twentieth century, is now not only a fixed part of Ukraine's cultural memory as mirror, prism, megaphone; "Shakespeare" also literally hovers over and helps protect Ukraine. In a magnanimous gesture of support, Michael Dobson, director of the Shakespeare Institute at the University of Birmingham, UK, donated funds he received from a prestigious award; these were used to purchase a drone that was named "Shakespeare."

Stretching back over more than forty years of my professional engagement with the topic of Shakespeare and Ukraine, the essays that follow examine some of the significant moments in 170 years of Ukraine's cultural history. Over this long stretch of historical time, Shakespeare, as the most translated and performed playwright in the world, has most frequently served to amplify – to make better heard – Ukrainians' fundamental assertions of identity, value, and allegiance. As Serhii Plokhy has argued, Ukraine's "claim to independence has always had a European orientation," in part because of its location, a "contact zone," "on the border of several cultural spaces."[27] Not conceived as an exhaustive study of the topic, this volume offers an introduction to the multifaceted and wide reception of Shakespeare in Ukraine that, today, continues to grow exponentially. It offers ample evidence that Shakespeare's works served in complex, multivocal, and varied capacities, among them, as cultural mediator and mirror, as the prism for a poetic feminist voice, as assertion of cultural and national identity, as solace, as subversion, and as tool for creating a new conceptual theatre. Only such a beloved hyper classic is able to perform such resonant, multiple functions.

2

Calibans All: Shakespeare at the Intersection of Colonialisms

With few exceptions, Shakespearean postcolonial criticism has limited itself to examining the way in which culture has been contested and negotiated on the battlefield of Shakespeare's work and reputation in North America, South Africa, the Caribbean, and India. For obvious linguistic reasons, only a limited number of scholars have ventured into the, arguably, even more complex terrain of Eastern Europe and especially Imperial Russia, where the colonizer-colonized relationships are, if not murky, then like geological formations which, when exposed, reveal seemingly infinite gradations of multi-layered strata.

This chapter provides a brief foray into this terrain, one which both confirms the difficulty of assigning a simple or single function to Shakespeare and the need for more supple and comprehensive theories of cross-cultural Shakespearean encounters. For this complex and contradictory relationship to Shakespeare, I take a remarkable moment as a synecdoche: the encounter of the African-American actor Ira Aldridge (1807–67) with the Ukrainian social revolutionary, poet, writer, painter, and former serf Taras Shevchenko (1814–61). The following scene occurred after one of Aldridge's performances of King Lear in St. Petersburg:

> Spread out from fatigue and half-lying in a roomy chair was King Lear [Aldridge], and over him, literally on top of him, I found Taras Hryhorovych [Shevchenko]; tears like hail were raining from his eyes; he articulated disconnected, passionate words of distress and grace in a muffled loud whisper, all the while covering the great tragedian's grease-painted face, hands and back with kisses.[1]

Aldridge's presence in the Russian Empire and Shevchenko's extraordinary viscerally-emotive response to his performance may be examined from at least three different perspectives: that of the aristocratic Russian,

Count Tolstoy, who invited and cultivated the friendship of both the Black actor and the Ukrainian painter-writer; Aldridge, the African-American actor playing in English with German actors to Russian audiences; and the Ukrainian Shevchenko, recently-returned to Russia from what was originally to have been a life sentence of exile. At the nexus of this triad is Shakespeare. A fourth perspective of this intercultural encounter, which I shall consider only in passing, is that of the German influence on "Russian" Shakespeare.[2]

Preceded by many other English writers, Shakespeare arrived late in the Russian empire, giving little indication of the vast ocean of future commentary. Never simple, the Russian relationship to Shakespeare evolved contrapuntally, rather than in any linear fashion. Often tamed, at times silenced, at others loudly appreciated but frequently simultaneously all three, Shakespeare in Russia reveals the constantly intersecting and problematic notions of colonizer and colonized. When Ira Aldridge arrived in St. Petersburg in 1858, Shakespeare's reputation, limited to a few plays and known to a small group, was in decline after only a brief period of glory in the 1840s. Shakespeare was the preserve of that tiny fraction of the population of the huge empire that was literate and that could afford to attend the theatre. Translators of Shakespeare were almost inevitably "Westernizers," that is, intellectuals who were interested in and willing to entertain or open up a dialogue with Western ideas, including the idea of a theatre. Thus, Alexander Sumarokov, the first translator of the "inspired barbarian" (as he called the Bard) is also notably referred to as the "father" of Russian drama, suggesting a necessary link between the creation of a native Russian theatre and interest in Shakespeare.[3] Sumarokov was also the initiator of a two-century long tradition of working from foreign, especially French or German, rather than English sources. Following P.A. de la Place, he "regularized" and transformed *Hamlet* (1748) into moralistic discourses and, among many other changes, made Polonius into the arch-villain of the piece.

Other early Westernizers include the German-born and educated tsarina Catherine II, who adapted *The Merry Wives of Windsor* and *Timon of Athens.* By adapting Shakespeare, following the advice of her correspondents, the *encyclopédistes* Voltaire and Diderot, Catherine wished to declare Russia a member of the Western cultural club and herself an enlightened ruler who partook of larger intellectual discourses and debates (although some of her other actions indicated otherwise: she was responsible for extending total serfdom from Russia to Ukraine in 1783). Shakespeare's only other champion in the eighteenth century, the historian Nikolai Karamzin, was also the first Shakespearean to fall victim to the censor. His *Julius Caesar* (1787) was confiscated and banned by Catherine, a ban which was not lifted until well over a century later.

Early nineteenth-century Russian intellectuals, taken with neo-classicism and sentimentality, did not find Shakespeare especially congenial. Although new translations began to appear (such as those by Ivan Veliaminov, Nikolai Gnedich, Stepan Viskovatov, Mikhail Vronchenko, and Nikolai Ketcher), the practice of working from adaptations and translations prevailed, as may be seen by the title page of the most notorious of such examples, Alexander Rotchev's *Macbeth. A Tragedy of Shakespeare from the Works of Schiller* (1830). A Frenchified and Germanicized Shakespeare subsequently was revered not as an early modern writer of tragedies but as a romantic melodramatist. From his beginnings in Imperial Russia, then, Shakespeare was doubly foreign: geographically and historically distant; his works were also mediated by foreign filters, contemporary translation practices, and literary fashions.

The zenith of Shakespeare's popularity in tragedy (knowledge of which was limited to only a handful of plays) came with a period of general Anglomania, the growth of the Romantic movement, and the development of a native Russian theatre in the 1830s and 1840s. Pushkin, the descendent of an Ethiopian general, is of central importance here. The first Russian writer to become enthralled by Shakespeare, Pushkin accepted Shakespeare as the inspiration and guiding hand for many of his works, at the same time as he fully believed in the "natural" and "untutored" quality of Shakespeare's genius. Also responsible for an outburst of tremendous enthusiasm for Shakespeare was Nikolai Polevoy's translation of *Hamlet* as embodied by two great actors, the wild, emotional Pavel Mochalov (1800–48) and the slightly-less-so Vasilii Karatygin (1802–53). Contributing to the acceptance of Shakespeare were Russian journals, which while at first derivative (reprinting articles about Shakespeare from French, German and English periodicals such as *The Spectator* and *The Edinburgh Review*), increasingly became an original and influential medium for the dissemination of knowledge about Shakespeare.

By the 1850s, however, Shakespeare's eclipse was hastened by the death of Mochalov and Karatygin and, in literary developments, by the turn to realism. Precisely at that moment, Aldridge arrived in the Russian Empire. Himself little known in Russia, in preparing for his visit Aldridge advertised the fact that he had played in Covent Garden and the Lyceum in London, had toured the British Isles and most of Europe (including France, Hungary, Serbia, Bohemia, and many German states), and that he was to present with but one exception (*The Padlock*), a repertoire entirely Shakespearean. The first Black actor to play white Shakespearean roles, he debuted in St. Petersburg on 10 November 1858 with *Othello*. The

novelty of a Black actor and one with almost an entirely Shakespearean
repertoire quickly aroused the interest of Petersburgers. Hitherto, no
single actor in Russia had made Shakespeare his preserve and, in fact,
few Shakespeare plays had actually been staged. The influential progressive thick journal *Sovremennik* [*The Contemporary*] excitedly commented:

> A black tragedian! That's certainly original! Although we don't understand
> a word of English, certainly we can't miss seeing a *black tragedian*! Added to
> which, the English Othello will have a German Desdemona – that indeed is
> strange and fascinating.[4]

Many of those who attended did so out of the curiosity expressed by
Sovremennik: for the exoticism of the Black actor playing in an unknown
language with a white actress responding in Schlegel's elegant translation of Shakespeare. In the absence of English actors, Aldridge played
with a German troupe,[5] thus initiating a tradition of bilingual productions (Tommaso Salvini and Sarah Bernhardt later followed this prec-
edent). Limited to only six performances (although later extended to
sixteen), Aldridge was permitted to play at the Imperial Circus Theatre,
a venue which may have contributed to many spectators' idea that they
were about to watch a freak, a sideshow, a comedy. Indeed, a number of
the reviewers subsequently admitted that they had come to gape and to
mock the spectacle. Arriving at the Circus simply to observe the oddity
of heroic characters played by a Black actor, many Russians nonetheless
seemed to have been swept away by the force of Aldridge's acting. After
the shock of the first linguistic dissonances, the majority, like French
writer and critic Théophile Gautier (then touring Russia), found themselves unperturbed by the disjunction, since they understood neither
German nor English. Indeed, he seemed dazzled by the performance,
remarking that from Aldridge's first entry on the stage, "he was Othello
himself, as created by Shakespeare, his eyes half closed as though dazzled
by an Afric sun, his manner orientally carefree";[6] yet, at the same time,
Gautier was surprised by Aldridge's restraint and dignity, characteristics
noted by other critics as well. Only the very few who understood both
languages, like the Russian correspondent from the *New York Herald*,
considered the performance comical. An Englishman, writing for one
of the St. Petersburg newspapers, also criticized Aldridge, attacking his
diction, melodramatic gestures, and facial expressions which, he argued,
destroyed Shakespeare's interpretations of Othello and Shylock.[7] Melodrama, however, was the preferred mode in the nineteenth century, not
only in Russia but in Britain and Western Europe as well. No one, however, seems to have been concerned that Shakespeare was, yet again,

being presented to the Russians by mostly foreign intermediaries. The German troupe (unnamed in the extant documents) and the German influence (dating back at least to Catherine II) seems to have been naturalized or at least regarded of little cultural threat. Instead, the focus was on Aldridge, whose presence sharply divided the Russian intelligentsia.

For liberal Russians, Aldridge presented much more than a curiosity or a touring Shakespearophilic missionary. As K. Zvantsov explained on the eve of Aldridge's arrival, his race and background, his Othello-like claim to be descended from a royal African line, as well as his "unfitness" for the stages of his native America, made Aldridge a natural symbol for the fate of his people; moreover, Aldridge could also serve as a convenient tool by which liberal democrats could attack the tsar and his repressive regime:

> In our contemporary history there is an event which creates a whole sphere of life and thought, i.e., the liberation of the Negro in the United States; this becomes something *internal,* not only for the enslaved people, but for all of us. That is why, for us, at this particular time, the role of Othello performed by this artist of genius, with all its subtleties of tribal and climatic character, has a universal mighty significance...From Othello is torn the deep cry, "Oh, misery, misery, misery!" and in that misery of the African artist is heard the far-off groans of his own people, oppressed by unbelievable slavery and more than that – the groans of the whole of suffering mankind.[8]

For Zvantsov and progressive Russian intellectuals, Aldridge presented an image of the strength of the human spirit and liberation from slavery, a liberation which was finally to come with the 13th Amendment to the American Constitution in 1865. Aldridge-Othello also spoke to their own, related issue, serfdom – just as, a few years later, French liberals would similarly read their injustices into Aldridge's performances. In Paris, Alexandre Dumas *père* would kiss the actor's cheeks and proclaim, "*Je suis aussi un Nègre.*"[9] For liberals in Eastern and Western Europe, the Black actor was perceived as a kind of mirror in which a variety of different, although related, ideals and hopes could be reflected. Adhering to many ideas of this group was the aristocratic Russian, Count Tolstoy, Vice-President of the Academy of Arts in Petersburg, at whose home progressive painters, singers, poets, artists, and literati gathered.

Just prior to Aldridge's arrival, the draft legislation for the abolition of serfdom was circulated. (It was promulgated in 1861.) Both his repertoire of characters "more sinned against than sinning" and his revisionary view of Lear, Othello, Shylock, and Aaron the Moor spoke directly to larger issues of freedom and justice. Reinterpreting these characters as victims and yet heroic figures, Aldridge was himself scripting a new kind of liberal Shakespeare (and anticipating the kind of Shakespeare for which, in 1999, British actor Hugh Quarshie has called[10]), most notably in his complete rewriting of Aaron the Moor and Shylock. Shakespeare's malevolent Moor was transformed into a noble victim brought to violence only out of desperation, while Shylock became (as one contemporary observed) not "particularly a Jew, but a human being in general, oppressed by the age-old hatred shown towards people like him, and expressing this feeling with wonderful power and truth."[11] Completely cutting act five of *The Merchant of Venice*, Aldridge added a final, mimed scene in which Shylock shuddered with horror at the Venetians' blithe sentence of his conversion to Christianity. In *Othello*, Aldridge attempted "vividly to convey to audiences the messages that racism is the green-eyed monster that destroys not just its victim but also its perpetrator and innocent bystanders."[12] His interpretation of the marginalized, the Jew, the Moor, the slave, the old man, encouraged the response of the intelligentsia in Russia and elsewhere of reading Shakespeare as a champion of the oppressed and downtrodden, rather than as the carrier of an imperial Western culture. Zvantsov was moved to think

> of the many generations of black people suffering under the whip of American slave-traders…All this has been represented by Shakespeare so truthfully, so powerfully, that, without the slightest exaggeration – one risks hating all his white heroes, or at least, the Venetians that surround Othello, not excluding, even Desdemona herself. It is a pity that even she is not black.[13]

Similarly, I.I. Panaev, writing in *Sovremennik*, praised the nobility and strength of Aldridge's interpretation, the first "real" Othello Russians had ever seen.[14] By presenting a series of noble and persecuted characters, Aldridge invited a thematic, socio-political reading of his performance. This anticipated audience response (so successful with sympathetic spectators like Zvantsov) was further extended by his only comic role, that of the slave Mungo in Isaac Bickerstaffe's *The Padlock*, a role which Aldridge deliberately took up right after playing Othello. Aldridge's repertoire thus created its own unstated but nonetheless effective narrative of the consequences of colonization. It also revealed Aldridge's wide spectrum of acting skill, from tragedy to comedy. The broad comedy of the slave was balanced by his ingenuity and native intelligence; when he was unjustly punished, spectators reportedly cringed. In taking up such roles, Aldridge was hoping to combat prejudice and to induce empathy and understanding:

> My great ambition has been to prove that my fellow countrymen are not
> deficient in intellectual ability but that circumstances and prejudice have
> been almost insurmountable obstacles. Oh that the time may hasten on
> when all distinctions may cease, when man may be estimated by his indi-
> vidual worth, and not by consideration of Caste or Colour.[15]

Although he played King Lear in white-face, Aldridge kept his black
arms and hands free of make-up, as if to insist – so Marshall and Stock
suggest – that he was a Black playing a white man. This tactic may have
also deliberately contributed to the perception that the injustices committed against the old king were analogues of those committed against
Blacks. Aldridge's awareness of the way that race could be effectively
exploited through Shakespearean characters may also be seen in the way
that he encouraged an Othello-like myth about himself as an "extravagant and wheeling stranger / Of here and every where," descended
from Senegalese African princes. Eliding his New York roots, Aldridge
referred to himself as the African Roscius. The combination of his own
exploitation of race and the liberal Russian championing of Aldridge and
Shakespeare as symbols of opposition to tyranny thus worked together to
conflate Bard, actor, race, and role.

If in progressive circles Russians admired Aldridge's performances and
used them to further their own, Slavophiles and supporters of serfdom
saw only "Savage, wild flesh in earrings" or, simply, "stupidity."[16] Similarly,
while Shakespeare's naturalization was perceived by Russian Westernizers
as a way of revealing Russia's growth into cultural maturity, the Slavophile
opposition regarded the domestication of the Bard as an intrusion and an
admission of backwardness and provincialism. Even worse, Shakespeare
by a Black American actor was an act of cultural colonization and, more, of
degradation. In Moscow, Russian actors at the Maly (Alexandrinsky) Theatre refused to perform with Aldridge. In direct response to this affront
offered by a Black performing Shakespeare, Vasilii Samoilov hurriedly
prepared Othello and Lear, deliberately performing these roles at the
Maly at the same time that Aldridge was acting elsewhere. But, notwithstanding the Russian's attempt to appeal to native honour, the auditorium
was not as full as at Aldridge's performances. Nor did Samoilov's performances, according to the reviewers, reach the same heights of power as
Aldridge, whom actors now began to study and emulate.[17]

While some audience members derided the "wildness" of Aldridge's
performances, in fact, the great majority were astonished by his
restraint, particularly by comparison with the usual melodramatic pos-
turings and declamatory style of Russian actors. Théophile Gautier,
who anticipated a "vigorous, somewhat uncontrolled, a little wild and

fierce" Othello, found, instead, a "decorous," "majestically classical" and "gentlemanly" Othello, whom he compared to English stage actor Charles Macready.[18] Count Tolstoy's daughter, Ekaterina, similarly disappointed by the lack of a lurid Othello, was, at first, "*unpleasantly*" put off by the "simplicity" of Aldridge's acting.[19] Some critics drew surprised attention to his unaffected gait, which resembled that of a "normal" person rather than a tragedian. Indeed, Aldridge has been credited, along with Mikhail Shchepkin (a Ukrainian-born serf until 1822, and one of the most famous actors in the Russian empire), with helping to encourage the growth of a realistic school of acting well before the advent of Konstantin Stanislavsky.

Aldridge's Lear comprised one of his greatest Russian successes. Some critics preferred his Lear to his Othello because, it was said, in the former he acted, while in the latter he was said to be "simply himself." Remaining in role as a feeble old man even after the play was over and after he acknowledged the audience's ovations, Aldridge particularly affected the Ukrainian bard, Taras Shevchenko. The latter had been invited to the home of the Count and Countess Tolstoy to meet Aldridge and hear his "recitations from Shakespeare"; thereafter he attended a number of Aldridge's performances.

Born a serf with a natural artistic talent, Shevchenko acquired his freedom from a reluctant master by the intervention of a small artistic circle, who raised the exorbitant sum demanded by auctioning off a painting donated by the portraitist Karl Bryulov. Shevchenko's new status of free man, not extended to his siblings, permitted him to study at the Imperial Academy of Arts which was otherwise barred to serfs. There, he obtained a good humanist education and learned French. Submitting his painting "The Death of Lucrece" as his fulfillment of the Academy's historical theme, within nine years Shevchenko himself became a lecturer there, a young bohemian-about-town, attending the theatre, discussing ideas, painting, etching, and writing poetry and plays. He was lionized as the brightest young poet of his day, especially for his book of poetry, *Kobzar* [The Bard], which, among others, dealt with Romantic themes of orphanhood, injustice, tyranny, and betrayal. From this period in the 1840s, the height of Anglomania and Romanticism, Shevchenko acquired his love of Shakespeare and melodrama – perhaps the only genre possible for a colonized people. (The subject of Shevchenko's aesthetics is discussed in the next chapter.) He saw a number of productions of heroic, melodramatic Shakespeare on the lively stages of St. Petersburg and, in 1843, took the most *Sturm und Drang* scene of the plays and illustrated it with an etching: "King Lear and the Fool in the Midst of the Raging Elements." (The politics of Shakespeare's and Shevchenko's fluctuating reputations are examined in Chapter Ten.)

Shevchenko's clandestine circulation of his sharp political satires aimed against tyranny and the tsarist family past and present, as well as the suspicion that he belonged to a secret organization, the Brotherhood of SS. Cyril and Methodius, earned him arrest without trial, a lifetime sentence as a private soldier, exile, and – most severely and at the personal insistence of tsar Nicholas I – a complete prohibition from painting and writing. Sent to the far reaches of the Russian empire, Shevchenko was later given some reading privileges and most frequently requested two books in particular from his friends: the Bible and Shakespeare in Nikolai Ketcher's translation,[20] both represented spiritual sustenance, longing for truth, and freedom and justice. For Shevchenko, Shakespeare was the apex of literary talent; thus, he conferred the epithet "Shakespearean" on works that he particularly admired. For example, in response to the public reading of Marko Vovchok's (pen name of Maria Vilinska) short stories, he shouted out "Shakespeare! Shakespeare!"[21]

Shevchenko's love of Shakespeare was, doubtless, tinged with some guilt. As a serf, he could hardly have had access to the Bard's works; only his freedom, provided by both Russian and Ukrainian friends, permitted his acquaintance with Shakespeare. As a Ukrainian, Shevchenko would not have been able to read the English writer in his own language, since, at the same time as Shakespeare was being translated, adapted, and censored in Russian, in the "provinces," most specifically in Ukraine, he was strictly prohibited in the Ukrainian language until the twentieth century. Not surprisingly, then, in his poetry, Shevchenko depicts himself as a hybrid, a "classically marginal or displaced figure – he is neither peasant nor nobleman, he can neither return to his past nor forget it nor deny it."[22] Like the hybrid Aldridge, Shevchenko openly drew attention to his roots, totally identifying his personal fate with that of his nation: Ukraine as *slavus-esclavus*.

Shevchenko met Aldridge shortly after his release from nearly ten years of exile, an exile fortuitously shortened by the death of the tsar and the constant lobbying of his friends, among them Count Tolstoy's family. Shevchenko's poetic works, however, continued to be banned in the empire, appearing in Ukraine only in 1905 (and still in censored form until the fall of the USSR in 1991). For Shevchenko, Aldridge was the embodiment of a Shakespeare whom he had treasured and committed to memory in exile. His comment in a letter to the actor Mikhail Shchepkin, that Aldridge "performs wonders" on the stage and shows us a "living Shakespeare," makes a great deal of sense.[23] In Aldridge, he recognized, as did other progressive intellectuals, not only the whole history of Aldridge's people (what the Russians saw) but also himself and

Figure 2.1. Taras Shevchenko's portrait of Ira Aldridge, 1858.

Source: Wikimedia Commons.

his own people's history. Shakespeare was the pellucid mirror in which receding colonialisms were discovered. Like Blacks, Ukrainian actors were confined by tsarist edict to a "song-and-dance" theatre of lower-class characters and caricatures, which served to confirm national stereo-types. Like Blacks in America, they also were prohibited from playing in or possessing their own Shakespeare. Shevchenko understood that even as Shakespeare spoke the language of the masters, he also gave voice to Aldridge, just as Russian Shakespeare had sustained Shevchenko in exile and provided the medium of this new friendship. With the help of fifteen-year-old Ekaterina Tolstoy, who acted as translator, Aldridge and Shevchenko exchanged songs and histories, both deeply moved by the other's narrative, each seeing himself in the other.

In spite of the language barrier, through gestures, song, and Shake-speare, Aldridge and Shevchenko became good friends, Shevchenko eventually drawing Aldridge's portrait, and Aldridge requesting a copy of Shevchenko's likeness from a mutual friend, the sculptor and artist Mikhail Mikeshin.

Figure 2.2. Mikhail Mikeshin's caricature of Taras Shevchenko forcibly restraining his emotions while witnessing a performance by Ira Aldridge.

Listening to an English he did not understand, remembering a Russian Shakespeare he had lovingly conned, Shevchenko watched Aldridge-Lear playing with actors speaking yet another language. As the Ukrainian's colleague M. Savychev relates, Shevchenko was unable to repress his feelings during many of Aldridge's performances. In one case, he expelled so many loud sighs and expressions of grief that Savychev's mother was obliged to flee from her box in embarrassment and return home before the end of the play.[24] Shevchenko's enraptured response to Aldridge's masterly control of his craft was also a keen response to the performance of injustice, as Mikeshin's caricature of Shevchenko indicates. Standing, his forehead lowered and his fists clenched as if to control anger as much as enthusiasm, the pudgy Ukrainian poet hardly seems like a revolutionary. Mikeshin's scribble alongside the cartoon comments, "Mutely enthralled by Ira Aldridge."[25]

As a metonymy of exile and solitude, of interconnected levels of colonizer and colonized (and thus a thoroughly Romantic situation), the encounter between Aldridge and Shevchenko suggests the complexity of Shakespeare's cultural work in the Russian empire: simultaneously solace, connection, pleasure, opposition to tyranny, and a mark of colonialism. Yet, notwithstanding the double colonialism (a Shakespeare acquired by Russian masters from Germany and France), Shevchenko's Shakespeare provided the lingua franca of their meeting in the highest social circles. If not free from imperialist taint, Shakespeare nonetheless could appear to present a counter to tribalism and intolerance.

Aldridge and Shevchenko's affinity for each other, expressed in their instant friendship, was also so regarded by the aristocrats of the Tolstoy household, although at least one account unknowingly portrays it as a natural alliance of subalterns. Ekaterina Tolstoy (later Mrs. Yunge), the intermediary by virtue of her knowledge of languages in the meetings between Aldridge and Shevchenko, later recalled that Aldridge

> was a sincere, good, careless, trusting, and loving child. His character was very similar to that of Shevchenko, with whom he became very close. It would happen that Aldridge would come in with his quick, energetic step and at once ask, 'And the artist?' That is what he called Shevchenko, for every attempt of his to pronounce that name ended with his shaking with laughter over his hopeless attempts.[26]

Post-colonialists and feminists will immediately recognize in Tolstoy-Yunge's easy conflation of the characteristics of the Black actor with that of Shevchenko the portrait of the subaltern or the "Other," possessing the characteristics of an amiable, emotional, and loving child, one man not at all distinct from the other.[27] Nearly fifty years later, in 1913, the painter Leonid Pasternak, father of the rather more famous poet and writer, Boris, recreated this scene in a drawing. From the imperial perspective, both are engaged in "exotic" and unusual activities: the Black as actor ready to declaim a text; the former serf, as artist briefly looking up from his work, their friendship clearly indicated by the friendly embrace. Shevchenko's own drawing of Aldridge (the oil painting he made has not survived) shows Aldridge's warmth and nobility, while his self-portrait at about the same time reveals a sensitive artist looking frankly but tentatively out of the darkness at the viewer.

The complexity of the originary intercultural and multilingual moment of Aldridge-Shevchenko's meeting and, more, its subsequent significance prevents any easy division into powerful and powerless, master and subaltern. If some Russian actors at first refused to perform with Aldridge, others were irrevocably changed by him. When Aldridge departed from St. Petersburg, he was presented with a massive bracelet inscribed "To Ira Aldridge, the great interpreter of the immortal Shakespeare, from the Russian Artists, St. Petersburg, 1858." If Aldridge was

Figure 2.3. Taras Shevchenko's *Self-portrait with Candle*, aquatint etching, 1860.

a victim of colonialism, he was also a "colonizer" or, as he was called by a number of Russians, a Shakespearean "propagandist." Travelling not only to large centres, he also toured provincial towns throughout the empire, popularizing Shakespeare's name and plays. Despite the fact that Aldridge hoped for a longer stay in the Russian empire, V.F. Adlerberg, the minister of the imperial court, refused permission, ignoring two petitions signed by various prominent figures urging the minister to relent. Among the signatories were Shevchenko and other friends of the Tolstoy circle.

While Aldridge's effect on the German actors was unrecorded, in addition to Russian actors and literati, he made a lasting impression on Ukrainian actors, playwrights and translators. Accompanying Shevchenko to some of his meetings with Aldridge, the writer and critic Panteleimon Kulish would go on to become the first major (and a prolific) translator of Shakespeare into Ukrainian. Convinced of Shakespeare's importance to Ukraine, Kulish translated thirteen plays, certain that Shakespeare could serve as a significant means by which Ukrainians could join the European high cultural table.[28] The young Ukrainian actor Ivan Karpenko-Kary (stage name of Ivan Tobi-levych), who later authored nearly forty plays, was so moved by his experience of seeing Aldridge perform that he was still recreating the Black's intonations and gestures thirty years later, passing them on to a younger generation of actors.[29] Taken together, these two examples of the power and influence of Aldridge on translation and perfor-mance ensured that Shakespeare would be rooted in Ukraine both as literature and as theatre or – in theatre theorist Diana Taylor's terms – both as archive and as repertoire. As she has explained in her influential book, the archive exists as tangible documents such as texts, letters, drawings, maps, and so forth. Performances, on the other hand, "function as vital acts of transfer, transmitting social knowledge, memory, and a sense of identity."[30] Indeed, she asserts, the repertoire "enacts embodied memory: performances, gestures, oral-ity, movement, dance, singing – in short, all those acts usually thought of as ephemeral, nonreproducible knowledge….The repertoire both keeps and transforms choreographies of meaning."[31] By continuing to re-enact and re-embody Aldridge's theatrical performances even decades after having witnessed them, Karpenko-Kary was passing on the meanings that had accrued to those events, their cultural mem-ory, and tradition. Aldridge had inspired the creation of a Ukrainian theatre – an almost unthinkable project in nineteenth century tsar-ist Russia. Karpenko-Kary would eventually become the founder and director of the first professional Ukrainian theatre in Russian-ruled Ukraine, the Teatr Koryfeiv (Theatre of Coryphaei; roughly trans-lated, Theatre of Star Actors).

After the death of Shevchenko in 1861, Aldridge toured Ukraine, including Kyiv, Kharkiv, Odesa, and Mykolaiv, bringing Shakespeare, sometimes illegally, to the stage. When *Macbeth, Richard III* and *King Lear* were banned throughout Russia by tsarist decree, Aldridge con-tinued to perform the plays by the simple expedient of not printing posters announcing the title of his performance. By the time the authorities discovered what he staged, he had already moved on to another city. With renewed waves of repression beginning in 1862, Aldridge was no longer welcome in Russia. Aldridge scholar Bernth Lindfors has persuasively argued that the sudden ban on his per-forming in St Petersburg arose because Aldridge was now "perceived as a symbol of the liberation struggle."[32] His repertoire and his per-son were thus generally understood as unwelcome counters, even possible threats, to tsarist authoritarianism and Russian imperialism. Nor could Aldridge return to the USA. His European perambulations

Figure 2.4. Ira Aldridge as Othello, Petersburg, 1858, the year that Aldridge met Shevchenko.

finally ended with his death in 1867 in Łódź, Poland, another country for which he symbolized opposition to tyranny.[33]

The example of Aldridge's travels throughout the empire and the responses that they elicited return us to the classic postcolonial questions: "Who can speak for the colonized? Who is the colonized? Who is the colonizer?" In the historical, poignant moment of the Shevchenko-Aldridge cross-cultural encounter, we recognize that history, identity, and memory coalesce. The ever elusive Shakespeare serves as mirror and prism: reflecting, refracting, problematizing, and, always, resonating.

3

"North by North West":
Shevchenko and Shakespeare

What did Shakespeare's works mean to creative minds in nineteenth century Ukraine? What did Taras Shevchenko mean when he would shout out, "Shakespeare! Shakespeare!" as an expression of extreme admiration? How did he understand the English playwright's works? This chapter addresses the still understudied dramatic work of Taras Shevchenko and the way in which it is underpinned by his concept of a "Shakespearean" aesthetic. Not lasting much more than four years, Shevchenko's brief experiment with drama was not highly regarded by many contemporary – or later – critics, despite the stage success of his *Nazar Stodolya*.[1] Indeed, while the publication of Shevchenko's *Kobzar* (1840) and the long poem *Haidamaky* (1841) suggested to writer and Shakespeare translator Panteleimon Kulish "the sound of the resurrecting trumpet of an archangel,"[2] Shevchenko's contemporaneous drama (to extend the analogy) might instead recall the feeble bleatings of a muted horn.

Shevchenko's Dramatic Oeuvre

Some confusion exists about the number of plays Shevchenko wrote. Only two are extant, a fragment in Russian verse from act three of a play titled *Nikita Gaidai* (published 1842) and a complete play in Ukrainian prose, *Nazar Stodolya* (1843). The original text of *Nazar Stodolya*, also written in Russian, has disappeared. *Nikita Gaidai* is probably the same play which Shevchenko earlier entitled *Nevesta* [The Bride], while *Nazar Stodolya* is most likely a re-working of a play to which he referred as *Danylo Reva*.[3] Another dramatic endeavour, *Slepaya krasavitsa* [Blind Beauty] (1842), seems to have been transformed into the poem *Slepaya*, composed in Russian. Finally, in a letter written during his exile, he outlined one other idea for a drama, a satiric vaudeville, but no such play has come down to us.[4]

The only complete play extant (*Nazar Stodolya*) and the excerpt from *Nikita Gaidai* strike most readers with disappointment. While Shevchenko's poetry is mellifluous, lyrical, expansive, and revolutionary, his Russian plays appear, in a word, thin. And yet his dramatic works are surprisingly revelatory of his aesthetic interests and concerns. Their study repays with an understanding not only of the poet's views of the drama but also of his role as a poet and especially as a "bard of the people." For what Shevchenko successfully achieves in his poetry is found writ large in his dramas. An understanding of the aesthetic impulse behind the plays may incidentally explain the reason why Shevchenko in English translation has never been a favourite with the Anglo-American reader.

The title of this chapter, drawing from Hamlet's phrase that signals he is mad only "North by North West," suggests that what follows is an oblique approach to Shevchenko's understanding of Shakespeare, one that is rooted in nineteenth-century Romanticism. The complex vectors of dramatic influence at play might be summarized by the expanded onomastic formula Shakespeare-Schiller-Ducis-Pixérécourt-Shevchenko.

Shevchenko and Melodrama

Shevchenko's aesthetic theory is nowhere openly stated, but we might fruitfully observe its nature by its consequences – more specifically, by its objects of admiration and imitation. The favourite device of New Historicists, the polysemous anecdote, is a useful way to concentrate and sharpen this focus. The first anecdote concerns an incident which occurred when the Black actor Ira Aldridge visited St. Petersburg in 1858 and subsequently toured Russia and Ukraine. Photographs of Aldridge show him in various distinctly theatrical, grandiose poses in the roles of Othello and King Lear. Aldridge appeared in a one-man show, speaking in English, and performing segments from *Othello*, "Shylock" (i.e., *The Merchant of Venice*), *King Lear* and *Macbeth*.[5] The focus of his performances was not on the text *per se* but rather on the text as a vehicle for the actor's expressive skill. As discussed in the previous chapter, Shevchenko responded with great emotion and enthusiasm to Aldridge's performances.

The frequently-cited anecdote about Shevchenko embracing Aldridge and showering him with kisses[6] has been frequently cited (including in the previous chapter) as evidence for Shevchenko's natural affinity for the Black actor whose personal history recalled Shevchenko's parallel fate. While undeniably true, it is notable that, in addition to Aldridge, the other great actors whom Shevchenko revered, Pavel Mochalov and Mikhail Shchepkin, were also emotional, even turbulent, in their acting style.[7] Mochalov's *Othello*, for example, was renowned for being "wild" and

Figure 3.1. Taras Shevchenko, *King Lear and the Fool,* 1843.

"terrible."[8] The affective power of theatre was one of the main sources of
pleasure. In terms of emotional extremes, we might also want to remind
ourselves that the only Shakespearean scene Shevchenko the artist chose
to illustrate with an engraving was the literal *Sturm und Drang* scene of
Lear and the Fool in the midst of the raging elements (1843).

This rehearsal of well-known incidents from Shevchenko's life is meant
not as biographical criticism, suggesting the poet's sympathy with the
downtrodden – one of the usual reasons for citing such episodes – nor as
evidence of Shevchenko's knowledge of Shakespeare. It is rather a means
of getting at what Shakespeare and "Shakespearean" aesthetics meant to
Shevchenko. For what seems abundantly clear from the anecdotes noted
above is Shevchenko's abiding interest in an affective art, an art which
focuses on morality, pathos, suffering – in other words, a mode completely
natural for Shevchenko, bearing in mind both his personal history and
that of his nation. It is, of course, the mode of melodrama, a mode that
dominated the theatres of nineteenth century Europe and Britain.

To identify melodrama as central to Shevchenko's works is to expand
the insight of critics such as Petro Rulin,[9] Oleksander Kysil,[10] and Valerian

Revutsky[11] who correctly identified *Nazar Stodolya* as melodrama, in contrast to the obfuscating categories of I. Pilhuk ("an historical-ethnographic drama"),[12] A. Pypin ("a romantic drama"),[13] and S.M. Shakhovsky ("a romantic oratorio").[14] For it is indeed melodrama, not tragedy, that Shevchenko wrote.

Today, for the most part, melodrama is loosely used as a term of contempt. In this chapter, I wish to employ it not in that denigrating fashion but rather as a neutral term which will assist in describing a genre as well as a particular aesthetic. In melodrama's defence, we should first recall that the rich variety of classics of melodrama includes such disparate plays as Schiller's *The Robbers*, August von Kotzebue's *Menschenhass und Reue* [Misanthropy and Remorse] (adapted and popularized in English as *The Stranger*), and Dion Boucicault's *The Colleen Bawn*, What these plays share is a fundamentally melodramatic view of life that differs from the tragic in many ways but particularly in one essential feature: in tragedy man is divided, in conflict with himself, while in melodrama he is "free from the agony of choosing between conflicting imperatives and desires."[15] In itself, this single-minded impulse is without special moral commitment: the villain is as uniformly dedicated to his cause as the virtuous heroine and courageous hero to theirs. Both types of characters are "whole," not capable of development, although they may be prone to sudden conversion.

A second, central feature of melodrama which arises from the first is its dependence on external pressures or adversaries for action: an evil man, a social group, a hostile ideology, an accident. The clear-cut quality of melodrama also necessitates its resort to extremity in incident, consequence, and solution. Scholar Peter Brooks refers to melodrama as the "aesthetics of astonishment," for it frequently moves from one crisis to another in an episodic fashion.[16] In bluntly delineating protagonists and antagonists, melodrama tends toward the moralistic. More importantly, in its pure form, it is the drama *of* morality: "it strives to find, to articulate, to demonstrate, to 'prove' the existence of a moral universe."[17] A drama of recognition, the reward of virtue in the concluding scene in comic formulas of melodrama is secondary to public recognition of virtue and either public punishment of evil or its conversion.

What melodrama entails, therefore, is the conflict between clearly opposing sides; melodrama invites, indeed only contemplates, binary oppositions. It is intent not on ambiguity, ambivalence, plurality or polysemy, those favoured modes of our times, but rather on the boldly stated oppositions between light and darkness, good and evil. Thus, the best in melodrama reaches toward the archetypal. But while grandiose, extreme and seductive on stage (it is an excellent vehicle for showing off a good actor, as Mochalov, Shchepkin and others knew), the verbal icon of melodrama in print appears shrunken and vapid. Drawing upon a polarized universe, melodrama does not end in a new society, as comedy does;[18] nor does it end with sacrifice, as does tragedy. Rather, it ends with "a reforming of the old society of innocence," with "confirmation and restoration."[19]

Shevchenko's early work follows precisely from such a melodramatic aesthetic: it is the rhetoric of absolutes, the story of true virtue assailed by evil external forces. By no accident does the latent image of Ophelia lie behind many of Shevchenko's works: the woman who feels too much (in contrast to Hamlet, the man who thinks too much), the pathetic (that is, suffering) rather than the tragic plot. The oppressive male world in Shevchenko's poetry generally destroys the victim, who is already subjugated, oppressed, silent, and marginalized. Ostracization, madness, and suicide (especially by drowning) are found in many of these (and in later) works, including *Prychynna* [The Bewitched], *Utoplena* [The Drowned], *Kateryna*, *Topolia* [The Poplar], *Slepaia* [The Blind One], *Vidma* [The Witch], and *Varnak* [The Convict].

Melodrama depends for effect upon what Brooks has called its "scandal": "excessive feeling."[20] Its open indulgence in exalted rhetoric and pure emotion both seduces and is the source of critical resistance and embarrassment. While melodrama refuses censorship and repression, particularly in the area of emotion, it is always based on raising deeply sincere (never false) emotions. Two examples, one from *Prychynna* and the other from *Nazar Stodolya*, will suffice as synecdoches:

> As she broken-hearted,
> Stood before him, had he sworn
> To return…O hated,
> Cruel lot! To meet no more
> Were the lovers fated?
> Slain did he and moveless lie,
> His dear face uncovered?
> Would her tears not burn his eyes?[21]   (*Prychynna*)

HALIA: You promised my mother on her deathbed to marry me to Nazar. What are you doing? How have I angered you? Why would you destroy me? Am I not your own daughter? (*Bursts out crying*).[22] (*Nazar Stodolya*, Act I)

Paradoxically, the openness of the emotions, the shooting-from-the-hip style which names antagonists and firmly commits the poet to certain ideas, have been described as the epitome of "manly" Ukrainian poetry[23] – even though feminist critics might define such a voice as "feminine" for its taking up the story of the marginalized Other. In Shevchenko's poetry, not only woman but that even more radically dispossessed being, the orphan, a being without visible sanction, carries the burden of the poet's message: the injustice, indifference, and amorality of the universe; the orphan becomes a symbol of revolutionary energy.

Shevchenko and Shakespeare

In examining Shevchenko's dramaturgy, his knowledge of the theatre, his friendships with actors, and his scattered comments in his letters and prose writings, scholars have drawn attention to his admiration of Shakespeare and especially his constant call, while in exile, for two books: the Bible and the works of Shakespeare in Nikolai Ketcher's translation. The mere placement of a discussion of Shevchenko's dramaturgy alongside his readings of Ketcher suggests (inaccurately) that Shevchenko was influenced by Ketcher's fairly serviceable prose rendition of Shakespeare. But the Shakespeare that Shevchenko as young-bohemian-about-town saw on the lively stages of St. Petersburg was not Ketcher's. In fact, Ketcher's translations were never staged during Shevchenko's lifetime, nor were they highly regarded by the *régisseurs* or actors. Shevchenko had not, could not have, read Ketcher's version of *Romeo and Juliet* (to which critics often compare *Nazar Stodolya*[24]), for in 1844 Ketcher had not gone beyond translating some of the English histories.

What Shevchenko knew as "Shakespeare" were the Russian adaptations and translations of the much-preferred Jean-François Ducis, himself a "barbarian" (as some of his own countrymen called him) adaptor and popularizer of Shakespeare on the French stage.[25] The admired actors of the day, like Mochalov, described the Ducis-based Shakespeare plays as "very effective and stageworthy."[26] Shchepkin acted in an adaptation of *Othello* taken from Ducis, as did Vasilii Karatygin and others.[27] What these plays had, and what the audiences wanted, was excitement that could arouse a whole spectrum of different emotions.

Ducis's Shakespeare, "imitée de l'anglais," as he put it on the title page to his *Hamlet* (1769), was a regularized Shakespeare in which confidants abound, unities and decorum are observed, and emotion consistently runs high.[28] The name of Ducis may in fact be taken as representing the whole influence of the melodramatic tradition on Shevchenko. Behind Ducis also lurks the "father" of melodrama, René-Charles Guilbert de Pixérécourt, who established the international standard for the genre, a genre which took all of Europe by storm. In France alone between 1797 and 1834, it is reported that thirty thousand performances of Pixérécourt's dramas took place.[29]

On the stages of St Petersburg, melodrama and vaudeville, along with generically-related opera and ballet, reigned supreme. Shevchenko might have seen the Ducis-based translations of Stepan Ivanovich Viskovatov, who turned *Hamlet* into a three-act play with Hamlet as king rather than prince. In the concluding scene, Hamlet rejects suicide in order to serve his nation. (If so, this would shed much light on Shevchenko's comment in one of his prose works that the ending of *Hamlet* is "earth-shaking."[30]) Or he might have experienced Alexander Gavrilovich Rotchev's transformed *Romeo and Juliet* (1825–7) which (like his own *Nazar Stodolya*) ends happily. Nikolai Gnedich translated and adapted *King Lear* from Ducis; his rendering was performed by Mochalov in 1838 and was possibly the source for Shevchenko's engraving. In Gnedich's adaptation Lear's madness is short-lived and he is reconciled with Cordelia in Act III.[31]

The common manner of approaching Shakespeare was not by working from an original but from an adaptation and translation. This system reached its properly-mocked apogee with one of Rotchev's works, which announced on its title page, *Macbeth, a Tragedy of Shakespeare, from the Works of Schiller* (1830). Even Nikolai Polevoy's translation of *Hamlet* (1840), a much-touted version, was scorned by the caustic Vissarion Belinsky as "Ducis-like" and as "romantic melodrama."[32] But, despite the scorn of the literary critics, it was the Romantic, melodramatic Shakespeare that continued to be played on both the Russian and the "provincial" (Kyiv, Kharkiv, Odesa) stages.

Thus it was not the "real" Shakespeare that the young Shevchenko admired and hoped to emulate.[33] His sympathies in fact were closer to the aesthetic theories of Friedrich Schiller, whose works he knew (although performance of Schiller's dramas was prohibited by the censor).[34] In particular, Schiller's essay entitled "The Pathetic" (1793), put forward an idea surely congenial to Shevchenko: the notion that the pathetic (suffering) is "the first condition required most strictly in a tragic author."[35]

The preface to *The Robbers* (whose title might have associatively suggested *Haidamaky* – that is, robbers or bandits) also raises another idea Shevchenko would have applauded: the stage as a moral, unifying force. As Schiller insisted, "it commands all human knowledge, exhausts all positions, illumines all hearts, unites all classes, and makes its way to the heart and understanding by the most popular channels."[36] Schiller goes on to argue the importance of patriotic writers who could create a truly national stage, which, in turn, would help create a nation.[37] Schiller's aims as well as his self-evidently Romantic rhetoric are indissolubly linked to the rise of nationalism. This would have been of great interest to Shevchenko who was creating and defending a national literature, language, and identity whose very existence was being denied.

The choice of melodrama, conscious or not, was the only possibility for a bard or prophet of the people. While crafting a work in the still fashionable genre that could be found on the St. Petersburg stages, Shevchenko's Romantic melodrama, *Nazar Stodolya*, did not break new ground in the same way as his poetry. The play, a technically superb melodrama, is a veritable catalogue of the genre's conventions and devices: Nazar, the courageous and handsome hero; Halia, the virtuous and thoughtful heroine very much in love with him; Khoma, the tyrant-father who attempts to trick his daughter into marrying an old rich Cossack *polkovnyk* (colonel) for his own gain; Stekha, the witty, clever housekeeper with an eye to her own material gain; and Ihnat, the solid, sterling friend who prefers drink to women. In addition to these stock characters, we have the *de rigeur* presence of musicians, songs, dancing, a minstrel, a supernatural setting (Christmas Eve), a snowstorm, and a ghost-inhabited inn.

In the extant fragment of his play *Nikita Gaidai*, there is a mysterious letter containing state secrets, a love affair, a secret mission, scheming Polish magnates, a well-intentioned but naive king, a patriotic and noble hero (Nikita), and his similarly-inclined beloved, Marianna. Both plays also contain a potentially incendiary background of historical events. Nazar and Nikita are Ukrainian patriots and firm believers in the Cossack brotherhood, egalitarianism, merit, and democracy (just as Ducis' Romeo believes in the brotherhood of all men and so cannot even hate the Capulets). Nazar refuses to bow before any authority. These are sentiments typical of melodrama, the democratic genre. And it is here that further links between the drama and the poetry may be seen. In poetry, as American scholar George Grabowicz has observed, "the ethos of the collective, of the group, often epitomized by the Cossacks…provides the perspective on the past and constitutes its moral measure."[38]

While these ideas are by no means foregrounded in *Nazar Stodolya* (where romance takes precedence), they penetrate the whole play and may suggest why the censor refused permission for its performance (if Shevchenko did indeed submit it to the Alexandrinsky Theatre). It is this commitment to the group, the heroic, the radically democratic values of melodrama, that creates the bomb of *Kobzar* and of later works. Within the genre of the drama however, these elements are not new but are part of the melodramatic aesthetic.[39] To the reader of Shevchenko's poetry, the plays appear to be alien creations, not in the least because *Nazar Stodolya* concludes happily, whereas Shevchenko's poetry is obsessed with destruction. There, suffering, incest, betrayal, injustice, and death predominate. And yet this is but a surface difference. The aesthetics of melodrama effortlessly accommodates both the tragic and the comic ending.

The easy traffic between Shevchenko's poetry and his drama is illustrated by the frequent stagings of his poetry on the one hand and on the other by his own transformation of the plot of *Slepaya krasavitsa* from drama into narrative poem. Shevchenko's poetic and dramatic works are of a piece, not only because the events portrayed in his poetry are similar to the plots and conventions of melodrama but, more importantly, because of the concord of his poetry with melodrama's morality and sensibility. Shevchenko's poetry is defiant: it espouses the concerns of the victim, the greatest victim being Ukraine itself, pictured again and again as virtuous, innocent and raped. The single voice, the "bard of the people," the "prophet" Shevchenko, speaks with unswerving commitment and moral certitude. In the apparent absence of moral or ethical norms, the poet insists upon the existence of and the need for a moral universe, if not now, then in some mystical future. It is by no accident that George Grabowicz has styled Shevchenko a "myth-maker," for myth-making is part of the melodramatic mode. As Brooks has observed, "Melodrama represents both the urge toward resacralization and the impossibility of conceiving sacralization other than in personal terms."[40] Notably, it is also easy to shift from the melodramatic point of view into satire, as Shevchenko does in his political poems. The same moral base is at work here, the same sharply drawn antagonisms and heartfelt anguish at injustice, the same absolutes, although more caustically expressed

Writing his plays in Russian for a Russian stage, Shevchenko could hardly have become the prophet of his people, although (as his two extant experiments with drama suggest) he could have been a successful writer of melodramas. But by transposing the aesthetic impulse of melodrama into Ukrainian poetry, Shevchenko could speak for and as the dispossessed. Forbidden from returning to his beloved Ukraine in his last years, Shevchenko was a true Romantic, not just intellectually apprehending but actually experiencing the exile, solitude, and suffering Western Romantics for the most part merely imagined.[41]

Shevchenko's Russian dramas and his prose works written in Russian proved his writerly skills. It was, however, by deciding to write in Ukrainian that he became a radical, throwing down the gauntlet to those who, like Belinsky, believed that great poetry could never be written in a "dialect."[42] Shevchenko's insistently Ukrainian voice challenged not only the critics but also political and cultural authority and hegemony, especially as symbolized by the "Little Father" himself, Nicholas I. That the tsar recognized the power of the word is evidenced by his own hand, which scrawled his approval of Count Orlov's severe assessment:

Shevchenko acquired among his friends the reputation of a great Little Russian writer and therefore his poems are doubly harmful and dangerous... because of his rebellious spirit and boundless insolence, he must be regarded as one of the main criminals.[43]

Sentenced to life as a private soldier and forbidden to work as an artist and writer, Shevchenko, the former serf, then the young, lionized poet of cultural circles, seemed himself to have lived one of the most outrageous of melodramatic plots imaginable.

4
Ophelia as Poet:
Lesya Ukrainka and the Woman as Artist

While the poetry and drama of Lesya Ukrainka (pseudonym of Larysa Kosach-Kvitka, 1871–1913) frequently stress the heroic – and this is the note which has been most constantly sounded by critics – its counterpoint, the tragic silence and opposition which meet women's voices, is of equal significance to her work. Indeed, without this counterpoint, her work might seem naively optimistic or bombastically heroic. Her oeuvre often focuses on the complexities of crisis: her figures are torn between systems, possibilities, roles, and desires. The last plot she began to formulate as she lay close to death was the story of an Arab woman who, partially Westernized, is forced to live out her life in an "Oriental," and now somewhat alien, environment. Throughout her works, Ukrainka examined a great variety of themes set in as many various historical periods; in all but a few, women occupy her full attention.

Most frequently lauded by critics for introducing Western themes and forms into Ukrainian literature, Ukrainka translated the power of these texts by focusing not necessarily on what she admired most but on what troubled her most. Well-known characters from classical works, including those of Shakespeare, acted as prisms by which Ukrainka interrogated and illuminated issues of great concern to her: the position of the woman artist in society, gender politics, and (more obliquely) the oppression of Ukrainian culture.

Ukrainka uses *Hamlet* throughout much of her creative career as a touchstone to examine her poetic calling, a calling often at odds with direct political activity. *Hamlet* thus becomes a palimpsest against which her works play, frequently recoiling from their source, melding with others, occasionally in harmony with it. Hamlet, part hysteric (as Freud argued), and part woman (as Goethe claimed), enamoured of words, rather than deeds, weak and passive in the interpretation of many nineteenth-century critics (such as Coleridge, Hazlitt, Lamb), seems to be a "natural" tragic hero with whom a female poet could identify. But it is not exclusively Hamlet himself, the poetic intellectual, with whom Ukrainka identifies. In Ukrainka's reading, the poet is also, and more especially, Ophelia: the woman who is abandoned, destroyed, maddened, and who sings to her death. Linked in Ukrainka's imagination to Sappho, but also to a number of other literary figures (including Juliet and Lady Macbeth), Ukrainka's Ophelia is much more than a delicate, pathetic figure of secondary importance; she becomes the focus of interest. Complexly allusive, this Ophelia gathers up the image of troubled artist, sensuous beloved, betrayed lover, and madwoman; *she* is "[t]he lunatic, the lover, and the poet…of imagination all compact" (*A Midsummer Night's Dream*, 5.1.7–8).

Ukrainka's poetic personas and her dramatic heroines, many of them madwomen, prophetesses and artists, have much in common with the views of late twentieth-century feminist theorists. To "speak otherwise" is in the nature of their fictional roles as are the firm opposition, violence, betrayal, or silence with which these characters are met. The additional and very real variable of the political context, especially censorship and prohibition of Ukrainian culture and language, also needs to be taken into account. Although cultural politics is not a focus of this chapter, it is an important element in understanding the way that foreign texts could (or could not) be appropriated in areas of Ukraine under Imperial Russian rule.[1] Ukrainka's poetic personas and her dramatic heroines are triply excluded from sources of power: as women in a male-dominated society, as "abnormal" artists in a "sane" society (even when they masquerade as Greeks or Hebrews), and as Ukrainians in an imperial Russian-ruled country.

The course of Ukrainka's creative work indicates a clear awareness of this complex exclusion; it is revealed in the tragic duality of her characters, both in the poetry and in the drama, characters who recognize themselves as mere voices in the wilderness, who cannot but must speak, write, create. In the struggle of poesis against praxis, creative endeavours against social action, an alternative position consistently surfaces: women's traditional silence and the peace and apparent freedom of oblivion. If not indicative of her deep-seated doubts about the role of woman as artist, then the constant return to these questions throughout her literary career suggest at the very least her awareness of the complexity and difficulty of such a role.

The fate of the artist is one of Ukrainka's life-long concerns, a concern which is perhaps most obviously expressed in her lyric poetry. It is in her derivative juvenilia that the images of Ophelia and Sappho are first fused. The Romantic poetry of Heinrich Heine, whom she also extensively translated in her youth, is everywhere apparent in her work of the 1880s. "Sappho" (*Сафо*, 1884), the first of many poems which deal with Ukrainka's struggling ideas about the woman as poet, as creator, bard, or prophetess, was written when she was thirteen:[2]

Sappho

Above the sea, on the cliffs,
A beautiful girl sits,
Radiant in a laurel wreath,
Holding a singer's lyre.

To her sad song
She plays accompaniment.
And with that song in her heart
Her great longing arises:

In that song she recalls her glory
Great, and the beautiful world,
Evil people, and love,
And betrayal, the sorrowful passion of her years,

Hopes and despair…The girl
Tore off her laurel wreath
And in the waves of the foamy sea
Found an end to her song.

Сафо

Над хвилями моря, на скелі,
Хороша дівчина сидить,
В лафровім вінку вона сяє,
Співецькую ліру держить.

До пісні своєї сумної
На лірі вона приграє.
І з піснею тою – у серці
Велика їй туга встає:

В тій пісні згадала і славу
Величну свою, красний світ,
Лукавих людей, і кохання,
І зраду, печаль своїх літ,

Надії і розпач…Дівчина
Зірвала лавровий вінець
І в хвилях шумливого моря
Знайшла своїй пісні кінець.[3]

In this early poem, Ukrainka is able to delineate, however crudely, the basic outlines of her conflict. While clearly as much a product of her teenage years as it is the fruit of Romanticism, this four-stanza lyric already makes a number of important connections which Ukrainka would continue to explore throughout her career. The Sappho about whom she writes is (as Ukrainka was to become) an acknowledged and successful creator (she is both crowned with laurels and sings of her own fame and glory); she has experienced love but has suffered and been betrayed. The sudden shift in tense, from present to past, in the last stanza seems intended to shock the reader, as does the final word in the Ukrainian original: *кінець* – end. The Romantic reverie of the first three stanzas is thus dramatically overturned by unexpected death, as the poet-singer is spurred to her death by her own poetic creations that bring to mind past injustices.

According to legend and literary tradition (including Ovid's *Heroides*), the great Sappho drowned herself when she was rejected by the beautiful young Phaon. In Ukrainka's account, Sappho is not an older, much experienced, woman rejected by a younger lover but pointedly a young girl betrayed by love; in other words, she is a type of Ophelia: an innocent, full of promise, destroyed before she comes to full flower. (Throughout Ukrainka's oeuvre, "song" and "poetry" are used synonymously; this synonymity further enhances the connections between Ophelia as singer and as poet, and the link between Ophelia and Sappho.)

It is possible to read "Sappho" as Ukrainka's mere aping of male writers' romanticized versions of the madwoman, for her image of Sappho might be interpreted as coinciding with the "sexual victimization, bereavement, and thrilling emotional extremity"[4] of Romantic literature as a whole, in which madwomen in particular are transformed into *objets d'art*,[5] yet to do so would be to read carelessly and without reference to her work as a whole. That the Sappho theme is more than a Romantic influence Ukrainka was merely imitating may be confirmed by jumping ahead to 1912 or 1913 (the dating is uncertain) and not long before her death, when Ukrainka again returned to this theme. Extant is part of the opening scene of an unfinished play entitled "Sappho and Phaon" which centres on the conflict between the calling of the woman-artist (creative expression and its public dissemination) and the demands of conventional love (modest, retiring behaviour).[6] Phaon sits idly by as

Sappho is engaged in writing a poem. Bored and ignored, Phaon urges Sappho to stop writing, at first out of apparent concern for her health: she looks pale. Then, as their loving conversation quickly deteriorates, Phaon moves on to some minor literary critique of her poem-in-progress. Finally, when it becomes clear that Sappho interrupts rather than abandons her work in order to respond to her lover's comments, Phaon raises the larger, real issue implicit in his earlier remarks: love songs, he remonstrates, should be private, for his ears only, and not trumpeted abroad. In a fit of anger, Sappho sarcastically offers him a piece of embroidery as a more fitting gift than a poem and then proceeds to destroy her "child" (as she calls the poem, and as the childless Ukrainka referred to her works), by erasing the wax tablet upon which the poem was being written. What Phaon demands from Sappho, then, is an analogous effacement of self, a betrayal of her poetic gifts. Although Ukrainka never finished this play, we may speculate with some confidence that such a Sappho would commit suicide because of the conflicting demands of love and of art rather than unrequited love, the latter being the reason proposed by one of the long traditions associated with her life and work.

The limitations imposed upon the female writer – the particular themes and subjects traditionally approved for women, which stressed modesty, not passion, the domestic, not the public spheres – deeply rankle Ukrainka. The vocation of writer sharpens this age-old conflict between gender and vocation, freedom of choice and socially-approved role. In this struggle, love is not a transcendent force which overcomes all such obstacles but, rather, is closer to Simone de Beauvoir's dangerous obstacle in the path toward self-fulfillment.[7] For Ukrainka, women in love consistently lose and at great cost: their identity and creativity are erased. What is indirectly suggested in the works (discussed below) which fall between these two treatments of Sappho is bluntly stated in her satirical poem "A Woman's Portrait" (*Жіночий портрет*, 1906). Here, Ukrainka bitterly and unequivocally attacks the idea of woman's surrender of self when in love.[8]

A Woman's Portrait

You are an honest woman; you don't sell
your beauty and caresses for money,

you don't give insincere kisses
for hapless greed, for luxury.

You are a proud woman; you didn't enter
a little lair, bound by friendly arms;

you took the hardest work for yourself,
silently carrying on for many years.

You are a good woman; you don't have tart words
for those who "fell low,"
even though you yourself suffered through misery,
even though temptation came close to you.

You are a sincere woman. That is why you bow
your head low, when you recall those
who sell themselves; you know how it was
both bitter and sweet for them, having fallen into slavery.
Because you sold yourself, too. Not for silver
And not for greed, nor for gifts,
but for that caressing warmth,
for dear things and for kisses....

It was the heart's hunger which drove you after him,
in whose eyes shine bright diamonds,
whose laughter seemed golden to you,
whose curls were as abundant as grape clusters.

Not your flesh, but your soul,
your talent and your mind you sold into bondage,
you set it into endless penal servitude,
and for you it is both bitter and sweet unto pain.

Жіночий портрет

Ти чесна жінка, ти не продаєш
своєї вроди і пестощів за гроші,
нещирих поцілунків не даєш
за лакомство нещасне, за розкоші.

Ти горда жінка, ти не увійшла
в кубельце, звите дружніми руками,
найтяжчу працю ти собі взяла,
несеш мовчазно довгими роками.

Ти добра жінка, слів терпких нема
у тебе для таких, що "впали низько,"
хоч злидні перетерпіла й сама,
хоч і тобі була спокуса близька.

Ти щира жінка. Тим своє чоло
ти хилиш низько, про таких згадавши,
що продаються; зняєш, як було
Їм гірко й солодко, в неволю впавши.

Бо продалась і ти. Не за срібло
і не ща ласощі, не за дарунки,
але за те пестливеє тепло,
за любі речі та за поцілунки...

Се ж голод серця гнав тебе за тим,
у кого в очах діаманти ясні,
чий сміх тобі здавався золотим,
а кучері були, мов грона рясні.

Не тіло ти, а душу продала,
свій хист і розум віддала в неволю,
у каторгу довічну завдала, –
і гірко й солодко тобі до болю.[9]

Through its repetitive strategy of praise – "honest," "proud," "good," and "sincere" – irony takes over, for this woman, too, has also sold herself. By satisfying her *голод* (hunger/ famine/ dearth) – the famished needs of love – woman becomes slave. Ukrainka thus makes the provocative claim that such an honest woman is but a variant of the prostitute; the lives of both types of women tell the same story. "Portrait of a Woman" is Every Woman's Portrait or, rather, the same story that is also no story, for the woman's individuality is dead, willingly effaced in her weak capitulation to the temptation of man's love.

The poignant sacrifice of woman's personal desires and talents, the "key act" of the angel-woman[10] is developed in yet another poem, "The Forgotten Shadow" (*Забута тінь*, 1898), which takes Dante's wife as its subject. The eternal fame of both Dante and Beatrice and Dante's transcendent love for a woman he hardly knew – the subjects of the first thirty-four lines of the poem – are, in the remainder of the poem, contrasted with the "forgotten shadow," Dante's wife:

The Forgotten Shadow

Somewhere, far down in history's depths,
A recollection of her still lives. Who is it?
'Tis Dante's wife! No other name remains

By which she still is known – as though she never
Possessed her own name.
This woman was not a guiding star,
But, like a faithful shadow, followed him
Who was the guide of "wretched Italy."
She shared with him the hard bread of exile,
She kindled the glowing fire upon his hearth
Within a stranger's house. And more than once
His hand, reaching out to seek support,
Was laid upon her assured shoulder;
Dear to her was his singer's fame,
But she did not stretch out her hand
To intercept a single ray;
And when the fire died out in the singer's eyes,
She closed them with her pious hands.
Yes, a faithful shadow! And where is her own life?
Where is her own fate, happiness and sorrow?
History is silent, but in my thoughts I see
The many sorrowful and lonely days
She spent in troubled waiting,
The sleepless nights, as dark as that trouble,
And as long as destitution; I see tears…
And walking on those tears, like pearly dew,
Into the land of fame – the lovely Beatrice!

Забута тінь

Десь там, на дні історії, глибоко
Лежить про неї спогад. Хто вона?
Се жінка Дантова. Другого ймення
Від неї не зосталось, так, мов зроду
Вона не мала власного імення.
Ся жінка не була провідною зорею,
Вона як вірна тінь ішла за тим,
Хто був поводарем "Італії нещасній".
Вона ділила з ним твердий хліб,
Вона йому багаття розпалила
Серед чужої хати. І не раз
Його рука, шукаючи опори,
Спиралась на її плече, запевне;
Їй дорога була його співецька слава.
Але вона руки не простягла,

> Аби хоч промінь перейнять єдиний;
> Коли погас вогонь в очах співецьких,
> Вона закрила їх побожною рукою.
> Так, вірна тінь! А де ж її життя,
> Де ж власна доля, радощі і горе?
> Історія мовчить, та в думці бачу я
> Багато днів сумних і самотних,
> Проведених в турботному чеканні,
> Ночей безсонних, темних, як той клопіт,
> І довгих, як нужда, я бачу сльози…
> По тих сльозах, мов по росі перлистій,
> Пройшла в країну слави – Беатріче![11]

Beatrice, the lovely Muse who leads Dante to a vision of heaven itself, becomes, in Ukrainka's version, the other woman who obscures for ever the devotion, sorrow, and love of the self-sacrificing, passive wife. As in "A Woman's Portrait," so here Ukrainka looks at the margins of history and literature; Dante's wife is like the other honest women in losing not only her story but also her name. Whereas literary tradition glorifies Dante's mystical experience, Ukrainka foregrounds the personal sacrifice women have made and have been expected to make. As Shoshana Felman observes about woman's roles at this time, "[f]rom her initial family upbringing throughout her subsequent development, the social role assigned to the woman is that of serving an image, authoritative and central, of man: a woman is first and foremost a daughter/a mother/a wife."[12]

Ukrainka's work challenges these socially-constructed roles. In looking for alternate models to emulate, Ukrainka appears to seek an active principle, one attentive to socio-political exigencies. Such action seems to preclude or at least question what her vocation demands: words, that traditional woman's weapon. While in some poems, like "Words, why aren't you tempered steel?" (*Слово, чом ти не твердая криця*, 1896), Ukrainka seeks, and recovers, a forceful role for poetry; in many others, doubts remain. "Avenging Angel" (*Ангел помсти*, 1896), which together with a number of other works written in the same year, draws from Shakespeare and focuses on this clash between words and deeds. Part of a cycle of poems entitled "Songs of Slavery" (*Невільничі пісні*), "Avenging Angel" brings together a variety of Shakespearean allusions: the nightmarish visions of *Richard III* (Clarence's prophetic dream of "A shadow like angel, with bright hair / Dabbled in blood" 1.4.53–54, and the series of avenging ghosts who visit Richard in his sleep in 5.3.118–176), the ghost scene in *Hamlet* (1.3.), and Hamlet's "antic" response to Polonius (2.2.191).

Avenging Angel

In the secret darkness in the middle of the night
A dubious guest often flies in to visit me;
He arouses terror by his glare and greets me,
His eyes shine brightly like the bloody star of Mars.

The dreadful messenger smiles at me,
I see both love and hatred in that smile:
On his white wings blood blushes,
Just as the evening star's crimson lies on the snow.

He speaks to me words terrible and great,
In his hands blazes a gleaming, flaming sword;
And in my heart, like a war cry,
Wild songs are aroused in me.

"Words, words, words!" to them my guest speaks.
"I am the angel of revenge, of deeds, not words,
Think not that thy brave song
Will stir others, but not thyself, to war.

"I give to thee this sword; though thou art weak,
My sword is not heavy for brave hands.
Dost thou fear death, punishment, suffering,
Thou, who was always free in thy soul?"

He passes me the sword, I want to take the weapon,
But my hand does not obey me,
And the fiery fury in my heart subsides:
"Go," I say to him, "I will not go with thee.

"I do not pity life, but I pity the human
Which dwells in me, which I in others see;
When I kill that, let punishment follow the sin,
I will not want to live out that shameful hour.

'Thy servant Corday, a brave Norman,
In tyrants saw a tyrants' whole age,
Yet even in the tyrant the man appeared to her,
When the mistress shrieked at the murder."
The midnight guest disappears, but that look and speech

Leave a bloody and terrible trace in my heart,
And in the daytime I see that strange guest,
And the unfinished conversation tears and oppresses my soul.

Ангел помсти

У темряві таємній серед ночі
     До мене часто гість непевний приліта,
     Він поглядом жахає і віта,
Мов зірка Марс кривава, сяють очі.

Всміхається мені страшний посланець,
     Я бачу в усміху ненависть і любов,
     На білих крилах червоніє кров,
Мов на снігу зорі вечірньої багрянець.

Він промовля мені слова страшні й великі,
     В руках палає меч осяйний, огневий
     І в серці, наче поклик бойовий,
Здіймаються у мене співи дикі.

“Слова, слова, слова! – на них мій гість мовляє,
     Я ангел помсти, вчинків, а не слів,
     Не думай же, що твій одважний спів
Других, а не тебе до бою закликає.

Даю тобі сей меч, дарма що ти не сильна,
     Мій меч не тяжкий для одважних рук.
     Чи то боїшся смерті, кари, мук,
Ти, що була душею завжди вільна?”

Він подає свій меч, я хочу взяти зброю,
     Але не слухає мене моя рука,
     І лютість огнева із серця геть зника:
“Іди, – кажу йому, – я не піду з тобою.

Не жаль мені життя, а жаль тії людини,
     Що у мені живе, що бачу я в других,

     Коли ж її уб’ю, хай кара йде за гріх,
Не схочу пережить ганебної години.

> Твоя слуга Корде, одважная норманка,
>   В тиранах бачила тиранів цілий вік,
>   Але й в тирані їй з'явився чоловік,
> Як над убитим крикнула коханка."
>
> Зника північний гість, та погляд той і мова
>   Лишають в серці слід кривавий і страшний,
>   І вдень мені в очах стоїть той гість дивний,
> А душу рве й гнітить нескінчена розмова...[13]

Although the avenging angel castigates the poet's fears and passivity, the dreamer's acknowledgement of the humanity in every being prevents her from taking up the angel's bloody challenge. Even a tyrant like Marat cannot be killed without regret. While Hamlet's question is whether or not to take up action against tyranny, this poem seems to be resolved in favour of passive resistance and a kind of humanitarianism. Yet the resolution is only rhetorical, for the poet concludes with the haunting impression of an unfinished conversation that "tears and oppresses her soul" (1.36) The dreamer thus appears to accept the position of a Turgenev-like Hamlet: an undecided, humane intellectual who is unable to take direct action; the dreamer accepts words (poetry, art), not duty, not violence. Her sphere of endeavour will be in the feminine realm of "words, words, words" (1.13), while the night-visitor, a "Mars," operates in the male world of violence or the "active" life. If the night visitor is Macbeth, the dreamer is Lady Macbeth, able to contemplate the deed of murder but incapable of carrying it out.

The scant criticism of this poem is singularly unhelpful but the poem begins to acquire clarity when viewed from a feminist perspective. When the angel-like Ophelia is suppressed, the figure which arises "like a bad dream, bloody, envious, enraged"[14] is a madwoman-witch, an angel of revenge – the author's double, the revolutionary, not the literary and passive self. When Ophelia / Dante's Wife / Woman is suppressed, then the demonic Lady Macbeth comes to the fore. Yet, as the poet insists, the conversation is unfinished. Neither the recognition of humanity and its concomitant response of passivity nor the act of violent rebellion are finally acceptable. The poem insists that no closure is possible; for woman neither role is truly acceptable.

Ukrainka's concern with the female writer's isolation, as well as with the lack of a clear, practical ability to respond to tyranny, is a recurring theme in her work.[15] At least in part, this awareness seems to have led to involvement in political radicalism and in the writing and translating of works (including those by Marx), which, in the early part of her career, took her away from more creative endeavours. But it may also have been partly responsible for her turn to drama. Drama, a more active, certainly more public art than poetry, could very well have served to allay some of Ukrainka's own tensions and doubts about her poetic ivory tower and, as such, may have been her compromise (as well as her strength, as she was to discover) between the world of words and the world of deeds.

Of her dramatic children, *The Azure Rose* (Блакитна троянда, 1896) remained Ukrainka's – although not the critics' – favourite. It, too, brings together the references to madness, Ophelia and Lady Macbeth. A psychological drama, it has an Ibsen-like theme: a young playwright, Orest Hruichev, is in love with an artist, Lyubov (a proper name which means Love; the diminutive "Luba" is frequently used in its place) Hoshchynska. Their relationship is thwarted by society and, more particularly, Orest's mother, who believes that Lyubov will become mad like her mother. Sharing this view, Lyubov, while apparently quite sane at the beginning of the play, is nonetheless frightened of eventually losing her mind and, as a result, of destroying Orest, just as her own mad mother had emotionally destroyed her father. A strong-willed woman, Lyubov is an artist whose talent is taken for dilettantism because of her sex (while Orest's skill at writing is encouraged); her passion and intellectual questioning are taken as evidence of madness. Unable to marry and bear children because of society's belief in inherited madness, and thus thwarted in the only role which the late nineteenth-century society approved for women, Lyubov has no choice but to turn inward.[16]

In Act I, her mother's photograph is the object of some discussion among her rather shallow friends, who inquire about the identity of a beautiful woman in Lyubov's photo album. Ostrozhyn, a journalist, observes that the woman looks like a star of the demi-monde or like an actress playing a madwoman. In one version of the text, Ostrozhyn's remarks are more specific: he compares the beautiful woman to an actress playing Ophelia, and then, correcting himself, suggests that she actually looks more like Lady Macbeth.[17]

Ukrainka's awareness of the theatrical posing of madwomen and, in particular, the imposing of Ophelia-like postures upon them, shows an early, uneasy recognition of what a century later Showalter found in her studies of Victorian photographs of madwomen: a romanticized style of expressing emotional distress revealed by an explicitly sexual, external, sartorial shorthand of garlands, white gown and flowing locks.[18] To some extent, Ukrainka appears to conform to this male, romanticized view of madness in her first play, when she has Lyubov emulate her own mother's image in her first mad scene (3.12). Dressed in a white peignoir in lieu of a wedding dress, and her hair loose, she announces her intention to marry Orest in this theatrical garb. Proceeding to declaim Juliet's passionate soliloquy, "Come night, come Romeo," Lyubov directs her clearly sexual soliloquy at Orest. She tells the assembled, uncomprehending group of witnesses to this event that she purposes to make her stage debut immediately after the wedding; Juliet will be her crowning role. The madness and sexuality of Ophelia fuse with the figure of Juliet, both victims of corrupt societies. The symbols of loss of control – the loose hair and clothing, the wild and overtly sexual behaviour – and the abandonment of "normal" or conventional modes of feminine behaviour mark her as mad; yet it is both assumed and real madness, like Hamlet's.

To paraphrase David Leverenz on Ophelia, Lyubov's madness is "not a question of repressed sexual desire, though certainly her anxieties, like Hamlet's, have to do with feelings denied. It is a question of what it means to understand oneself when the price is falseness to others."[19] Submitting to familial and social duty to authority and forced to abandon her own desires, Lyubov's madness is the result of the impossible attempt to obey contradictory impulses. Lyubov's passionate and "unmaidenly" responses in Act III and elsewhere confirm for the psychiatrist, Dr. Protsenko (the apparent *raisonneur* of the play), that Lyubov is mad; hers, he believes, is a madness which is the result of too much strenuous intellectual work, too much unsupervised reading. In her deliberately provocative statements, in her passionate search for an independence from the yoke of middle-class love, Lyubov both fascinates and yet horrifies her beloved, Orest, and the other middle-class characters of the play, who finally and simply do not understand her internal struggle. While he loves her, Orest wants to make her only his Muse; he calls her his "Beatrice." Like the other characters in the play, he fails to perceive the true nature of her struggle.

Lyubov's perception of the hollowness of society is allowed direct expression only in the mad scenes, just as Ophelia in her mad scenes can finally reveal the underlying corruption of the Danish court, her grief, and the tensions she has experienced trying to solve the incompatible demands of duty and of love. For madness, as Maurice and Hanna Charney have pointed out, "allows woman an emotional intensity and scope not usually expected in conventional feminine roles."[20] The sexuality of Ophelia and Lyubov, the attack on social conventions, their rage, frustration, and sorrow are all "permissible" in the throes of madness. Thus, when, in an apparent non-sequitur, Lyubov turns to her weak-willed friend Milevsky and queries, "Does your wife often wash her hands?" she is not questioning her hygiene but is obliquely glancing at Lady Macbeth's obsessive hand-washing after the murder of Duncan. Syanya

Milevska has murdered no one but herself by marrying, for Milevsky, a shallow and thoughtless character, can hardly be the object of Syanya's devotion, only of her desire to conform to bourgeois ideals.

The frustration with such comfortable and false ideals spills over in scenes of hysteria which are completely incomprehensible to her friends, family, and physician alike. Overhearing many of the vicious remarks which Orest's mother, Maria Hruicheva, makes about her, Lyubov later responds with a self-conscious posturing, even when she is most hysterical: *"nur ein kranker Mensch ist Mensch"* [*sic*; only a sick person is a person] she insists in Act III.13. Intending to shock her immediate audience, Lyubov also directs the unseeing eyes of society at its own darkness.

In act IV, Strindberg-like, Orest and Lyubov begin to exchange traditional gender attributes: as Orest becomes ill, passive, and "femininely" weak because Lyubov has attempted to repress her love and has left him, Lyubov, on the other hand, acquires strength, determination and purpose, even as she uses these in a distinctly and traditionally feminine way.[21] She chooses to go mad to escape the impasse posed by the conflict between society's expectations and her own desires. Later, in a scene of disturbingly cool reason, Lyubov again chooses to commit suicide, this time by using drugs (a contemporary variant of drowning), but also encourages Orest to follow her. She thus both fulfills her society's beliefs in inherited madness and also rebels against that society by progressively stepping out of it: at first through partly feigned madness, then through suicide.[22] In attempting to suppress her love for Orest throughout the play, Lyubov resembles Ophelia who is forced to comply with her father Polonius's wishes and to deny Hamlet her love.[23] Orest, in turn, echoes Hamlet's words from Act I, scene two (11.141–42) when he promises always to love Lyubov and to care for her so that "the winds of heaven/[Will not] Visit her face too roughly" – Hamlet's phrase describing his idealized view of his father's love for his mother, Gertrude. The theme of madness, the internal struggle and mental anguish of the lovers, the hostile environment, the tragic conclusion of the play all recall moments from *Hamlet*, most especially (to paraphrase Leverentz once again) in the "extraordinary and unremitting array of 'mixed signals' that separate role from self, reason from feeling, duty from love."[24] For Lyubov, the tragedy lies in the fact that even her beloved Orest fails to understand her. He wishes to marry her but can only conceive of their traditional, socially constructed, roles: he will be the protector, the breadwinner, the artist; she, his Muse. Lyubov's vision of taking up a different path, expressed through the idea of love as an extraordinary azure rose, seems dangerous and baffling to him.

Lyubov's madness allows Ukrainka to explore in a more oblique, literary, and safe way many of the issues found in her earlier verse, but it also permits Ukrainka the possibility of disassociating herself from this assault on society. Like Ophelia, Lyubov could be (and was) interpreted as merely an unbalanced, pathetic creature. While unpopular with nineteenth- and many twentieth-century critics, *The Azure Rose* seems to foresee contemporary feminist concerns and, in its particular use of madness, anticipates the idea of the madwoman as a heroine, "a powerful figure who rebels against the family and the social order; and the hysteric who refuses to speak the language of the patriarchal order, who speaks otherwise."[25]

The poem "To Be or Not to Be?" (also written in 1896) suggests an alternative to madness, oblivion, suicide: the escape offered by art. First printed in the cycle of poems entitled "Thoughts and Dreams" (*Думи і мрії*), this is the first poem that carries an overt reference to *Hamlet* in its English title, "To Be or Not to Be?"

To be or not to be?

Hold, my heart, hold! do not beat so madly.
Calm yourself, my thoughts, do not fly so wildly.
Do not beat your wings in empty space.
You, my guilt-seeing Muse do not blind
Me with the fire of your immortal eyes!
Give me your hand, hug me to your bosom.
I gave you everything that I had,
Give me your great counsel.
Look: around us are great fields newly ploughed up,
And wild thickets, and steep precipices,
And dark, quiet waters. Look:
There are no highways, only here and there
Confused footpaths leading to obscurity.
Over there are people – a meagre few – ploughing those fields,
Over there, from the thickets, is the barely-heard knocking of a hatchet,
From the high precipices echo eagles' cries,
Only the quiet waters always silently stand by,
And, only sometimes, does a rock break off from its summit,
Fall and disappear into the dark, quiet waters, –
The trembling circle separates and disappears.
    Tell me, my unearthly counsellor,
Whither into space should I give myself?
Should I take off the silver-gold

Of my lyre and temper it into a plough,
And tie up these wings with the strings
So that a shadow will not fall on the narrow furrow?
Should I take up a place next to those people,
Plough up the fallow, and sow, and then –
And then await the harvest, but not for myself?
Or, should I throw myself over there, into the thicket,
And from the wild labyrinth carve a road
With a hatchet and a fine saw in my hands,
Until some rotting, great trunk
Falls and chokes me among the dark thickets?
Or, should I, eagle-like, fly up high,
Way above all the precipices, into limitless space,
Snatch bright lightning from a cloud,
Break off the golden wreath of a star
And blaze up in light during midnight?
But, what if in a second that light goes out,
Like a meteor, and the darkness seems even blacker,
Even more terrifying than it was before?
And what if no strength remains,
The fire scorches my wings and I'll fall
Like a rock, which breaks off in the precipices,
There, into the dark water, into the deep,
Into the cold water where, not for long,
The circle will tremble on the surface of the water?
You are silent, proud Muse! Only her eyes
Were inflamed by fire, with a great sweep the variegated wings
were lifted up
And clapped...O sorceress, stay!
Take me with you, let us fly together!

To Be or Not to Be? ...

Стій, серце, стій! не бийся так шалено.
Вгамуйся, думко, не літай так буйно!
Не бий крильми в порожньому просторі.
Ти, музо винозора, не сліпи
Мене вогнем твоїх очей безсмертних!
Дай руку, притули мене до свого лона.
Тобі я віддала усе, що мала.
Подай мені великую пораду.
    Дивись: навколо нас великі перелоги.
І дикі пущі, і високі кручі,

І темні, тихі води. Подивись:
Шляхів нема, а тільки де-не-де
Поплутані стежинки йдуть на безвість.
Он люди – мало їх – орють ті перелоги.
Он з пущі ледве чутно стук сокири.
З високих круч луна орлиний клекіт,
Лиш тихі води все стоять мовчазно,
І тільки часом камінь з круч зірветься,
Впаде і кане в темних тихих водах, –
Розійдеться і зникне круг тремтячий.

     Скажи мені, пораднице надземна,
Куди мені податись у просторі?
Чи маю я здійняти срібло-злото
З своєї ліри і скувати рало,
А струнами сі крила прив’язати,
Щоб тінь не падала на вузьку борозну,
Зайняти постать поряд з тими людьми,
Орати переліг і сіяти, а потім –
А потім ждати жнив, та не для себе?
Чи, може, кинутись туди, у пущу,
І в диких нетрях пробивать дорогу
З сокирою в руках і з тонкою пилою.
Поки який гнилий, великий стовбур
Впаде й задавить серед темних хащів?
Чи, може, злинути орлицею високо,
Геть понад кручі, у простор безмежний,
Вхопити з хмари ясну блискавицю,
Зірвати з зірки золотий вінець
І запалати світлом опівночі?
А що, коли те світло миттю згасне,
Як метеор, і темрява чорніше,
Страшніше здасться, ніж була раніш?
А що, коли не стане в мене сили.
Вогонь обпалить крила й я впаду,
Неначе камінь, що зірвався з кручі,
Туди, у темні води, в глибину,
В холодну тишу, і недовго буде
Тремтіти круг на площині води?

     Мовчиш ти, горда музо! тільки очі
Спалахнули вогнем, барвисті крила
Широким помахом угору здійнялись
І сплеснули…О чарівнице, стій!
Візьми мене з собою, линьмо разом![26]

Although written in blank verse and shaped by a series of questions like Hamlet's soliloquy, Ukrainka's "To Be or Not to Be?" deviates radically from its famous namesake. For Ukrainka, "To be or not to be" is not a question of metaphysics but a question of creativity. The poem, an apostrophe to her Muse, raises some of the same questions as "Avenging Angel," but in a different key. The poet seeks advice, refuge, and finally mystical transportation from her Muse. Should she join the people who plough and gather the harvest? Or, should she fly like an eagle, above the precipices, into limitless space and snatch a lightning bolt from a cloud, encasing herself in fire? The "not to be" is thus transformed into the quotidian practical activities of working, harvesting for others, and of being "lost in the thicket."[27] "To be" is equated with poetic fancy, Romantic transmutation, great ambition but also with solitude, fear, and self-destruction. The poet's assertion of her desire to fly with her "sorceress," poetry, and her clear preference for art over duty and social responsibility seem to bring this topic to its close, and yet it ends with yearning, not with resounding affirmation.

Whereas "To Be or Not to Be?" draws on its resonances from Hamlet, "Adagio Penseroso," part IV of a cycle of poems entitled "Rhythms" (*Ритми*, 1900), turns directly to Ophelia and the figure of the female poet for whom madness, silence, and oblivion are lulling and magnetic possibilities. The five-stanza poem begins with the poet wishing that she could flow with the water like the mad (*bezumna*, literally, without a mind) Ophelia, bedecked with flowers.

Adagio Penseroso

Oh, I should like to float upon the water
Like Ophelia, garlanded, mad.
My songs would float in my wake,
agitated like that gentle water,
    Always farther, farther...
And the water would slowly
fold me in its light waves
Like a child in thin swaddlings.
And would rock me, like a dear dream, so quietly, quietly...
    I, so powerless, would let myself be carried and hugged,
floating with a quiet, barely audible song,
descending into an azure, bright water
always deeper, deeper...
    Later, on the waves
there'd remain only the indistinct echo

of my songs, like a memory that fades of
a forgotten ballad of olden days;
it contained something sorrowful and bloody,
yet how to recollect it? The song echoed
long ago, long ago…
    And even later the echo would disappear,
and on the water only my flowers would rock,
those that didn't follow me to the bottom of the river.
They'd float until, in a quiet cove, they'd fasten onto white water lilies;
there they'd stay. Over the drowsy waters
inert branches of weeping willows would bend,
into the quiet shelter the wind would not blow,
from the sky onto the lilies and the flowers,
which I, mad, had gathered, would descend only peace, peace.

Ритми

IV (Adagio Penseroso)
    Хотіла б я уплисти за водою,
немов Офелія, уквітчана, безумна.
За мною вслід плили б мої пісні,
хвилюючи, як та вода лагідна,
все далі, далі…
    І вода помалу
мене б у легкі хвилі загортала,
немов дитину в тонкий сповиток.
І колихала б, наче люба мрія,
так тихо, тихо…
    Я ж, така безвладна,
дала б себе нести і загортати,
пливучи з тихим, ледве чутним співом,
спускаючись в блакитну, ясну воду
все глибше, глибше…
    Потім би на хвилі
зостався тільки відгук невиразний
моїх пісень, мов спогад, що зникає,
забутої балади з давніх часів, –
в ній щось було таке смутне, криваве,
та як згадати? Пісня та лунала
давно, давно…
    А потім зник би й відгук –
і на воді ще б колихались тільки

мої квітки, що не пішли зо мною
на дно ріки. Плили б вони, аж поки,
в яку сагу спокійну не прибились
до білих водяних лілей, – там стали б.
Схилялися б над сонною водою
беріз плакучих нерухомі віти,
у тихий захист вітер би не віяв;
спускався б тільки з неба на лілеї
і на квітки, що я, безумна, рвала,
спокій, спокій...[28]

Here, the verbal portrait that Ukrainka paints most closely resembles the sensual languor of Delacroix's lithographs of *La morte d'Ophélie* (1848) and Everett Millais's *Ophelia* (1857). Yet, of note, is Ukrainka's peculiar deviation from the nineteenth-century idyllic view of the drowning madwoman: the echoes of her song recall both sad and bloody events of an antique ballad. It is this hint of violence along with the conditional tense of the poem which jars and, further, which suggests that oblivion and erasure will not mark the final point of rest in the cycle. In fact, the remaining four lyrics which conclude the sequence move away from this nadir to attempt once again the heights already observed in "To Be or Not to Be?" While there is something forced about the remainder of this sequence, "Adagio Penseroso" almost seems to persuade the poet herself; the sensuous images linger in the mind long after the rest of the poems emphasize the positive alternative, striving for a Keatsian ecstasy and faith in the poetic calling.

Ukrainka's complex, allusive, and radical use of literary figures such as Ophelia and Sappho in her search for a new path for the woman as artist deserves a much fuller study than this chapter allows. In her plays, seventeen of which follow *The Azure Rose*, Ukrainka explores versions of passionate but, ultimately, destroyed woman: the prophetesses Cassandra and Tirtsa, the religious martyr Priscilla, the uncompromising apostle of Christ, Miriam, the proud Lady Macbeth-like Dona Ana, and the selfless Dolores. These are women torn between the demands of love and their own beliefs, desires, and principles. Most audaciously, in *The Nobleman's Wife* (*Бояриня*, 1910), set in the seventeenth century, Ukrainka has her heroine, Oksana, literally die from nostalgia for her Ukraine. Having followed her husband to Muscovy where boyar customs demand a harem-like segregation of women, Oksana suffers both national and gender domination, and seems almost to will her own death. Banned from 1920 to 1989, this play was politically too dangerous to publish until the fall of the Soviet Union.

In Ukrainka's last and most popular play, *The Forest Song* (*Лісова пісня*, 1911), she returned once again to a version of the Sappho / Ophelia / Woman's Portrait story. The forest nymph, Mavka, at first a Muse, betrays herself: she abandons her poetic gift, her playfulness, her forest, in order to dwell among the miserable, toiling human race – all for love. But, in the practical world of reapers and sowers, Mavka's love for Lukash seems brazen and her desire for songs, affection, and play, at best, childish. As her woodland friend, the Forest Elf, reminds her in a phrase reminiscent of "To Be or Not to Be?" she betrayed herself by giving up "dwelling in high tree tops / And came down low to walk in baser paths."[29] When Lukash also betrays her by marrying Kylyna, a deceitful, clever peasant-widow, Mavka is taken by Him Who Dwells in a Rock to sleep in forgetfulness "[i]n depths profound, in blackness, damp and cold,"[30] images reminiscent of the drowning Ophelia in "Adagio Penseroso." Eventually managing to free herself through her love for Lukash, Mavka, dressed in black and covered in an opaque grey veil, returns to Lukash's cottage to be greeted by his wife, who calls her insane. When Kylyna expresses the desire that Mavka stand "amidst [her] charms and spells," the nymph is transformed into a willow tree – the very tree from which Ophelia fell and was drowned.[31] By the end of the play, Mavka becomes the poet-singer, a type of native Ukrainian Ophelia, taking on the attributes of her spiritually-destroyed mortal lover, Lukash.[32] She will bear witness to, and herself sing of, love, betrayal and death:

Mavka

> I'll answer them
> with the quiet rustling of my willow branches,
> with the gentle voice of a delicate flute,
> with the sad dew of my boughs.
>   I'll then sing through
> all that you sang for me,
> in the early spring when you played here,
>   Gathering dreams in the grove…
> Play, my beloved, I beseech you!

Лісова пісня

> Я обізвуся до них
> шелестом тихим вербової гілки,
> голосом ніжним тонкої сопілки,
> смутними росами з вітів моїх.
>   Я їм тоді проспіваю
> все, що колись ти для мене співав,
> ще як напровесні тут вигравав,
>   Мрії збираючи в гаю…
>   Грай же коханий, благаю![33]

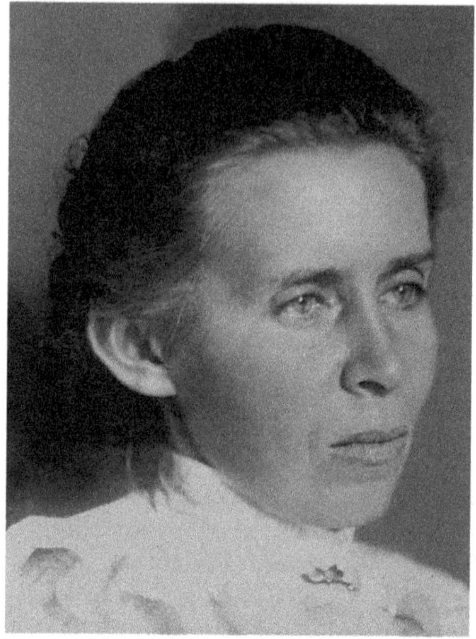

Figure 4.1. Last photo of Lesya Ukrainka, Kyiv, 1913.

Source: Photo by Yuri Teslenko. Courtesy of the Museum of Outstanding Figures of
Ukrainian Culture, Kyiv.

Racked with tuberculosis, Ukrainka at various times fled the damp climate of her Western Ukrainian home for Germany, Italy, Bulgaria, Egypt, the Crimea, and Georgia.[34]

While engaged in curing her body, she constantly observed – as her extensive correspondence attests – woman's condition.[35] What she found were Ophelias. For Ukrainka, the central Shakespearean text of *Hamlet* spoke yet again of the high cost of woman's love and of the erasure of her identity. The female creator, implicit in Ophelia and explicit in Sappho, was, in the eyes of the world, an odd and presumptuous being only fully acceptable when romanticized and destroyed. Always clear-eyed, Ukrainka believed that nothing short of a revolutionary restructuring of society would change this state, and yet, like her own heroines, she was compelled to continue to tell her story.

5

Periphery Against Centre: *Hamlet* in Early Soviet Ukrainian Poetry

---

The question of Shakespeare's impact on the Slavic world looms in importance above all others dealing with Western influence on the cultural and artistic life of these nations.
(Constantine Bida, "Shakespeare's Entrance into the Slavic World")[1]

Constantine Bida's assertion about the importance of Shakespeare for the Slavic world made more than half a century ago continues to have a particular application for Ukrainian culture. More than simply a method of broadening aesthetic sensibilities or awarenesses, the use made of Shakespeare in Ukrainian literature has invariably been tied to important junctures in Ukrainian history and politics, as well as culture. The appropriation of Shakespeare by way of translations, adaptations, and performances, as well as the more particular use of themes, characters, and images in Ukrainian literature may be considered (following the polysystem theory of Itamar Even-Zohar) not only the "periphery's" "interference" in the dominant literary system but, moreover, often a direct challenge to the "centre" and its ideological and aesthetic assumptions.[2]

Shakespearean works have proved to be more than just a rich source for Ukrainian writers. Incorporated into a new setting, they become what Jean Howard and Marion O'Connor have called "a site of…struggle conducted through discourse."[3] Such a process is, as Even-Zohar observes, an "indispensable" object of study "for an adequate understanding of how and why transfers occur, within systems as well as among them."[4] While the latter aim is beyond the scope of this short study, the former, an examination of the site of struggle conducted through discourse, will be the object of this chapter, which will examine the particular case of what was considered a "peripheral" literature until 1991 – peripheral, of course, because of its status as a national literature in a (then) stateless Ukraine.

American literary scholar Bohdan Rubchak has pursued the matter of periphery challenging centre beyond the usual Bakhtinian interest in young, peripheral genres and forms, when he addressed the notion of literature as a whole as a "peripheral system with regard to central social systems." Literature, argued Rubchak,

> in itself can aspire to social centrality either directly or indirectly or by pretending that it is a basic component of a given central social system. Such cooperation of literature into a system ordered according to social hopes and expectations frequently occurs when that central social system suffers a crisis and must be ideologically resuscitated, as for example in totalitarian systems, revolutions, émigré groups…or enslaved nations, whose own social systems are either incorporated in the new central systems of the occupier or liquidated by him altogether.[5]

Rubchak's analysis and his emphasis on "social hopes and expectations" provide a useful context for understanding *Hamlet* as a metaphorical megaphone. In the case of Ukrainian literature, allusions to *Hamlet* were frequently linked to a need to affirm Ukraine's uniqueness and its separateness from the dominant literary system – Russian – by emphasizing Ukrainian ties with, and an affinity, for Western culture. Shakespeare in Ukrainian literature thus could pose an oblique challenge to the prevailing conservative aesthetic of the Soviet Union and, especially, to its political system; Shakespeare could be a means of attacking "canonicity,"[6] both political and literary. In Stalinist 1930s, the time of the purges, *Hamlet* could also be used to mask such affiliations and, instead, by castigating the Danish Prince, confirm loyalty to the centre. Because of the constrictions of space, this chapter will focus only on the work of three poets active in the early Soviet period who employed *Hamlet* to engage with the cultural and political realities of their volatile times: Maksym Rylsky (1895–1964), Mykola Bazhan (1904–83), and Yevhen Pluzhnyk (1898–1936).

Translated into Ukrainian at least fourteen times, *Hamlet* has, not surprisingly, proved to be one of Shakespeare's most popular plays in Ukraine and the inspiration for much literary creativity from Taras Shevchenko (1814–61) to Lina Kostenko (1930–), as well as the subject of literary criticism, and, of course, performance; as in the West, *Hamlet* is regarded as the quintessential Shakespeare play. Two major areas of interest for Ukrainian writers may be delineated: the image of the mad Ophelia – the woman who feels too much, an image that appears, for the most part, in nineteenth-century Ukrainian literature and discussed in the previous chapter and the image of the delaying intellectual, Hamlet, the man who thinks too much. It is this latter image that became the focus of early Soviet Ukrainian writers' interest: their treatment of Hamlet acts as a barometer of their times and of their specific ideological orientation.

During the 1920s, the heady days of the early Soviet period, Ukrainian writers turned to *Hamlet*, as they also turned to other Western European models of art and theories of aesthetics, marking the culmination of a process of Europeanization that had begun long before in the nineteenth century. The 1917 Revolution, as Canadian scholar George S. N Luckyj pointed out, freed Ukrainian writers from "the constant preoccupation with the problems of national freedom, revolution, and self-fulfillment"[7] for a study of aesthetic questions. Strict censorship that had forbidden Ukrainian books and newspapers and stymied theatrical performances was no longer enforced, making possible the efflorescence of a national culture.[8] Thus, in the years after 1917, Ukrainian writers worked in a new creative space. The variety and complexity of different aesthetic viewpoints are reflected by the burgeoning of different literary groups: the Symbolists, Futurists, Neoclassicists, *Lanka* (the Link), and VAPLITE (Free Academy of Proletarian Literature). The excitement of creating a new culture is evident in the heated polemics about art and culture and in the distinguishing features that were to make it "proletarian."[9] The poet and translator Maksym Rylsky expressed this excitement in the following way:

> But to love or not to love that
> Which grows around us and in us ourselves,
> That creates us, and that we ourselves create,–
> Only a blind man, in whom instead of blood
> Black ink flows in a dead stream,
> Worries about questions like this.[10]

The leader of VAPLITE, Mykola Khvylovy (1893–1933), a poet and short-story writer, initiated the important Literary Discussion (1925–8), "the last free debate to take place in Soviet Ukrainian Literature,"[11] involving hundreds of writers who debated literary theory and ideology through pamphlets and books, at meetings, and in the lecture hall. Khvylovy's response to the times and to the creation of a Ukrainian Communist culture was two-pronged: to orient his fellow-writers to the "mighty civilization" of the West – to Goethe, Darwin, Byron, Marx, and Shakespeare – and to free Ukrainian literature from what he perceived as a dead centre, the Russian influence.[12] The two approaches were closely intertwined. Khvylovy urged his colleagues to look to Europe and its literary traditions because, as an idealistic communist, he felt that it was necessary to directly and unreservedly reject "the 'Russian road.'"[13] Russian literature, he claimed, was "passive-pessimistic," had "reached its limits and stopped at the crossroads."[14] In no event should Ukrainians follow the path of Russian literature:

> This is absolute and unconditional...
>
> The essence of the matter is that Russian literature has weighed us down for centuries. Being the master of the situation, it accustomed our psyche to slavish imitation. For our young art to nourish itself on [Russian literature] would mean stunting its growth. Our orientation is toward the art of Western Europe, toward its style, toward its reception.[15]

In *Thoughts Against the Current* (*Думки проти течії*, 1926), Khvylovy responded to the question, "To which Europe should we look?" with the following much-quoted response:

> Take whichever you like: past or present, bourgeois or proletarian, the ever changing one. For indeed, Hamlets, Don Juans, or Tartuffes existed in the past, but they also exist today; they were bourgeois, but they are also proletarian; you may think they are immortal, but they will also be capable of change.[16]

A similar sentiment was voiced by the avant-garde Ukrainian stage and film director Les Kurbas, who staged the first Shakespearean production in Ukraine (*Macbeth*, 1920), and whose experimental work is the subject of the following chapter. Kurbas argued that Ukrainian literature and art had reached "a vital and most important turning point. It is directed straight toward Europe...without any intermediaries or authoritative models. This is the only path for our art."[17] It is important to stress that, in the case of Khvylovy, this anti-Russian stance "was not so much a product of Ukrainian nationalism as of revolutionary internationalism. Khvylovy was convinced that the global revolution would never succeed if one nation, in this case, the Russians, attempted to monopolize it."[18] The method of achieving this goal, however, varied with each literary group.

Following Khvylovy's lead, the poet, scholar, and translator Mykola Zerov (1890–1941), part of The Neoclassicists, encouraged writers not only to look to the West but also to carefully study the sources of Western civilization and culture. By examining history, literary forms, subjects, and themes, Ukrainian literature would become internationalized. Like Zerov, poet, translator, and literary critic Maksym Rylsky (1895–1964) enthusiastically turned to the Western literary tradition; his poetry is replete with allusions to Dante, Heine, Byron, Homer, and, above all, Shakespeare. Indeed, of all Ukrainian writers of the first half of the twentieth century, Rylsky was most influenced by Shakespeare, even though he imagined him as an "actor, drunkard, dreamer and thinker" in his poem "Shakespeare" (*Шекспір*), written in 1920. Often quoting from Shakespeare in his letters, Rylsky even more frequently alluded to Shakespeare in conversation, so much so that, recognizing his own habit, he began to make fun of himself by using the catchphrase, "You should read Shakespeare," even when it was not appropriate for the occasion.[19]

Rylsky, "an unsurpassed master of the subjective lyric,"[20] began his career as one of the very promising young Neoclassicists. George Luckyj has characterized Rylsky's early work as presenting a "static beauty of life."[21] By the mid-1920s, however, Rylsky began to turn to social themes, and by the 1930s, his works became a "realistic presentation of the new socialist reality."[22] Rich in imagery, Rylsky's early poems are about love, nature, and art. In the poem "Shakespeare," the speaker, Shakespeare, boasts of his "unvanquished downpour of words, / Love, torment, tenderness and rage / Characters [made] from steel and from silks," which have presented readers with "the eternal in the momentary."[23] As is evident in this poem, but also in his critical writings, Rylsky, the translator into Ukrainian of *King Lear* (translated in the early 1930s but not published until 1941) and *Twelfth Night* (also translated in the early 1930s but not published until 1950), an avid sonneteer himself, admired the range and depth of Shakespeare's poetic inventiveness, the spectrum of emotions evoked, and the complexity of his characters.

The greater part of Rylsky's own poems written on Shakespearean themes appeared in the 1920s: as well as the aforementioned "Shakespeare," these include "Falstaff" (*Фалстаф*), and "The Danish Prince [Under a Wave of Despair]" (*Принц Данський (під хвилю зневіри)*). These early poems were also (almost without exception) neglected by Soviet scholars. In the introduction to volume 1 of Rylsky's works, the critic Oleksandr Biletsky even deemed it necessary to defend the early poetry, explaining that Rylsky's work should be understood within the context of the "childish sickness of leftism" of the 1920s to which other writers were prone but which Rylsky had avoided.[24]

Rylsky wrote his early work during the exciting years when the Communist Party had not yet attempted to take complete control of cultural development and when Ukrainian culture received state support. This short-lived period, when artists and writers were conscious of creating a whole new cultural universe, was marked with the stimulation of experimentation and discovery, a creative atmosphere I have elsewhere termed "jubilant experimentation."[25] Translation of foreign works into Ukrainian, prohibited under the tsars in the latter half of the nineteenth century, now instantly became a widespread activity when authors of all periods were simultaneously introduced into Ukrainian culture; thus, among others, Sophocles and Shaw, Molière and Wilde – the ancients and the moderns – all became part of the intoxicating cultural mix. It is also at this time that Ukrainian writers turned specifically to the image of Hamlet. The use that they made of Shakespeare's character is an indicator of their aesthetic and political positions and of the specific, rapidly changing politics of the 1920s and 1930s.

Rylsky's first poem on the *Hamlet* theme appeared in 1919. Although his collected works were published in 1960, this poem was not republished until 1995, in the newly independent Ukraine. Only a single fragment had appeared earlier,[26] since the full text of the poem could be easily construed as questioning political orthodoxy; such a stance would have put Rylsky in serious danger. The fragment published during the Soviet period was inspired by Hamlet's exchange with Polonius (in 3.2.11.376–82 of *Hamlet*), a significant moment in the play for Rylsky (indeed, he lamented the cutting of this scene in a production staged in 1955).[27] In this scene, Polonius, attempting to mollify the mad Prince, agrees with every change of his mercurial mind. Thus, a cloud resembles a camel, a weasel, a whale. Rylsky substitutes Shakespeare's swallow for the weasel, suggesting a progression of creatures that represent three elements – land, air, and water. The apparent arbitrariness of Hamlet's shifts in interpretation mirrors the arbitrariness and chaos of the political landscape when nothing seemed secure or stable. In 1919, the Bolshevik revolution had turned into civil war. Total chaos engulfed the country; authority collapsed as six different armies (the Ukrainian, Bolshevik, Whites, Entente, Poles, and Anarchists) fought on its land.

This same episode from *Hamlet* was taken up once again in a lyrical poem of the same period: "Like Hamlet I Scrutinize the Clouds" (*Як Гамлет придивляюся до хмар*), published in the collection *Under Autumnal Stars* (*Під осінніми зорями*, 1918; reprinted with only half of the original poems in 1926). Here Rylsky clearly used Hamlet as a vehicle for considering his own art. Comparing himself with the Prince, and his uncooperative pen with the "fawning, lying" Polonius, Rylsky considers two paths available to the poet, that of submission to flattering "nobles" and of resistance, or the embrace of truth and art.

> Like Hamlet I scrutinize the clouds,
> And my pen, my treacherous Polonius,
> Pours into the word a strange magic,

The red gleams of the holy sun.
Don't listen, prince, to the unnecessary words
Of the fawning-lying nobles,
Why would the clouds need this noisy song?[28]

The transition in Rylsky's work (or to employ the interpretation of Soviet scholars, the moment when he "freed" himself from his earlier "Parnassian" poetic self[29]) came in the mid-1920s and is marked dramatically by a poem on another Shakespearean theme, "Falstaff." In this poem, Hal, now Henry V, ascends the throne and begins to solemnly address his people when a fat, unsavoury figure with a red nose pushes his way through the thick crowd. But Falstaff, "the old man," is repudiated by Henry. In the second stanza, Rylsky similarly repudiates his own youth; his past is an "unclear blot," which unashamedly calls itself his friend. Like Henry, Rylsky orders his past (here one reads his political and literary "follies") to "Go away! I don't know you."[30]

Near the end of the period in 1929, Rylsky wrote his last poem on the *Hamlet* theme: "The Danish Prince," published in *Echo and Reverberation* (*Гомін і відгомін*), according to Soviet scholar M.S. Shapovalova, one of Rylsky's "saddest poems."[31] Rylsky pours out his bitter thoughts about what he believed were unjust critical remarks and a lack of understanding of his poetic quest. Contemplating an escape from such a despondent spiritual state, he turns to thoughts of *Hamlet*. His desire to flee, to cease thinking, to eat and sleep is a type of non-being. But merely voicing these sentiments seems to turn the tide.

For, as Hamlet reminds us, to sleep and feed is to be but a beast (4.4.35):

Let's say it's really thus. These are nerves, perhaps spleen…Escape to the
   Crimea! Not think, eat, and sleep!
But remember: Where is Polonius, O Prince?
   He's at dinner.
He's eating?
He's being eaten.[32]

The mordant, cynical reminder of the fate of Polonius suggests what passivity and inertia could lead to. By 1928, the Soviet Cultural Revolution was in full swing and Stalin was firmly ensconced in power (a subject discussed in subsequent chapters of this book).

Rylsky's poems chronicle the rise and fall of Ukrainian writers' attempts to challenge the centre during the period of the early Soviet regime. A restrained, philosophical writer deeply rooted in Western classical traditions, in 1929 Rylsky despaired for all writers, as well as for himself, for by 1927 a pro-Soviet organization, the VUSPP (the All-Ukrainian Association of Proletarian Writers), was formed to combat the spread of "nationalist" ideas (or the perception of such ideas) in literature. The Communist Party's control and surveillance of literary activities had begun. By 1932, all literary organizations in the USSR were dissolved.

A more trenchant attack on passivity, and particularly on Hamlet, was soon to appear in the 1930s under Stalinism when the centre asserted firm control of all cultural discourses and institutions. Typical of this period is Mykola Bazhan's (1904–83) poem "The Death of Hamlet" (*Смерть Гамлета*). Like Rylsky a poet and translator, Bazhan "overcame" (so, according to Soviet scholars) "certain formalistic and constructivist tendencies" from the 1920s and became a socialist realist.[33] As L. Novychenko remarked, "The Death of Hamlet" clearly established Bazhan as a Party poet at an opportune time.[34] Lazar Smulson characterized the poem as Bazhan's entry into the "path of devoted service to the socialist fatherland."[35] In fact, Bazhan was probably responding to a specific danger, for the critics O. Levada and A. Chepurniuk publicly criticized Bazhan's early work for its "nationalist themes," for its failure to "measure up to the demands of the working class,"[36] and for its failure to realize "the catastrophe which awaits those who have departed from the broad path of the proletarian revolution."[37] These were seriously dangerous accusations that could have literally grave consequences.

Avoiding explanation, Shapovalova merely obliquely commented that "The Death of Hamlet" is "one of the poet's sharply topical key works of the 1930s."[38] This was, of course, the time of the purges, when over one hundred leading scholars, writers, and other intellectuals were executed or sent to labour camps, and a new nationality policy was declared: outstanding works of Ukrainian scholarship and literature were removed from libraries and bookshelves; plays were banned and scores of theatres closed; and the number of Ukrainian schools was drastically reduced.[39] Bazhan chose the path of compromise with the state and thus ensured that, unlike others, he survived the Stalinist period.

In addition to "The Death of Hamlet," Bazhan's poems on Shakespearean themes include "And the Sun Is So Transparent" (*I сонце таке прозоре*) and "In Stratford-upon-Avon" (*У Стратфорді на Ейвоні*). "The Death of Hamlet," a monologue in the "pamphleteering style,"[40] transformed the philosophical questions of *Hamlet* into questions about the class struggle. It is a deeply satiric work and clearly the work of a Party poet, who turns the Shakespearean character into a paragon of evil. As Ukrainian scholar Nataliya Torkut and Yuri Cherniak have pointed out, *Hamlet*, as "a generally acknowledged masterpiece" and thus a high status work of literature, could not be completely ignored, but its various "semantic valences" could be singled out and employed "for reaching relevant ideological or aesthetic objectives."[41] In Bazhan's interpretation, Hamlet becomes a mean-spirited, hypocritical, spineless creature. Hamlet's doubts, a great moral failure "in the crucial moment of the great social battle," are thus viewed as "equal to betrayal."[42]

"Hamletism" or hesitation, doubt, and lack of commitment are, according to Bazhan, the greatest kind of evil. He writes of Hamlet:

> In a trance of problems, dilemmas and deceit,
> And you hear someone calling "comrade!"
> And you hear someone whispering "sir!"
> And Hamlet recovers [his senses],
> tries briskly
> To respond both to this and to that.
> As if to say, look –
> here is the right
> This is the left side of my face.[43]

Hamlet thus becomes a symbol of the uncommitted, hesitant intellectual who is torn between the old, bourgeois system (suggested by the term of address, "sir" – *пан*) and the new, communist system (suggested by "comrade"). A Janus-like figure who seems to look to both the old and the new, Hamlet – according to Bazhan – actually only looks backward. His evil lies in his attempt to please all sides. With this view of the Prince, Bazhan followed the Party line in refusing complexity and embracing binaries; he willingly commits Hamlet to death so that a new, "real" (rather than effeminate) man might spring up from the battle of class struggle: "Die, black Prince of fear / So that a man might be born from the battles." Humanism is a mirage; no one has patience in these times for a divided being. The only humanism permitted, according to Bazhan, is the humanism of Lenin, and class will be the guide to all – love, hate, and war. Class will teach Soviet citizens "to look the enemy in the eye / Will teach us to shoot the enemy in the forehead."

Defending Bazhan's clearly Party-inspired militant poem, Yuri Surovtsev argued that Bazhan does not judge Hamlet, the humanist of the Renaissance, rather, the poet judges "Hamletism," the psychosis of division. The type of Hamlet Bazhan criticizes, attested Surovtsev, develops ethically from inactive indecision to a submission to evil. Bazhan's Hamlet is a type of man possessed of "decadent morals and psychology."[44] Decadence, ambiguity, doubt, passivity, and ideological impurity are all connected in both Bazhan's and Surovtsev's conception of Hamlet. (The concept of Hamletism and its reception in the late 1930s and during wartime is discussed in Chapter Nine.) In 1957, a few years after Stalin's death, a "definitive" article on Bazhan in volume 2 of the history of Ukrainian literature characterized his poetic stance on Hamletism, thusly:

> The poet has painted a sharply satirical portrait of the typical image of a hideous bourgeois-intellectual-individualist with his depraved morals, spiritual desolation, false humanity…'Hamletism ' in such circumstances worked with fascism as the cynical position of "neutrality."[45]

A survivalist, Bazhan here appeared to directly support the Stalinist waves of repression of the 1930s, as well as to concede the necessity of the earlier purges of the 1920s that had been directed against "inactive, opportunistic, lax, or otherwise unfit members" of the Party. By the 1930s, the purges were aimed at those who had made "ideological mistakes" or who had "ideological failings" (that is, those who challenged or disagreed with Stalin). Hamlet and Hamletism had thus become symbols of those who were purged: the intellectuals, who refused to accept simple responses to complex questions, who hesitated to carry out or support Stalin's terror.[46] Khvylovy, who regarded "the Octobrist simplifiers and vulgarizers"[47] as the real enemies of proletarian art, despaired:

> Our watchword is: reveal the duality of the man in our time, show your true self. If you are a revolutionary, you will often split your "I." But if you are a citizen or a servant, let us say, in one of the departments, you are in fact a Gogolian hero even if you feel like the king of all creation.[48]

Recognizing the direction of the untenability of Soviet intellectual life under Stalin, Khvylovy committed suicide.

The reception of the tragedies of Shakespeare – both their interpretation and their performance – fell to its lowest nadir in the history of the Soviet Union, as the very idea of the genre of tragedy was replaced with a new Soviet genre, "optimistic tragedy." (Chapter Eight further explores this new genre in the Stalinist state.) Shackled by ideology, literary criticism became descriptive rather than analytical. Formulaic phrases, like mantras, initiated every work. Marx's and Engels's love of Shakespeare was praised while Western views of Hamlet were castigated as Freudian, Protestant, melancholic, romantic, or merely aesthetic[49] – that is, simplifications. "Shallow psychological interpretations"[50] were vigorously attacked, while Soviet views were lauded for recognizing and stressing the "plebeian" origins of Shakespeare, for emphasizing the "realism" of his work, for his use of folk elements (songs, superstitions, rites, and fables), and for reflecting the class struggle of the Renaissance. A.A. Smirnov's *Shakespeare: A Marxist Interpretation* summed up the view of

Soviet scholars of the 1930s: "The basic characteristics of Shakespeare's point of view and style – his militant, revolutionary protests against feudal forms, conceptions, and institutions – remained unaffected throughout his life."[51] Soviet Shakespeare was imagined on the literary and political barricades – or at least by styling his works as such, they could continue to be performed and studied.

The "chronicles" fared best in Soviet criticism of the 1930s,[52] while the comedies often fared worst, in part since the pluralistic thinking suggested by humour (particularly by the polysemy of puns), as well as the virtues of compromise and compassion found in Shakespeare's comedies,[53] were not only antipathetic but also potentially subversive and dangerous in such a political climate. As Frederick Ahl has observed, "Pluralistic thinking has a tendency to discover humour because it is ever aware that a given word or idea does not belong exclusively to one field of reference or to one context."[54] But pluralism is exactly what was being rooted out in the late 1920s and 1930s. It is not surprising that Zerov had to be purged, for he argued that "we must protest against group-mindedness, group-patriotism, and group-exclusiveness. We must protest against the belief that in a literary group we have the sole criteria of truth."[55] In complete opposition to Zerov's and Khvylovy's views were those of Stalin, who, in a letter to Lazar Kaganovich, the then-Secretary of the CP(B) U, warned that the extreme views of Khvylovy and his followers must be controlled; only then "is it possible to transform the rising Ukrainian culture and Ukrainian social life into a Soviet culture and Soviet social life."[56] Thus, on 3 November 1937, Zerov, along with Les Kurbas and over one thousand other intellectuals, artists, writers, and performers, was shot by firing squad in the Far North, having been accused of anti-Soviet activities – accusations sparked by his concentrated focus on classical and aesthetic ideas. Rehabilitated in the 1958 (five years after the death of Stalin), Zerov's works were still published only in a few excerpts until 1990, when a two-volume edition of his poetry was finally permitted publication under the more liberal conditions of glasnost. His collected works of literary criticism only saw the light of day in 2003, in an independent Ukraine, when another period of cultural renewal had begun. (The experimental work of stage and film director Les Kurbas is the subject of the following chapter.)

While Rylsky more obliquely indicated his awareness of the awful fate of his contemporaries, the poet Yevhen Pluzhnyk (1898–1936), another victim of the purges, directly responded to Bazhan's party line in a courageous but quixotic gesture. Solitude, melancholy, division of the soul, the struggle of the powerless individual born in the wrong time – these were some of the dominant themes of the personal, lyrical poetry of Pluzhnyk. He approached the subject of the Danish prince in a poem entitled "He Walks…Always Walks" (*Ходить…все ходить*), which appeared in his last collection of poetry ironically entitled *Equilibrium* (*Рівновага*), written in 1933–4 but not published until wartime (1943). This collection contains a number of poems about historical and literary personages and it is through them, for the most part, that Pluzhnyk examines the idea of metaphysical balance. In two reflective, lyric poems, "I've Already Tired" (*Я вже натомився*) and "My Soul! Once Again You Stand on the Brink" (*Душе моя! Ти знов стоїш на грані*), Pluzhnyk analyses his ennui and the division in his own soul. This psychological-philosophical subject matter also reappears in a poem about Hamlet, which resembles these latter poems in tone as well as in subject matter. The poet sees the prince constantly walking, lost in thought, undecided whether to be or not to be. Just as Pluzhnyk attempted to revive himself, to spur himself to action in "I've Already Tired" and "My Soul," so the speaker in "He Walks" urges the Danish prince to take control of himself and to quickly complete his forgotten soliloquy. The speaker recognizes that his time, like Hamlet's, is out of joint ("God ! Oh, My God! What an age!").[57] Not believing that Hamlet is "fascist" or a "collaborator" (Pluzhnyk directly addresses Bazhan in his poem), or that he is evil because of his indecision, Pluzhnyk ultimately pleads for the values of reflection, for sympathy for the Prince who is not unlike the poet: not attuned to his time, powerless, suffering, struggling, alone. The poem ends with the uncertainty of being, a reflection of the anguish of the poet striving to live and write ethically.

Pluzhnyk's lyrical, contemplative poetry is concerned with metaphysics and his apprehension of the poet's relationship to life and his society is individualistic, free, independent, and, moreover, skeptical– a dangerous attitude to hold at this time.[58] The 1930s did not countenance the luxury of Pluzhnyk's position. Only complete commitment was permitted and Pluzhnyk, like many others, was arrested and sentenced to death by firing squad. Although his sentence was commuted, he was then exiled to the Solovetski Islands in the Far North where he died of tuberculosis.

As Pluzhnyk was writing his last few poems, the "new man" of Soviet society, its "positive hero" was being enshrined.[59] In complete opposition to Hamlet, the new Soviet hero was single-minded and determined, subordinating everything, even his personal life, to the great ideal.[60] (Chapter Eight examines this new Soviet hero as represented in the dramatic works of Oleksandr Korniychuk.) A close study of the models of early Soviet Ukrainian literature ironically reveals a fear of the collective on the one hand and, on the other hand, a desire, or more accurately, a necessity, "to demonstrate the indispensability of the leader and the Party."[61]

Soviet formulaic literature reveals the centre's reassertion of control. As Canadian scholar Myroslav Shkandrij has pointed out, the influence of Russian civilization and the influx of Russian specialists into various republics of the USSR were defended as "a historically progressive phenomenon,"[62] as, for example, in Ivan Le's *A Novel of the Lowlands* (*Роман міжгір'я*, 1929), printed in enormous numbers in 1930, 1931, 1932, 1934, and at regular intervals thereafter until the fall of the USSR.[63] Non-formulaic literature, or literature that portrayed life "as something irreducible, unforeseeable, something that escapes the grasp of the most sensitive and intelligent individual or Party" challenged "the tidy right-wrong equation" that was required.[64] In addition to the dangers of humour, subversive elements of fiction included "excessive" delving into psychology. Soviet critics developed a theory of personality that refused to admit that the psyche was a battleground of conflicting forces; instead they insisted on the "positive hero" always being calm, composed, stern, and very deliberate in his actions.[65] When the worst sin of society is individualism, the vacillating Hamlet, so divided in his soul, and perhaps the most individualistic of Shakespeare's creations, must, by logical extension, become the object of attack.

It should be noted parenthetically that the negative view of Hamlet and of Shakespearean works as a whole in the 1930s was not a new phenomenon. Earlier, Tolstoy had criticized Shakespeare for the lack of balance and harmony in his works, taking as his starting point a didactic theory of art. As Bida has pointed out, morality, not aesthetic considerations, often prevailed in Slavic literatures.[66] "The deeply complex Hamlet-like individuals" were not admired by Slavic literati,[67] for whom "the role and the significance of the poet is…conditioned by his relationship to society in which he lives, to his nation, and to his country."[68]

Also at the back of this conservative aesthetic was Lenin's central article "Party Organization and Party Literature" (1905), which continued to form the basis of Soviet literary policy. Espousing a pragmatic theory of literature, Lenin argued that "one cannot live in a society and be free from that society. The independence of the bourgeois author, artist, and actress is merely a pretended independence from the money-bag, from the bribe, from being kept."[69] Literature must be subordinated to the Party and to the government and should be used as a weapon of the socialist state. Like Tolstoy before him and Stalin after him, Lenin's concept of literature was utilitarian and didactic.

The equating of Hamlet with Hamletism was not seriously or significantly challenged until the 1970s, when, in a reversal of the notion of

Hamletism (by then firmly entrenched in both the Ukrainian and Russian lexicon), the Danish prince suddenly became a symbol of clear moral vision, of a positive affirmation of life and of high principles. By 1980, the leading Ukrainian poet Lina Kostenko was safely able to write in her collection of poetry entitled *Uniqueness* (*Неповторність*, literally, the Unrepeatable):

> And what of Shakespeare? He lives in Hamlet.
> And this is the only answer for us: to be!
> Whether mankind travels the cosmos, or with oxen,
> Whether it has a goose quill in its hands, –
> The mighty of immortal staves sail through Eternity,
> Like icebreakers on the Dnipro.[70]

At the end of the 1980s, Mikhail Gorbachev, General Secretary of the Communist Party of the Society Union, initiated a new era of glasnost. Calling for reinvigoration rather than change, nonetheless, it became possible to conceive of a reorientation of the relationship between centre and periphery. Hamlet once more became a positive figure, while many writers, including Khvylovy, Pluzhnyk, and Zerov, who had been relegated to obscurity since the 1930s, were "rehabilitated" and moved to the centre. The canon of Soviet Ukrainian writers was reassessed and the writers themselves reranked. Khvylovy and Pluzhnyk, among others, were now said to have marked the apex of early Soviet Ukrainian literary life.

The use of *Hamlet* by Soviet Ukrainian writers reveals the impossibility of Soviet cultural policy that could not permit Ukrainian Soviet writers to be simultaneously culturally independent of Moscow yet politically and economically tied to it. Appropriated by all sides of the ideological, national, and aesthetic debates of the last 150-odd years of Ukrainian history, Shakespeare and his *Hamlet* show no signs of exhausting their use. President Zelensky's evocation of Hamlet in the first days of the Russian invasion of Ukraine in 2022 shows how large a role Shakespeare continues to play in the Ukrainian cultural psyche.

6
Shakespeare Right or Wrong?

In an interview in *Gambit* in 1970, Edward Bond remarked that, as a society, "we use the play [*King Lear*] in a wrong way. And it's for that reason I would like to rewrite it so that we now have to use the play for ourselves, for our society, for our time, for our problems."[1] For Bond, "wrong" Shakespeare is academic Shakespeare, while "right" Shakespeare is a transformed and contemporary Shakespeare. Bond's clear-cut division of approaches to Shakespeare is quintessentially modernist in its rejection of "museum" Shakespeare in favour of a reworked classic for our time. His division of approaches into right and wrong also points to the main line of argument that will be explored here: the idea of style – the central issue of modernism – as not just an interpretive and ideological tool but also a moral one. Les Kurbas's 1924 radical reconception of Shakespeare's *Macbeth* in the early Soviet period will be the focus for this exploration.

Within the general trend of modernizing Shakespeare on Western stages from the 1960s on, *Macbeth* has been employed as the trademark avant-garde play, its primitivism and anarchism being particularly attractive characteristics. These were also some of the obvious attractions of this play for the high modernist period. The great Ukrainian stage and film director Les Kurbas (1887–1937) conceived a production of *Macbeth* in terms almost identical to those championed by Edward Bond. For Kurbas, it was particularly important that the performance not "decline" into literature but that it remain theatre. The text should therefore remain only one of the materials at the disposal of the creative actor; it was to be a tool, not a tyrant.

A polymath, Oleksandr (Les, as he preferred to be known) Kurbas was an actor, director, playwright, translator, pedagogue, theorist, filmmaker, and musician. Himself an "epoch" in the Ukrainian theatre – as one of his contemporaries referred to him[2] – Kurbas influenced hundreds of theatre artists and designers to this very day. Having studied in Western Europe as well as in Lviv (Western Ukraine), Kurbas was not interested in a world limited to the adulation of Moscow and St. Petersburg. Spearheading a theatrical movement away from Russia, "the dead centre" (as he styled it), he attempted to create not just a great Ukrainian theatre but a magnificent theatre that would astonish the world. This ambitious goal, one he held since his early student days, would be initiated by a necessary first step: performance and analysis of the great classics, including Shakespeare – an impossibility until the twentieth century because of harsh tsarist censorship. At the height of the prohibitions, during the reign of Alexander II (1855–81), in a secretly distributed Circular in 1863, the Minister of the Interior, Pyotr Valuev, infamously declared that "no separate Little Russian [i.e., Ukrainian] language ever existed, does exist, or ever could exist." A little over a decade later, the 1876 Ems Ukaz banned the importation and publication of all books in, and translations into, Ukrainian, including the Bible and Shakespeare. In 1881, the teaching of Ukrainian in public schools and in conducting church sermons in Ukrainian were prohibited. In 1888, a decree banned giving children Ukrainian names at baptism. All theatre performances were banned; all Ukrainian books in print were removed from the shelves of libraries; even Ukrainian folksongs, when publicly performed, had to be sung in Russian or in another foreign language. At century's end, some concessions were made, including permission to create travelling theatre troupes which were nonetheless prohibited from performing in politically sensitive areas. Other restrictions remained in place up to 1917, limiting subject matter and genre: domestic and folkloric themes only but no satire, history, romantic verse plays, or plays of urban life. Upper and middle-class characters were required to speak Russian; peasants and children, Ukrainian. Further, Ukrainian plays were allowed only if a Russian play was staged first on the same night and consisted of the same number of acts. Such constraints encouraged both national stereotypes (the Ukrainian equivalent of the stage Irishman), and generic ones: sentimental and melodramatic plays with obligatory musical and dance numbers featuring large choirs dressed in authentic embroidered shirts.

Since both foreign and native Ukrainian drama endured a simultaneous prohibition, the ability to finally stage Shakespeare, even in a time of great crisis, meant that his works had become inextricably associated with national and cultural revival.[3] Shakespeare first appeared on the boards in Ukraine in the swirl of world war, civil war, and revolution. With his Young Theatre (Molodyi Teatr) Kurbas began preparing to stage *Romeo and Juliet* in 1918. Everything was ready for performance; the roles had

Figure 6.1. Les Kurbas, 1919.

Source: Volodymyr Hrycyn/Yosyp Hirniak Archives, New York, New York. Courtesy of
Virlana Tkacz.

been cast and the costumes, props, and set design completed when General Denikin's forces attacked Kyiv and ransacked the theatre.

While for Western Europe the First World War ended in late 1918, it was not over until late 1920 in Ukraine and was complicated by civil war punctuated by proclamations of Ukrainian independence. According to British historian Edward Acton, the year 1919 was very like the period of European economic collapse following the Black Death. In twelve months alone, the population of Kyiv fell by a third. Regions were cut off from one another, while governments came and went. Kurbas took a truncated, starving company, the Kyidramte, to the countryside where it was possible to obtain food. In a town fifty miles from the capital, Bila Tserkva, right at the vectors of a number of fronts, Kurbas decided to set aside his plans for *Romeo and Juliet* in order to take up another Shakespearean play: *Macbeth*. Banned under the tsars, its regicide and general brutality were particularly congruent for the anti-monarchical revolutionary and early Soviet period in which the barbarism of war was playing out. Despite the anarchy and extreme privations of civil war that caused some of his actors to pass out from hunger, Kurbas prepared

Figure 6.2. Program from *Macbeth*, directed by Les Kurbas, Kyidramte, 1920.
For the First Time on the Ukrainian Stage!

the first Ukrainian Shakespeare production with both trepidation and excitement, finally staging the play on August 20, 1920. On the verge of this very first performance, Kurbas addressed his company with the following words:

> Everyone for everyone! Everyone for the production! Don't wait until work is placed in your hands. Help the property manager, the costumers, the machinists. We are doing a great, historical deed for Ukrainian theatre and culture. Throw your whole soul and energy into the fire of creative work on *Macbeth*.[4]

The actors understood that they were doing much more than just performing a play by Shakespeare; their production was the equivalent of a proclamation of cultural independence and an assertion of Ukrainian identity.

The 1920 *Macbeth* was a fairly straight-forward, if sardonic, interpretation of a play that Kurbas continued to contemplate, mining its depths in two other redactions. Ukraine's independence, proclaimed in 1918, was short lived, swept away by the creation of the USSR. Once Kurbas was able to return to the capital, he founded a new company, the Berezil Artistic Association, and began to achieve the artistic scope of endeavour about which he had long dreamed. Berezil was the archaic name of the month of March, and thus signalled spring, renewal, revolution. The Berezil was created with an ambitious agenda: to produce plays; carry out theatre research; experiment with stage design, performance, and audience response; publish a journal; and set up a theatre museum, the first in Ukraine. Studio-labs were created, each of which had a specific focus, from village theatre to opera. Becoming pedagogue as well as director, Kurbas organized lectures on, among other topics, world history, art, music, theatre, aesthetics, literature, philosophy, biology, psychology, and anything new – books, plays, and theories (such as the then very new Freud). The actors were also obliged to undergo rigorous physical training, including fencing, acrobatics, ballet, juggling, roller skating, and trapeze-walking. His new actor was to be a fit, intelligent, cultured being who created his role by being at the very apex of his technical craft. At its height, the Berezil with close to 400 members, included six studios, directorial labs, and various research committees, including a "psycho-technical" committee studying applied psychology in order to develop new teaching methods in the theatre.

Desiring more than just to broaden the genre, period, and subject matter of Ukrainian theatre, Kurbas intended to rethink the whole grammar of theatrical conventions, indeed, of theatrical representation itself. Preparing his audience for his audacious new production of *Macbeth* in 1924, he argued against a revived pseudo-classical Shakespeare: "Our approach to Shakespeare naturally must be the approach of our day. The restoration of Shakespeare in the manners and customs of his time is formally impossible and in essence unnecessary. The whole value of the scenic embodiment of a classical work in our day lies namely in the ability to present a work in the refraction of the prism of the contemporary world view."[5]

By 1924, when relative political stability followed the cessation of war and with the Soviet government's active policy of Ukrainianization to help convince the population to embrace communism, aesthetic questions came to the forefront. Polemical debates erupted concerning the relationship between politics, art, and nation; stylistic questions were raised about realism and modernism, and the repertoire itself was under significant debate. Was Shakespeare needed in the context of this new political entity? For Kurbas, the answer was, unreservedly, yes. Much could be learned from the masterly construction of his plays. Shakespeare and the classics were particularly useful in focusing attention on style – in Kurbas's view, the central issue of modernism. He turned once again to *Macbeth*.

Before proceeding to examine this remarkable production, it is perhaps necessary and useful to explain that I regard the avant-garde as both a radical, ground-breaking offshoot of modernism focused on experimentation and process and, also, as the expression of a left-wing political stance aimed at repudiating bourgeois culture. In Eastern Europe, this repudiation meant the rejection, for the first time, of "the national character and didactic pathos of earlier literature," as well as the erasure, as in other Western modernist projects, of the boundaries between art forms and genres, between "high" and "low."[6] This double task may be seen in the work of Kurbas; thus, in his view, his 1924 production was both left and right, that is, inspired by a left-wing ideology but thoroughly "correct" in its view and use of Shakespeare.

Shortly after the premiere of Kurbas's *Macbeth*, one of the actors in the production, Vasyl Vasylko, recorded in his diary that the production was like a "bomb [that] went off, throwing such sparks into the audience that even on the second and the third day [all of] Kyiv shouted 'gvalt.'"[7] From the point of view of Vasylko and many of the actors, as well as a good portion of the audience, *Macbeth* was a tremendous success, as the thundering ovations indicated. (Chapter Seven analyses the audience response to this production.) But not everyone loved the production. Those critics who detested the production accused Kurbas of "sacrilege," "vivisection," and serious "error."[8] Why did this production elicit such sharply-polarized responses? In interviewing theatrical historians in 1995 in Kyiv, I was surprised to learn that this production continued to have many detractors. What was it about the style which led critics, then and more recently, to categorize it in moral and religious terms as "wrong" and "blasphemous"?

First, let's consider the production.[9] The *Macbeth* which opened on 2 April, 1924[10] presented a full-frontal attack on the illusionist theatre. Disruptions, contrasts, juxtapositions, minimalist costumes, montages of stage action, atonal music – these were to help ironize the moral tale of an ambitious man. Kurbas employed various techniques to create a Cubist Expressionist production,[11] which would reflect his views about audience, actor, and artwork. A self-conscious creation of fragments to be reassembled by the spectator, this production (as one of the sympathetic critics observed) intended to wipe out the remnants of the bourgeois theatre.[12] While only twenty-three pages of the director's copy have survived, they reveal a consistency in their cuts; these appear to be excisions aimed at simplifying the emotional range of the play by omitting small choral scenes and, most importantly, by eliminating Macbeth's heroic concluding speech.

The whole production was austere and harsh. In Vadym Meller, the scenographer, Kurbas discovered a like-minded friend and colleague who shared his artistic interests and could translate them into reality. Like Kurbas, Meller studied in the West. After a very successful first exhibition, he had been invited to show his works in the Salon d'Automne together with Picasso, Gris, and Braque.[13] For the 1924 *Macbeth*, Meller created enormous screens (4 x 4 meters high), bright green shields of stretched canvas, on which giant modernist red block letters announced "Castle," "Precipice" (the translator's word for "heath"), and so forth, recalling both medieval-renaissance locality boards,[14] and, in their typeface, contemporary political posters. Their starkness urged the audience to creative completion: to imagining what each of these locations might be like. Their size dwarfed the actors and diminished their usual centrality on stage, suggesting that the characters were subject to forces other than their own individual wills, to other discourses, interpretations, and frames. Raised or lowered when needed at the sound of a gong, the screens served as more than background. Lowered at the same time, they indicated the simultaneity of the action in different parts of Scotland. At other times, they moved in slow, stately rhythm to underscore the emotions of the actors; to emphasize tension, the dynamics of the action; or even to interfere in the action – as, for example, when they physically blocked off Macbeth's attempt to follow Banquo's ghost – represented by a searchlight beam.[15] Fragments of furniture, chairs, and a throne were, like the screens, lowered and raised when needed. The actors, often lit by the harsh light of projectors, moved in a restrained way, and the whole rhythm of the production followed this general style.[16]

Like the stylized and bare stage which both suggested place and yet also mocked any such certainty, so the costumes were spare and theatrical, emphasizing the duality of the actors (as characters and as people) and of their time frame (both time present and past). Wearing either militarized garb or contemporary work clothes very like those worn by many people in the audience, the actors were distinguished from them by only a few ancillary articles: stylized bits of medieval or renaissance clothing, such as tunics and cloaks, decorated with appliques in a modernist interpretation of heraldic designs.

At the centre of this production was the "naked" actor – the major experiment in this version of *Macbeth*. Kurbas's challenge to the actors was to display the perfection of their technique by engaging, then disengaging in their roles, at will. The pure craft of acting was laid bare

Figure 6.3. Macbeth and the Witches from *Macbeth*, Act IV, directed by Les
Kurbas, 1924.

Source: Ukrainian State Museum of Theatre, Music, and Cinema Arts.

without the attendant "mysteries" of sustained, realistic character, illu-
sory sets, grand costumes, extensive music, and numerous props.[17] In
renaissance fashion and with similar effect, actors' roles were doubled
or tripled. Thus, Yosyp Hirniak, for example, played Donalbain, the
Murderer of Banquo, and the Doctor. Each role carried over associations from the previous one, contributing to the idea of the tentacles
of guilt reaching into all parts of the realm and limiting the audience's
habit of dividing the characters into goodies and baddies. The mechanism of acting itself was openly displayed: each actor came on stage at
his or her own pace, sometimes greeting the audience and assuming a
role only when he or she was properly positioned. Similarly, after performing his part, the actor exited as "himself." Thus, in the first scene,
the witches came on stage wearing wide blue-grey trousers and red wigs.
Mysterious little electrical lights flickered in their costumes and around
their eyes when they uttered their prophecies. A surreal violet blue light
was used to emphasize their horrible grimaces. Like priests, they held
censors in their hands, thus immediately announcing the bitingly satirical thread of the interpretation. But, after this eerie scene, the screen

Figure 6.4. Macbeth (Ivan Marianenko) and Lady Macbeth (Lyubov Hakkebush) from *Macbeth*, directed by Les Kurbas, studio shot, 1924.

Source: Ukrainian State Museum of Theatre, Music, and Cinema Arts.

with the word "Precipice" disappeared from sight, the violet light vanished, and the witches calmly left the stage as actresses who had done their "number."[18]

The sleepwalking scene was performed with the same emphasis on actor in and out of role. Lyubov Hakkebush proceeded to centre stage, where she placed her candle, took off her mantle, shook her head until her long dark hair tumbled over her shoulders, and only then proceeded emotionally to "Out, damned spot!" Similarly, after Macbeth delivered his powerful soliloquy in act 1, scene 7, he seized his dagger and turned to go to kill Duncan. Taking a few steps, he resumed his identity as Ivan Marianenko the actor.

The "engagement-disengagement" technique proved to be extremely hard on the actors. Actress Iryna Steshenko, who played one of the witches, wrote in her memoirs of the difficulty of maintaining a balance between restraint and involvement in the role,[19] while Lyubov Hakkebush, who played Lady Macbeth, was admonished at rehearsals for descending into pathology and bad taste in creating the sleepwalking scene.[20] Indeed, the inclination to overdo their acting segments was one of the dangers of this technique. As Kurbas reminded them, all acting, he emphasized, proceeds from thought, not emotion.[21]

The "engagement-disengagement" principle was repeated again and again in the production, thus isolating and drawing attention to key moments in the play, as well as to the points of transition – forcing the audience and the actor to a cerebral response to the play and to a focus on the constituent parts of theatre. Every aspect of the production was placed in quotation marks, every theatrical convention was questioned, including the idea of the tragic hero. The traditionally heroic Macbeth was portrayed by Ivan Marianenko (hitherto noted for his tragic roles) as a common, unimaginative soldier, dressed in contemporary clothes, including sloppy puttees. This Macbeth combined simplicity of character with single-minded cruelty; his doubts were not indicative of a conscience but were rather a revelation of his fearfulness, a fearfulness revealed right after the regicide, when he threw himself at his wife with the very same knife he used to murder the king. King Duncan was presented as a drunken fool, whose death at first seemed, if not deserved, then at least not completely reprehensible. Both Macbeth and his wife counted on the fact that most of Scotland would not discover their crimes, and the knowing rest would keep silent out of fear. More austere than her husband, Lady Macbeth was not a romantic young beauty but a mature woman without passion for her husband, who seemed, rather, to be annoyed by his fearfulness. Ugly and sharp-featured, she was in love only with power and herself. When Macbeth left to kill Duncan, she followed him, comfortably holding the dagger like a practiced killer.[22] The Macbeths were understood as products of their time – a Scottish Middle Ages that Kurbas interpreted as inherently and instinctually spiritually hollow, vicious, and cruel.

The only moment which contained a remnant of traditional tragedy was the sleepwalking scene. Dressed in white, Hakkebush seems Ophelia-like in photos taken of this scene. While in the rest of the production she was costumed in restrictive, unattractive clothing (a dark, shapeless three-quarter length robe over a white shift, pleated at the bottom, vaguely recalling a Ukrainian peasant's costume) and a severe headpiece (a white kerchief held in place by a metal band), in this scene, she wore only a long white shift over which her long, unfettered hair cascaded. Robbed of the dignity of her usual severity, she was subject to the hallucinations of an imminent assassination on herself.[23] The consequences of her past cruelty were apparent in the stark contrast to previous scenes.

Figure 6.5. Lady Macbeth (Lyubov Hakkebush) sleepwalking scene from *Macbeth*, directed by Les Kurbas, 1924.

Here, she was palpably terror-stricken by her inability to achieve real power or to control events.[24] That this was not a scene of pathos is suggested by the response of the drama critic I. Turkeltaub, who faulted Hakkebush for being too mannered and her acting too cold.[25]

Grappling towards a new relationship with the audience, Kurbas wished to break down drama into its constituent subsystems, forcing the audience to reexamine the individual materials of the theatre and, then, to reconstitute them into a new whole. He employed some devices to destroy traditional audience expectations and engagement (as, for example, the engagement-disengagement device), while others were to draw the audience in at moments when they least expected it. Thus, for example, he had the witches wired so that small electric lights lit up as they moved in their deliberately exaggerated "witchy" way. But, when it came for Banquo and Macbeth to speak to the weird sisters, the witches were lit up from behind, casting huge shadows onto the audience. The thanes spoke to these shadows and thus to the audience which, after being alienated and amused by the odd beings, now just as suddenly found itself implicated in the dark world of *Macbeth*.

Figure 6.6. Amvrosy Buchma as The Fool/Porter in *Macbeth*, directed by Les
Kurbas, Kharkiv, 1924.

The closest link between actor and contemporary audience was provided by major additions to the text: three intermedia and dumb shows.
The Porter (played by Amvrosy Buchma), called the Fool in Kurbas's
production, appeared in the intervals between the acts. During the first
interval, Buchma was dressed in fool's cap and traditional fool's clothing,
with exaggerated make-up, including a bulbous nose which occasionally lit up. The Porter's costume linked him to the old Vice of medieval
drama, the attendant of the Devil – a connection confirmed and developed in an additional mimed sequence following 1.3 (that is, just after
Macbeth and Banquo first encounter the witches) in which cardinals
cavorted on the stage and then turned into devils by the simple expedient of revealing their cowls on which were painted devilish faces.

Buchma, as Porter, performed clownish tricks, acrobatic jumps and
dance-steps, after which he always spoke with individual members of the
audience. In her memoirs, fellow actor Natalia Pylypenko compared
Buchma to a rubber ball that flew across the stage, seemingly weight-
less and unpredictable, at one time flying up to the ceiling, at another
descending by the trap door and shooting up again.[26] He made seemingly

impromptu speeches on contemporary political and social issues (such as the deposition of the tsar, the League of Nations, various religious superstitions, even backstage theatrical disputes); these were Kurbas's analogy to Shakespeare's references to the Jesuits' equivocations. Every day, the director insisted, the jokes and references had to be changed. Actor Stepan Bodnarchuk was responsible for transforming items in the morning newspaper into couplets by nightfall. In this, as in other elements of the theatricality of the production, Kurbas was consciously reaching back to the rich, old medieval and renaissance traditions of the audience-actor relationships. In permitting the Fool some creative freedom, Kurbas was also consciously drawing upon English fools like Will Kempe renowned for his impromptu conversations with the audience and his extempore comic remarks. Buchma also shared with Kempe the lively combination of acrobatics, wit, and physical clowning.

In the fourth act, during the intermedia referred to as "Haymaking," Buchma entered as a peasant, reaping energetically as he went and singing a harvest song. Here, from the scenes of bloody-mindedness, Kurbas moved the audience in a Shakespearean manner to consider the apparently undisturbed (or compliant) common man. Rather than any sentimental or folkloric association, the simplicity of the peasant's task both contrasted with the violent, over-the-top actions of the main characters but also connected them. For, of course, the Reaper was also the Grim Reaper, mowing down "the rays of light, [and] extinguishing them with his broad sweeps."[27] Fatigued by the work, he would then approach members of the audience sitting on bleachers in front of him and take cigarettes from them; thus, he connected the main plot and the intermedia to reality itself. (These intermedia, and another possible source of inspiration, cabaret, are examined in Chapter Eleven.)

The Fool's third and last appearance occurred in the final moments of the play, when Macduff comes out carrying the head of Macbeth. Still wearing his Fool's makeup – the mocking, grinning face – Buchma came in costumed as a bishop, in gold tiara and white soutane. He then crowned Malcolm to the solemn music of an organ ironized by the delicate sounds of the piccolo and the rougher harmonium. Just as he did so, a new pretender approached, killed the kneeling Malcolm, and took the crown. Without pause, the bishop once again intoned the same words, "There is no power, but from God." As the new king began to rise, a new pretender murdered him, and the ritual was repeated once again.[28]

The mixture of burlesque, acrobatics, buffoonery, and Grand Guignol – linked to Futurism and Dadaism of the West – was intended to focus attention on and interrogate the material and form of the theatre in the most radical way by employing a world classic – hence a text regarded with some piety. While in some quarters the production was acclaimed as a "great triumph" and a work of genius,[29] in others, it was simply "a scandal."[30] The Kyivan audience, which had recently endured a Macbeth-like period of rapid and bloody exchanges of power (eleven between 1917 and 1920), was forced to exercise a very renaissance type of activity. This "history" play induced the spectators simultaneously to apprehend Ukraine, Shakespeare's England, and Macbeth's Scotland. Shakespeare was their contemporary. It invited the audience to consider who was the subject of the satire. Was the production intended to be prophetic? Destructive of political powers? How were the issues of silent complicity linked to the issue of power, loyalty, and fear? These questions were particularly topical, considering that Lenin had just recently died (21 January 1924) and the backroom power struggles, already well in process before his demise, continued, suggesting the possibility of further violence and political chaos. How could it be that the bloodiness and ineffectualness of the tsar (Duncan) was, in the end, indistinguishable from the Soviet power that took his place (the Macbeths and the Malcolms of the world)? Where was the morality of the new regime? Was it possible that regicide was neither romantic nor heroic and that evil was simply banal, repeatable, and unconnected to ideology?[31]

Kurbas's intention – to problematize all the elements of theatre (the classic, plot, role, character, hero, time, space, acting, prop, costume) – was, as has already been noted, an attempt to reconceive the whole notion of theatre. In his view, this was the only right way of going about the task of creating a new Ukrainian culture and of staging a classic. Whether one considers him a naive convert to the new Soviet order or an aesthetic idealist, nonetheless it is certain that Kurbas believed that the struggle had to be, could only be, the struggle to reinvent all systems, and this aim could only be achieved by constant experimentation. The avant-garde style was intended to make audiences think critically and to unite them in analytical thought through their complicity in the action. Devices which broke down the conventional barrier between stage and audience, actor and character, were, in Kurbas's logic, rupture on behalf of a new communion. But this harmony could only be achieved by the special cooperation of the audience which had to fill in the hermeneutical gaps. It required then not a suspension of disbelief but a very special and shared belief – a belief in the possibility of forms emptied of traditional associations and codes in order that they be recreated and filled with something entirely new.

Contemporary critics and spectators unsympathetic to modernism focused on the discontinuity and unpredictability of the production. They found it cold, exclusionary, and elitist. Even with his pre-production articles, puffs, and his brief statement of purpose before the curtain, Kurbas was not entirely successful at creating the kind of new audience-actor relationship he intended. The vociferous polemic launched in the press (which lasted over two months) was in part a debate about the modernist style and its relationship to the notion of the classic. Kurbas was accused of "blasphemy" in his treatment of Shakespeare, of completely annulling a theatrical classic, of presenting a "cold" and unfeeling production,[32] and of showing life as it shouldn't be, instead of how it should.[33] Shakespeare in his hands, according to the critics, was simply Mr. Wrong.

But what was "right" Shakespeare? In an article castigating the production, Yakiv Savchenko defined the "correct" tradition of staging Shakespeare as, first of all, a realistic recreation of Elizabethan theatre; secondly, as a tradition of strong actors playing in a heroic-romantic style; and, lastly, as a production which centres all the attention on the main characters.[34] "Right" Shakespeare, then, appeared to be very close to old traditions and conventions of the commercial theatre. Savchenko's prescriptions suggested the unity between audience and stage of a simple garden variety based on the idea of the stage as representing reality or, more accurately, a heightened reality. The idea of style as potentially right or wrong seemed to rest on the bedrock of a particular understanding of community and, further, on the strength of the social fabric. Considering itself under ideological siege from within and from without (not having yet recovered from world war, civil war, and revolution), the "right-thinking" Bolshevik polemicists of the Soviet Union in 1924 had little tolerance for a notion of theatre (or art) that was not unifying or celebratory of great deeds. Ironically, in a country in which God was proclaimed dead, only moral and religious terms could be found to convey the depth of their condemnation of modernist Shakespeare.

By 1934, with Stalin firmly in power, some of Kurbas's peers publicly attacked his *Macbeth* for being too bourgeois; for taking the "bourgeois aesthetic" to its "absurd" conclusion by not reflecting objective reality but only hinting at it, by presenting a system of signs, marks and ideas instead of concrete reality; and, finally, for creating overly abstract forms.[35] True experimentation, viewed as art for art's sake – the principle really under attack here – was a movement that did not strike deep roots in the East, where art had always generally been approached from an ethical (religious or social) perspective.[36] The critics' offensives were, in part, a reflex regression to ethical models of criticism developed over the past two centuries (and perhaps most notoriously found in Tolstoy's critique of Shakespeare). The traditional, ethical approach to the arts also fed naturally into the new political terminology of error, heresy, and deviation.

The Futurist Mykhail Semenko accurately pinpointed the cultural crisis of his time as a crisis of theory.[37] With little thought given to the part culture would play in the Revolution, its leaders had no consistent cultural policy, let alone a theory. Lenin's only interest in culture, for example, was exhibited by his insistence that cities be plastered with slogans and that statues be erected to revolutionary leaders. The latter in particular evoked the most conservative of tsarist and neoclassical cultural habits. The avant-garde was appalled. But this conservatism or regression was of a piece with other kinds of turnings-back. For the Commissar of the Enlightenment, Anatoly Lunacharsky, as for Lenin, the classics were national property and thus to be tampered with at peril. Lunacharsky's slogan, "new content in old forms" – must have given the modernists pause in their belief in a new order, as must have the critic Turkeltaub's slogan, "Backwards in art and culture."

Already by the late 1920s, the rhetoric of morality (Kurbas called it "cheap demagoguery"[38]) – modernism was wrong and destructive – soon drowned out intellectual debate. The unpredictability of modernism and its apparently cyclical view of history could hardly co-exist for long within a new, official master narrative: the story of scientific, inexorable progress toward a new paradise on earth. In such a narrative, in which the answers were already known, what point could experimentation possibly serve? Among the first to welcome the revolution, the avant-garde had few allies. Generally dismissive of the old ethnographic school, of the bourgeois, and of much of the intelligentsia, the Ukrainian avant-garde worked itself into a political corner from which, by the 1930s, there was little possibility of escape. This corner became quite tight indeed following the first Soviet Writers' Congress of 1934 when socialist realism became the only method of creating artistic works.

The 1920s debates concerning *Macbeth* usefully points out many of the broader difficulties with modernist Shakespeare and the modernist project – at least in Ukraine. While modernism provides freedom in opening up space and, especially, time, and attempts simultaneously to distance and to draw in, often only its discontinuities and ruptures are immediately apparent. By contrast, the mimetic approach to the theatre, although only a convention and without objective validity is, as Benjamin Bennett astutely pointed out, a "communal initiative": "if the realistic begins by being discredited, if it is recognized from the outset as mere convention, then the conscious decision to accept that convention is undoubtedly communicative, shared with others, a communal process." What is crucial, then, continues Bennett, "is not meaning, but *style* as the token of an ethical decision repeatedly taken in the theatre."[39]

Conservative, academic, or commercial theatre with its apparently easy acceptance of "ordinary reality" thus functions in a seemingly harmonious manner; it provides a readily identifiable common ground for actor and audience. Such a desire for clearly defined and understood concepts of communion was most obviously found in the first years of the Revolution. Thus, Nikolai Evreinov's staging of *The Storming of the Winter Palace* on the third anniversary of the October Revolution with at least eight thousand participants and one hundred thousand spectators (whose participation, observes Lars Kleberg, "was merely a question of degree rather than kind"[40]) was both an expression of this conflation of life and art and a harbinger of things to come. Inspired by the artistic precedents created during the French Revolution and by the ideas of Richard Wagner and Romain Rolland, such huge spectacles, mass festivals and glorifications of revolutionary leaders, it is true, did not last very long. But that does not mean that the desire for such "realism" and the communion which underlay it disappeared, rather, it found a less obvious outlet in the theatre's return to "realism" as the officially approved approach to art in the Soviet Union.

Rather than foreground the audience-actor connection, Kurbas's modernist productions presumed that the audience wished to co-create a new ground for interpretation and communion while creating a semiotic earthquake where nothing remained stable or certain. Modernism optimistically endowed the audience with the desire to work while at play, to think critically, and to question in an individual way in order to achieve a long-term project of a new community. Thus, for many Ukrainian modernists, it was commonplace to think of the theatre as the church of literature, the best expression of collective ceremonial thinking.[41] Here, we may see that the modernists themselves reverted to religious and, in other cases, to moral terms. For both camps, this emotion-laden terminology revealed the deeply-engrained belief in the monumentality and potency of the classic for our culture. Yet modernism was also deeply skeptical of its communicative tools and signifying practices, as the interrogations of Kurbas showed. Using rhetoric while also drawing attention to its manipulations, modernism had enormous political and subversive force[42] – a fact which goes some way to explaining both Stalin's and Hitler's detestation of it.

Modernism's idealistic conception of the audience and its occlusion of the psychology of viewing – the perhaps overwhelming need for harmony, what perhaps we really like in mimesis – doomed Ukrainian modernist productions to a specialized or special audience. It is perhaps not surprising after all, that, in 1995, Ukrainian theatrical historians remained uncomfortable with what one critic called Kurbas's "fireworks," his "whimsies,"[43] his too intellectual, too contemporary production.[44] Tired of political interpretations of plays and anxious to rejoin the European community, Ukrainian theatrical artists and critics seemed, at least in the 1990s, happiest with a psychological realism.

7

The Perfect Production: Les Kurbas's Analysis of the Early Soviet Audience

Audiences mattered in the Soviet period.[1] Recognizing the effectiveness of theatre above all other arts in its ability to influence the masses and to inculcate a socialist consciousness, the Bolsheviks (later, the Communists) made planned, strenuous efforts from the very beginning to "regulate the theatrical market" – as censorship and control were euphemistically and commonly described. By the 1930s, they achieved a stranglehold on all aspects of theatrical activity, including repertoire, personnel, and artistic style. Theatre directors were open to attack, dismissal, arrest, and execution. It was imperative for the literal survival of their companies that their productions be supported by a strong proletarian audience base and that they demonstrate their clear ideological positions. A firm understanding of the audience and its needs was thus a serious issue that went far beyond concerns with box office receipts.

One way in which theatre directors could negotiate the treacherous political terrain and prove that they were, in fact, presenting comprehensible productions well-received by workers was by seeking solid empirical evidence confirming their claims. Few, however, appear to have done so. Indeed, Willmar Sauter laments the fact that neither today nor during the early Soviet period was "even the question of who visited the theatres…empirically surveyed."[2] As this chapter will show, however, audiences were indeed empirically and thoroughly studied by the Ukrainian director Les Kurbas (1887–37). His use of a broad spectrum of tools and approaches, including behaviourist analyses and questionnaires, remains, to date, still one of the most forward-thinking and all-encompassing methods of studying the process of creating theatre.

Shakespeare and the Early Soviet Stage

One of the most frequently reiterated laments of the early Soviet period was that there was "a crisis in the theatre." This did not mean the absence of theatre. On the contrary, theatre groups sprang up everywhere like mushrooms, including and especially in the villages. The "crisis" was, rather, located in the fact that the pre-revolutionary drama and theatre hardly seemed equipped to speak to the new era just emerging from the Bruegelesque crucible of world war, civil war, and revolution.

In this context, there was small interest in Shakespeare in Russia. The turn away from staging his works was already noticeable in the last two decades of the nineteenth century and continued well into the Soviet period with only a few notable exceptions. Instead, throughout the 1920s, the place of the world classics in the new Soviet order was continually and hotly debated,[3] with some demanding that they be discarded as useless relics of a bourgeois past, others that they be "rehabilitated" to suit the contemporary moment and in the absence of contemporary Soviet "Shakespeares."

It was not in Soviet Russia but in Ukraine that the most remarkable Shakespeare production of the 1920s (and, arguably, of the whole Soviet period) was produced. As has already been noted in the previous chapter, under the tsars all performances and translations of Shakespeare into the Ukrainian language had been banned by nineteenth-century decrees and circulars (in 1863, 1876, 1881). After the tsarist reforms following the 1905 Revolution, the first Ukrainian stationary theatre was finally permitted in Kyiv, a momentous event in importance for Ukrainians not unlike the impact for the Irish made by the founding of the Abbey Theatre. Since Shakespeare and other foreign writers had hitherto been prohibited, Ukrainian directors and actors were, unlike their Russian counterparts, eager to perform them.

The great Ukrainian stage and film director Les Kurbas intended to produce the whole Shakespearean canon, although, for a variety of reasons, he was able to prepare only four plays (*Romeo and Juliet, Macbeth, Othello*, and *King Lear*) and do preliminary work on five others (*Hamlet, A Midsummer Night's Dream, Twelfth Night, Timon of Athens*, and *Antony and Cleopatra*).[4] In the process, he laid the foundations for modern Ukrainian theatre and film, educating and influencing hundreds of actors, visual artists, musicians, directors, and scene designers. Kurbas was convinced that the Ukrainian theatre urgently first needed to acquire mastery of the world classics along with the stylistic variety they represented; this "catch up" stage of acquisition would eventually lead to the creation of a distinct theatrical Ukrainian "voice" or idiom. What Kurbas admired most about writers such as Sophocles and Shakespeare was their "good bones," that is, their dramaturgical structure and effectiveness in moving audiences. As he observed, "Classical dramaturgy is at base important and still useful to the present day in its structural aspects, which have arisen out of a certain understanding of the laws of human reception. It is maximally educative."[5]

If the unwritten rules of human response could be catalogued, analysed, and understood, then it might be possible to create great contemporary plays and productions that would resonate with the same kind of power as the classics. Expressionism, Cubism, and Constructivism were among the then current "isms" of great appeal. All of these, however, were alien and unknown to many in the audiences Kurbas faced in the 1920s. These were a heterogeneous group that reflected Kyiv's multicultural and class realities and included the intelligentsia, peasants, and workers; literates and illiterates; Russians, Ukrainians, Jews, Germans, Poles, Georgians, Armenians; and others. Some had never seen any theatre before. How could the perfect production be created that satisfied, moved, and enchanted such mixed audiences?

Les Kurbas and the Audience

As a true man of the theatre (actor, director, playwright, translator, sometime composer, and costume designer), Kurbas paid serious attention to affect and the resulting bond it creates among spectator, actor, and the work. Rejecting the idea that art is merely the union of form and content, he observed that, rather, it consists of content, form, material, creativity, and reception (*сприймання*) – a clear reference to the observer's role in art.[6] Later, he went further by describing art as a communal activity: it was, he explained, that special form of a relationship among people in which they are made to feel, share, and experience one single worldview.[7] Such a definition anticipates and chimes with the concept of "theatre event" introduced into Western performance criticism in the 1980s: the idea that the actor and the audience constitute an "inseparable entity, and have to be understood and analysed as a mutual relationship."[8]

From his earliest days in the Young Theatre, his first theatre collective, Kurbas set out to inform, shape, and understand spectators' reactions to his productions. He is unusual in the history of theatre in his all-encompassing efforts to do so. We may see this on one level in his sometimes mocked practice of appearing before the curtain dressed as Harlequin to explain the aims of a production and, more generally, the goals of his theatre company. The choice of costume may not simply be an attempt to present an instantly recognizable theatrical figure. As the exhibition at the National Gallery of Canada, "The Great Parade: Portrait of the Artist as Clown" (2004) has shown, Harlequin was also a trickster who, like his diabolical progenitor, Hermes Trismegistus, linked the rational with the irrational world.[9] In this earlier period of creativity, Kurbas frequently referred to theatre as a temple, to the importance of returning to its ritual origins; to the necessity of presenting both the diabolical and the beautiful on stage; and to the joy of playing.[10] He invited spectators to be receptive to transformation, to be drawn into the action, to forget the self, and become co-creators of the production.

By the time that he founded the Berezil Artistic Association[11] in 1922, however, Kurbas gave way to a more intellectual and sophisticated apprehension of the theatrical event and, consequently, of the relationship among actor, audience, and work. His engagement with the question of the audience is also reflected in a broader range of attempts to reach out to them and, in turn, to attempt to understand and analyse their response. On the most basic level, we may see his attempt to inform and shape opinion by his careful placement of productions puffs and interviews in both the Soviet Ukrainian and Russian press, most notably on the eve of his radical production of *Macbeth* in 1924, a clear indication of Kurbas's jitteriness about a possibly negative or uncomprehending audience response. His nervousness obviously continued up to the very moment of its premiere on 2 April, when he decided to send out actor-manager Stepan Bondarchuk to justify to the spectators the radical tampering with a world classic.

Another level of engagement may be seen in his common practice of sitting in the audience, observing their expressions at first hand and listening to their comments. Such a custom permitted him to assess spectators' immediate and unreflective response. He also had members of the Berezil take turns as note-takers. A copy of the play-text was brought to each performance and the reactions of the spectators were noted in the margins of the text. According to actress Iryna Avdieva, who occasionally served in this capacity, the following categories were employed: active attention, passive attention, disengagement, indifference, coughing, movement, noise, laughter, applause. Occasionally, when things did not go according to plan and the audience laughed at a point in the action where they shouldn't, Kurbas could be seen rubbing his forehead in annoyance and mumbling, "Not this, not this."[12]

A deeper analysis of audience response, however, would require something more than general notations about audience laughter, puzzlement, or applause. In the pursuit of such a more empirical understanding of affect, Kurbas made a practice of distributing detailed questionnaires after every performance. This practice is generally in tune with the significant scholarly aspect of the Berezil which needs underscoring. Not simply a theatre company but rather closer to a theatre university, the Berezil produced dramatic and musical shows (including opera); carried out theatre research; experimented with stage design, performance, and audience response; published a journal, "Theatre Barricades" (*Барикади театру*); and set up the first theatre museum in Ukraine. At its height when it had a membership of around 400, the Berezil embraced six studios: three in Kyiv, one each in Bila Tserkva, Boryspil, and Odesa, as well branches in villages and towns within Kyiv's perimeter. Its widely experimental and ambitious range also encompassed a children's theatre, a touring model peasants' theatre, as well as a Jewish section.[13]

On the more scholarly side and in addition to an extraordinary variety of lecture topics covered in the classroom (e.g., world history, art, music, theatre, rhetoric, aesthetics, literature, philosophy, biology, medicine, psychology, fencing, classical ballet, juggling, tightrope-walking, acrobatics, roller-skating), Kurbas created a number of research committees, such as the psycho-technical committee studying applied psychology in order to develop new teaching methods in the theatre. The creation and distribution of detailed questionnaires conforms to this sustained interdisciplinary and multidisciplinary research, the results of which would have been discussed and analysed in research committees and in the directors' lab.

It is a little known fact that there are hundreds of extant questionnaires from Kurbas's productions in the archives of the Ukrainian State Museum of Theatre, Music, and Cinema Arts (in Kyiv). We know from published accounts and archival sources that this can be only a miniscule number of the many thousands of questionnaires which the Berezil distributed. In an article published in 1924, for instance, "S.B." (probably Stepan Bondarchuk) reported that over forty thousand questionnaires had been distributed by the Berezil during the previous theatre season. None of the extant questionnaires have received any scholarly attention, although they provide a fascinating snapshot of the early Soviet Ukrainian audience, their sense of identity, their understanding of theatrical forms, their preferences, and their thoughts about theatre's relationship to ideology.

During my visit to the Kyiv archives in 2000, I transcribed thirty-seven extant questionnaires which had been distributed on 14 November 1924 after a revival of one of the performances of Kurbas's *Macbeth*, that is, at a performance given seven months after the premiere of what was considered a scandalous production.[14] The responses offer a glimpse both of the kind of remarkably detailed analysis in which the Berezil was engaged, and a lively picture of the mixed audience that attended. From our twenty-first century point of view, inundated as we are by telemarketers, opinion polls, and other (too many) sorts of surveys, we might be astounded by the scope and detail of this early practice, as well as by the willingness of the audience to respond, often in great and critical detail.

History of Theatre Questionnaires

Before turning to a discussion of the questionnaires and in order to contextualize and assess Kurbas's achievement in this area of audience analysis, a brief sally into the history and practice of distributing theatre surveys is required.

A cousin of Darwin's, Sir Francis Galton (1822–1911), is generally considered the inventor of the survey/questionnaire, first using this form of information gathering in 1874 for a work on heredity.[15] It seems logical to assume that the more widespread practice of distributing questionnaires is linked to the rise of sociology as a scientific discipline (it was first taught at universities in the early 1890s). When, exactly, the practice was transferred to the realm of theatre has not yet been discovered.

In imperial Russia, the earliest documented example of the distribution of theatre surveys was undertaken by the Nevsky Society, formed to produce a cheap but "morally healthy" alternative (i.e., non-alcoholic) entertainment for workers. The Society eventually designed basic questionnaires in 1896 "to make the theatre more responsive to its public's needs."[16] Although some of the excerpts from respondents were published in the Russian press,[17] it is unlikely that the young Kurbas (nine-years-old and living in faraway Western Ukraine, then under Austro-Hungarian rule) would have known about this practice.[18]

It is also unlikely that Kurbas knew about two other examples of the uses of theatrical questionnaires, one carried out by the Mobile Public Theatre from Petrograd (led by Pavel Pavlovich Gaydeburov and Nadezhda Fedorovna Skarskaya) that toured the front and distributed questionnaires there in September and October of 1917.[19] Nor would it have been likely that he knew about the director Alexander Bardovsky's use of behaviourist studies carried out at the Leningrad Youth Theatre in 1917 which, observing the reactions of so-called "typical" children, compiled the results into a "general survey."[20]

A better known example of such a practice was that of Vasilii Fyodorov, the assistant director of Vsevolod Meyerhold, whose distribution of questionnaires is recorded as having taken place during the 1924–5 season and after it was established by the Berezil.[21] Fyodorov was interested in analysing the reactions of spectators and, in order to do so, created a chart encompassing twenty possible reactions of the audience running the gamut from silence to coughing to laughter. He published some of his findings in 1924 to some lively and critical debate,[22] particularly from Mikhail Zagorsky who attacked the behaviourist approach as sociologically useless.[23]

Rather than treating the audience as an *object*, Zagorsky called for more rigorous, empirical studies that considered the audience as *subject*. The alternative he proposed was questionnaires, a practice he himself had briefly undertaken during the theatrical season of 1920–1, and whose 186 extant surveys he analysed and first made more generally public in his article-rebuttal to Fyodorov. The unavoidable conclusion he came to in that essay was that there was no single performance and no single spectator[24]; in other words, the auditorium is not formed of a homogeneous group but, rather, is constructed of a variety of constituents, a conclusion "rediscovered" by Western scholars in the late twentieth century.[25] Opining the absence of empirical audience research, Zagorsky underlined the importance of asking questions about the social composition of the audience, its class groupings, and their distinct responses to this or that play, theatre, and its approach to "academic" or to "left" shows.[26] What Zagorsky proposed as an ideal – the union of the separate fields of audience reception (essentially demographic questions) and reception research (behaviourist questions) – was, in fact, already a well-established practice at the Berezil. Indeed, Kurbas's synthetic, broad-based, and sustained efforts at empirically understanding the audience both outside and inside the auditorium were unique and innovative, though apparently as unknown to his Russian counterparts as to scholars writing today.

The Berezil Questionnaires

Let us now turn to the questionnaires and recall their purpose, which, for Kurbas, was to understand the nature of his audience: its composition, responses, and preferences. By analysing the results, he hoped to grasp the underlying "rules" of audience reception intuited by the great writers of the past. In turn, this would enable him to create contemporary equivalents of classical masterpieces that would have the power to move his audiences. At the same time, the responses to the questionnaires could furnish the director with empirical evidence of a supportive proletarian base and thus justify his theatrical experimentation in the face of Party charges of incomprehensibility and ideological deviation.

The twenty-four questions of the Berezil questionnaire were divided into four parts: 1) Who are you? 2) Our production; 3) Our theatre; and 4)

Theatre in general. The first set of questions (Who are you?) address seemly straightforward demographic issues:

1. Your social status (worker, peasant, worker-*intelligent*, etc.)
2. Your profession
3. Your age
4. Nationality
5. Your education (what level you've completed)
6. Do you act or have you ever acted on stage?
7. Do you often attend the theatre?

The difficulty of assessing and subsequently responding to the audience and its preferences becomes apparent when we begin to analyse the responses. To the first question (social status), one third identified themselves as "workers": their professions included plumbers (the largest number represented), itinerant workers, a hemp-worker, lathe-operator, telegraph operator, stage electrician, hotel-worker, former baker, and two students. A few either refused to record their status or were unsure of it, leaving blanks and, instead, permitted their response to the second question, their profession, to stand as a response to the first.

The second largest group, 18 per cent, identified themselves as "*trud-intelligent*" – "worker-intelligentsia," a label that included teachers and students. One wag avoided the *trud* (work) part and identified himself as an "*intelligent*," and, by profession, as a "poet dilettante." Twelve per cent identified themselves as peasants, although in this category many seemed to have acquired a surprising degree of literacy: one, who identified himself as an agricultural worker had completed a secondary education, while another with the same educational background and who considered himself of the same class, was, by profession, a teacher. On the other side of the scale were two peasants who had completed only a few lower grades of schooling, yet listed their professions as copyists or clerks.

The respondents varied in age from seventeen to forty-five, though nearly half were in their 20s. A number of them, however, refrained from indicating their age, including a group of five friends who responded all together on one form.

Not surprisingly, nearly 62 per cent identified their nationality as Ukrainian; 10 per cent Russian, 5 per cent Jewish, 2 per cent Greek, and 2 per cent "Slavic." The group of five answered this question by responding, in Ukrainian, that they were five people "of different [but unspecified] nations." It should be noted that the language of response was not always identical with the claim to nationality (the "Slav" wrote in Ukrainian; a number of Ukrainians in *surzhyk* – a mixture of Russian and Ukrainian – or in Russian). As has already been suggested, the educational background was variable: from a few grades of trade school, to secondary schooling, to a claim of a "high" education.

To question 6 (Do you or did you ever act?) 62 per cent responded negatively although one respondent was clearly tempted by the siren call of the stage, since he observed that although he had never acted, he might. Of the 27 per cent who had experience with the stage, one identified himself as the director of a drama group, another, pointedly, as a member of a Ukrainian drama group. Also in this group were a plumber, a stage-electrician who "occasionally" acted, and a hotel-worker who claimed that he "acted and went to the theatre every day." Were these bit parts that were performed on a daily basis? False claims? Responses made to annoy the survey analysts? In any case, correlating these responses to acting experience with their status yields no truly satisfying generalities: worker-plumbers were as likely to have had some acting experience (or claim to it) as *trud-intelligents*, Ukrainians as often as Russians.

To question 7 (Do you often attend the theatre?), 51 per cent said "yes" (though this affirmative response was qualified in some cases with reference to financial constraints); 32 per cent indicated that they attended infrequently; 2 per cent of the respondents were in the theatre for the first time in their lives, and another 2 per cent for the first time in the Ukrainian theatre. Interestingly, there seems to have been no necessary correlation between educational background and frequency of attendance at the theatre; peasants with little or no education as well as the intelligentsia were as likely to attend.

Two general conclusions may be drawn from these responses to the first series of questions: one, that the Berezil appeared to have a core of youthful Ukrainian supporters of various backgrounds, status, and professions, something which confirms the claims that Kurbas himself made throughout the 1920s; and two, that the Berezil productions drew a very mixed audience, a fact which would make it difficult (and increasingly so) to create a production that would be comprehensible and satisfying to all.

The second series of questions centred on the production of *Macbeth* and asked the following long list of questions:

1. Did you understand and like the content of today's play?
2. What parts of the content of today's play were not comprehensible?
3. What did you like about the actors' performances?
4. What did you not like about the actors' performances?
5. What is your opinion about the constructions (stage decorations)?

  6. What is your opinion about the costumes?
  7. What is your opinion about the music?
  8. What is your opinion about the dances?
  9. What is your opinion about the lighting?
10. What did you like best about today's show?

A brief synopsis sketching out some of the key features of Kurbas's remarkable production of *Macbeth* is in order here; a fuller analysis is found in the previous chapter of this volume and in an extensive analysis in my *Shakespeare in the Undiscovered Bourn*.[27] Shakespeare's Scottish play, produced two months after the death of Lenin, was, as Kurbas explained, "fractured by the prism of the contemporary revolutionary world-view," that is, it became a totally contemporary, tragic-farcical, blood-soaked Cubist-Expressionist Shakespeare – one unlike any other seen before anywhere (East or West) at that time. In Yuri Boboshko's words, this was "not a 'costume' drama but a national tragedy full of contemporary meaning."[28] The production interrogated every single theatrical convention, from props to the idea of the tragic hero. The designer, Vadym Meller, created enormous bright green screens of stretched canvas on which giant modernist red block letters announced the locality of each scene. Raised or lowered when needed at the sound of a gong, the screens served a variety of functions. Lowered at the same time, they indicated the simultaneity of the action in different parts of Scotland. At other times, they moved in slow, stately rhythm to underscore the emotions of the lead actors, to emphasize tension, or even to interfere in the action. Fragments of furniture, chairs, and a throne were, like the screens, lowered and raised when needed.

The most radical experiment of this production involved the creation of character. In Renaissance fashion and with similar effect, actors' roles were doubled or tripled, contributing to the spreading of guilt in the realm. The great test for Kurbas's actors was to be able to display mastery of their technique by engaging and then disengaging from their roles at will – a repeated strategy that isolated and drew attention to key moments in the play, in effect, making them like operatic arias, or separate "numbers," set apart from the rest of the action.

While these tactics intellectualized and distanced the play from the audience by stressing the omnipresence of evil, others (such as backlighting the witches) drew the audience into the violent, corrupt world of feudal Scotland. Created by Kurbas, three mimed interludes involving the Porter/Fool were interspersed between the acts of the play; these drew the audience further into the play, destroying the idea of the audience as fourth wall. (This cabaret-like technique is discussed in Chapter Eleven.)

The Fool's last appearance, which occurred in the final moments of the play, when Macduff comes out carrying the head of Macbeth, caused a major scandal. Still wearing his Fool's makeup (the mocking, grinning face) actor Amvrosy Buchma came in costumed as a bishop and proceeded to crown Malcolm to the solemn music of an organ that ironically contrasted with the delicate sounds of the piccolo and the rougher harmonium. Just as the Fool/Bishop completed the ceremony, a new pretender approached, killed the kneeling Malcolm, and seized the crown. Without pause, the bishop once again intoned the same words, "There is no power, but from God." As the new king was about to arise, a new pretender murdered him, and the ritual was repeated once again.

Keeping in mind the extraordinary departure from traditional ways of staging Shakespeare and (as we have seen) also the demographic range of spectators, it is remarkable that over 62 per cent responded positively to it and claimed to understand it. Despite the radical transformation of this classic, one respondent commented that of course he liked the production and, anyway, how could one not like Shakespeare? The group of five (mentioned earlier) took this opportunity to solemnly and formally greet the Berezil with its success and to wish the company the determination required to continue along their courageous experimental path. Only 8 per cent admitted to a partial understanding of the production; of these, one noted that, in any case, he didn't understand the Ukrainian language. Others left blanks, but 24 per cent complained: some that this was an old play and that new contemporary playscripts were needed; another regretted the absence of the *narod* (the people) on stage; yet another that the production was too "mystical," and, in perhaps the harshest critique, one remarked that the production was about as alien as a piece of junk at a Jewish bazaar.

Among the favourite parts of the play, the most frequently cited were the Fool's appearances, the mass scenes, the witches, the killing of Duncan, the elasticity of the actors' expressions, the coronation scene, and the scenes with the ghosts and spirits. These positive responses, we may guess, came from those who enjoyed the theatricality of the production, while those who responded negatively to many of the same elements appeared to have been proponents of realism: in this regard, they negatively cited the actors' grimaces, their "weird" acting, ponderous gestures, and characterization of their roles.

The austerity of the stage décor, the costumes, and the music received a similarly divided response along with some expressions of genuine puzzlement. A few partisan voices were heard ("The music was wonderful because our rector – Butsky[29] – composed it"). One of the few questions which elicited near unanimity was in response to the dances carried out by the witches. The contemporary abstract movements à la Bronislava Nijinska[30] elicited many blanks. Of the only eight responses to this question, most categorized the dances "very bad," while some even disputed that there were any. By comparison, most responded positively, and with enthusiasm, to the lighting effects, even when condemning the sustained level of stage darkness.

The majority were very knowledgeable about past productions of the Berezil. Nearly half had seen at least two of their other shows, while one enthusiast had seen "almost all." *Jimmie Higgins* and *Macbeth* were both cited as favourites: the former because of its "clear illumination of the class struggle" and because of its lifelikeness; the latter, because it was more comprehensible; both, for their "working class spirit." Two, however, held the opposite view: the Shakespearean production was far removed from workers' understanding.

In response to the last question of this section of the survey (How does Berezil differ from other theatres?), some responded by remarking on the "new pathways in art" that Berezil was carving out; others, that proletarian audiences attended this theatre and that it was closer in spirit to the masses; still others cited clarity (of purpose, one assumes); ideology; simplicity; stage sets; originality, freshness, untiringly revolutionary work on the development of form; new productions; absence of kitsch; and richness of representation. One irritably responded: "I've answered this question many times before and you yourselves know the answer." Only one peasant claimed not to find any difference among the productions of the various theatres of the city.

The bewildering variety of responses, the range of audience constituencies, preferences, and critique doubtlessly made interesting fodder for discussion at the Berezil research committees and theatrical labs. There was, however, one more and final part of the questionnaire, three questions about theatre in general that could more specifically help shape the Berezil's choice of repertoire for the immediate future. These were the following:

1. Which kinds of theatrical productions do you like best (opera, drama, theatre of the pre-revolutionary type, drama of the revolutionary type, the circus, film, etc.)?
2. Based on what kind of life would you like to see a play?
3. What else would you like to tell us about our theatre?

Nearly half of the respondents made film either their first choice of preferred production or one of their top preferences. This was followed by 37 per cent who chose theatre of the revolutionary type.

Another 18 per cent made opera their first choice but, surprisingly, only two of the same people who did so also chose pre-revolutionary theatre as a second choice. The status of those who made opera their first choice reveals another interesting detail: three were peasants with little education, two were plumbers, and two were young students. Anyone attempting to make simplistic ideological connections between higher education, class status, and the high art of opera would have been stymied by such results.

One conclusion to be drawn from this part of the survey was that film appealed to the widest constituency, being either the first choice or one of the top preferences of Ukrainians, Russians, and Jews (the Greek respondent didn't specify any preference); peasants and plumbers, students, migrant workers; and teenagers and adults. In the future, the majority of respondents wanted to see shows taken from contemporary life, from the class struggle of the proletariat, from the period of the civil war, from revolutionary life, from real, everyday life, and from the life of the Ukrainian people.

The final question of the whole survey presented the general rubric of "What else would you like to tell us about our theatre," a catch-all question that, after an already lengthy survey, we might imagine, could lead to a lot of blanks. In this case, it resulted in an outpouring of commentary. A sampling:

- "Go away"; "You destroyed the old theatre and gave us nothing nice in return";
- "Wonderfully organized mass scenes";
- "In the current atmosphere, it's not necessary to repeat 'O God' so often. Although you use it [the phrase] ironically, the Red Army masses and the workers don't understand. The plays [reflect] the contemporary spirit. The acting superb – especially Macbeth and his wife, and others";
- "Obviously, your theatre is not yet fully formed. Your theatre is a questing theatre. As a quest, it pretty much satisfies me. A complete rupture with the old methods, original treatment of plays, method of collectivization – all that is good";
- "Your theatre is far removed from the understanding of the worker and in many plays you jump ahead by many decades and by doing so you disconnect yourself from the worker; but sometimes, for example, with *Macbeth*, you go too far back and that is not understood [either]. Give us contemporary workers and workers' understanding";
- "Either I understood nothing, or you will understand nothing";

- "Your theatre wouldn't be so bad if you had sets, [and] the curtain came down after every part. There's nothing more to say, I don't feel like saying anything more, but I will say more next time. For now, this is enough";
- "A couple of questions. I don't know how you will answer them. Maybe in the newspaper: 1) What do you achieve by and what do you mean by the absence of decorations and 2) What are your next projects?" [scribbled at the top of the page another afterthought: "Provide an answer in the press"];
- "More mass scenes, more from the life of the revolutionary civil war";
- "I have nothing more to say about this play. Except for one scene, the lighting should be brighter. Not enough music in the *entr'acte*, which in my view is indispensable, and that's why I beg you to trouble yourself about this";
- "In today's show the clown was pointless. It doesn't harmonize with the whole character of the play";
- "I like your theatre but our audience still hasn't lost the habits of the old theatre and doesn't understand [your theatre], for which purpose, in my opinion, you should organize lectures in workers' clubs and explain what your theatre is trying to do."

The deeply engaged, even when negative, response of the audience brings the theatre event of 14 November 1924 curiously alive. We hear the audience's directly expressed advice, their sincere comments (sometimes technical, sometimes homespun), their harangues, their critique, their hopes. Above all, we see their expectation of a real response from the Berezil. If Kurbas wanted a thinking and co-creating audience, he was getting one.

The Consequences

The publication of the results of the season's questionnaires was eagerly and anxiously awaited. Writing about the prepublication hype, Oleksander Kysil emphasized the broader significance of such surveys: theatre, he noted, more than all the other arts, was intimately tied to communal life and thus it was imperative that its effect on the audience be understood.[31] Supporting this view, the young theatre inspector Yuri Smolych also urged all theatres to follow the example of the Berezil in employing both behaviourist studies and questionnaires to study their audiences.[32]

The questionnaires offered both the promise of a convincing refutation of the Communist Party's charges against the Berezil of being too experimental and thus inaccessible to the masses, as well as the means of securing the theatre's survival. This was threatened by the Party's major decision that same year (1924) to "systematically regulate the chaos of the theatre market" by limiting the burgeoning number of theatres throughout Ukraine to only nine.[33]

When the analysis of the season's 55,552 questionnaires[34] was finally published, it confirmed the results indicated by my meagre sampling analysed above: the Berezil attracted a predominately youthful, vocal audience that represented a broad social spectrum, though with a considerable and growing, proletarian base. Divisions between those who supported the new, experimental approaches and those who continued to prefer the old ethnographic theatre remained, a fact well noted both by the Berezil detractors and its supporters.[35] Nonetheless, the evidence of the questionnaires doubtless assisted in more than just prolonging the existence of the Berezil. Its place as an exemplary theatre supporting communist ideals (but, as Kurbas insisted, not Communist) with innovative methods and techniques was acknowledged by Party officials, and it was soon moved to the recently-established new capital of Ukraine, Kharkiv, to become its premiere model theatre. Kurbas was decorated as People's Artist of the Republic and the Berezil was to participate in the prestigious Paris *Exposition internationale des arts décoratifs et industriels modernes* in 1925 as well as at the New York International Theatre Exposition in 1926. Kurbas and his Berezil were at their zenith.

Below the level of officialdom and in the directorial labs and research committees, where there was the usual ongoing critical assessment of productions, first principles, and ideas, the questionnaires received especially close scrutiny. Since the stakes were high, it was imperative that future productions continue to attract proletarian audiences. Shortly after the publication of the findings, the detailed platform of the Berezil was published, outlining its basic principles and intentions, and laying claim to creating theatre on the basis of the "new scholarship" (which, one assumes, included audience analysis).[36]

On the individual level, perhaps swayed by the respondents' comments, by his continuing quest for new creative challenges, and by his desire to reach a wide audience, Kurbas decided to turn his created efforts for the next two years almost exclusively to film.[37] When he returned to stage direction, it was to forge a strong relationship with the writer Mykola Kulish whose plays focused precisely on the topics which the majority of the respondents to the questionnaires most desired: contemporary plays about everyday life in Ukraine, about life in the revolutionary period, and about civil war.

However, Kurbas's return to the theatre coincided with stricter controls, embodied by the proclamation of the "Theses about Theatre

Criticism"[38] that urged the proletariat to take over leading roles in the cultural revolution, to take command of, as well as critically to rework, all of the classical heritage of the past, and to destroy all "harmful" works of the bourgeois-feudal period. Works that were saturated with the spirit of the class struggle were to be actively promoted. Experimental productions were implicitly condemned on the basis of incomprehensibility. Evidence of poorly digested cultural politics in the theatre was to be followed up to its source, "uprooted" and "persecuted." Content was henceforth all-important: only socially significant works were to be permitted. So-called "academic" (formerly imperial) theatres were to be responsive to Party directives, and private theatres and collectives were exhorted to "democratize" their work by getting rid of "recidivism."[39] Because theatre "was an important factor in popular education, an active weapon in the cultivation of a socialist consciousness of the popular masses" the Party resolved that, above all else, it had to be accessible, which meant comprehensible and "realistic not avant-garde."[40]

Attacks on the Berezil and on Kurbas in particular continued in tandem with praise throughout the 1920s. At the officially organized lengthy debates, the "Theatrical Discussions" of 1927 and 1929, which marked the culmination of the decade's polemical, sometimes vitriolic, disputes about the purpose and function of theatrical art and its relationship to the audience, the shift in power from directors and theatre companies to their audiences was made evident. It was confirmed at decade's end with the creation of repertoire committees that cemented audience control over all aspects of productions, including choice of repertoire, personnel, and style.[41]

After a rehearsal literally at gunpoint, Kurbas was relieved of his post as artistic director of the Berezil in 1933. A few months after moving to Moscow to direct Solomon Mikhoels in *King Lear* at the State Jewish Theatre, he was arrested, imprisoned, exiled to the Far North, and, finally shot, on Stalin's express orders, in 1937, the same year that "Uncle Joe" ordered thirty thousand other executions and the "cleansing" of all Ukrainian educational, cultural, and scientific institutions. Kurbas's papers, films, maquettes, and diaries were destroyed and even his name was prohibited from being mentioned until Stalin's death. His "rehabilitation" came only in the late 1980s with glasnost and the disintegration of the USSR. The declaration of an independent Ukraine in 1991 finally made it possible for his legacy of innovative productions, theoretical articles, and audience analyses to receive their long-overdue attention.

8

In a Crooked Mirror: *Hamlet* as Intertext in the USSR 1934–1943

From the very beginning of the establishment of the USSR in 1922, theatre was regarded as essential to military and political struggle. Indeed, "culture" as a whole constituted "one of the primary spheres of revolutionary contestation, like politics and economics."[1] But what was the most effective arsenal to deploy in such a struggle? What should be retained from the old canon? What renounced? What, if anything, adjusted to fit the times? The attitude to the European classics, and Shakespeare in particular, was fraught with historical, value-laden palimpsests.[2] A playwright familiar to the small literate circles of imperial Russia for well over a century, Shakespeare occupied a complex position in the literary system, reflecting, among other things, a long-standing "love-hate" relationship with the West. Many Bolsheviks wished to sweep away all such pre-Soviet and foreign works from the repertoire; others argued vehemently for their retention. Still others expected that the cataclysmic political and social changes that had come about after the First World War, Revolution, and Civil War would result in the birth of new, Soviet Shakespeares. These events, it was hoped, would bring about a *Soviet* classic. Just as Shakespeare had become a symbol of Englishness, so a Soviet classic would become a potent symbol of "Sovietness," embracing revolutionary grandeur, powerful emotions, and heroic conflicts. The new Soviet "Shakespeare" would thus render the English Bard redundant. But Soviet Shakespeares proved either slow to be born or were stillborn, yet the desire and the hope, periodically reignited, lived on.

After the death of Lenin (1924) and having finally overcome all his opponents towards decade's end, Stalin consolidated his power as General Secretary of the USSR. He turned to creating a socialist offensive on every front, including with his "Cultural Revolution" (1928–32) aimed at "proletarianizing" art and culture. It was expected that a new, great Soviet culture would not just mobilize popular support, it would consolidate and amplify the prestige of the new Soviet state both inside and outside the USSR. Repeated assertions about Soviet cultural superiority were made, along with the claim that the great works of the past were given more careful attention in the USSR than they were in their own native countries. Shakespeare was supposedly "neglected" in England but attracted great interest in the Soviet Union.[3]

Rather than examining the ways in which Shakespeare was used as a dissident, obliquely allegorical, or otherwise subversive text that challenged the Soviet regime,[4] this chapter will examine the other "side": that is, the uses and limitations of Shakespearean intertexts by an official writer, ideologue, true believer in the aims of the Communist Party and a favourite of Stalin, Oleksandr Korniychuk (Russian: Korneychuk). In Ukrainian scholar D.T. Vakulenko's generous assessment, Korniychuk directed his whole creative being toward the contemporary moment: "[H] is artistic works are documents of the period, they hold up the mirror to life, although sometimes the mirror is crooked and has no backing."[5] But Vakulenko also conceded that Korniychuk was a "sincere propagandist who did not always differentiate demagoguery from socialist politics…nonetheless, he has his place among those creators devoted to the people and the creation of a new Soviet literature, one of the first founders of its ideological-aesthetic principles."[6]

More particularly, this chapter will examine the ways in which the simultaneous effort to both remember and forget Shakespeare in the process of groping toward the creation of a new Soviet aesthetic (here understood as the theory by which cultural works were judged) ultimately confirmed and even more deeply rooted Shakespeare in Soviet culture. It will argue that one important factor in the success or failure to supplant Shakespeare lay in the Soviet attitude to, and treatment of, time: its inexorable or "systematic" prolepsis – "'knowledge' of the future-that-is-already there" – which made socialist realism an "impossible aesthetic."[7] In contrast to scholars who have considered reworkings of classical texts as "a contemporary obsession" intent on exploring "the possibilities of performance in the present, to explore the present itself,"[8] this chapter argues that the Soviet reworking of *Hamlet* was not an obsession with the present, nor with a nostalgia for the past, but rather, with the future.

Stalin and Theatre

Despite the plethora of challenges in governing and controlling a huge multinational state, even the smallest detail of culture received Stalin's careful attention.[9] His influence was "indisputably decisive" in this area, a zone in which he took a special interest.[10] "Bloody Tyrant and

Bookworm," as well as "Editor-in-Chief of the USSR" (as historian Geoffrey Roberts variously styled him[11]), Stalin unilaterally permitted, prohibited, transformed, or encouraged cultural endeavours at will throughout the length and breadth of the USSR, including in its largest republic, Ukraine. Taking an extraordinary interest in every aspect of theatre, Stalin read, annotated, and edited plays in manuscript, conferred privileges on theatre artists, ordered theatre openings and closings, commented on the décor, censured reviews, and judged prizes.[12] Each and every comment of his "became the subject of rumours, myths and decisions that affected careers and even lives.[13] The centrality of theatre was reflected in a variety of ways, including with newly-created awards (Meritorious Artist, People's Artist of the USSR) as well as in the number of arrests of theatre artists before, during, and after the Great Terror.[14]

In 1932, Stalin successfully wooed Maxim Gorky out of exile, marking him for the position of leader of Soviet literature and "consolidator of literary forces," – another strategy aimed at legitimizing the regime.[15] Showered with many privileges, Gorky became the first head of the Writers Union and a powerful force in the USSR, largely responsible for initiating a major shift in the Soviet theatrical repertoire. The Bolshoi, Stalin's favourite theatre, was elevated in rank; the Moscow Art Theatre, held up as a model for theatres in all republics of the USSR; and Stanislavsky's system became theatrical dogma. The days of avant-garde experiments of theatre directors like Les Kurbas were over. All independent cultural organizations were abolished and the massive Soviet censorship machine, along with internal passports, was introduced. Theatre was brought under Party control through the appointment of communists as producers and administrators; Party officials and proletarian representatives from factories and unions served on "artistic councils" in order to prevent any deviations from the Party line.

The turn to the classics like Shakespeare usefully dovetailed with the long-standing and rooted conviction among the old intelligentsia that the theatre's purpose was to educate and improve the spectator. It was in Gorky's apartment in October 1932, at a meeting to which Vyacheslav Molotov, Kliment Voroshilov, and Lazar Kaganovich were also summoned, that Stalin first used the famous phrase "engineers of human souls" to describe the function of writers. Urged to suppress their need for individual expression, writers were, instead, to serve the greater cause of perfecting socialism. Marrying the technological with the religious, Stalin's phrase, which became an oft-repeated mantra, revealed the depth of the significance that he attributed to culture. Indeed, "the production of souls," he insisted, was "more important than the production of tanks."[16] At that same meeting, Stalin appears to have laid out the basic elements of the theory of socialist realism before it was formally and publicly articulated in 1934 at the First Soviet Writers' Congress.[17] Contending that "an artist's head" should be full of "the theories of Marx and Lenin....And if he shows our life truthfully, on its way to socialism, that will be socialist art, that will be socialist realism."[18] Of all the genres, he declared, plays were the best suited for the mobilization of the masses.

Unlike Lenin and Trotsky, Stalin was not a huge admirer of Shakespeare nor did he appear to have much knowledge of his works.[19] Hamlet is the only Shakespearean character that Stalin ever mentions by name. Likely imbibing the idea of a weak Hamlet already in the formative years of his youth, he appears to have upheld this conviction throughout his life.[20] Thus, for example, in 1940, in reviewing the screenplay for *Law of Life* (directed by Boris Ivanov and Aleksandr Stolper), Stalin commented:

> There is a demand for works to represent the enemy for us in all his most important aspects. Is this right or wrong? Wrong. There are different ways of writing – the way of Gogol, or of Shakespeare. They have outstanding heroes – negative and positive. When you read Shakespeare or Gogol, or Griboedov, you find one hero with negative features. All the negative features are concentrated in one individual. I would prefer a different manner of writing.[21]

In 1947, Stalin again identified Shakespeare with negative characters. Criticizing Sergei Eisenstein's portrayal of Ivan the Terrible in the second part of his film on this subject, Stalin commented that the filmmaker should have shown both the necessity for the tsar's cruelty and the reason for his ultimate failure as being insufficiently cruel. In Eisenstein's creation, Stalin remarked, the tsar came out "as indecisive, like Hamlet. Everyone suggests to him what should be done, but he can't make a decision himself."[22]

Noting that there were two types of romanticism, bad and good, Stalin affirmed that "Gorky's idealisation of man was the idealisation of the new man of the future, the idealisation of the new social system of the future"; this approach and this character type, Stalin asserted, would move the USSR forward.[23]

The First Soviet Writers' Congress

Shortly after the discussions in his apartment, Gorky penned his 1933 essay "On Drama," in which he castigated the continuing impoverished state of Soviet dramaturgy and invoked the need for a "socialist heroism" or "revolutionary romanticism,"[24] – phrases that seem inflected by the meetings with Stalin. An admirer of Shakespeare, Gorky urged writers to create a new character type that had hitherto never before appeared in the literary canon: a hero that was "straightforward, clear, and large."[25] Such a hero would educate spectators in the high principles of socialism and its morality; thus, he would not only represent but would also *create* in the audience, the qualities of the New Soviet Man. Following the example of Lenin, this hero was required to be a "teacher, activist, and the creator of the new world," and, in order to "describe this hero with an appropriate power and intensity of language," playwrights were urged to "learn from the unsurpassed masters of this literary form, and, above all, from Shakespeare."[26]

The following year, the formative 1934 First Soviet Writers' Congress put the final stamp on the end to creative experimentation in the arts. A mammoth portrait of Shakespeare, like a venerated icon, stared down at the gathering, at which Gorky advised writers to emulate the Bard while employing the method of socialist realism, now the only permissible way to create aesthetic works. In his keynote address Andrey Zhdanov, Stalin's spokesman, described this method as "a combination of the most stern and sober practical work with a supreme spirit of heroic deeds and magnificent future prospects."[27] Literature was to have two functions: "*both* to depict life in its messy particularity, in its mundane, practical detail, *and* to idealize…Citizens were to be transformed – assimilated – by inspiring themselves into the master narrative of history."[28] Literature must be "truthful" in its portrayal of reality, in its "revolutionary development, and its ideological remoulding and education of the toiling people in the spirit of socialism."[29] Much could be learned from the classics.

The conjunction of contradictory impulses – celebration and imitation of Shakespeare, on the one hand, control, on the other – suggests the complex, uneasy, and unpredictable alliance of Shakespeare with communist ideology. While the Writers' Congress was taking place, Stalin was holidaying, probably deliberately absent so that he could distance himself from debates while, at the same time, "exercising remote control over its proceedings, vetting keynote speeches and receiving regular updates from Kaganovich and others."[30]

As Katerina Clark has pointed out, in the 1930s culture was "*always* in the purview of the Soviet leadership, and *especially* of Stalin….Even in the most critical moments of inner Party struggle or of the terror [the late 1930s] or of [the Second World] war, not only did the routine apparatus of control over cultural matters function, but decisions were taken at the highest levels on cultural issues of a fairly minor order."[31]

It was at this time that the great project of translating Shakespeare into all the languages of the Soviet Union began. This was justified as a way of presenting its citizens with the world heritage that – it was claimed – had been previously denied them; but it was also one of the many means of creating a common, homogeneous Soviet culture as defined by the Party. By 1966, Russian Soviet scholar Roman Samarin could boast that the translation project had resulted in more than five million copies of Shakespeare's works in twenty-eight languages of the Soviet Union.[32] Despite occasional local opposition, Shakespeare was also brought, sometimes forcibly, to the many stages of the various republics of the Soviet Union. Critic Pavel Markov justified such decisions of the Repertory Committee by asserting that the Committee "does not permit the performance of plays which are socially insignificant or harmful, and it assists the theatres in the correct interpretation of a play."[33] Joseph MacLeod went further in completely collapsing the values of the USSR with Shakespeare. By closely examining Shakespeare's works, he insisted, we may discover the Bard's "high regard for the ordinary man, in his weakness and in his strength," thus "we scarcely know whether it is Shakespeare or the Soviet Union that we are describing."[34]

Already part of the Russian intelligentsia's cultural toolkit under the tsars, Soviet Shakespeare was thus introduced to and became known by a wide swath of Soviet peoples. Primarily esteemed as a writer of tragedies, he was best known for *Hamlet,* a play that had, since the nineteenth century, made the deepest impression on Russian culture and the Russian psyche.[35] If the Soviet desire was ultimately to out-Shakespeare Shakespeare, then the play to beat was *Hamlet.* But there were hurdles; among them, the need to address or redress the long tradition of interpreting Hamlet as a divided hero or what Ivan Turgenev called a "superfluous" man – an intelligent, educated aristocrat alienated from his milieu and constitutionally incapable of action.[36] Moreover, there was no room in the USSR for "mystery, uncertainty, and doubt"; following Marxist-Leninist principles meant that "[a]ll valid questions" were to "have definite answers."[37]

A Soviet "Hamlet"

Our investigation begins by focusing on this image, depicting surely the most famous theatrical gesture of all time: a man holding a skull:

The man looks intently at what he will inevitably become. The living contemplates and addresses the dead. It is an immediately recognizable scene to most people around the globe and includes "the most famous theatrical prop in the history of drama, possibly in the history of Western culture."[38] It appears to be an image taken from one of the best known scenes of Shakespeare's iconic play, *Hamlet,* commonly accepted as the

Figure 8.1. Yuri Shumsky as Platon Krechet, Ivan Franko Theatre, Kyiv, date unknown.

Source: Courtesy of the State Theatre, Music, and Cinema Museum of Ukraine, f-44030.

most translated play in the world. As Marvin Carlson has pointed out in his influential study: "Who does not immediate recognize, in whatever pictorial style he may appear, the dark habited young man gazing contemplatively into the sightless eyes of a skull he is holding?"[39] Taking up the skull identified by the gravedigger as that of the royal jester, Yorick, Hamlet meditates upon the circle of man's life: his great ambitions, his loves, frolics, pleasures, and his ultimate common end. The heart of Shakespeare's play, this is an extraordinary scene of multiple memorializations: the memorialization of a specific life – that of a successful and beloved professional fool, a friend of princes. It is also a nostalgic memorial to the past – the time of Hamlet's innocent, happy youth undefiled by knowledge of murder, betrayal, and, of possible adultery – and, more specifically, a memorialization of the court of Hamlet Senior.

In broader terms, of course, the man-and-skull *gestus* (that is, the linking of the action of picking up the skull with the gesture and attitude of contemplation) is also a scene of the memorialization of all of the history of mankind, a reminder of the human graveyard in which we will all meet, and where heroic, significant figures such as Alexander the Great mingle with annoying, punctilious lawyers and simple rustics, a place where victims are not differentiated from perpetrators, the weak from the strong. It is a scene that has continued to haunt audiences because of its primordial, atavistic, and undeniably powerful truth.[40] Linking image and movement, it is a moment in any production of the play in which the audience often seems to hold its breath. To a great extent, the power of this scene derives from a rare conjunction of time present, past, and future into which the audience is forcibly interpolated. Framed by its multiple layers of theatrical, biographical, critical, and interpretive pasts, the scene unfolds in a present that was already a past, that immediately becomes part of its history and yet also looks forward to the time to come: to our future, our ends.

A metonym of Shakespeare's works, of Shakespeare, and of Theatre itself, this scene is perhaps one of the most salient examples of collective remembrance as public recollection. More than any other, it haunts theatrical history; its gestures are anticipated and repeated in productions of *Hamlet* by countless actors. Since the nineteenth century, when Edmund Kean likely first represented the Danish Prince directly addressing the skull, the combination of gesture, attitude, and prop have, by its repetition, become a memorialization of both Hamlet the character (himself deeply concerned throughout his play with the issue of memory and forgetting) and all of the actors – male and female – who have ever played this role. It may usefully be studied in Diana Taylor's terms as a *scenario*: that is, as a meaning-making paradigm, the "enactment of 'embodied memory'" (performance, gestures, movement) which has been transmitted throughout the ages and which forces us to situate ourselves in relation to it.[41] As Taylor also points out, the scenario always predates the script and allows for a different ending.[42]

With these ideas in mind, let us go back to our first image and to Soviet Shakespeare; for this is not a scene from *Hamlet* but a photo still from a production of *Platon Krechet*, a play by Oleksandr Korniychuk. The photo shows not a portly, staid Prince Hamlet in contemporary dress but an idealistic Soviet surgeon, Platon Krechet, as played by Ukrainian actor Yuri Shumsky.[43] The play's author, his biography, and his relation to the centres of power are central to our discussion. Korniychuk (1905–72) was an omnipresent and, for a time, nearly omnipotent figure in Soviet cultural life. A dramatist and writer, Korniychuk was also a Party activist, a Hero of Socialist Work, a five-time and subsequent winner of the Stalin Prize (1941, 1942, 1943, 1949, and 1951) and twice head of the Writers Union of the Ukrainian SSR (during the war and after, until 1953); he also served as a correspondent for propaganda papers in occupied Ukraine during the Second World War and, among many other high-ranking posts, held the position of Deputy Commissar of External Relations for the Ukrainian SSR (1944).[44] Korniychuk wrote in Ukrainian, but his works were almost immediately translated into Russian and, as a consequence, he was often considered (and treated) as a Russian Soviet playwright.[45]

In his heyday, many articles and a "literary portrait" were written about Korniychuk; a subway station in Kyiv was named after him, as well as streets in the Ukrainian cities of Kolomyya and in Nizhyn.[46] Korniychuk's literary opinions were widely and constantly cited and understood as having been sanctioned by the highest powers in the state. Keenly aware of political opportunities, Korniychuk always "swam with the current and always came up dry."[47] In Pierre Bourdieu's terms, Korniychuk had a feel for "the game."[48] Thus, typically, Korniychuk, who always courted power, dedicated his first creative work, the short story *He Was Great* (1925), to Lenin, on the first anniversary of his death. His other early works were deployed against "bourgeois Ukrainian nationalists and other enemies of the people."[49] Later, Korniychuk became one of the first to create a play in which Lenin appeared as a character (*Pravda*, 1937), thus helping to initiate what has been called a tradition of "Leniniada" – works featuring Lenin as the main character.[50]

Korniychuk skyrocketed to fame in the late 1920s, when his second-place win in a state competition garnered the attention of Stalin himself[51] and when the dearth of good Soviet plays was one of the constant refrains of Soviet dramatic criticism. It was an opportune moment; Korniychuk's artistic ambitions dovetailed perfectly with the long-held Soviet desire to create new Shakespeares. Through his own plays, Korniychuk aimed to challenge and supplant the Bard by re-codifying his works and revealing their gaps and omissions. His aim was to become a Soviet classic, to create Soviet literary models for emulation, and thus to out-Shakespeare Shakespeare. These ambitions are most clearly illustrated by *Platon Krechet*, first written shortly after the Holodomor (the great man-made famine that killed millions) was underway in Ukraine (1932-33) and was published in 1935.

If, as Pierre Bourdieu argues, theatre can only work when there is total connivance between the audience and the author,[52] in the period under study, the only audience that mattered was an audience of one. Stalin's approval meant immediate success: permission to produce, translate, and even reproduce the work in other media.[53] With evident support "from above," Korniychuk's play was immediately widely published, translated, and hurried onto the all stages of the USSR, including the Moscow Art Theatre, in the late winter of that same year.[54] Revised and republished in 1941, then turned into Stalin's favourite medium, film, in

1942, it received the State Prize from the Council of the People's Commissars of the USSR.[55]

Platon Krechet

Korniychuk's hero, Platon, is a driven, hardworking, self-sacrificing surgeon and researcher whose idealistic, noble nature is suggested by his name (Platon trans. Plato; Krechet trans. gerfalcon). Sensitive to beauty and music, Platon dedicates his life to improving the lot of Soviet society. His antagonist, Arkady Pavlovych, the director of the hospital at which Platon works, is portrayed as an envious, opportunistic, pessimistic colleague. More significantly, he is an obstructionist to progress, a "shard of the pre-revolutionary intelligentsia than cannot withstand the onslaught of socialist reality."[56] Briefly, the plot unfolds like this: Platon operates on an unknown man dying of stomach cancer. Although, typically, he selflessly works throughout the night (and therefore misses his own birthday celebrations), Platon is unable to save the doomed man who, unbeknownst to him, is the father of Lida, the gentle, beautiful architect with whom he has just fallen in love. When she discovers that her father is dead, Lida accuses Platon of murdering him through his insistence on employing innovative but untried surgical techniques. But all ends well. The death of Lida's father is balanced by a life saved (an important communist official is saved by Platon); his rival, Arkady, is discredited, and Platon gets his girl.

The play's language is simple, unadorned prose with sentimental, melodramatic overtones. The culminating moment of the whole play in its 1935 version and the key passage for our purposes is Platon's direct address to Death while looking at skull:

> We are not always strong enough to halt your coldness – your eternal laughter. You are inexorable in closing the circle [of life]. You destroy geniuses of the people in times that are the most difficult for them…You stop hearts full of burning yearnings. (*Picks up the skull.*) Who gave you the right throughout the centuries of night – closed to us forever – to carry your smile into our day?… Who gave you the right to end the happiness of man with your breath?…
>
> I challenged you to do battle. Today, you are victorious, brutal…But tomorrow, which of us will be the victor?…Who?…You?…Or, I?[57]

Shorn of any metaphorical richness or philosophical debate, Platon's speech is a direct attack on death, a very challenge to its existence, for the heroic young Soviet surgeon expects, if not to overcome death right away, at the very least (in the words of a Canadian television advertisement preventing strokes), to "make death wait." Dedicated to the people, Korniychuk's Platon is the new Soviet man: an exemplary figure who models the "correct" relationship between the individual and society, the person and the collective, and the past and the future. In the 1935 version, Pavlo Berest, the Chairman of the Executive Committee of the Party, tells Mariya Tarasova, Platon's mother, that her son is an even better healer than Jesus Christ.[58]

In act two, scene one, Platon explains: "For a million years mankind has been robbed of the sun. We are restoring it. For the first time in history, death is retreating in our country. I believe, Comrade Berest, that the day is not far away in which we will destroy premature age forever and will tear away time from death; we will restore those millions of sunny days to future generations." To this, Berest responds, "Millions of sunny days… That will be the most humane monument to those old Bolsheviks who perished too soon."[59] The best way to memorialize those who died for the Revolution is by destroying mortality itself. As Shakespeare scholar Hester Lees-Jeffries insightfully reminds us, "memory and remembering are not primarily about the past, but rather about the future. Remembering is the way in which one conceives of and expresses the relationship between past and future time, in the present; remembering the dead is central to this."[60]

Contemporary commentators immediately recognized in Platon his resemblance to the Danish Prince. For "Who, but Hamlet could stand beside Platon?" inquired Soviet Ukrainian scholar Rostyslav Kolomiyets.[61] Not a highborn prince divided in his thoughts, this ordinary but idealized positive hero, born to the working classes and educated under the new Soviet system, is endowed with agency. He struggles to realize his lofty ideals. In this case, they are high indeed – of Faustian proportions and well beyond the usually more practical dreams of the "positive hero." As a builder of socialism, Platon served as a model for emulation by the masses (thus anyone, in any profession, could be a Soviet hero), just as the play in which he figured was intended to be a model for literary replication. Idealistic yet unique, ordinary yet extraordinary, Korniychuk's Platon appeared to have addressed the aporias of both Zhdanov and Gorky's formulas for socialist realism.[62]

By employing Shakespeare's most famous scenario as an intertext, Korniychuk boldly proclaimed himself a Soviet "Shakespeare." His play required a forgetting of the "universal" Bard or, more accurately, a remembering of only a part of his most famous work while simplifying, condensing, and generalizing it into a model of socialist realist melodrama. Platon's unhesitating agency was thus an oblique comment on the inadequacies of both Shakespeare and pre-Soviet systems of thought.

Death is the enemy that will be ultimately vanquished by Soviet scientific methods.[63] The scenario's usual – and seemingly incontrovertible – ending is thus reduced, recoded, reimagined, and rendered optimistic by a hero who projects no weakness or vacillation in his titanic struggle to overcome life's ultimate opponent. Unlike Hamlet, Platon invites the spectators to contemplate not their inevitable ends, by viewing an image of the past (the skull), but rather humanity's glorious future. Shakespeare's play is reduced to a scenario and, more particularly, to a familiar, but nonetheless potent image; the complex temporality of the tragedy is transposed into collective time, while the central character is made to stand for a new myth of an immortal Soviet people.

As many scholars have pointed out, socialist realism and its positive hero were to be understood through the project of a new ontology that attempted to do away with the notion of death. In this view, the individual loses the status of a separate existence and melts into a collective "body." Death loses its importance; instead, it acquires an "über-individual sense"; there can be no tragedy since the collective is immortal; its immortality ensures the realization of the idea of communism, of progress toward a greater, better future.[64] Indeed, this is a future already known; it is, in Régine Robin's terms, a "systematic prolepsis…a process that by definition blocks an authentic anticipation of the future and confuses the interpretation of the past. This manipulation of time in fact produces its own closure."[65]

Korniychuk's play was greeted with great acclaim, including by that of Maxim Gorky.[66] In the wake of the horror of the deaths of millions from the Holodomor, his play offered a happy and welcome vision of the brave new world toward which all these and other sacrifices were a necessary prologue. Barely a month later (in January 1935), *Platon Krechet* also became the subject of a series of orchestrated debates, one of which was held during a meeting of the Ukrainian Association of Marxist-Leninist Scholarly Research Institutes.[67] A number of prominent literary figures, among them the literary critic Samiylo Shchupak (editor of *Literaturna hazeta*, Literary Newspaper) and Ivan Kulyk (head of the Association of Ukrainian Writers) disputed whether this play was "not yet Shakespeare" (the position taken by the former) or whether it was already Shakespeare (the position of the latter).[68]

The repertoire of the Ivan Franko Theatre in Kyiv, which premiered this and most of Korniychuk's other plays, was one in which the classics occupied a central place; it was soon designated an "academic" theatre.[69] Its audiences would have known some of Shakespeare's works and would have appreciated both the Shakespearean intertext and the Soviet playwright's ambitious intentions. As Hnat Yura, the Franko's Theatre artistic director, explained, "In the process of appropriating the classical tradition" the Theatre aimed both "to preserve those traditions of actorly art, and, at the same time, to discover new means by which to display our heroic reality."[70] Korniychuk's plays became "the foundation" for that theatre's "mastery of the socialist realist method."[71]

Korniychuk, the "infant marvel" (according to MacLeod[72]) was soon declared a Soviet classic and his play became required reading for Soviet students.[73] He was lauded for having created a new archetype: a man shaped by the Soviet power and dedicated to the people.[74] Hamlet dies, but Platon lives and challenges death![75] As Vladimir Torin observed in 1939, in all his works Korniychuk dealt "with the burning questions of the day from the point of view of the Communist Party, of which he is a member."[76] Reprised in the spring of 1941, *Platon Krechet* received an approving review on 18 March in the Party newspaper, *Pravda*: "Korniychuk surrounds his heroes with an atmosphere of lyrical goodness and heartfelt sympathy. There are many warm, bright colours on his palette. *Platon Krechet* is a play of great optimism. Not by accident is the play full of references to the sun, nature, and the happy song of the earth."[77]

Hamlet at War

The Franko Theatre left Kyiv for Moscow on their summer tour in June 1941, bringing with them Korniychuk's repertoire which included another Shakespeare-inspired play. Stalin himself came to see *In the Steppes of Ukraine,* a comic-satiric re-working of *Romeo and Juliet* with a Shakespearean device: a play-within-the play. In this work, the two lovers, Halya (Juliet) and Hryts (Romeo), the offspring of the antagonistic heads of two collective farms (one a socialist, the other, a communist), rehearse scenes for a production of Shakespeare's *Romeo and Juliet.* Shakespeare's tragedy is thus ingeniously both "inside" and "outside" Korniychuk's play. The memory of Shakespeare's tragic ending acts as a counterpoint to the "outer" Soviet play which ends happily, and so thus (as in *Platon Krechet*), obliquely critiquing the failures of earlier, pre-Soviet responses to life's conflicts and implicitly laying claim to Soviet aesthetic and ideological superiority. Necessarily sprinkled with Shakespearean quotations, Korniychuk's comedy dissolves all antagonisms in general reconciliation and happiness, which embraces even the Mercutio figure (Oleksy), who is not only alive but is married off at play's end.

The day after the Franko Theatre's production, the Second World War broke out. It is not hard to imagine why positive, uplifting dramas quickly proved inadequate in the face of the cataclysm of the war.

Enemies were no longer fictional obstructionists (like those in *Platon Krechet*) sabotaging the march of progress or mildly contestatory antagonists (as in *In the Steppes of Ukraine*). With death all around, it was more difficult to pronounce the certainty of one day conquering it. Within three months of the war, after the devastatingly successful invasion of the USSR by Nazi German forces for which the Soviets were unprepared, Korniychuk quickly penned his *Partisans in the Steppes of Ukraine* (*Partyzany v stepakh Ukrayiny*). It was a semi-tragic or "optimistic" tragedy and a sequel to *In the Steppes of Ukraine* (*V stepakh Ukrayiny*), dedicated to the twenty-fifth anniversary of Soviet rule in Ukraine. Like *Platon Krechet, Partisans* was rapidly turned into a film (1942) with incidental music by Sergey Prokofiev – perhaps the only reason it is remembered today, if at all.[78]

The story revolves around a group of Ukrainian peasants who, knowing of an imminent Nazi attack on their village, decide to fight the Germans in any way they can, including cudgelling the enemy to death and burning their own crops. Self-sacrificing, heroic, courageous, the peasants are successful in overcoming the boorish Germans, and in discovering and identifying the traitor in their midst. In this play, but with notably a different emphasis, Korniychuk attempted once again to recode the semiotic field of the man-and-the-skull episode of Shakespeare's play; but the grim circumstances of war required a different approach. Here, Ostap, one of the old villagers, takes up a skull he has found on the field. Rather than using this occasion to prognosticate a great Soviet future free of death as in *Platon Krechet,* here the man-and-skull scenario is used for more particular ends: to prefigure an eventual victory of the *narod,* the people.

In Act II of the play, the stage direction tells us that "*Ostap enters carrying a spade. In his hands he has a skull,*" Part gravedigger, part Hamlet, Ostap exclaims:

Wherever you dig, there are nothing but bones and skulls. (*Sits down, looks around.*) This was some Christian soul that perished; near him there is a large crucifix, a gold one even, – it glistens! Everything else has rotted away, turned to dust, but the gold still shines (*Looks at it,*) Ah! Poor fellow, they hacked at your head from all sides. You were a good Cossack, I can see, and you fought stoutly. And your enemies paid for it and left their own bones here. Otherwise they would have taken the crucifix away. It's evident that Saint Peter has let you into paradise long ago because you fought well for Ukraine. It may be that the Germans will cut us down here, too. If it that happens, we shall meet, you and I. (*Lies down, puts the skull under his head, yawns, and crosses himself.*)[79]

Ostap promptly falls asleep and experiences a long semi-comic dream in which he dances, drinks heavily with the saints in Paradise, and converses with the now re-embodied skull. When he is rudely awakened, Ostap interprets his vision as history and as prognostication of the future:

> The Fascists will meet their end very soon....This Cossack (*takes up the skull*) told me that the Tatars killed him here, but first he cut an enormous number of them to pieces. He told me that in those days also there was a great enemy invasion of our soil. But our people stood their ground and routed them. He said that now, too, our people will resist. That means we'll beat the Germans.[80]

The war and destruction visited on this land – Ostap's monologue suggests – will nonetheless result in a "happy ending": the *narod* will expel its invaders and, ultimately, will emerge victorious. As Chasnyk (trans. Garlic), chairman of the Death-to-Capitalism Collective Farm, insists, "All the people are rising, as they did in olden times against Genghis Khan."[81] As the play nears its end, Ostap's advanced age prevents him from following his younger, more energetic peasant-partisans into further guerilla incursions. Lying down on the ground and using the skull once again as his pillow, he awaits his inevitable death by the Germans but not before repetitively calling upon his absent children to commit acts of revenge: "Fight the godless ones as this Cossack did. Fight with fire, earth, and water...Amen. *Rifle and machine-gun fire can still be heard in the distance,*"[82]

More forcefully, Halushka (trans. Dumpling; chairman of the Quiet Life Collective Farm) insists that his fellow peasant guerillas – and the audience – obey only "one law, which is a sacred law" – the law of revenge.[83] He orders his fellows, "Wherever you meet the enemy, destroy him, annihilate him, as best you can. If you have nothing in your hands, then strangle him, kill him without fail."[84]

Cannily avoiding representation of the true chaos of the first few months of war and the absence of any leadership, *Partisans of the Steppes* (sometimes translated into English as *Guerillas of the Steppes*) created a new official myth *before* the fact, as Valentyna Kharkhun insightfully has pointed out.[85] In this play, Korniychuk imagined the villagers – old as well as young men, women and children – immediately preparing to fight for Stalin; organizing themselves into unified, strategically effective partisans; successfully subverting Nazi efforts; happily studying how to throw grenades; and carrying out such improbably hyperbolic acts as killing sixty-two Germans at "a go."

No longer focused on international communism's great (deathless) future, Korniychuk revisited the man-and skull scenario, reworking it primarily as a reminder of the Ukrainian past which predicted its future: the heroic endeavours of ordinary people, their patriotism, love of the land, Christian identity, and victory over the invader. Previously taboo topics and sentiments (such as Christianity and Christian concepts and love of the fatherland of Ukraine rather than the USSR) were now "rehabilitated" and mobilized for the cause.[86]

Touched up by Stalin himself, Korniychuk's play was quickly disseminated in both stage and film versions throughout the USSR.[87] In audaciously fashioning the myth of the partisans *before* they were actually doing the work of blowing up fascist efforts and smoking out collaborators, Korniychuk's play was literally a work to be emulated; in philosopher J.L. Austin's terms, these were performative utterances that created reality.[88] The play's heroes were imagined as the people's avengers, not vacillating Hamlets but focused destroyers of the enemy. In showing an immediate groundswell of organized peasants working heroically against the Germans from the first moments of war, the play, performed at the front and on various major stages, created a new official myth that took root in the mass consciousness even before the war ended.[89] It was a myth that was to endure and, indeed, to be codified and constantly repeated in official narratives that still today do not brook alternative accounts.[90]

In ambitiously taking up theatre's most easily identifiable scenario – the man-and-skull – Korniychuk counted on the palimpsest of all of the resonances of that potent moment to enter into his audience's consciousness. Korniychuk was attempting to use interpolated learning to change its semiotic field, As Jay Winter and Emmanuel Sivan argue, "The distortion and selection of visual memories…is easier than in the case of verbal ones."[91] Korniychuk, in his dogged ambition to be a Soviet Shakespeare, by distorting, selecting, and re-coding the Bard's most famous scenario, was also creating the official model of the Soviet war play. Revisionist, prognostic, optimistic, it intended to be what Alon Confino calls a "sociocultural mode of action."[92] As a vehicle of "remembrance," *Partisans* helped create a "fictive kinship" that linked the people and the state in an all-encompassing, unifying positive myth of collective, spontaneous, organized action against the invader.[93]

But the grim progress of the war necessitated further alterations to Soviet aesthetic formulas and models and further drastically limited the functions that the man-and-skull scenario could be made to perform. As the Nazis penetrated ever deeper into Soviet terrain, literature and the theatre were enjoined to take up their "holy duty" of bringing forward victory. "Culture" was to be mobilized as a "mechanism" for raising the citizens' consciousness and wielded as a "weapon" against internal and external enemies.[94] *Pravda* castigated writers for failing to march in step with the heroic Red Army and urged them to fulfill their duty by presenting patriotic images of the daily battle for freedom.[95] Korniychuk once again responded to the challenge, this time answering with *Front* (1942; film in 1943), written at the express request and under the watchful eye of Stalin himself.[96] The timing of its publication was of central importance: the siege of Stalingrad when the outcome of the war's end was still unforeseen. An attempt to excuse Soviet military defeats and lay the blame on the uneducated old guard of Bolshevik officers, the play significantly first appeared in four instalments in *Pravda* (August 24 to 27, 1942), where it was also praised for "displaying the manliness of spirit, heroism, and the humanism of the Soviet people"[97] and "hailed as a masterpiece among masterpieces because it staged the slogans of Stalin's party exactly."[98] Korniychuk, the trusted propagandist, once again contributed to wartime myths, this time by completely eviscerating his intertext.

In *Front*, we no longer see a skull on stage. Instead, we have a scene imagined by Krykun (trans. Loudmouth), a war correspondent, who explains to Soviet officers and soldiers that his wide readership is the result of his skill at fabulation, not at reporting truth. The resemblance to Korniychuk, intended or not, is curious, if not ironic. Krykun recounts the fictitious story he intends to publish: the response of a Soviet general who has just learned of his son's death. He imagines his face: "His eyes do not hold any tears. No, I didn't see any tears. His eyes burned with the holy flame of revenge. He said, firmly, 'Sleep, my little son, peacefully and do not worry. I will avenge you. I swear on the honour of an old soldier.'"[99] Foregrounding message above any artistic efforts, Korniychuk responded to Stalin's call for "art" as weapon. The man-and-skull scenario vanished to be replaced by the simple message of revenge. Elsewhere, too, in 1943–4 – in posters, literary works, and films – extreme images and messages appeared urging Russians to kill not just Nazis but *all* Germans – women and children –, to completely annihilate the enemy.[100]

At the Shevchenko Theatre in Kharkiv, *Front* was produced along with documentary war footage and concluded with a song: "Svyashcennaya voyna" – Holy War.[101] In the fight for survival, there was no longer any room for remembering or forgetting Shakespeare. The message of theatre was now reduced to the idea of kill or be killed; it was also focused on the immediate *present*. The man-and-skull scenario was not, after all, infinitely malleable; it had reached the limits of the cultural work it could perform. Not *Hamlet* but *Macbeth* and the bloodlands of Scotland were now more appropriate to the task. As we recall, in the Scottish play, Malcolm counsels Macduff to turn his inconsolable grief over the slaughter of his whole household into active revenge. Once Maduff so persuaded,

Malcolm approvingly responds, now "The tune goes manly." (*Macbeth* 4.3.235).

Alon Confino has usefully pointed out that "the crucial issue in the history of memory is not how a past is represented but why it was received or rejected…[T]o make a difference in a society, it is not enough for a certain past to be selected. It must steer emotions, motivate people to act, be received: in short, it must become a socio-cultural mode of action."[102] In his ability throughout his career to respond to the needs of the moment, to stir emotion, and to manipulate (and create) cultural memory, Korniychuk was eminently successful. But if many of the myths that he created survived the collapse of the Soviet polity, most of his work has, since 1991, been relegated to near oblivion. Korniychuk's uses of the Shakespearean intertext laid bare the paradoxes of socialist realist drama – the unidirectional vector of forward-marching time with its positive hero – and showed how it required, under volatile and constantly changing political circumstances, a concomitant and constant revision, excision, and further simplification.

Eleanor Rowe has pointed out that Russians have long had a "proprietary attitude" to *Hamlet,* treating it more as a Russian, rather than as a world, classic.[103] In an eruption of multiple productions after Stalin's death in 1953, *Hamlet,* the play that had been reviled by the Great Leader, returned to its prominent spot in Russian cultural life, its appeal undiminished, even strengthened – confirming Susan Bennett's thesis that, "By performing (including writing) a text which in some or other way makes reference to an already existing (thereby value-laden) text, the production and reception of the "new" text necessarily become bound to the tradition that encompasses and promotes the old."[104] Korniychuk's uses of the *Hamlet* intertext reflect the complexity of Bennett's inquiry: is "containment" "an inevitable effect of re-articulating the past" or can "a new text, by way of dislocating and contradicting the authority of tradition" produce "a 'transgressive knowledge' which would disarticulate the terms under which tradition gains its authority?"[105] It is an inquiry made even more complex by Soviet politics. Although Korniychuk eventually fell from his pre-eminent literary perch, his models of socialist realist drama did not entirely disappear. In the post-Stalinist 1950s, both critical interpretations and stage productions of Shakespeare's play presented a heroic prince, a man of truth and conscience. Most famously, Boris Pasternak, who had spent years translating the play, referred to it as "not a drama of weakness, but of duty and self-denial.…*Hamlet* is the drama of a high destiny, of a life devoted and preordained to a heroic task."[106] The hesitant, weak Dane of Turgenev seemed to have dissolved; in his place stood Hamlet and, shadowing him, his ghost, Platon Krechet.

Epilogue

Stefaniya Andrusiv has claimed that "no regime guarded its monopoly on the word as much as the communist regime. And no other succeeded to such an extent in brandishing language and shaping it to its own purpose."[107] Similarly, Sarah Davies and James Harris have argued that

> Stalin's words deserve as much scholarly attention as his deeds; in a sense, his words *were* his deeds….To a degree we are only now coming to realize, Stalin *literally* imposed his rhetoric upon the country he ran. To understand the nature of the dictator's power, we need to be attentive to the various ways in which he deployed words in the struggle to create and impose a compelling vision of the world.[108]

Bringing his many years of experience as a writer, journalist, and editor before the Revolution to his assiduous editing of film scripts, historical works, decrees, slogans, up until the very last months of his life, Stalin nonetheless generally preferred that his own words not be published and never without official sanction. Instead, "behind the scenes, he commented regularly on artistic affairs and his words often circulated quite widely, leaving a strong imprint on Soviet discourse."[109] As the decade unfolded, his "utterances came to be surrounded by a growing aura of sanctity and received correspondingly reverential treatment."[110] Such a behind-the-scene approach may perhaps explain the repeated anecdote, undocumented in print, of Stalin's questioning of the need for *Hamlet* during the Second World War.[111]

Over seventy years after Stalin's death, busts and plaques memorializing the *vozh'd* once again appeared throughout Russia. Not simply preservation or restoration of his memory and his place in Russian history but active and aggressive defence has been the recent norm. A case in point was the response of the Russian government to director Armando Ianucchi's satirical film *The Death of Stalin*, Launched in early 2018 with the purported intent to serve as a volley against Western politics and growing European populism, the film met with a barrage of Russian criticism and outrage at its apparent ridicule of Soviet leaders. It was banned in Russia allegedly not because of censorship but, Russian Culture Minister Vladimir Medinsky, claimed, rather for having crossed a "moral line between critical analysis of history and the mockery of it."[112]

The ban on Ianucchi's film was followed not long after by the announcement of the cancellation of all of the activities of the British Council, including the proposal to erect a monument to Shakespeare in Moscow (discussed in Chapter Ten).[113] These prohibitions are signals of related issues: the long-standing love-hate relationship with the West, the potency of culture, and, more particularly, the political uses of Shakespeare. Culture thus continues to hold its pre-eminent place as a player of considerable weight and of immeasurable importance in shaping the public's imaginarium, in reflecting its values and its aspirations to its citizens and to the world.

9

Hamlet, 1943

In the previous chapter, we saw how the Mona Lisa of Shakespeare's canon, *Hamlet,* served as a potently resonant intertext reflecting the Stalinist regime's aspirations and values. This chapter examines the first Ukrainian production of Shakespeare's play from the opposite position of the ideological divide. Yosyp Hirniak, its director, and Volodymyr Blavatsky, the lead actor, conceived of this production that premiered on 21 September 1943 as a declaration of war against art as propaganda and as an assertion of Ukrainian cultural identity.[1] It was, for them, also a faithful mirror of Ukraine's tragic situation in 1943.

The stage history of *Hamlet* in Ukraine is the history of delay – not the delays of Hamlet but those of history. The repeated attempts at performing *Hamlet* form a narrative of efforts to gain political and cultural agency, and the desire to follow new pathways and so denying the imposed rhythms of an imperial drum. *Hamlet* was an especially dangerous play to possess, asking too many questions and providing no answers, probing the nature of evil both as a political and as a metaphysical problem, examining the relation between action and intention, word and deed, the individual and his society. The location for the 1943 production, in Galicia (Western Ukraine), the region often referred to as the Ukrainian Piedmont, suggests something about the nature of the act of staging Shakespeare.[2] Lviv, its centre and an ancient city, was held at various times in the past by Turks, Swedes, Austrians, and Germans; it belonged to Poland from 1919. During the Second World War, Lviv was almost constantly occupied alternately by the Nazis and the Soviets. (The city was formally ceded to the USSR in 1945.) Working under conditions of Nazi occupation (30 June 1941 to 27 July 1944), theatre artists regularly experienced "moral shock" and "psychological trauma," as Valeriy Haydabura, who interviewed some of the survivors, has shown.[3] Theatres were bombed during performances and people summarily shot outside the Lviv Opera Theatre, as its pock-marked façade attests to this very day. While traumatized by Nazi atrocities, the actors also lived in fear of the opposite: a return of Soviet forces that had been equally barbaric. As historian Richard Stites has pointed out, "the grim unholy war of Russian atrocities" is, even now, still "less well-known to the general public inside and outside the country [Russia]":

> This part of the war was largely hidden from the public; the final campaigns were couched in triumphalism and the rhetoric about heroic liberators of enslaved peoples and inmates of the Nazi death camps of Poland. The rhetoric was by no means fake but it also obscured the story. Between 1939 and 1941, while the USSR was an ally of Hitler, about a million and a half Poles, Ukrainians, Belorussians, Jews, Lithuanians, and others were forcibly deported to the arctic North, Siberia, and Central Asia. In the nightmare of nocturnal arrests and searches, looting, cattle cars, resettlements, and executions, almost 300,000 people perished.[4]

To stage Shakespeare in the Ukrainian language during wartime was a mark of cultural, if not of political, nationalism. To produce *Hamlet* was to join in the world of nations. How did this come about? How was this possible in such circumstances?

1943

The year 1943 marked a decisive shift in the war in the East. The Germans were successively beaten back by the Soviets, most notably in Stalingrad in February. A whole series of Soviet victories followed in the late summer and early fall of 1943, when a major Soviet counter-offensive, involving 40 per cent of the Red Army infantry and 80 per cent of the tanks, was launched to recapture Ukraine, a significant source of food and manpower.[5] In addition to fighting the Soviet troops at the front lines, the Germans were also being attacked behind the front lines by Ukrainian nationalist, Polish (*Armija krajowa*), and Soviet partisans. Between June and October 1943, the Nazis publicly executed 1,541 Ukrainian insurgents in Galicia in an effort to maintain control over the region.[6] In the wake of their defeat at Stalingrad, the Nazis launched a massive propaganda campaign in June 1943 as part of their declaration of "total war."[7]

Hamlet was produced in the Fall of 1943, the second year of the Nazi occupation of Galicia, at the Lviv Opera Theatre (LOT) – the institution's name forcibly changed by its occupiers from the Ukrainian Theatre of the City of Lviv.[8] Although air raid alarms went off more and more frequently and street roundups, violence, and executions continued to take place, the Theatre was nonetheless abuzz with the sound of performers and workers – numbering nearly 600 – energetically working from morning until night, appreciating every uncertain day of their existence.[9]

Although after 1942 art by the enemy (including the art of earlier epochs) was prohibited, as were religious, nationalistic, and Marxist works,[10] Shakespeare, a special but conflicted case, passed the muster of Nazi censors.[11] *Hamlet* was considered *"Hochst umstritten"* – the most disputed – but permissible under certain, controlled circumstances.[12] Early on in the war, a special issue of the Nazi journal *Wille und Macht* was wholly dedicated to justifying Shakespeare as an author appropriate for the German Reich. Here Shakespeare is described as an "exceptional" Englishman with a Nordic outlook; his works, a German trust and part of their *Geisteskultur* (spiritual culture), were only best understood and performed in Germany. Shakespeare's tragedies were described as manly and uncompromising.[13] Hamlet – it was argued – was neither English nor Danish; he was, in fact, German; he was a German thinker, poet, dreamer, as well as in every sense a fighter.[14]

German permission to produce *Hamlet* both at home[15] and in occupied Lviv should thus be viewed in the light of cultural imperialism (*Germanisierung*) on the one hand and on the absence of any coherent Nazi policy on the other.[16] Notably, a standing German State Theatre for German civilians and troops opened in Lviv in the summer of 1943 with H.H. Ortner's *Isabella von Spanien*, and, as late as 1944, the theatre loving Nazis were still developing plans for an extended German theatrical life in that city.[17]

The director of the 1943 *Hamlet*, Yosyp Hirniak, had been a leading actor of Les Kurbas's famous Berezil Artistic Association in Kharkiv (in Soviet Ukraine). Arrested in 1933, interrogated, and sent to the taiga, unlike Kurbas who was executed in 1937, Hirniak managed to return to Ukraine in 1940, finally making his way to Lviv in 1942. Bringing the Berezil's fresh ideas about theatre to Western Ukrainian audiences,[18] he began to introduce an ambitious repertoire including world classics. Among these was *Hamlet* – the play that Kurbas had began preparing in 1933 with Hirniak in the lead role. Kurbas's tragic fate prevented the realization of this dream but Hirniak intended to take it on, this time not as actor but as director. Like Hirniak, actor and artistic director Volodymyr Blavatsky had also worked with Kurbas at the Berezil but only briefly (from August 1927 to February 1928),[19] returning to the travelling troupes of Galicia. Tying both men together was their profound dedication to the goal of developing the Ukrainian theatre and to continuing the work of charismatic director Les Kurbas who had created remarkable productions in challenging and hostile conditions.

Figure 9.1. Yosyp Hirniak, *Hamlet*, souvenir brochure, Lviv, 1943. Artist: Semen Hruzbenko (Solomon Gruzberg).

Blavatsky and Hirniak's shared project could be only guardedly and selectively revealed in 1943. When, for a published interview, Blavatsky was queried about the influence and guidance of the director on his interpretation of the role of Hamlet, Blavatsky laconically replied that "we were in agreement about the conception, we had a unified view in this respect. Together we looked for a common language, we shared an idea about the role and the play."[20] What agreement, what common concept, Blavatsky prudently omitted to publicly spell out. Much later, in 1971, in correspondence with the actress Orysia Steshenko, Hirniak explained that in preparing *Hamlet* he had consciously followed Kurbas's example of putting difficult and important works on the Ukrainian stage to create a "real" Ukrainian theatre and "not the one I found in my fatherland,"[21] Moreover, Hirniak continued,

My second goal, in that terrible time, was to represent a person who has God in himself, but who throws away a world created by God. Added to that was the fact that I believed that Hamlet condensed in himself much that, under the conditions of occupation at the time, lay under dozens of prohibitive seals and censorship. But oh, how one wanted to talk it out![22]

In the midst of war and under the watchful eye of the German occupational army, in Lviv Hirniak began organizing a three-year theatrical studio that would train actors in both Ukrainian and world classics. As Richard Stites has observed, "Sad and terrible as it is to say, the war seemed to unleash creativity and create a kind of relieved joy."[23] Freed from the brief period of Soviet-imposed theatre and rhetoric with its "operatic, stylized, melodramatic, posed, monumental, utopian, and panegyric" style,[24] Hirniak turned to Shakespeare. As much a desire to confirm the possibility of classics in Ukrainian and thus the possibility of Ukraine, Hirniak's *Hamlet* was also an attack on the prevailing aesthetic of other theatres. For Hirniak and Blavatsky, as for their mentor, Kurbas, the Moscow-sponsored revival of ethnographic plays like *Marusia Bohuslavka* and *The Zaporozhian Kozak Beyond the Danube* (*Запорожець за Дунаєм*), prominent in the repertoire both before, during, and after the war on Soviet territory, was Uncle Tom-ism and, moreover, a destruction of spectators' growing sophistication of their aesthetic taste. But, while such examples of ethnographic theatre have been much maligned, and with some good cause, even Hirniak later agreed that it had "saved its people [Ukrainians] from complete catastrophe" during the nineteenth century, when the printed and spoken word were banned.[25]

The Soviet-sanctioned performance of ethnographic plays was meant to suggest support of Ukrainianization. While reluctant to employ the discourses of nationalism in the early part of the war because of separatist fears, Stalin allowed these some foothold in 1943 when it became clear that, in the war against the Nazis, nationalism was a much stronger motivating force than communism.[26] Thus the glorification of brotherly love among all Slavic nations turned more evidently toward encouraging Ukrainian pride in their heritage.[27] To confirm this new discourse in the political arena, prominent Ukrainians were awarded high Soviet Ukrainian government posts. Among them, the playwright Oleksandr Korniychuk (discussed in the previous chapter) was named minister of foreign affairs.

Stalin's offhand questioning of the necessity of producing *Hamlet* in 1941 at the Moscow Art Theatre resulted in the immediate withdrawal of the play from the repertoire and an implicit ban of the play for the rest of war. It is generally known that Stalin detested Hamlet, mostly, it has been suggested, because he is a character who thinks. Certainly, Hamlet's formidable intelligence and his ironic questioning of authority were also significant factors. *Hamlet* as play and as character could hardly serve Stalin's self-image as a man of action, "the steel one." From very early on in his political activism, Yosif Dzugasvili took on meaningful pseudonyms but this, his last, as Stalin, curiously made him identify with the Russian victors, not with their Georgian victims. However, *Hamlet* was not completely absent from the stage,[28] nor was Stalin above permitting Shakespearean motifs when they suited his cause. Such adapted Shakespeare or, more accurately, Shakespearean motifs, could be found in Korniychuk's *Partisans in the Steppes of Ukraine*, awarded the State Prize in 1941 and discussed in detail in the previous chapter. Along with Korniychuk's *Front*, first performed in Moscow on 19 October 1942 and subsequently performed in forty theatres throughout Ukraine, *Partisans* became, according to the official account, part of the "spiritual armour of the Red Army"[29] and, ironically, was released as a film in "Shakespeare's" month, April, in 1943.

Stalin was not the only one to feel that *Hamlet* was a threatening or, at the very least, inappropriate play to stage during the Second World War. For Andrey Sinyavsky, the "superfluous hero" was "more suspect" than the clear-cut negative enemy, since the latter was "like the positive hero… straightforward, and in his own way, purposeful."[30] In the massive propaganda "explosion" which the Second World War unleashed,[31] there was little room for characters who questioned commands or vacillated before they acted. Nor were any psychological subtleties countenanced. An article published in *Krasnaia zvezda* (Red Star) in 1942 concluded with a citation from Konstantin Simonov's poem "Kill Him!" if your home is dear to you: an injunction to kill without mercy or hesitation any perceived enemy.[32] Created during the "Great Patriotic War," the "Great Fatherland War," or the "War of National Liberation" (as the Second World War was variously styled by the Soviets), the Soviet Information Bureau churned out, in a variety of media, black and white characterizations of the two opposing sides: the peace-loving Soviets on the one hand, and the brutal, imperialistic Germans on the other. Most often, the suffering of the Soviet people was the main topic, especially the killing of women and children and, by extension, the rape of the land.[33] Rather than glorifying the masses, by 1942, Soviet Russian propaganda turned to embrace the individual, the courageous individual, the hero – an essentially non-Soviet, even anti-Soviet, value system.

Outside of Russia, Soviet propaganda was considerably more circumspect in its use of a nationalist and individualist discourse even before the war. Just before its outbreak, in 1937, Les Kurbas, along with the left-wing playwright Mykola Kulish, and the Georgian director Sandro Akhmeteli were labelled "seriously dangerous" types who propagated nationalistic theatre, and theatrical circles in these republics were singled out as harbouring "nests of spies and imperialists."[34] Nor did this view change in 1943. To harness the minorities and to suggest the unity of the various nationalities against German imperialism, Stalin permitted one major film epic per nationality. Some nationalist sentiment could be acceptable if it was balanced by the theme of friendship between the minority nationalities and the Great Russian nation. Such "friendship" also needed to be projected into the past where, if necessary, historical facts were changed.[35] In 1942 and 1943, Stalin released a "flood" of medals, including some posthumous ones, such as the 1943 medal awarded to the seventeenth-century Cossack Hetman Bohdan Khmelnytsky, who had joined forces with Russia in an effort to defeat Poland.[36]

While long-dead military leaders were lauded, contemporary Ukrainian artists were strictly controlled. As Argyrios Pisiotis notes, Soviet culture from 1941 to 1945 "became predominantly Russian."[37] The poetic films of Oleksander Dovzhenko, whose loving rendering of the Ukrainian landscape seemed excessively patriotic, were suppressed by Stalin himself, and publishers were informed that none of Dovzhenko's work could be published.[38] Dovzhenko wrote in his diary on 28 November 1943 about the prohibited scenario for *Ukraine in Flames*: "I wrote the story honestly, just as it is and the way I see life and the suffering of my people. I know: I will be accused of nationalism, of Christianity, of all-forgiveness, I will be sentenced for ignoring the class struggle."[39] In a Hamletesque entry, on 18 December 1943, he wrote about two truths, one real, the other fabricated, yet the latter is the one in which people were urged to believe.[40] Reviewing this period from the distance of the 1960s, the Ukrainian actor-director Hnat Yura recalled working in theatrical "brigades" on the front lines, where, he argued, what was needed were

> not psychologically deep cogitations, but the resolution of problems tied to the fate of a whole nation; not intimate scenes of personal sufferings but the emotions and feelings of the popular masses and their representatives, whose will unfailingly aims at victory – not of personal conflicts, but of the liberation of the whole nation.....The tragedy of our times is different from the tragedies of the times of Shakespeare. Ours should reflect the spirit of our historical epoch, [they] should be optimistic.[41]

Unlike the cinema, the theatre was notoriously unreliable as a tool of propaganda, a fact noted by Nazis and Soviets alike. While the content, the performance, and the context of film presentations could be controlled, theatrical productions could not. As early as 1924, Stalin himself had argued that "[t] he cinema is the greatest means of mass agitation,"[42] while P. Poluyanov declared that "the curse" of the theatre is "the unrepeatability of the spectacle."[43] Cinema, on the other hand, could not only be easily controlled, it was also more economical in its use of artistic resources and had the added bonus of the potential for an infinite auditorium.

Wartime theatrical and cinematic propaganda was certainly not the prerogative of the Soviets or of the Germans alone. Hirniak and Blavatsky were also well aware of the strong appeal of an affective aesthetic in Ukrainian circles even before the war. In 1939, right-wing Ukrainian nationalist Natalia Gerken-Rusova had published a short monograph entitled *Heroichnyi teatr* (Heroic Theatre) in which an "*Ars militans*" was proposed. Castigating both melodramatic, ethnographic drama and bourgeois drama dedicated to everyday life as "*Ars vulgaris*" – decadent, anti-patriotic, anti-nationalistic works – she proposed in their stead an "*Ars arma pro patria*"; this was to be patriotic drama, political, historical, and spiritual in content and style.[44] Art for art's sake, she concluded, was always a motto of declining epochs and unsuitable for the contemporary moment that required a heroic, ideologically committed theatre. Foreign models and anti-nationalistic "*art humain*" with its internationalist "pseudo-moralism" were unnecessary and must be extirpated.[45]

In such an aesthetic and political atmosphere, the Hirniak-Blavatsky *Hamlet* acquires a more radical reading. By no means "*Ars arma*," *Hamlet* is more often associated with the disease of Hamletism, psychologism, decadence, weakness – even pusillanimity.[46] To choose to produce *Hamlet* would seem to be an evasion of major proportions of the need to act. Evasion of duty or worse was the official reason the Soviet Russians avoiding staging *Hamlet* during the war. As N.N. Chushkin openly explained, "the very idea of showing on stage a thoughtful, reflective hero who takes nothing on faith…seemed to some people almost 'criminal.'"[47]

Hamlet's plot and, more especially, its thoughtful, anguished protagonist who struggles to act ethically in a corrupt world, spoke directly to the wartime circumstances. Poised between the Scylla and Charybdis of two competing and terrifying ideologies, Ukrainians turned to *Hamlet* to protest the inhumanity of the times and to voice their despair at their diminishing hope of finally achieving independence. The play traditionally associated with questions about the meaning of life and the value of action spoke to the historical moment in a pointed way, since there seemed to be little possibility of any meaningful action or escape from the consequences of the clash between Fascism and Communism. For Hirniak and Blavatsky, *Hamlet* was Ukraine's mirror; it allegorically represented Ukraine and its destiny: to be swallowed up either by the Nazis or by the Soviets. The atmosphere of fear evoked by the first scene of Shakespeare's tragedy, the military references made throughout, and, in particular, the

Figure 9.2. Playbill, *Hamlet,* souvenir brochure, Lviv, 1943.

allusion to the senseless invasion of a "little patch of ground" in Poland held special reverberations for the audience of the 1943 production. By then, Galicia was the battleground for a number of armies.

Preparing for the Production

Hirniak and Blavatsky understood the burden they had taken up by preparing to stage the first Ukrainian *Hamlet,* Shakespeare's most famous play, one that had endured for hundreds of years and sparked an ocean of commentary. Both anticipated that *Hamlet* would be the great event of the season and a test not only of their talent and skill but also of the maturity of Ukrainian theatre as a whole. Preparations for the production were thus made with great care and much trepidation.

For Volodymyr Blavatsky, the opportunity to play "every actor's dream" meant the obligations, as well as the pleasures, of the role. The role of Hamlet, he contended, presented an epochal moment in the life of an actor; to act this part well, he first had to understand it himself, to dig

Figure 9.3. Volodymyr Blavatsky as Hamlet, souvenir brochure, 1943. Artist: Semen Hruzbenko.

into the role, and to imagine himself performing it on stage.[48] Blavatsky immersed himself in as much of the available critical literature as he could, in Russian, German, and Polish; ironically, nothing in Ukrainian could be obtained. In a lengthy interview with Bohdan Melyansky, Blavatsky described the rollercoaster of his emotions as he began to study the text and then became overwhelmed by the mountain of scholarship on the topic. The challenges of the role were compounded by the fact that Blavatsky was also directing operas and operettas at LOT and, so his study of Hamlet was mainly confined to late evenings.[49] He and his fellow actors worked so hard on the language, gestures, intonations, that they no longer could discern whether they had succeeded or not. But, finally, at the rehearsals that lasted several months and which British and French POWs were permitted to attend,[50] Blavatsky managed to return to his original intuitions about the character by reminding himself of Kurbas's oft-stated advice to discover the joy derived from play (*радість з грання*).

While Blavatsky was contemplating the interpretive history of the play, the LOT's first great challenge was to commission a new, theatrical, rather than literary, translation of the play. (By 1943, there were already six translations into Ukrainian of the play.[51]) Mykhailo Rudnytsky, a professor of foreign languages in Lviv from 1939 to 1941, was appointed to create such a stage-friendly translation. In addition to his scholarly works, the multilingual Rudnytsky was also a literary critic, prolific author of various genres, and seasoned translator. Well-travelled throughout Europe, he had also been in England, where he witnessed a number of theatrical productions. Rudnytsky thus was an obvious choice for the task of preparing a world classic. Some Ukrainians knew of another element of his biography. From 1922 to 1925, Rudnytsky had been a professor of the underground Ukrainian University in Lviv. More problematically, because life-threatening in 1943, was the fact that he was partly of Jewish descent. By June 1943, the Nazis had completely liquidated the Ghetto, proclaiming in the fall that Lviv was *Judenrein* – "clean," free of Jews. For Rudnytsky, working on *Hamlet* provided creative solace and escape from grim reality. In a letter to Blavatsky, he referred to the translation project "as a blessing," while sometime later he recorded that "[i]n the course of the whole war I did not have a more pleasant job than that of translating *Hamlet,*"[52]

As well as translating the play, Rudnytsky was also deeply immersed in other aspects of the preparations for the production. His mini-lectures on the canon of Shakespeare's works, as well as on *Hamlet* in particular, ensured that the ensemble became familiar and comfortable with the conventions and traditions of English theatre.[53] At the first reading of the translated play to the performers, he also offered many suggestions about the delivery of the verse, of appropriate gestures, and also explained illuminating historical details.[54] Working with the performers, he made some adjustments to his text. The final version was an instant success. Regarded not only as having fulfilled the requirements of clarity, comprehensibility, and theatrical suitability, it was also hailed as a model worthy of emulation for future stage translations of foreign classics.[55] Lost for over sixty years, the text was rediscovered in the twenty-first century, and the text finally published in 2008 in Lviv, on the eve of the 120th anniversary of the birth of Rudnytsky (1889–1975). Reading the translation in the twenty-first century, Ukrainian actor-director Bohdan Kozak concurred with the opinion of the 1940s: the text was brilliant, poetic, lively, at times sharp, sarcastic, witty, and most certainly theatrical.[56]

Oddly, Rudnytsky, who had been so deeply involved in the preparations for the production of the play, failed to appear at the premiere on 21 September 1943. Ola Hnatiuk, scholar and former diplomat in the Polish corps, speculates in her 2019 book *Courage and Fear* that Rudnytsky disappeared from the city since the publicity generated by the event (including his name prominently featured on posters) might have easily resulted in someone probing too deeply, discovering, then denouncing him for his Jewish heritage.[57] Instead of attending the opening, Rudnytsky quietly returned to view a later performance, after which he wrote to Blavatsky praising his "remarkable" acting and restraint, especially for

Figure 9.4. "Hamlet on the Ukrainian Stage." Volodymyr Blavatsky depicted
on the cover of the souvenir brochure, *Hamlet*, Lviv, 1943. The allegorically
positioned Lviv Opera Theatre totters in the background.

avoiding what he termed the unnecessary pathos, pseudo-philosophical
fatuousness, and saccharine tone typical of so many other (European)
productions. He also noted that Blavatsky's interpretation reminded him
of a production of *Hamlet* that he saw in London many years ago.[58] Rudnytsky justified his absence from the premiere by the fact that the day
was windy and rainy, and, besides, he wasn't feeling well. These weak
excuses suggest (as Hnatiuk also argues) that he avoided the city when
the publicity about the production was at its height and thus the risk to
his life became too great.[59]

Carefully sifting archival documents and printed sources, Hnatiuk presents a fascinating view of the Lviv Opera Theatre as a place of refuge for
a handful of Ukrainians of Jewish descent. Among others engaged in the
Hamlet project was Semen Hruzbenko (Solomon Gruzberg), whose Ukrai-
nianized name masked his roots and who, thanks to friends, among them
Ostap Tarnavsky, survived the Nazi occupation. An artist, Hruzbenko created the memorable drawings of the actors published in the press and in
the souvenir booklet of the production curated by Tarnavsky.[60]

The Premiere

Weekly articles published in August in *Lviv News* (*Львівські вісті*) anony-
mously penned by Ostap Tarnavsky built up audience expectations for
the production.[61] Finally, the day of the premier, 21 September 1943,
arrived. Of this theatrical event, Ivan Nimchuk wrote:

> Finally we, too, have received our holy-day: a production of *Hamlet* in the
> Ukrainian language. How many theatres in the world have staged and are
> staging this living tragedy of a living person, how many people admired this
> work of genius, how many scholars around the world have added their com-
> mentaries to it, thereby enriching the literature about Shakespeare, but
> hitherto the everywhere-abnormal circumstances under which our nation
> lived did not permit Ukrainian theatres to stage this play.[62]

Nimchuk's reference to "abnormal" circumstances was an allusion to
conditions under both the Austro-Hungarian and the Imperial Russian
empires. Under Austro-Hungary, Ukrainian productions and translated
texts needed the approval of the censor. It was often long in coming, if
it came at all. As we have seen in previous chapters, tsarist ukases and
decrees in the last quarter of the nineteenth century prohibited the performance of all and any work in Ukrainian, including Shakespeare.[63]
Censorship continued in the Stalinist period.[64]

The celebratory, even jubilant, nature of the 1943 theatre event was
widely expressed by audiences, critics, and actors. So for example, in his
memoirs, Oleh Lysiak recalled with considerable pride this "Great Day"
for Ukrainian theatre as a "monumental" and "unforgettable event."[65]
Italian, Spanish, French, Czech, and German newspapers made note
of the production, while French prisoners of war, among them some
theatre critics, brought copies of their national newspapers to show the
Ukrainian actors.[66] Dr. G. Hauswaldt writing in *Krakauer Zeitung*[67] (25
September 1943, no. 230), admiringly referenced the achievements of
the director (Hirniak), the designer (M. Hryhoryev), and the actors; he
singled out Blavatsky for bringing to the role of Hamlet "an excellent and
persuasive liveliness and strength."[68] Later, Blavatsky recorded that the
theatrical ensemble's *Hamlet* was the "crowning" of all of their activities of
the past three years in Lviv; they had successfully passed the Shakespeare
test, the test of the ensemble's, and the Ukrainian theatre's, artistic maturity.[69] Their success must have also come as a great relief.

The significance of a Ukrainian *Hamlet* was not lost on the Ukrainian
populace, who attended the twenty-five performances in massive numbers, many coming from outside Lviv.[70] Some of them could also interpret

the various strata of discourses layered on the production not simply by contemporary political events but also by history and biography – especially those of Rudnytsky, Hirniak, and Blavatsky. Ukrainian reviews of the 1943 *Hamlet* production are buoyant, triumphant witnesses and not as cautious as one might expect from articles subject to the Nazi censor – although it is a truism that freedom of the press grew in proportion to its proximity to the battlefront. Bohdan Melyansky's review, published after thirteen performances, outrightly expresses astonishment at the mere existence of the production: "It's strange that it's possible." Seemingly unaware of the possibly nationalistic connotations of his review, Hauswaldt expressed his entrancement with the "unforgettable music of the Ukrainian language." Praising the theatre ensemble's full range of artistic endeavour, he pronounced that, "without doubt," the production "exceeded ordinary ability" and conveyed a complete, unified impression. Although, as Hauswaldt observed, Hamlet may be played in an ecstatic fashion, Volodymyr Blavatsky's interpretation evaded such "clever passion" and instead showed the hero expressing and complying with his fate.[71]

Hauswaldt's brief review appeared in the Nazi-censored newspaper which regularly carried articles about the cultural life of the *Generalgouvernment* (the German name for the zone of occupation), alongside pieces which emphasized German strength, resolution, and invincibility. Employing what Zbyněk Zeman has called "black propaganda" (pretending to be what it is not), the paper frequently attributed to British sources the imminence of German victory.[72] The headline for September 25, 1943, for example, reads, "The striking force of the German Waffen in the East is not to be overlooked," according to a purportedly "British" authority. In the context of this newspaper, Hauswaldt's positive review may suggest that the actor's craft overcame any possible political-historical interpretation for a non-Ukrainian spectator; it also appears to confirm Blavatsky's claim that many Germans who knew no Ukrainian nonetheless came to see the play, some of them returning a few times. Alternatively and more probably, Hauswaldt (and his readers) may have interpreted the defeat of the individual (Hamlet) by greater forces as ultimately conforming to the Nazi myth of invincibility: the divided hero "complies" with his fate, that is, his destruction by a superior force.

More detailed and hence more revelatory than the reviews of Hauswaldt or Melyansky are those of Ivan Nimchuk. Nimchuk published four pieces about the production: three reviews and one lengthy article on the eve of the premiere. The number of the articles reflects the importance he attributed to this theatrical event and also reveals his continuing

amazement and delight at both its continuing success and at its very existence.[73] In addition to reviewing the production just before and right
after the premiere, Nimchuk also dedicated a detailed article in the literary monthly *Our Days* (*Наші дні*), complete with Hruzbenko's drawings
of the main actors and a detailed description of their very careful preparation of their roles. Like Rudnytsky, Nimchuk also had a suspect background, in his case, that of a Ukrainian nationalist. Nimchuk's nationalist
leanings began early, when he was the editor in Vienna of, first, *Renaissance of Ukraine* (*Відродження України*) in 1918 and then *The Ukrainian
Flag* (*Український прапор*) from 1921 to 1923. From 1925, he edited the
Lviv newspaper *Deed* (*Діло*) (chief editor 1935–9) and, as a result of these
endeavours, he was imprisoned for two years by the Soviets in 1939 in the
infamous Lubyanka prison. Thus, both translator's and critic's names
carried specific, potentially life-threatening connections for them. Their
common victory, in having *Hamlet* performed in Ukrainian, doubtless
contributed to their euphoria.

In his first review of the production, published five days after the
premiere, Nimchuk began by referring to the celebratory, even sacral,
character of this production (*свято* – literally, holy-day). This *Hamlet*,
Nimchuk was at pains to stress, finally helped "place" the Ukrainian theatre and, by extension Ukrainians, on the world stage. Emphasizing that
Hamlet is the "living tragedy of a living person," Nimchuk was referring to
something more than the "timelessness" of the play, rather, he was referring to its literally mimetic qualities of the play – elements that could only
be hinted at but which he develops a little more fully and courageously a
short time later in the article in *Our Days* (*Наші дні*). Prudently acknowl-
edging the importance of Goethe's interpretation to the play's reception, Nimchuk briefly reviewed the range of historical opinion about its
main character, eventually coming to his conclusion that *Hamlet* is the
most problematic of world classics because it raises the most problems,
its richness lies in ideas, emotions, and in the surprising range and shifts
of Hamlet's moods. Nimchuk said as much as was possible under the censor's gaze. The stress in each of his articles on the contemporaneity of
Hamlet is tempered by his reference to its timelessness and its universality.
The carefully placed reference to Goethe's point of view (although one
not necessarily shared by the Nazis) and the praise of the Schlegel-Tieck
translations (preferred by Hitler) seemed to yield primacy to German
thought, scholarship, and *Geisteskultur*. The bland allusion to the "hitherto everywhere-abnormal circumstances" that prevented earlier Ukrainian *Hamlets* also seemed calculated to flatter the Nazis – as if the German
occupation were "normal" and, moreover, because of the permission to
produce Shakespeare's work, perhaps even better than at other times.

Nimchuk's phrase could even have been read by the Germans (unlikely to know the history of past attempts to stage a Ukrainian *Hamlet*) as a reference to the immediate past, that is, the Soviet occupation. All in all, there seemed to be nothing politically objectionable here. Blavatsky's acting style was compared favourably compared by German spectators to Willi Beigel and Rudolph Ferau,[74] comments which were again suggestive of the cultural deference paid to the occupant. The souvenir booklet of the production, produced after the premiere, played up the flattery, with the blunt observation that the Ukrainian theatre revived only with the advent of the German army.[75]

Calculated flattery seems to have dulled the censor. All the signs of a grand premiere were here. The auditorium of the magnificent, classically designed Lviv Opera Theatre was filled with spectators who exuded an excited, anticipatory mood. When the play began, a "growing tension" was felt, which "overflowed" and was finally released by "spontaneous ovations at the end of the third act."[76] Described by Nimchuk as a "realistic" production with only a "hazy" hint of romanticism, Hirniak's *Hamlet* centred on an active and resolute hero, "full of purpose and passionate individuality, who is destroyed 'by circumstances that were stronger than he was.'"[77] Nimchuk's brief précis was, no doubt, read by the least skilful Ukrainian reader as not only the plot of *Hamlet* but also, by the late fall of 1943, as the evident and imminent tragedy of Ukraine.

In his brief overview of the centuries' old power of the play and its draw for actors, directors, and scholars, Nimchuk focused on the archetypal appeal of Hamlet, whom he likened in this respect to Faust, Don Quixote, and Prometheus. As we have already seen, for many, only heroic characters came to mind in wartime. But Hirniak was right in choosing *Hamlet*, in recognizing the heroics of the divided self, of the doomed, inner struggle, over heroic posturing and facile solutions. Pointedly, the souvenir brochure underlined the fact that only the transformed, reeducated actor, not the ethnographic one, could play this "actor's dream."[78] Restraint rather than emotional melodrama was the leitmotif of the whole production.

Keying his Hamlet to the times, Blavatsky attempted to create a complex, kaleidoscopic portrait of an intellectual. Displaying a full spectrum of emotion from strong will and firm intellect to melancholia, from apathy to action, from sudden fits and starts to self-castigation, and traversing the borders between conscious and unconscious madness, Blavatsky's Hamlet struggled with the insane truth of life in 1943. Although "tragically broken" and "disillusioned" (so according to Nimchuk[79]) by his sudden knowledge of evil and corruption, Blavatsky's Hamlet was, nonetheless, no weakling; rather, his was a "contemporary, strong-willed, not decadent interpretation."[80] More given to facial expression than verbal emphases, Blavatsky made few, economical, gestures, an intellectual restraint inherited from his days under the tutelage of Kurbas. He presented a "clear" and fully-rounded character[81] or, rather, two: the youth who flinches from ugliness, from the repellent events of life, and is thus ready to commit suicide or to die without regret if fate so wills it; and the wiseman-philosopher, twice as old in age, ruminating on metaphysical issues. Masking both, suggested Nimchuk, was a "third" Hamlet: the player, who flirts with the fringes of madness. Although suffering from tuberculosis and from nervous disorders associated with the dangerous conditions in which he was performing, Blavatsky was particularly strong, confident, and sharp in those scenes that offered scope for biting satire and for directly attacking hypocrisy and corruption: the encounters with Rosencrantz and Guildenstern, with Polonius, and Osric. In "The Mousetrap" scene, Blavatsky permitted himself only minimal facial expressions, and no sense of mad delight. This was a Hamlet who, like Hal, knew them all but who, unlike that royal predecessor, could not script an easy solution to the spiralling violence of events.

Duality and deception provided a major interpretive line for the whole production, focusing on two centres of interest, Hamlet and Claudius, with the minor characters reflecting one or the other character. Opposing the intellectual and strong-willed Hamlet was Bohdan Pazdri's Claudius: although a carouser and a duplicitous villain given to great anger, he was represented as being fully in control of events and insidiously aware of how to rule effectively. Claudius's effectiveness as a ruler was best proved by his swift, unhesitating handling of Laertes' (Serhi Dubrovsky) rebellion. Yet Pazdri also knew how to move the audience to near sympathy in the kneeling scene, "almost, Nimchuk admitted, 'moving some' to believe in the sincerity of his repentance.[82] Hirniak had briefly toyed with the idea of making up Pazdri to look like Stalin, an effect that doubtless would have endeared this production to the Nazi censor. When Pazdri's gaunt physionomy resisted such an effort, Hirniak abandoned the idea. Then, upon reflection, he realized that it was all for the best, since his intention to centre on Hamlet's battle with evil as a whole was perhaps better met without the specific reference. Hirniak also later admitted that in Hamlet's hesitations and delays in committing revenge both he and Blavatsky saw, as in a mirror, the position of Ukraine that found itself between the two evils of Bolshevism and Nazism.[83]

Claudius's Queen, in the interpretation of Vera Levytska, was unaware of her husband's evil. Her personage and actions, observed Nimchuk, involuntarily explained, at least in part, why Claudius was tempted to

Figure 9.5. Scene from *Hamlet*, souvenir brochure, directed by Yosyp Hirniak, 1943. Scene design and costumes: M. Hryhoriyev.

commit fratricide. From the photos of the production, it would appear that Nimchuk was referring to the dark-eyed, elegant beauty of Gertrude/ Levytska. In approvingly noting Gertrude's passivity, he appeared to be praising her interpretation of the Queen as a patient, uninquiring, and supportive wife. Only in the closet scene did she lose this "pale" quality. Reversing an oft-acted interpretation of the closet scene, Blavatsky/Hamlet was so completely restrained in his encounter with his mother that Gertrude, not he, was driven into an angry frenzy. Spontaneous applause greeted the scene's close.

According to Nimchuk, Eliza Shasharovska as Ophelia was much more complex than Gertrude, although his description (a naive beauty brought up to respect traditional forms; a tender, timid, virginal character) suggests that she had much in common with the Queen. In the scenes of madness, Shasharovska worked up so much passion that she shed copious tears, carrying her audience's sympathy with her, a sympathy doubtless magnified by the fact that Shakespeare's songs were replaced by those of the native Ukrainian composer Mykola Lysenko.

Ophelia's father, Polonius (Ivan Hirniak, no relation to the director), revealed a divided self like Hamlet. At home, he was a wise, goodly, worldly father; at court, a "reptilian courtier," fawningly servile but (at least for Nimchuk) insufficiently comic. Although the opportunity was there, Hirniak refrained from using the reference of Polonius's name to satirize the Poles (again, unlike Korniychuk's vulgar display of such sentiment in the wartime film *Bohdan Khmelnytsky*). Laertes (Dubrovsky) mirrored his father's tendency to indulge in rhetorical phrases recited in a high dramatic style. A noble but hot-tempered youth, he was self-assured, passionate, but a too-quick defender of his family's honour. In allying himself with the evil king, he distanced himself from his noble, chivalric nature. Horatio, as Nimchuk observed, is often bland in performance, but in Ivan Lisnenko's interpretation, he came across as a straightforward, sterling character with a gentle heart, who completely understood and sympathized with his beloved Hamlet. The spectators were put in no doubt why this friendship had withstood all tests and had survived all of Hamlet's disillusionments.

In the smaller roles, the inseparable pair, Rosencrantz and Guildenstern (V. Korolyk and V. Shasharovsky), were interpreted as good-hearted middling men but also narrow-minded Philistines and careerists. The Ghost (E. Kurylo), speaking in an effectively resonant voice, persuasively rendered the raging figure of a spirit. Osric (Stepan Kryzhanivsky), without a thought or will of his own, was the quintessential flatterer. M. Melnykova as the Second Player, playing opposite Yaroslav Helias, the First Player, presented "the well-imitated pathos" of the disloyal, oath-breaking wife in "The Mousetrap" scene. Petro Soroka gave an "interesting and fully-rounded creation" as the wiseacre First Gravedigger.[84] Prudently, Nimchuk said nothing more about this crucial scene of skulls, bodies, and ambiguous causes of death, one which would have been frequently, literally, replayed in the daily lives of its wartime audience. The medieval-themed costumes safely removed any obvious contemporary references to tyrants, rotten kingdoms, military threats, and powerless individuals. The set, austere, due to the difficulty of obtaining materials, consisted of a painted medieval-looking stone wall with a rounded arch framed by heavy curtains emblazoned with lions, while the properties were limited to just a few chairs and a table.

In this large cast, the notable omission was Fortinbras. No reviewer makes reference to his absence, although in an extended piece in *Our Day*, Nimchuk commented that the play gives great scope to directors as well as actors, the director displaying his talent by the creative cuts he makes in this sprawling play. The souvenir booklet provides an accurate précis of Shakespeare's play (including the ending), but other than blandly noting that the text was cut in an agreement made between translator and director, no further explanations are given. No doubt the contemporary parallels between the foreign occupational forces and Fortinbras' military presence at the end of the play were too close to reality and cutting them may have been a prudent act of self-censorship, or perhaps they were even made at the insistence of the Nazi censor. Nimchuk's (and Hirniak's) silence on this point is eloquent.[85] In this same review, Nimchuk baldly and boldly reiterated that *Hamlet* centres on a character who is our living contemporary.

That the production succeeded in its intent is indicated by the fact that the audience spontaneously and wildly applauded when Hamlet stabbed Claudius, twice, in the last scene of the play. The play ended with the lights slowly dimming on the dead Hamlet, as solemn music accompanied Horatio's speech ("Goodnight, sweet Prince"). After thirteen sold-out performances, Bohdan Melyansky reviewed the production for *Lviv News*, observing that this production stirred the spectator "by its soul": the audience apprehended it "sincerely" and "experienced it deeply."[86] In a lengthy interview, Blavatsky claimed that overwork was responsible for his slip at the première, when he began Hamlet's famous soliloquy with the words, "Is it good or evil," instead of "To be or not to be." Perhaps. Or it may have been a brief moment of bravado that could not be acknowledged. Rather than the metaphysical issue of being, this Hamlet, for at least one performance, posed the question about evil and action as directly as could be.

Hauswaldt's concluding commentary in his review, "*Im ganzen ein stark nachhaltiger Erfolg*" (on the whole, a strong, effective outcome), seemed to predict that this was a *Hamlet* which would live on in theatrical memory. It was one which also, he noted, showed that the Lviv Opera Theatre wanted to display a broad-based artistic face. In a brief notice after the fifteenth performance of *Hamlet*, Nimchuk recorded the "unprecedented, simply record-breaking success of this play."[87] Blavatsky had reached the "heights of artistic playing" and the production itself should signal to other, especially provincial theatres, that spectators wanted "not cheap, light diversions, but serious, spiritual food," provided by great classics, foreign or Ukrainian. Pull up your repertoire was the advice he gave to other theatres.

Not everyone was enamoured of the production. Yosyp Hirniak pointedly refused to write about his work on the play.[88] Trained in the exigent and perfectionist school of Kurbas, used to ensemble acting of the highest order, Hirniak could privately acknowledge the political import of his production, but the aesthetic was, in his view, not yet quite up to the mark, notwithstanding the audience's and reviewers' responses.

Soviet Lviv

By 1944, the Soviets were once again in control of Galicia. Ukrainian national consciousness, circumspectly encouraged by Stalin in the last two years of the war, was repressed immediately after, and the old familiar slogans of internationalism (the brotherhood of nations, the glorification of the Soviet, particularly Russian, state) was invoked. In a Lviv reoccupied by the Soviets, the first productions ordered on the boards were *Rosiiski liudy* (Russian People), *Partyzany* (Partisans), *General Briusylov*, and *Nazar Stodolya* – a return to the pre-1943 repertoire, a mixture of Soviet Russian propaganda about the unity of the national minorities, and nineteenth-century ethnographic drama. In his orthodox account of this repertoire, O.O. Kulyk observed that "[T]here was something symbolic in the choice of this [*General Briusylov*] production, because it was the armies of the eighth Russian Army led by General Briusylov that liberated Lviv from German-Austrian usurpers exactly thirty years before."[89]

In 1945, an All-Union Communist Party regulation "Concerning the Repertoire of Drama Theatres and the Means for Its Improvement," demanded, among other items, that the works of "foreign bourgeois playwrights," and historical plays, especially those about kings and tsars, be removed.[90] While orthodox Stalinists referred to the subsequent period of Ukrainian theatre as "socialist idealism" and as marking "the triumphal forward path of Ukrainian theatre,"[91] Yosyp Hirniak (by that time an emigrant to the USA) sadly named this period "Korniychukivshchyna," his neologism referencing the second rate work of Korniychuk and, more broadly, depicting post-war Soviet Ukrainian theatre as grey and bland provincialism.

Ukraine, like the rest of the USSR, had to await Stalin's death in 1953 and the Thaw of the Khrushchev years before another *Hamlet* could be seen on its stages. Then, stage and film directors throughout the USSR rushed to put on the play about the Danish prince. But official Soviet theatre histories, right up to the collapse of the USSR, remained silent about or denied that any Ukrainian theatre had existed during the war. Officially sanctioned theatre histories and overviews of the repertoires of the various republics of the USSR, including those of Kirgiz, Belarus, Georgia, Azerbaijan, Turkmen, Uzbekistan, Kazakhstan, all offered variants of the same, seamless stage history. To read one is to read them all. Such official theatre histories convey the image of a single, unified Soviet people, happy to take up plays that actively celebrated "Russianness," even in such far away and culturally alien places as Buryatia.

Memorialization or, indeed, analysis of the Soviet participation in the Second World War, continued to serve as a flashpoint for hot polemical debate even after the fall of the Soviet Union.[92] The struggle against fascism was, and is, part of a highly politicized mythology reaching back to the war itself and whose theme is the loyalty of, and unity, amongst all Soviet peoples. Soviet theatre history was not immune to these debates nor to the unwillingness to examine, challenge, let alone shatter, established Russian narratives. Problematic productions, such as those of *Hamlet*, were glossed over, while others reinterpreted to make them appear to conform to acceptable pre-war categories of social realism or romantic-heroic action. Korniychuk's *Partisans* and *The Front*, along with Simonov's *The Russian People*, were cited again and again as the most popular and successful plays of the war period, produced, and supposedly lauded, throughout all the territories of the USSR.

In 1956, Yaroslav Helias, invited to play the part of Hamlet, was proclaimed the first Ukrainian to do so. He was an excellent choice for the role, having already had experience with the play. The First Player in Hirniak's production in 1943, he now aptly took on the part of a young man who struggles to come to terms with erasures of memory, with deception, corruption, betrayal, and mortality. Helias's Hamlet endured an unspoken dialogue with the past – the 1943 production that could not be acknowledged to have taken place. Fittingly, Player had become lead actor, and thus took up in a very literal sense the issues of Shakespeare's text: the relation between acting and doing, playing and playing along. In Ukraine today, during yet another barbaric war, *Hamlet* remains a potent, necessary, and very political play.[93]

10

Commemoration as Amplification: The "Universal" versus the National Bard

What happens when the "universal" Bard, Shakespeare, confronts a "national" Bard? In their "Introduction: Shakespeare and the Cultures of Commemoration," Ton Hoenselaars and Clara Calvo propose that "[a] serious study of commemorative practices involving Shakespeare – preferably with an international focus, and comparative in scope to include the afterlives of other artists – is likely to enhance our appreciation of the dynamics of authorship, literary fame, and afterlives in its broader socio-historical contexts."[1] Similarly, Marijan Dović and Jón Karl Helgason suggest that "an investigation into the asymmetries and tensions between the national and international levels of canon-formation might be one of the most inviting tasks for future research on cultural sainthood."[2] This chapter aims to contribute to such projects by analysing aspects of the complex and sometimes intersecting Soviet strategies of rituals of commemoration, containment, amplification, and celebration of two types of bards. Focusing primarily on the "universal," Shakespeare, and the "national," Taras Shevchenko (1814–61), each of whom posed particular challenges to the authorities and ideologies of the multinational Soviet state, this chapter will also glance at commemorations of Alexander Pushkin and their use as ideological weapons.

Monuments, Politics, and Public Spaces

On 12 October 2017, TASS, the Russian news agency, announced that a Shakespeare monument was to be erected by 2019, not far from the centre of Moscow and next to the Old English Court Museum, the location from 1556 to 1649 of the first English trading and ambassadorial office in Russia.[3] The British Council's proposal to initiate and fund this monument reflected the close cultural links between Russia and the UK that had developed and grown despite rising tensions on the international front, particularly in the wake of the Russian annexation of Crimea and the invasion of eastern Ukraine in 2014. A tangible public marker of Anglo-Russian cultural exchanges, the proposed monument could be perceived as a cultural mediator and even as the apogee of a plethora of wide-ranging activities of the Council, which were first initiated in 1959 and had continued with ever-expanding energy, notably during the two Shakespeare anniversary years of 2014 and 2016.

As the Russian press indicated, the monument was intended to help "popularize the literature [sic] works of the English writer" (TASS).[4] Both the announcement of the memorial and its ostensible purpose may have come as something of a surprise to scholars aware of the two-centuries-long Russian engagement with Shakespeare, a surprise, both because there seemed to be hardly any reason to popularize such an already familiar literary figure in Russia but also a surprise to learn that a monument to Shakespeare did not already exist in the capital. But yet another shock was to come: on 17 March 2018 plans for the monument were suddenly cancelled in tandem with a ban on all Council activities in retaliation for the UK government's expulsion of Russian diplomats and its assertion that Russia was to blame for the poisoning of former double agent Sergei Skripal and his daughter Yulia on British soil.

In announcing the ban on the Council, Dmitry Peskov, Vladimir Putin's presidential spokesperson, opined:

> We see how the country of Byron and Shakespeare, the country of Conan Doyle, a country which once was a shining empire with the deepest political traditions of democracy, turned into a country whose politicians, mildly speaking, make irresponsible statements. This is a problem. This is a reflection of a very hostile policy.[5]

In invoking these literary figures, Peskov turned their iconic names and status against their own country. In so doing, he employed a formidable weapon, culture, which had been a staple of Russian power relations both within its borders and with those outside it for well over a hundred years. Never a minor player, culture (conceived as "high" culture) was, particularly during the Soviet era, one of the primary spheres of "contestation, like politics and economics. It was a locus for struggle, an arena in which power (hegemony) could be won or lost."[6]

Lenin himself was behind the decree of 14 April 1918, "On the Dismantling of Monuments Erected in Honour of the Tsars and Their Servants and on the Formulation of Projects of Monuments to the Russian Socialist Revolution." Published in the newspaper *Izvestiia* [The News], the decree specified that sixty-six "outstanding persons in the field of

Figure 10.1. Ceremonial unveiling of the Shevchenko monument in Petrograd, 1 December 1918. Sculptor: Janis Tilbergs, Latvia.

Source: Wikipedia Commons.

revolutionary and social activity" were to be honoured with memorials. Celebrating an oddly mixed group of Russian and foreign revolutionaries, social activists, writers, poets, philosophers, scholars, composers, and performers, these monuments were to include, among others, Marx, Engels, Spartacus, Danton, Robespierre, Bakunin, Dostoevsky, Scriabin, Garibaldi, and Shevchenko but not Shakespeare.[7] By appropriating public space – streets, squares, parks – for new monuments, Lenin signalled power: the political and conceptual transformation of the state by way of symbols that conveyed key concepts. Serving the purpose of propaganda rather than immortalization, the proposed monuments were to include "agitational inscriptions" that presented brief biographies and pointed didactic (propagandistic) messages for the masses.[8] By toppling tsarist monuments and replacing them with new Soviet ones, the Bolsheviks were rewriting history and reimagining the future in a symbolic yet tangible form. Such changes to Soviet urban spaces, which created new memories and suppressed others, were aimed at reframing cultural memory, national consciousness, and identity.[9]

In announcing and subsequently cancelling the project of a Shakespeare monument in Moscow, the Russian government was signalling the interrogation and potential rupture of a relationship with a Western power that had been carefully cultivated over a number of decades. Rather than a mediator, culture was now being wielded as a weapon.[10] Lenin had understood the power of such a tool. The unveilings of Soviet monuments to special individuals were large public occasions framed and punctuated by a variety of performative acts, including rousing music and many speeches. Deliberately organized as political events that frequently took place on Sunday mornings, they presented a revolutionary punch back to the ritual of churchgoing. But in the rush to carry out Lenin's plans, artists creating the busts and bas-reliefs used terra cotta or plaster, materials that quickly began to deteriorate. Despite this inauspicious beginning, the appetite for statues and monuments did not abate in the coming decades, indeed, one of the major, visible legacies of the Soviet Union to this day are the numerous monuments (especially of Lenin) that dot the urban landscapes of the territories of the former USSR.[11] Included in this number are monuments dedicated to Shevchenko.

Habituated as Shakespeareans are to the manifold and extravagant commemorations, celebrations, biographies, and studies of Shakespeare around the world since David Garrick's Jubilee (1769), they may be surprised to learn that the intensity and number of rituals, monuments, biographies, paintings, institutions, films, and other modes and tools venerating Shevchenko, the Ukrainian national Bard, exceeds even Shakespearean bardolatrous proportions. According to the web-based interactive map of sites indicating Shevchenko's monuments, by 2014 (the 200th anniversary of his birth) there were 1064 monuments, each serving different objectives. These are found not just in every major city of Ukraine but also in thirty-two other countries, including Russia, Georgia, China, Kazakhstan, Azerbaijan, Tajikistan, Turkmenistan, Uzbekistan, Poland, Belarus, the Czech Republic, Hungary, Romania, Montenegro, Slovakia, France, Germany, Italy, Greece, Cuba, Estonia, Lithuania, Denmark, Bulgaria, Macedonia, Moldova, Australia, Brazil, Argentina, Paraguay, the UK, the USA, and Canada. As well as memorial statuary, institutions, schools, streets, subway stops, parks, medals, other places and objects were named after him or his works, including an asteroid: 2427 Kobzar (The Bard, the title of Shevchenko's first book of poetry, which acquired such symbolic force that it came to be applied to Shevchenko himself).[12] Indeed, globally, it appears that there are more monuments in honour of Shevchenko than that of any other poet in world literature. As in the case of Shakespeare, Shevchenko's afterlife has also been one of intensive procreativity, spawning manifold works in all areas of endeavour. Matching this fecundity, scholarship has created a gargantuan body of works, Shevchenkiana. And like Shakespeare, whose name stands as shorthand for British culture, so Shevchenko is the

Ukrainian sign: "the name-metaphor which encodes the entire history of the nation for all Ukrainians in past, present, and future."[13]

The National Bard

Before turning to a comparison of the commemoration of bards, it is useful to pause here in order to rehearse Shevchenko's life-story, well-known to Slavists but less so to Shakespeareans. A poet, prose writer, playwright, ethnographer, folklorist, political figure, as well as a gifted painter, illustrator, and an Academician of the Imperial Academy of Arts, Shevchenko's mantle as national Bard of Ukraine derived from his consistent and vocal championing of the Ukrainian language, history, and culture. The arc of his life offered a compelling narrative for Bolshevik purposes, which needed little or no adjustment to fit the new ideological imperatives. An orphan child of serfs, Shevchenko showed early promise as an artist. His master, Pavlo Engelgardt, recognized his talent and intelligence; hoping to augment his prestige by possessing his own private artist, he apprenticed Shevchenko to a Russian painter while they were in St Petersburg. In that city, Shevchenko encountered his fellow countrymen who, moved by his situation and impressed by his ability, organized a campaign to buy his freedom. Russian painter Karl Bryulov offered up one of his paintings in a lottery with the prize money going to that cause, finally making it possible for the twenty-four-year old to be permitted to study at the exigent Imperial Academy, where he came to receive many awards and where he joined a sophisticated circle of St Petersburg artists, bohemians, and intellectuals.

A deep admirer of Shakespeare, Shevchenko was inspired in 1843 to create a powerful etching of King Lear with the Fool during the storm. As we have seen in Chapter Two, when the African-American actor Ira Aldridge performed as Lear in St. Petersburg, Shevchenko was so emotionally moved that he showered him with tears and embraces, recognizing a deep bond between them, one which arose in part from the shared psycho-social legacies of slave and serf. Shakespeare's works thus provided the mirror by which the two could recognize each other's histories and from which their friendship developed. Shevchenko's portrait of Aldridge seems to reflect this deep sympathy and affection.[14]

At the same time as he was painting, Shevchenko was writing prose, plays, and, especially, verse. His first collection of poetry, *Kobzar* (1840), had already gained him instant fame. After graduating from the Academy, he made three trips to Ukraine between 1843 and 1846 as a member of the Kyiv (Kiev) Archeographic Commission. There, he was deeply stirred by the fate of his still-enserfed siblings and relatives and was equally affected by the landscape, especially by the condition of historical and architectural monuments, which had either been destroyed by tsarist authorities or permitted to decay, thereby erasing Ukrainian history. These he decided to capture in a series of etchings.

Penning angry political-satirical narrative poems that attacked the tsar and mocked the tsarina, Shevchenko also joined the clandestine Brotherhood of Saints Cyril and Methodius (also known as the Ukrainian-Slavic Society), dedicated to Christian spiritual fellowship, the liberalisation of the Empire, and to the creation of a federation-like union of Slavic nations. Shevchenko's political poems and activities changed his fate. Imprisoned and then exiled to the Russian military garrison in Orenburg near the Ural Mountains, he was prohibited, by tsar Nicholas I's express order, from writing, drawing, and painting. Subsequently sent to a remote harsh penal settlement in Kazakhstan, he nonetheless continued to write and draw, hiding his work in his boots. Allowed to have only two books, he requested a copy of the Bible and the works of Shakespeare in Nikolai Ketcher's Russian translation. (As discussed in earlier chapters, translation of Shakespeare into Ukrainian was forbidden.)

Amnestied two years after the tsar's death in 1857, then re-arrested, and finally re-released and sent to St Petersburg, Shevchenko was prohibited from returning to Ukraine. While under the watchful eye of the police, he continued to write, paint, and work on engravings until his death on his forty-seventh birthday and just a week before the emancipation of serfs was proclaimed. Buried in St. Petersburg, a few months later his remains were repatriated to Ukraine, as he had expressly wished. First by train, then by wagon, and, finally, by boat, Shevchenko's remains were taken through various towns in Russia and Ukraine, seen and mourned by thousands, until they reached their final resting place on top of a hill in the town of Kaniv overlooking the Dnipro River. The tall mound containing his remains and topped by a large wooden cross became a place of commemoration and pilgrimage for a wide spectrum of Ukrainians from peasants to intellectuals, who treated it as a "sacred place" that held the equivalent of a relic, a cultural saint.[15] Most significantly, Shevchenko's reburial on 22 May 1861 had coincided with celebrations of the abolition of serfdom, linking Shevchenko, his life and works, and his love of his country to this event and thus endowing the reburial site with tremendous symbolic significance and potency.

Early Soviet Commemorations

While Shakespeare celebrations were permitted in Russia in 1914 and Russians happily began formulating their contributions to worldwide commemorations as seen, for example, in Israel Gollancz's *A Book of*

Homage to Shakespeare (1916), Ukrainians were still subject to significant obstacles to translating and performing Shakespeare in their own language.[16] Strict tsarist censorship also affected Shevchenko commemorations. Lenin's inclusion of Shevchenko in his list of notables to whom Soviet monuments would be erected arose as a deliberate political gesture and response to the tsarist authorities who, up to the very end of the imperial regime, had refused all requests for the erection of such a monument.[17] Fearing the possibility of uprisings and demands for independence, the authorities sent out police units to prevent demonstrations and any sign of commemorative acts at the Shevchenko burial site.[18] Lenin was purportedly delighted by this act of oppression, since it created an ideal opportunity to underscore the contrast between the repressive imperial tsarist regime and the enfranchisement that the Bolsheviks had promised.[19] His decision to include a monument to Shevchenko, not Shakespeare, signalled his recognition of the revolutionary, anti-tsarist elements of the Ukrainian's impassioned poetry.

Shevchenko's biographical arc – from serf to defiant Bard – was particularly useful for the Bolsheviks, although, during their first two occupations of Ukraine, Russian Bolsheviks tore down and trampled portraits of Shevchenko and burned copies of his books. Lenin's policy on monuments, however, put a halt to such attacks and, instead, harnessed Shevchenko for Bolshevik purposes. Indeed, as Anna Makolkin has pointed out, his life and works formed "the ideal propagandistic plot for the life of a revolutionary in the utopian Marxist-Leninist state. He was the ideal model of a revolutionary, a fighter for the oppressed and an ideological ally of the new state."[20] "Ideal model," "hero," "icon," and "prophet" are some of terms that have been employed over the past century to describe Shevchenko.[21] All draw attention to the significance of affect in the project of nation-building. Perhaps the most fruitful term, however, is "cultural saint," a concept that is the focus of a fascinating study by Dović and Helgason, who explore cultural sainthood as a type of civil religion, in part duplicating the symbolic and social role once played by religious saints. As they point out, the cultivation and veneration of important cultural figures "decisively contributed to fostering a common symbolic imaginarium, stabilizing shared memories, and maintaining social cohesion of the emerging communities."[22] For stateless or minority ethnic groups, such commemoration of cultural saints is an essential survival tool. When official confirmation of such a figure came, it was celebrated as a national victory.

Shakespeare had no such cachet for the Bolsheviks in 1918. As we have seen in a previous chapter in this book, throughout the early Soviet period of the 1920s, heated polemical debates erupted concerning the fate of the culture and literature of the "bourgeois" past. Since Shakespeare had been the possession of literate Russian elite circles for over a century, for some Bolsheviks and their followers his works should therefore swiftly make their way to the cultural scrapheap. Shakespeare's precarious status was not assisted by suggestions that he was "the spokesman of a decadent aristocracy" or by theories of the aristocratic authorship of the works, notably those proposed by Vladimir Friche, who attributed the plays to the Earl of Rutland.[23] In the volatile decade of the 1920s, mass demonstrations, agitprop productions, and the active search for homegrown Soviet playwrights made commemorations of Shakespeare of marginal interest to Russians. (The desire for a Soviet "Shakespeare" is explored in Chapter Eight.)

If during this early Soviet period Shakespeare was generally ignored in most parts of the USSR, both he and Shevchenko could now be openly and officially endorsed in Ukraine. With the formation of the USSR in 1922, draconian tsarist cultural decrees were no longer enforced. The nationality issue had ostensibly been solved by the creation of the revolutionary state that was to consist of equal nationalities battling the inequality of class. An explosion of translations of works of world literature into Ukrainian followed. Theatre companies sprang up, and art and culture experienced a great efflorescence. Ukrainians, for whom Shakespeare had been forbidden, were finally able to take on the universal Bard through the remarkable prismatic productions of Les Kurbas discussed in Chapter Six. These innovative, experimental productions symbolized a national and cultural victory, as well as homage to, and ownership of, Shakespeare.[24] As for Shevchenko, in 1925, the Kaniv area where he was buried was declared a state sanctuary (*derzhavnym zapovidnykom*). Understanding the powerful resonance of Shevchenko for Ukrainians, Anatoly Lunacharsky, the Commissar for the Enlightenment, proclaimed: "Shevchenko is great because he is the poet of the Ukrainian nation, but more than that, the poet of the people [*narod*], and beyond all things else: he is a deeply revolutionary poet and in his spirit, socialist. The greatest glory for every country, nation, is to create the universally human."[25] A temporary monument was now permitted to be erected in Kyiv in 1923 and a film about his life was made in 1926.

In 1929 in Kharkiv, briefly the capital of Ukraine, the city council approved plans for a Shevchenko monument. Postponed several times, it was not unveiled until 1935. In between these two dates lay the horrors of collectivization, famine, political arrests, and executions. Commemorative activities were no longer permitted spontaneous expression; instead, they were placed under the control of the Party. In 1934, the Department of Culture and Propaganda of the Communist Party of Ukraine published a document known as "The Theses of 1934," which declared Shevchenko "a bourgeois democrat" and "an ideologist of petit-bourgeois peasantry with nationalist and religious remnants."[26] Yet, despite this damning appraisal, within a year the memorial was erected. The monument's sixteen figures represented characters from Shevchenko's works, as well as participants of the Revolution and builders of the Soviet Union, all spiralling around the central figure of the poet. Many of the actors of the Berezil Artistic Association had posed for these figures. In April 1934, the workers of the Kharkiv Steam-engine Factory purportedly requested that the Berezil Theatre be renamed the Shevchenko Dramatic Theatre.[27] Such celebratory, symbolic activities seemed to proclaim a victory for the national cause and the defeat of the policies of oppression of the Ukrainian language and culture that had been the norm in the last half of the nineteenth century.

The reality was more complex. Even as Kurbas's actors had served as models for the monument, the artistic director himself was "relieved" of his post, and his actors were forced to renounce his theatrical experiments. After moving to Moscow at the invitation of the great Jewish actor Solomon Mikhoels, Kurbas concurrently began to prepare productions of *King Lear* and *Othello*, On his way to rehearsals, he was arrested, imprisoned, and eventually executed during the great purges of 1937.[28] The renamed Shevchenko Theatre thus both glorified Shevchenko but also erased the work of the avant-garde Berezil. Kurbas's name was excised from all theatrical histories and lexicons. Reference to his directorial work became a "prohibited" and "dangerous" zone that could only be safely discussed after his full "rehabilitation" which came with the fall of the USSR in 1991.[29]

The year 1935 is worth pausing over as one of the watershed years in terms of Soviet commemorative practices. Stalin, now firmly in power, initiated a major paradigm shift which reflected a retreat from proletarian (and egalitarian) internationalism of the 1920s and marked a return to the idea of the continuity of "great-power" traditions. The turnaround was made evident in attitudes to cultural icons. No longer just revolutionary or Civil War heroes, Old Bolsheviks, or Red Army commanders, but now pre-revolutionary heroic figures were brought to the fore. Their biographies and creative legacies were recycled, reinterpreted, and adapted in order to shore up the regime's legitimacy, to instill national pride, and to mobilize mass support for Stalin. A vast swathe of activities across the whole USSR was launched to commemorate "symbolic contributors" to the USSR.[30] The most prominent among them was another national bard, Alexander Pushkin, one of Russia's greatest poets.

Figure 10.2. Shevchenko monument in Shevchenko Park, Kharkiv, 1935.
Unveiled on 24 March 1935. Sculptor: M. Manizer. Architect: Y.G. Langbard.
Photographer: V. Rudenko

Source: Courtesy of the Taras Shevchenko Museum, Toronto, Canada.

The triangulation of Shakespeare-Shevchenko-Pushkin helps clarify the functions of Soviet commemorations and their use as ideological weapons. Like Shakespeare, Pushkin had been omitted from Lenin's list of notables earmarked for monumental propaganda. Indeed, the Russian poet, who had spent the last years of his short life in an official position at the court of the tsar and who depended upon the ruler for his financial welfare, could not easily fit the bill of a revolutionary. His legacy had been quietly observed in small circles up until 1935, when Stalin launched remarkably extensive commemorative activities that involved all levels of society and every corner of the USSR. In that year, Stalin proclaimed: "Comrades, life has become better, life has become more joyous."[31] Two years of preparation resulted in a massive Jubilee in 1937, probably the largest and most prominent cultural event of the 1930s. After a long drought, Pushkin had reentered the literary canon and was memorialized with renamings of institutions, streets, and squares. Publications, statues, and scholarship followed. Pushkin busts were even placed alongside those of Stalin.[32] The carefully scripted celebrations of this cultural saint were intended to show that "life had become more joyous," yet, tellingly, the height of these celebrations in 1937 coincided with the Great Purges.

Under Stalin, official propaganda – including commemorative practices – reverted to celebrating tsarist Russian heroes, Russian patriotism, and Russian national pride. National feeling was restored as a more stable, sure, and more comprehensible way of unifying the wide spectrum of the masses and of promoting state-building than some of the more abstract theories of Marxism promulgated since the 1920s and not always understood or embraced by the larger, mostly poorly educated populace. Russians were elevated by Stalin to the status of the "Great Russian People," becoming, in effect, the first among equals in what David McDonald has termed the Soviet state's "fairy tale of the brotherhood of nations," the "brotherhood" in which Moscow nonetheless was unquestionably at the centre and the top of the hierarchical pyramid.[33] Indeed, as Rolf Malte has argued, "Moscow saw itself as the standard-prescribing centre of the country. Its celebration experts saw themselves as the regulators of a union-wide culture of festivities. To that effect, they tried to influence how celebrations were run everywhere, to exert control, and to shape regional circumstances to meet their standards."[34]

Although the message of the central Party-controlled media was "unmistakably Russocentric," curiously, "High Stalinism did not reverse the policy of nation-building in non-Russian regions. In the mid-1930s ethnicity became reified, and all officially recognised Soviet nationalities were to possess their own 'Great Traditions': founding fathers, literary classics, and folkloric riches. In other words, indigenous cultural agents were allowed, and often encouraged, to articulate their people's heritage."[35] The elites of the various republics were given some cultural autonomy as a way of containing political-nationalist sentiment. Commemoration of the past was acceptable, as long as it did not conflict with Soviet Russian narratives or Soviet Russia's cultural hierarchy. Yet, as historian Serhy Yekelchyk has observed, this was an ambiguous and even dangerous strategy: the constant affirmation of the peoples' ethnic differences was simultaneously a cornerstone of ideology and a time bomb.[36]

The limits of non-Russian commemorative practices may be seen in the unhappy experience of one Ukrainian publishing house that took the opportunity of the 1937 Pushkin celebration to reprint *New Verses of Pushkin and Shevchenko,* originally published in 1859 (thus during Shevchenko's lifetime). A swift response in the form of a scathing attack came in the Russian journal *Literaturnoe obozrenie* [Literary Review], in which the book was deemed an "unnecessary...pulp publication... [of]

no interest or worth, and a photographic reprint of a defective edition in a luxurious velvet cover at an inordinate cost."[37] This aggressive attack suggests that the book's publication was interpreted as "an expression of resistance against the cultural imperialism of Great Russia" and, moreover, as an unbelievably presumptuous assertion that Pushkin's work had anything in common with Ukrainian poetry.[38]

If Shevchenko was not permitted to occupy the same ground as Pushkin, he could still be celebrated separately. In 1939, Soviet Ukrainians were permitted to commemorate the 125th anniversary of his birth on a scale hitherto unknown in Soviet times. Its ritual elements followed the pattern of the Pushkin celebrations. On 7 March 1939 (two days before Shevchenko's birthday), a decree of the Praesidium of the Verkhovna Rada SRSR proclaimed the goal of eternally memorializing Shevchenko's memory.[39] Among the many acts of commemoration were the renaming of Kyiv University and the Kyiv Opera House, the publication of a complete edition of his works, and the erection of three imposing monuments (in Moscow, Kyiv, and Kaniv). The unveiling of the Kyiv monument was attended by some two hundred thousand participants who listened to speeches delivered by various highly placed dignitaries, including Nikita Khrushchev, the new deputy for Ukraine. Throughout the 1930s, Shevchenko's burial site had been enlarged by new memorials and museums. In 1939, a large sculpture was finally installed there. Until that anniversary year, Shevchenko had been "the poet of peasant rebellion" within the Soviet literary canon (despite his academic achievements); from 1939 onward (and particularly during the Second World War), however, official documents glorified him as the "great son of Ukraine" – the founder of its national literature and the father of the nation. If it were not for the emphasis on Shevchenko's "revolutionary-democratic" views, Yekelchyk drily observes, "this interpretation could have been mistaken for a piece of Ukrainian nationalist propaganda."[40]

Dović and Helgason remind us that what is essential in commemorative practices is the *official* validation of the status of the cultural saint because confirmation most strongly ties canonization to political power and provides the legitimization of new elites, "enabling the redistribution of symbolic, cultural, political, and even economic capital."[41] Official endorsement is achieved by various means, including multiple "baptisms" of the type that occurred in 1937 for Pushkin and 1939 for Shevchenko: the renaming of places, institutions, and events, as well as the appearance of the "saint's" name on stamps, coins, and other objects. These formed part of the rituals of remembrance, indoctrination, and simplification. The last of these, simplification, was an essential means by which the masses could be brought on board; the heroic figure was reduced to particular, repeated slogans.[42] Thus, in 1939, Shevchenko was celebrated with the mantras of "courageous internationalist," "egalitarian," "champion of the poor and the exploited," and "friend of Russia."[43] His biography, as well as his literary and creative legacy were, like those of Pushkin, selectively adjusted and simplified. And, like the Pushkin commemorations, Shevchenko celebrations were carefully controlled. The beautiful new edition of his works was heavily bowdlerized: politically-charged poems were entirely omitted while others were trimmed of their inconvenient expressions of Ukrainian national consciousness and of anti-Moscow references. Aspects of his life and work were completely distorted or even falsified.[44] The official line continued to emphasize the social and anti-tsarist (anti-imperialist) aspects of his work and legacy and his close relationships with Russians. No mention was made of the terrible purges of 1937 in which thousands had perished, among them theatre artists, scholars, and approximately eighty percent of professional Soviet Ukrainian writers.[45]

Shakespeare's Rising Red Star

In the meantime, Shakespeare's star, which had dimmed in the 1920s, began to flicker once again. In 1934 at the First Writers Congress, Maxim Gorky counselled Soviet writers to imitate Shakespeare while using the method of socialist realism. As we saw in Chapter Eight, socialist realism was now the only permissible way to create aesthetic works. In his keynote address at the Congress, Andrey Zhdanov had emphasized that this method would combine "the most stern and sober practical work with a supreme spirit of heroic deeds and magnificent future prospects."[46] The enthusiasm for Shakespeare of Gorky, as well as that of Marx and Engels, presaged the initiation of the great project of translating Shakespeare into all the languages of the Soviet Union. Once prohibited, Shakespeare was now becoming available to all. At the same time, translation was also one of the many means of creating a common Soviet culture as defined by the Party.

Commemorations of Shakespeare, however, posed particular challenges. As has already been suggested, Shakespeare's position in the Soviet Russian literary system was by no means simple; among other things, he was often a barometer of a long-standing and fluctuating "love-hate" relationship with the West. When not linked to national identity or state-building, celebrations of "hyper-canonical" writers like Shakespeare are often fuelled by a desire to demonstrate the cultural superiority of the great powers on a global scale.[47] Shakespeare commemorations in the Soviet period could serve such a purpose, that is, as assertions of superior Soviet intellectual power (by claiming that no other nation admired Shakespeare or understood him as well as the Soviet Union), while simultaneously acting as friendly overtures to the West.

Among the few studies of Shakespeare that appeared in the 1930s, Vladimir Kemenov's essays and Aleksandr Smirnov's book, *Tvorchestvo Shekspira* [Shakespeare's Creative Works], began to turn the tide against what were now termed the earlier "vulgar sociological" approaches. "Popular humanism" was emphasized as residing at the core of Shakespeare's most representative works. The tragedies in particular were regarded as having exposed the struggle between two social orders: the "protest of the exploited classes against the nascent power of capital."[48] In 1937 Mikhail Morozov became the head of the Shakespeare Kabinet, an institution attached to the USSR Theatrical Society, founded in 1934. The first anthology of essays on Shakespeare appeared in the *Shekspirovskii sbornik* [Shakespeare Collection] and the first conference was held in Moscow in 1939, with Mikhail Bakhtin as one of the speakers. Still, there were obstacles to viewing Shakespeare as an out-and-out progressive. The interpretation of his history plays presented many problems. One of the many sticking points was the representation of the masses, including the particularly difficult case of the viciousness of Jack Cade's popular revolt in *Henry VI, Part II*. And there still remained some niggling questions about authorship. With the world careening towards war and the USSR's secret pact with Germany, in 1939 there was still little reason for widespread Shakespeare commemorations.

The Cold War

By the end of the Second World War, the political and cultural terrain experienced another shift. On 26 August 1946, the Central Committee resolution "On the Repertoire of Drama Theatres and Measures Toward Its Improvement" signalled the need to purge apolitical plays, idealizations of the past, and western plays with "bourgeois morals." In January 1947, the representatives of the provincial Communist Party committee attacked "such contaminating capitalist poison as *Othello*."[49] If Mikhail Morozov's monograph *Shakespeare on the Soviet Stage* (1947) attempted to serve in the two capacities of partial bridge to the West and restatement of the "exceptional Soviet understanding of Shakespeare," by 1949, a "violently adverse review" attacked Morozov and others "for primitive formalism and Anglo-American methods of barren philology." As a result, Morozov then "went out of his way to attack the West and its bourgeois critics and theatrical workers," including accusing the USA of "using Shakespeare as an excuse for her aggressive acts; the individualism which the Americans saw in Shakespeare…was merely a subterfuge intended to justify 'subjugation of other people.'"[50] Also caught in this political net was Smirnov, who was attacked for his "liberal predilection for bourgeois civilisation."[51]

Since Shakespeare fortunately had the imprimatur of Marx and Engels, he was not entirely pushed into the background but continued to be tolerated, even when, once again, Stalinist ideologues reverted to preferring to celebrate the pantheon of national classics established by the pre-revolutionary intelligentsia. This approach embraced aspects of the early Romantic idea of the ideal national poet as "authentic, non-derivative, sublime, and yet deeply rooted in his own world and speaking for his people."[52] Accordingly, the Soviets continued to celebrate national poets in elaborate rituals of remembrance that also stressed the notion of the "friendship of peoples" within the larger state.[53] Rather than attacking Shakespeare, writers launched offensives against Western scholarly approaches to his works, calling them, among other things "falsifications."[54]

In the Soviet cultural teeter-totter, as Shakespeare fell, Shevchenko rose. The Shevchenko Museum opened in Kyiv in April 1949. The complete works were issued in a large volume edition, in a luxurious format with a print run of one hundred thousand. In 1951, on the occasion of the ninetieth anniversary of Shevchenko's death, he was the only subject of the first three pages of *Literaturna hazeta* [Literary Newspaper], the official organ of the Soviet Ukrainian Writers' Union. The front-page headline read "Forever Alive," a phrase "usually exclusively reserved in Soviet public discourse for the founding father of the Soviet State, Lenin."[55] In newspaper articles, radio programs, speeches, and at meetings, Shevchenko was glorified as a "revolutionary democrat" and as "the founder of Ukrainian literature." It was claimed that he possessed a "great and burning" love for the Russian people and a hatred for "*all those who bowed before the moribund idealistic art of the West.*"[56]

But who owned Shevchenko? Who had the right to commemorate him? The significance of this cultural saint and of monuments to his memory as symbols of identity, ownership, and power came to the fore in 1951, when a statue of Shevchenko was gifted to left-wing Canadians by the Soviet Society for Cultural Relations Abroad. Erected in the Taras H. Shevchenko Memorial Park near Toronto, for a considerable time the huge bronze sculpture occupied the eye of a storm of controversy, as Ukrainian nationalist émigrés protested against Soviet appropriation of Shevchenko and against the Soviet occupation of Ukraine. The monument was even briefly held under 24-hour police protection – a reminder of the affective power of such sites, which are the locus for articulating and, in this case, for contesting the ownership of a national culture. Similar polemical contestation of the ownership of Shevchenko surrounded the unveiling of monuments to Shevchenko elsewhere and, as will be seen below, well into the future. Indeed, as Dović and Helgason have noted, one of the most important features of national poets is their international and competitive dimension: "[T]hey validate a particular ethno-linguistic or "national" group and demonstrate that group's cultural and intellectual autonomy *to others*."[57] Both the West and the Soviets "wanted to position Shevchenko as a transnational figure of liberation, but to control his meaning each side had somehow to centre him in its own world. In this hall of mirrors the rival Shevchenkos struggled to achieve a distinct identity."[58]

Convergence: Shakespeare and Shevchenko, 1964

The year 1964 marked the waning moments of the so-called Thaw, roughly the period that began with Nikita's Khrushchev's rise to power after Stalin's death in 1953 and ended in October 1964, when Khrushchev was ousted. During this time, censorship was loosened and a variety of scientific and cultural exchanges with the West were initiated.[59] It was also the year that marked two significant birthday anniversaries: Shakespeare's 400th and Shevchenko's 150th. In this context, Soviet celebrations of Shakespeare could be seen, at least in part, as one of the friendly overtures to the West.

The anniversary celebrations of both bards need to be examined in light of the political context and the consequent creation of new Soviet rituals. The early 1960s had seen tensions among the left and right wings of the Communist Party, particularly in their response to the efforts of the "creative intelligentsia" to obtain some artistic freedom. The number of witnesses to the heady days of the revolutionary years was dwindling. Khrushchev's public denunciation of Stalin had brought about a sense of an ideological vacuum, if not uncertainty. In response to the pressures of the times, the Party turned away from traditional revolutionary rhetoric and instead concentrated on ideological assault: a focused effort to create a homogeneous *Soviet* culture based on a system of new, scripted rituals, though often grafted onto older, traditional customs and celebrations. These newly created *prazdniki* (holiday celebrations) centred on a number of important principles, including the internationalism of the new rituals, the maximum utilization of everything progressive in national or popular traditions, the struggle against remnants of bourgeois nationalism, the alleged universality of the new rituals, the synthesis of the logical and the emotional in every ritual and celebration, the expression of progressive ideas, and the connection of the new festivities with the whole system and way of life.[60]

As this author has pointed out elsewhere, Shakespeare's long ties to Russia meant that he could be employed within the context of such new rituals.[61] Shakespeare was useful in multiple ways: he could provide aesthetic sustenance to the intelligentsia and create a sense of a common Soviet high culture; he could also be perceived as a comforting symbol of notions of conservatism (especially to Khrushchev, who detested modern art). Shakespeare celebrations could be interpreted as a gesture of internationalism, even as they formed part of a new effort for the USSR to gain a "back door" to power.[62] They offered another way to gain recognition in the West by way of publicity and visibility while emphasizing Soviet world supremacy on the cultural front. Such "multivocality" (to use sociologist Christel Lane's term) can only be achieved "if a symbol is deeply embedded in a people's culture."[63] Shakespeare, with his venerable history in Russia but without any overtly nationalistic baggage, could fulfill precisely such complex functions, meaning different things to different parts of the Soviet polity. Such a complex role, it should be noted, continues to the present day in Russia.

In 1964 the broad-spectrum, extensive Shakespeare celebrations included theatrical productions, films, translations, dissertations, bibliographies, scholarly books, articles, critical reinterpretations, and a biography – all of which reflected a genuine esteem for Shakespeare and also mirrored the slightly more open atmosphere of this period. The celebrations were capped by a gala event at Moscow's Bolshoi Theatre, the venue for many important past congresses of the Communist Party. In 1964, Shakespeare's oversized image, like that of a huge icon, hung both outside the theatre and inside, in the very place where images of Lenin and Stalin had once dominated the cavernous stage. In this symbolic political space, dozens of speakers, honoured artists, scholars, poets, playwrights, and translators occupied the stage and faced a packed auditorium of over two thousand. In the imperial box sat Chairman of the Council of Ministers, Nikita Khrushchev, First Deputy Premier, Anastas Mikoyan, and Foreign Minister, Andrey Gromyko. Not by chance was the British film company Pathé permitted to record this event for world consumption, which seemed to confirm the Soviets' claim that no one better understood, loved, or venerated the works of Shakespeare than the Soviets. Shakespeare was proclaimed "A Writer of the People," an "exponent of the folk tradition" and of "progressive tendencies of the democratic strata of society," although admittedly and regrettably, "he never actually adopted a revolutionary outlook."[64]

Shevchenko was more useful in that last capacity, as a revolutionary. On Sunday, 8 March 1964, the eve of Shevchenko's birthday, the newspaper *Pravda* announced the coming "Shevchenko Days in Ukraine" that

were to include the unveiling of a new bronze statue in his honour, which
was to take place in the presence of representatives from the "fraternal
republics," as well as from Cuba, Japan, and Italy.[65] Official celebrations
of Shevchenko at the newly-erected monument in Kyiv included the presence of the whole Ukrainian Party Politburo as well as Khrushchev himself, who had just won the Soviet Shevchenko Prize for his contributions
to "the development and strengthening of Soviet Ukrainian culture."[66]
An all-union celebration was held in Moscow, where a Shevchenko monument was erected across from the Ukraïna Hotel. Shevchenko's biography again proved useful: he "could stand as a model of solidarity between
the peoples of Ukraine and Russia, he wrote in both languages, received
his artistic training in St. Petersburg, and maintained close ties to both
cultural worlds."[67]

Statues of Shevchenko were also erected in three other Ukrainian
cities, while a town in Kazakhstan, his place of exile, was named after
him. The "baptism" of the cultural saint continued. A plethora of works
marked the 150th anniversary of his birth: over 250 titles, including studies of his language, his commentaries, his relations with other national
cultures (including his love of Shakespeare), dictionaries of his vocab-
ulary, bibliographies, and an illustrated calendar indicating month by
month the important events of his life and afterlife, particularly in the
Soviet Union.[68] The last phase of festivities came towards the end of May
with a joint plenary session of the Executive Boards of the Association of
Writers of the USSR and of the Association of Writers of the Ukrainian
SSR, attended by writers-representatives from all the "fraternal republics" as well as "many" (unnamed) foreign cultural workers, representatives of UNESCO, who proclaimed the genius of "the son of Ukraine"
and "the revolutionary poet-democrat," Shevchenko.[69]

The extensive celebrations of both bards appeared to suggest a convergence, if not an equivalence, between the two. The differences, however, were important. Volumes such as Roman Samarin's *Shakespeare in the
Soviet Union*, first published in Russian and then translated into English,
include only Russian scholars as contributors. As we have seen, the largest and most impressive of the Shakespearean celebrations were held in
the centre, Moscow. While Ukrainians and other national groups were
not excluded from such Soviet Russian celebrations, when they did participate, it was in a secondary capacity and as representatives of their
ethnicity. As a ritual, the Moscow gala looked both outward, to the West,
and inward, to pasting over the fissures of Soviet society. *Pravda* made
only laconic references to other Shakespeare festivities in Kyiv, Vilnius,
Tashkent, Tbilisi, Baku, Minsk, and nameless "other cities" of the USSR;
the "real" commemorations were those held in Moscow.

The reportage about the Moscow Shakespeare gala appeared on the bottom front page of *Pravda* on 24 April, under the title "Soviet People Celebrate Shakespeare." In it, Shakespeare was praised for his life-affirming humanism. Like Shevchenko, he was also presented as a mediator between cultures. Among the speakers cited in the article, Ukrainian playwright Oleksander Levada underlined the significance of the "meeting" of Shevchenko and Shakespeare in that anniversary year, comparing this conjunction to Galileo encountering Michelangelo.[70] For his part, the Kirgiz writer Chinghiz Aitmatov underscored the importance of Russians and the Russian language in first giving Shakespeare to the people of the East (but occluding all references to the imposition of Shakespeare on local culture). Russian Soviet scholar Roman Samarin could boast that the translation project had resulted in more than five million copies of Shakespeare's works in twenty-eight languages of the Soviet Union. Yet Shakespeare had sometimes been forcibly brought to the many stages of the various republics of the Soviet Union. Uzbek "nationalists," for example, resisted Shakespeare, arguing that his works were foreign to them. Countering with a series of syllogisms, Soviet "progressives" insisted that

> the Uzbek Theatre should not develop on levels to which the oppressed people had been kept, but should work up to higher levels from the best tradition of folk art. As there was no tradition of Uzbek drama, their drama must obviously be founded on the best tradition of national life; as the Revolution was based on the worker and peasant, and the worker and peasant are international their heritage obviously included the great works of all nations; so they proceeded to stage Goldoni, Lope de Vega, Gogol, and *Hamlet*.[71]

Shakespeare was thus one more tool by which local culture was eroded and homogenized into a Soviet "high" culture model.

On 9 March 1964 (the birthday of Shevchenko), *Pravda* hailed him not only on its front page, reminding its readers of Lenin's respect for the Ukrainian bard and of his decision to memorialize his life and work with a monument but also on two subsequent pages, where an illustration of Shevchenko was accompanied by the headline "genius-son of Ukraine" and followed by the mantras "poet of freedom-loving humanity" and "the living fire of poetry." A quotation from Khrushchev was found at the top of the front page, in which he referred to Shevchenko as not just a Ukrainian poet but as "a poet-revolutionary" and "the friend of workers of all nations."[72] Other sanctioned celebrations were held in Minsk, Tashkent, Tbilisi, Dushanbe, and Yerevan. However, while official celebrations attempted to co-opt both Shakespeare and

Shevchenko to the Soviet cause, unsanctioned commemorations sprung up on alternative symbolic dates as a way to resist Soviet mantras. Thus, for example, poets, writers, students, and other dissidents created their own tradition, gathering together not on Shevchenko's birthday but on 22 May, the anniversary of the day on which his body had been moved from its place in St Petersburg and reinterred in Ukraine. These prohibited acts of memorialization symbolized the need to "return" Ukrainian culture and language from its appropriation by its Soviet Russian masters, reclaiming Shevchenko "as a symbol of the nation, rather than of socialism and of Ukraine's ties with Russia."[73] The place of Shevchenko's burial in Kaniv served as a special locus for pilgrimages and even martyrdom. In 1978 the Ukrainian Oleksa Hirnyk burned himself alive on Shevchenko's grave in protest against the Russification and colonization of Ukraine.[74]

Abroad, the dynamics of competitive commemoration were revealed once again in 1964, this time in Washington, DC, where a Shevchenko monument was erected through the efforts of Ukrainian nationalists in a ceremony that attracted over one hundred thousand people of Ukrainian descent and included the participation of former president Dwight D. Eisenhower. It was a commemoration, Savage has argued, aimed especially at influencing the American foreign-policy establishment with speeches that decried Soviet oppression and called for an independent Ukrainian state.[75] Meanwhile, patriotic Soviet Russian dissidents were also questioning the primacy of the Soviet myth of the friendship of peoples (among Russians, Ukrainians, Belarussians, Georgians, and others) which, in their view, led to the diminution of their Russian great heroic past because of the competing cults of different cultural saints. As Yekelchyk has noted, "In the final analysis, Soviet authorities never fully reconciled the Soviet peoples' multiple national histories....Tracing the various nations' historical trajectories as leading into the Russian Empire and the Russian-dominated Soviet Union thus inescapably involved the constant affirmation of the peoples' ethnic difference," an ambiguous and deeply problematic strategy.[76]

Conclusion

As we have seen, mass celebrations and commemorations formed a significant part of the Soviet ideological system from the earliest years of the state's creation. These rituals articulated, defined, and amplified social and political relations within the USSR and its relations with the outside world. Morphing into more and more carefully scripted events over the course of the decades, in tandem with the shifting political landscape, these festivities also embodied fluctuating ideological positions relating to history, nationalism and internationalism, as well as art and culture. Monuments and especially commemorative anniversaries crystallized these moments and sharpened the battle over the past and the way it interpreted the present and gestured towards the future.

After the collapse of the Soviet Union, official Shevchenko commemorations in Russia dwindled, although, in 2012, president Vladimir Putin, in discussions with then Ukrainian president and pro-Russian supporter Viktor Yanukovych, announced "with great fanfare" that the two countries would celebrate the 200th anniversary of Shevchenko's birth together. But, on the day of the anniversary in 2014, Putin was silent. The Kremlin website made no mention of Shevchenko. According to a Reuters report, in Crimea, invaded by Russian troops, pro-Russian activists attacked a small group of Ukrainians near a monument to Shevchenko. One was whipped; others were intimidated and mocked.[77] The great divisions in the view of Ukraine and, more particularly, of its future – with the European Union and the West, or with Russia – continued to be replayed in connection with its commemoration of the national Bard.

At the same time as Shevchenko continued to be a flashpoint of controversy, Shakespeare in Russia helped to build strong bridges with the West, particularly during the important anniversary years of 2014 and 2016. Extensive celebratory events, exchanges, theatre productions, and published works suggested the possibility of a normalization of the relationship of Russia with the West and, further, that culture could rise "above" politics – could perhaps even serve as a mediator rather than a weapon. The Russian government's sudden announcement in 2018 to prohibit the British Council's activities in Moscow and its refusal of the proposed Shakespeare monument, however, suggests an altogether different, more confrontational, use of bards and one that harkens back to Soviet-era uses of culture as a potent weapon.

Coda

With the fall of the Soviet Union and Ukraine's declaration of independence in 1991, a process of de-communization began: statues of Soviet leaders and generals were removed, and streets, metro stops, and buildings were renamed. What started as a gradual process of divestment of the Soviet past took hold more firmly in 2014 during the EuroMaidan (also known as the Revolution of Dignity), in which demonstrators, supporting closer ties with Europe and the West, repudiated their president (Yanukovych) and his intent to turn Ukraine back toward Russia. The shooting of unarmed demonstrators, the invasion and annexation of Crimea, the support of pro-Russian separatists in eastern Ukraine, and, finally, the brutal and unprovoked full-scale war that followed in 2022 rapidly accelerated this process of de-colonization, linking it more closely to de-russification. Russian missiles and drones attacked not just cities and villages but repositories of culture, history, and memory. Museums, galleries, churches, monuments, and schools were bombed. In the small, quiet town of Borodyanka, just north of Kyiv, not only were civilian buildings destroyed, but the town's Shevchenko monument came under targeted attack: the plinth was shelled and the poet's head was hit with bullets. The symbolism of such an attack was obvious. The founder of the modern Ukrainian literary language, Shevchenko is also the most important public symbol of Ukraine. As already noted above, Shevchenko is the Ukrainian sign: "the name-metaphor which encodes the entire history of the nation for all Ukrainians in past, present, and future."[78]

Such wanton destruction of Ukrainian cultural heritage as well as the "all-out Russification of Ukraine's occupied territories," including the abduction of children, provided still more fodder for rapid de-russification.[79] Ukraine's urban landscape, saturated with statues of famous Russians, also included many Soviet era monuments to Pushkin that had been erected in order to impress upon Ukrainians their ties with Russian culture. American scholar Edyta Bojanowska noted that "[c]hildren recited his poetry around the time of Russia's annexation of Crimea," while Russian actors who supported the full-scale invasion of Ukraine read verses by the Moscow-born bard."[80] Pushkin thus became a symbol of Russia's invasion and a reminder of its imperial legacy. Two months after the war began, a poll carried out by the sociological group Rating indicated that 76 per cent of Ukrainians supported the renaming of all material objects, places, and figures associated with Russia.[81] In December 2023, a Ukrainian panel discussion on the topic "Should something be done with Pushkin?" was directed at the fate of the Pushkin monument and street in Odesa.[82] The panel's question opened up the broader issue, also faced by other countries, of how to deal with a fraught history. In this respect, the heated debates echoed those in the USA to taking down statues honouring the Confederacy; in Canada, to those who created and abetted the residential school system; and, in Britain, to their historical complicity in the slave trade. The continuing brutality of the war in Ukraine, including in mostly Russian speaking areas in the east, galvanized the desire for the removal of all reminders of Russia.[83] On 20 September 2024, the governor of Odesa announced that the city's statue of Pushkin was to be removed.[84] Meanwhile in Kharkiv, only about thirty kilometres away from the Russian border, the 1935 statue of Shevchenko was meticulously sandbagged from top to bottom to prevent its destruction by Russian missiles and drones.

Figure 10.3. Shevchenko monument in Borodyanka, Ukraine, showing the scars of war, 11 April 2022.

Source: The State Emergency Service of Ukraine. Government of Ukraine. Creative Commons.

This careful attention to monuments (whether as destruction or as support) reminds us yet again of their symbolic potency and their power to evoke and amplify emotion, identity, affiliation, and values. Whatever their purpose, celebration of bards is always a political act.

Figure 10.4. Shevchenko monument in Kharkiv sandbagged to withstand the war's destruction, 2022. Ukrainian flag placed at the bottom.

11

Antic Dispositions:
Shakespeare, War, and Cabaret

Writing for the *New York Times* in 1981, Frank Rich began his witty review of a production of *Shakespeare's Cabaret* with the following: "As theater lyricists go, William Shakespeare is hard to beat. He may even be better than Lorenz Hart."[1] Hart was, of course, the lyricist half of the famous American song-writing team of Rodgers and Hart, contributing to such well-known compositions as "Blue Moon" and "Bewitched, Bothered, and Bewildered." The pairing of Shakespeare with cabaret, formerly infrequent and considered rather cheeky, is now commonplace. Shakespeare's anniversary year of 2016 harvested a particularly large bumper crop. Just a few examples will suffice to give a flavour of these productions. At the British Library, Spymonkey, described in promotional material as the "greatest clowns working in Britain today," presented an evening of "genius comedy," "a cabaret with a hilarious and joyful mash-up of clown and Shakespeare."[2] The Cambridge Arts Theatre reprised what *The Independent* described as "one of the best things to come out of the RSC": a "comic concoction of hilarious sketches and show-stopping numbers."[3] On the other side of the pond, Chicago's Shakespeare Theatre celebrated with *Shakespeare Tonight!*, "a captivating marriage of Shakespeare and cabaret."[4] Still further afield, The Puzzle Collective's "Shakespeare Cosplay Cabaret" urged Australians to "get ready for a night of music, dancing, circus, slam poetry, Shakespeare and superheroes!"[5]

As these descriptions suggest, the notion of cabaret is now generally associated with soufflé-light diversions that cleverly bring together the "high" and the "low" and thus appeal even to those who don't particularly care for the Bard. But how can such a genre function in wartime or in the horror of its aftermath? What purposes might it serve? This chapter maps out some of the connections between the characteristics and strategies of the early avant-garde cabaret and its subsequent use when married with Shakespeare – not for the purposes of light entertainment, distraction, nor of morale-boosting propaganda but as direct engagement with, and, indeed, reflection of the madness of war. In this approach, I take my cue from Kenneth Burke's late 1930s essay, "War, Response, and Contradiction."[6] Burke takes as his point of departure a debate between Malcolm Cowley and Archibald MacLeish that unfolded on the pages of *The New Republic* concerning two broad ways by which art may approach the subject of war. The first, championed by Cowley, are works that emphasize feelings of horror, repugnancy, and hatred. These, Burke contends, are "extremely militaristic attitudes" that may easily be turned inside out; indeed, they "might well provide the firmest basis upon which the 'heroism' of a new war could be erected."[7] Instead, Burke upholds the position of MacLeish who argued that the depiction of a "human" war – that is, a work that deals with the totality of the experience of war not just its horror – is more "socially wholesome" and the "soundest deterrent to war." In the words of MacLeish, such works contain "neither morality, nor text, nor lesson."[8] This, second, more complex, way, Burke suggests, combats tribal instincts. Taking this argument further, I propose that, in today's world, the Hamletsque "antic disposition" of cabaret – its grotesque, satirical, adversarial, yet playful and intelligent nature – may be one of the few ways to respond critically and with authenticity to war, fake news, and the madness of its strongman adherents.

Originating in Bohemian Paris in the last quarter of the nineteenth century, cabaret originally functioned as an intimate venue for avant-garde artists, intellectuals, writers, and their friends to exchange and to debate ideas, smoke, drink, recite poetry, perform songs, sketches, improvisations, avant-garde dramatic works, and, usually, eat. They created and performed for each other and directly to each other in an often raucous performance space that was the centre of heady experimentation. Satirically attacking topical issues in culture, morals, and politics and lampooning authority in its various guises and places, the cabaretists of the late nineteenth and early twentieth century created an alternative space to that of traditional, established theatres. Dissent was their leitmotif; conventional thinking, their target. Combining "intimacy and hostility," "participation and provocation," laughter and utopian hopes, they shadowed the fragmentation of the world and its imminent upheaval in the Great War.[9]

Rather than inhabiting or growing into a specific hide-bound genre, early cabaret displayed a number of salient features that would continue to figure throughout the following decades and beyond: satire, parody, song, improvisation, topicality, and playful impudence. It also engaged in a mutually-influential and constantly evolving dynamic with other popular entertainments. At the turn of the last century, that meant drawing from vaudeville, circus, puppet shows, carnival, and music hall. Reclaiming the importance of this genre of small forms[10] for theatre history, scholars such as Harold Segel, Laurence Senelick,[11] and particularly Lisa Appignanesi have exhaustively described and analysed the origins, dissemination, and later offshoots of cabaret, a fact which makes extended discussion of its history unnecessary here. As they have shown, the cabaret gave birth to some of the most electrifying innovations in twentieth-century performance art. It provided "the earliest podium for the expressionists, the DADAists, the futurists; it was a congenial forum for experiments in shadowgraphy, puppetry, free-form skits, jazz rhythms, literary parody, "naturalistic" songs, "bruitistic" litanies, agitprop, dance-pantomime, and political satire."[12]

Cabaret's rapid cultural acceptance and subsequent peregrinations from Paris to Petersburg and beyond revealed its inclination to shape-shifting, as each country introduced its own distinctive tonalities and accents to the genre, though everywhere it tended to draw its participants from peripheral groups whose outlook remained ironic.[13] In Germany and Austria, for example, some of cabaret's playfulness morphed into more serious political and aggressive humour and took on the name of *Kabarett*. There, the presiding genius was the spirit of the clown who anarchically scoffed at everything with simultaneously joyful and derisive laughter.[14] In this vein, the inimitable Munich clown, Kurt Valentin, wildly popular with audiences, deeply influenced the work of Bertolt Brecht. Erwin Piscator, too, fell under the spell of the cabaret in the 1920s. In Zurich, the Dadaist Cabaret Voltaire was a haven for those who opposed war: international artists and writers, some of whom had been eyewitnesses of the destruction, and others, who presciently escaped before the devastation began. Safely in Switzerland, they engaged in anti-logical experiments employing outrageous costumes, masks, and dance aimed at freeing up the imagination from the constraints imposed by tradition and convention. In Budapest and Prague, the cabaret scooped up nationalist sentiment with its desire to overthrow the dominance of German culture. In Poland, though less strident, it mocked both smug conservatives and Young Poland modernists. In imperial Russia, the cabaret leaned more heavily toward the theatrical; some of the best-known cabarets presented a large dollop of mini-plays, skits, and tableaux.

Topical, improvisional, impertinent, fluid in content and adaptable in form, the cabaret was the "perfect medium for hard times."[15] As Appignanesi has observed, its initially small size endowed the cabaret with a certain status of independence, while its potency derived in large part from the dynamic, and sometimes volatile, relationship between performers and spectators whose roles could be reversed at any moment.

Such a porous demarcation line between audience and performer held out the continual expectation and encouragement of experimentation, enhanced by improvisation with its possibility of an immediate response to "hot" current events. Song endured as a central component of the cabaret and as another powerful democratic weapon by which to ridicule authority and hypocrisy; at times it even served as a call to action, to protest, and criticism.[16]

In the confused, violent years of world war, civil war, and revolution that ultimately brought an end to the Russian empire, cabaret strategies attracted into its creative vortex many extraordinary talents, among them, the directors Nikolai Evreinov, Vsevolod Meyerhold, and Les Kurbas. Still the least well known of these in the anglosphere, the multi-talented Kurbas (1887–1937) was an actor, director, playwright, translator, pedagogue, theorist, filmmaker, and musician. As we have seen in Chapter Six, he was the first to introduce Shakespeare to the Ukrainian stage.[17] Through his subsequent innovative, experimental productions with his Berezil Artistic Association, he laid the foundations for twentieth-century Ukrainian theatre and film. Born in Western Ukraine, educated in Vienna, and well-versed in the traditions of world theatre, Kurbas spearheaded a theatrical renaissance which at first centred on the staging of the classics – not as an end in itself but rather as part of the process of national and cultural self-discovery through dialogue and debate with foreignness. A life-long voracious reader and polymath, he was deeply influenced by the ideas and the works of a plethora of thinkers, artists, and creators from Henri Bergson and Edmund Gordon Craig to Arnold Schönberg, Paul Cézanne, D.W. Griffith, and Albert Einstein. He was also inspired by the cabaret.

Just as he arrived in Vienna in 1907 to pursue his university studies in philosophy and philology, the famous Fledermaus (Bat) cabaret was founded.[18] Multicultural Vienna was a "natural" for cabaret, with its strong national traditions of music, theatre, and tart comedy. Kurbas became a frequenter of the Fledermaus, the "in" place of the time, which featured the highly praised sketches, monologues, and poems of Peter Altenberg. Described by one scholar as a "most notorious drunk and arch bohemian, flâneur and lover of prostitutes,"[19] Altenberg was also the central figure of café culture and of the cabaret scene, not just in Vienna but, arguably, in all of Austria. He memorably insisted that the cabaret was "the art of doing small things in the theatre the way really big things are done"[20] – that is, cabaret was not insignificant or minor in purpose but, rather, it was theatre reduced to its essential components. This quintessence of theatre, as it was embodied in the cabaret form and developed by Altenberg and another famous cabaretist, Frank Wedekind, was among the important early influences on Kurbas.

Figure 11.1. Les Kurbas, c. 1910s.

Moving from Western Ukraine to Kyiv in 1916, Kurbas encountered a robust cabaret culture which flourished in the basements of hotels, restaurants, and derelict buildings. These locales were filled with artists from various national groups, many of them arriving in droves during the civil war, hoping to escape the hunger and chaos that ruled in Russia. New cabarets were constantly springing up, such as the Harlequin Mini-Theatre founded by a group of artists that included future filmmakers Sergei Yutkevich and Grigori Kozintsev, the latter well-known to Shakespeareans as the director of the 1964 Soviet film of *Hamlet* and the 1971 *King Lear*. The KhLAM Club (an acronym for Artists, Writers, Actors, and Musicians but literally meaning "trash") was celebrated for its political and artistic diversity, attracting even Bolshevik commissars. The Art Cave (Lyokh Mystetstva), organized by Ukrainian and Russian poets and actors headed by Les Kurbas, presented new poetry, art, stylized dance, music, mini-plays, and sketches.[21]

The collapse of the tsarist empire had finally enabled aesthetic experimentation and released bottled-up political satire. The appeal of Shakespeare's *Macbeth* in this anti-monarchical revolutionary period is self-evident. We have already seen, in Chapter Six, how after having staged *Macbeth* in 1920, Kurbas continued to rethink the play in subsequent redactions. Using the play as a tool for interrogating the whole concept of theatre, in 1924 he created a third, radical reinterpretation.[22] Opening on 2 April 1924, two years after the creation of the Soviet Union and a few weeks after the death of Lenin, this was a tragi-farcical *Macbeth* – one unlike any other seen before anywhere in the old Russian Empire or, for that matter, in Western Europe. Anticipating a backlash from his spectators who might expect a pseudo-classical Shakespeare, Kurbas explained in interviews published in advance that it was neither necessary nor possible to revive a "museum"' Shakespeare; instead, he conceived of Shakespeare as a prism through which the contemporary revolutionary world-view would be refracted.[23] I have examined this remarkable production in detail elsewhere.[24] In coming back again and again to rethink the elements of this extraordinary production, I am fulfilling Yakiv Savchenko's prediction, made in 1924, that Kurbas's *Macbeth* could, and should, have many scholarly works written about each of its scenes.[25] Here, in this chapter, I will rehearse only some of the major features of the production previously noted in order to better contextualize a focus on those characteristics linked to cabaret, hitherto an unexplored but significant progenitor.

The stage was painted black. Decorative scenery was rejected and replaced by enormous movable bright green screens of stretched canvas on which giant modernist red block letters announced the locality of each scene. Going a step beyond the concept of self-supporting screens, Kurbas had "living" screens form an essential part of the dramatic action, even serving as a kind of character. Raised or lowered when needed at the sound of a gong, the screens sometimes indicated the simultaneity of the action in different parts of Scotland; at others, underscored the emotions of the lead actors; emphasized tension; and even interfered in the action. Props, too, acquired their own life, flying down or up, as need be. The musical score also surprised with its jarring mixture of Anatoli Butsky's contemporary atonal creations, Ukrainian folk songs, excerpts from Pietro Mascagni's *Cavalleria Rusticana*, and a Schubert military march. The porous boundary between stage and auditorium, fiction and reality, was consistently underscored. Most of the actors were dressed in contemporary workmen's clothes with stylized medieval accessories, suggesting the simultaneity of time past and time present. After a gong rang out announcing each sequence, the work lights came on and the actors entered as themselves, each at his or her own pace, occasionally greeting the audience. Only then did they engage in their roles. In effect, the actors presented a series of isolated, discrete "numbers," as in a cabaret performance. Repeated throughout the production, such an "engagement" and "disengagement" with a role drew attention to the broader notion of theatricality. Suspending traditional drama's fluidity of action, the cabaret tactic of discontinuity invited the audience to interrogate its expectations of theatrical conventions both on stage and in life. Focusing on the skill and labour of the actor, the strategy encouraged a cerebral response to the play on both sides of the footlights, since the actors – as in cabaret – were required to be both performers and spectators to each other, as well as to the audience.[26] (Kurbas's careful attention to the responses of the audience is discussed in Chapter Seven.)

The political and philosophical arc of the production echoed the cabaret attitude, provocatively addressing the audience as complicit collaborator in the events through an ironic, parodic "commentary" at the centre of which was the Porter, here, renamed the Fool. He usurped the primacy and the focal position in the play traditionally assumed by Macbeth. Like the jeering, disdainful Viennese cabaret clowns, Kurbas's Fool mocked political, religious, and moral pretensions in three separate, extensive appearances resembling cabaret mini-plays that punctuated the intervals between the acts of Shakespeare's play. The central organizing principle of the whole production was a montage of contrasts and analogues that emphasized the themes of hypocrisy, cycles of violence and destruction, and their consequences.

During the first interval, actor Amvrosy Buchma was dressed in fool's cap and motley clothing with gaudy, overstated make-up: a white face, crimson lips, and a large bulbous nose which, combined with his exaggerated gestures, linked him to circus clowns, silent film, and Dada. The allusions to the Harrowing of Hell plays in Shakespeare's Porter scene were literalized: pitchfork-carrying devils suddenly appeared on each side of the stage. When the Porter/Fool threatened them with his fist, they lifted up their heads and were "transformed" into a cardinal and a Jesuit priest by the simple trick of flicking back their cowls on which had been painted grotesque, gaping faces. Organ music solemnly announced the end of this episode that marked the world of *Macbeth* as hellish, hypocritical, fantastical, and mad. Clerical authority was mocked with aggressive buffoonery, part of the production's continuum of subversion that included the opening scene in which outrageously "witchy" witches, bathed in an eerie violet light, entered bearing liturgical censors traditionally used by priests to purify a sacred space. Not only were the witches shockingly appropriating the gestures and tools of clerics, but they also seemed to be endowed with mysterious powers, suggested by the fact that they were electrically wired. The Porter was visually and thematically connected to the witches. His nose, also wired, occasionally

Figure 11.2. Final scene of *Macbeth*, directed by Les Kurbas, 1924.

lit up, drawing attention to his clownish proboscis and mingling the audience's feelings of horror with laughter.

Upon his first entry, the Porter-Fool cavorted across the stage using wild, unpredictable acrobatic leaps and grotesque dance steps. As in cabaret, he made impromptu speeches to the audience, interspersed with carefully rehearsed satirical couplets on topical social and political issues gleaned from the morning's newspapers. These were created by fellow actor Stepan Bondarchuk who was tasked with reading all the latest news and transforming juicy stories into punchy couplets. Each evening brought fresh comments and jokes about current events, religious superstitions, and even backstage theatrical disputes, thus transforming the stage into a kind of cabaret revue which blurred the vicious political landscape of Scotland with that of volatile contemporary Soviet Ukraine. Explaining the significance of the use of such strategies to members of his directorial lab, Kurbas insisted that mini-plays were to be created only when they substantively contributed to the themes of the original play.[27] In this case, the contemporary references were conceived as analogues of the historically distant references to Jesuitical equivocation and hypocrisy. History and contemporaneity, fiction and reality were conflated in a simultaneity of time and space. Through cabaret strategies Shakespeare became their contemporary.

In his second appearance, in the fourth act, the Fool entered as a peasant-reaper, singing a traditional Ukrainian harvest song and miming the act of mowing the whole stage as if it were a field. As he methodically did so, he clipped away shards of stage light. With each movement, the stage visibly darkened. Seemingly overcome with fatigue from his hard work, he approached the members of the audience who sat on bleachers in front of him and engaged in spontaneous exchanges with them, occasionally asking someone for a smoke. The futility of revolutionary political change, the enormous human cost of the recent bloody events (including the consequences of eleven changes of government in Kyiv), and the common man's compliance out of fear and inertia were brought home by the unexpected disjunction between the folksong – with its theme of the pleasures of seasonal bounty – and the symbolic destruction wrought by the Grim Reaper-Fool who indiscriminately and unemotionally destroyed the light of hope, the light of life. This sequence moved the action of the tragedy away from the great figures who committed violent deeds to those who lived within the world of the strongman's creation: the common man, unable to shape events, afraid, and perhaps even unwilling to be disturbed by what he could not change. In essence, this scene brought to the foreground the collusion of the thanes in Scotland's tragedy: their inaction that led to the murder of Lady Macduff, her family, and the unnamed many others of the play.

The Fool's third and last appearance, which occurred in the final moments of the play when Macduff comes out carrying the head of Macbeth, caused a major scandal. Here, Kurbas looked into the future, a future built on a society's acceptance of violence as the central tool of change. Still wearing his Fool's makeup (the mocking, grinning face) Buchma came in costumed as a bishop. He then crowned Malcolm to the music of an organ whose solemnity was ironically undercut by the delicate sounds of the piccolo and the coarser sound of the harmonium. Just as he did so, a new pretender approached, killed the kneeling Malcolm and seized the crown. Without pause, the Fool-Bishop once again chanted the same phrase: "There is no power, but from God." As the new king was about to arise, a new pretender murdered him and the ritual was repeated once again. Unmoved by all, only folly survived the madness of the moral wasteland of a state founded in violence and dominated by a series of identically self-interested strongmen. Such an explosive political conclusion to the play directly attacked the legitimacy of those in power through the provocative strategies of cabaret coupled with the potency of a world classic. With this final scene, the production gave the lie to the newly developing Soviet narratives that mythologized and aggrandized the Revolution and its aftermath. Using satire, grotesque, exaggeration, clowning, and discontinuity, Kurbas made the Fool the central figure of the tragedy. Only he, as the embodiment of folly, could survive the viciousness of the Scottish world, a world that resembled the contemporary moment in which Lenin's death, rather than bringing a halt to violence, instead unleashed a series of new power struggles. The production thus raised troubling questions about the consequences of bloody exchanges of power as the basis for a new society. It looked both backwards and forwards in time, bringing together medieval Scotland, the very recent past, and, eerily, even seemed to predict the Stalinist terror to come.

Rather than a "safe" production that confirmed classical ways of presenting Shakespeare or a rousing propaganda piece that presented a clear ideological message, the 1924 *Macbeth* attempted, in its yoking of the power of the classic with the strategies of cabaret, an examination of the ethics and the consequences of war, violence, and revolution. Such a powerful analysis could only be achieved with the use of a classic whose radical revision would provide a salutary shock to its audiences. Indeed, the fallout from, and polemical debates about, the production continued to reverberate throughout Kyiv for weeks and months to come,[28] for, as Simon Barker has pointed out, "A Shakespeare read provocatively for uncertainties, hesitations and contradictions – and against the smoothing narratives of war and nation…is a very unsettling experience indeed."[29]

Standing at the point of origin of avant-garde Ukrainian Shakespeare, Kurbas's 1924 *Macbeth* is an iconic production that remains deeply embedded in Ukrainian theatrical history not only because of its far-reaching investigation of theatrical practices (here, only touched upon) but also because it was rooted in the fertile ground of a cultural renaissance, one which gave rise to a whole spectrum of wild and jubilant experimentation.[30] But Kurbas's work in the Ukrainian theatre had grave consequences for its creator. He was charged with ignoring the building of socialism, directing Ukrainian theatre toward nationalist goals, creating incomprehensible formalist productions, and – most improbably –, conspiring to overthrow the government. Arrested in 1933, he was executed in 1937 on the personal orders of Stalin.[31]

Acerbic cabaret fared little better. De-toothed for nearly seventy years, cabaret's legacy was restored with the fall of the USSR (1991) which ushered in another period of cultural efflorescence. Growing up at the end of the millennium, young urban Ukrainians felt finally liberated from Soviet censorship and from the requirement of serving the state. Like the avant-garde of the 1910s and 1920s, at first they turned to pure aesthetics as a way of showing their rejection both of politics and of the endemic

Figure 11.3. Dakh Daughters and their "Freak Cabaret."

Source: Courtesy of the Dakh Daughters.

corruption that had characterized both the Soviet period and its aftermath. And, like Kurbas and his contemporaries whom they admired, this generation (as musicologist Maria Sonevytsky has argued) reached out into the wider world, no longer experiencing the need to be defined as "Ukrainian" but simply as artists.[32]

Among the most provocative of the many inheritors of cabaret's legacy is the Dakh Daughters, created in 2012 in Kyiv. Their self-styled "freak cabaret," growing out of a project aimed at ruthlessly testing the borders of theatre and music, was inspired by early Parisian cabaret.[33] Made up of seven professional actors, musicians, and dancers who play on fifteen different instruments and sing in different languages (Ukrainian, English, French, German, Russian) and in various Ukrainian dialects, the women are made up to look like actresses from the silent film era: white faces, smoky eyes, and blood-red lips. Their performance pieces draw from a variety of traditions, including Dada, the avant-garde, silent film, and the early cabaret. They also borrow lyrics from authors they find inspiring, among them, Shakespeare, Taras Shevchenko, and Joseph Brodsky, as well as "low" poets like Charles Bukowski, described by one source as "the king of the underground" thanks to his antics and deliberately clownish performances.[34]

The group's name is important in signaling their primary connection to theatre: they are first and foremost "daughters" of the theatre; more specifically, they are all actresses from the small independent (non-commercial), experimental Dakh Centre for Contemporary Arts run by its creator, artistic director, and producer Vlad (Vladyslav) Troitsky. His Dakh Theatre has developed a mixture of ritual, masks, dance, mime, drumming, and haunting music to tackle a wide-ranging theatrical repertoire including adaptations of Gogol, Dostoyevsky, Pirandello, Sophocles, Sarah Kane, Marius von Mayenburg, Martin McDonagh, and Shakespeare (*Richard II, King Lear,* and *Macbeth*).[35] The Dakh Daughters are also involved in other groups, including DakhaBrakha (a folk music quartet embracing different styles) and Perkalaba (a combination of Hutsul-folk, ska, and punk rock).

Like the Dadaists of the Zurich-based Cabaret Voltaire of the 1910s, the Dakh Daughters' took an adversarial stance aimed at negating the entrenched spirit of corrupt politics and belligerent attitudes. The multi-instrumentalists Nina Haretska, Ruslana Khazipova (Perkalaba), Tanya Havrylyuk (Tanya Tanya), Solomia Melnyk, Anna Nikitina, Natalia Hanalevych, and Natalia Zozul (Zo) explained their intention to open up "a space on the border of theatre and music" and cross "all possible limits in genres and styles."[36] Optimistically, they claimed for their ultimate goal "life-affirming performance about love, freedom and beauty which, at the end of the day...will save the world."[37] That beauty, in their interpretation, is revealed in high octane performances, in outrageous, boisterous, shifting, dynamic rhythms and song. From cabaret, the group has inherited the transgression of generic and cultural boundaries, the centrality of song and/as performance, the defiant humour, satirical edge, spectacle, and dissent. Bizarre and hyper-energized, centred in contemporary hipster counterculture, their freak cabaret returns us to the concept of the antic in the *OED*'s many definitions as grotesque gesture, dress, shape, movement, fantastical clowning, and theatrical representation.

The band's first hit song, "Rozy/Donbass" (Roses/Donbass), seen by 4.3 million viewers on YouTube[38] and now their signature song, opens with the ponderous chanting of the first quatrain of Shakespeare's Sonnet 35 in which the speaker insists upon the flawed nature of all existence – human, natural, and cosmic:

> No more be griev'd at that which thou hast done:
> Roses have thorns, and silver fountains mud;
> Clouds and eclipses stain both moon and sun,
> And loathsome canker lives in sweetest bud.

Combining Shakespeare's words with those of a Ukrainian folk song (about a woman going mushroom picking), a punk spirit, rap rhythms, and percussive sounds, the Dakh Daughters' collage is punctuated throughout with the raspy, shouted-out repetition of the word "Donbass." "Roses/Donbass," the song's title, alludes to the way in which the city of Donbass in Eastern Ukraine had been mythologized during the Soviet period as a city of a million roses, one for each inhabitant. It was, in fact, the industrial region of Eastern Ukraine, the centre of steel and coal production and the stronghold of the then president, Viktor Yanukovych. Going further back, its history is more sinister: it was also the area that, arguably, suffered most from the Holodomor, the mass starvation during the famine of 1932–3. The menacingly-chanted refrain of "Donbass," part of the aggressive cabaret style, looked backward in time reshaping history with cabaret madness. In retrospect, it was also as uncannily predictive as Kurbas's 1924 *Macbeth*.[39] The song, it must be emphasized, was written *before* the occupation of Crimea and the invasion of Eastern Ukraine. Indeed, the Daughters had publicly insisted on their rejection of the political in favour of an art-for-art stance or what musicologist Maria Sonevytsky has called "the privilege of political ambivalence."[40] When the song was created, in 2012, Donbass was undergoing a wide-ranging renaissance that included the opening of riverside cafés, bars, clubs, opera, theatre, a new soccer stadium, and a state-of-the-art international airport. In an online website, the Dakh Daughters explained the creative process:

We started creating the composition even before the Dakh Daughters band was born. While working on the School of non-theatrical art performance for GOGOLFEST-2012 in Kyiv….Then, in fact, we sang Shakespeare's sonnets (and not only the 35th, which was the basis of the composition Roses). We did this performance together with the DakhaBrakha band and other actors from the Dakh Theatre.

Marko Galanevych, joking at the rehearsal, attached the word *"Donbass"* to some lines of the sonnet, and it stuck to these musical sketches that we had already put together. And the folklore part, the children's song, Shakespeare's sonnet, and peculiar vocalizations filled it, as our various songs usually fill it when everyone brings some idea of their own and we put it together into one coherent canvas. Everything was fast and natural for us….The song was not intended as a special emphasis on events in the country. It was created a year before the Maidan and a year and a half before the war [on Donbas]. Therefore, we consider it prophetic to a certain extent.[41]

In late 2013, the Dakh Daughters were invited to bring their freak cabaret to the makeshift stage of the Euromaidan – the locus in central Kyiv for the massive protests against the government of president Yanukovych and the place where, shortly thereafter, presidential snipers fired and killed nearly seventy unarmed citizens. Here, their cabaret strategies, reinterpreted by the many hundreds of thousands of demonstrators disillusioned with power and tired of corruption, acquired a darker resonance, one that was cemented after the invasion and the war which followed. It is now a song that is both indelibly stained with the fact of war and also serves as a kind of anthem for disenchanted youth. The thousands of lives that had been taken or displaced at the point of invasion in 2014, became in 2022–3, and in 2023–4, millions. Cities, towns, hospitals, schools, universities, cultural monuments, museums, and libraries have been attacked, damaged, or destroyed. According to statistics provided by UNESCO, 125 religious buildings, twenty-nine museums, nineteen monuments, thirteen libraries, one archive, 144 buildings of historical or artistic importance, and 3793 educational institutions have been damaged or destroyed.[42] Theatre basements, often sought out as a place of refuge, have not always been able to guarantee safety. The complete destruction of the Donetsk Academic Regional Drama Theatre in Mariupol is one of the great tragedies of the war in which hundreds, including children, perished – despite the fact that, even from airspace, the word "Deti" (Children), etched in enormous Russian letters both in front of and behind the theatre, was easily visible. Not just human life, cultural memory is being destroyed. The Kherson Museum of Art was completely looted; its collection of fifteen thousand art objects was seized and taken away in five trucks. Chillingly, at the start of the war, the Russian Information Agency Novosti published Timofei Sergeitsev's article, "What Russia Should do with Ukraine," calling for a complete erasure of Ukrainian identity. Even the word "Ukraine," he wrote, cannot be allowed to exist. The war is justified, he asserted, because the re-education of Ukrainians is not possible.[43]

Music, poetry, theatre – these are the tools that help Ukrainians survive the barbarities of the current war. Performing throughout Western Europe during the war, the Dakh Daughters have been received by enthusiastic audiences. As one French reviewer noted, Ukraine is on fire, but the Dakh Daughters continue to sing, chant, and rap their "poetry of anger," their "frenzied hope," set to the rhythm of the drums of war.[44]

Despite the constant threats to their very existence, yet another cabaret was born in Kyiv. *Bunker Cabaret* is a show created by the Hooligan Art Community, an independent theatre company; its members, like the Dakh Daughters, are part of the first generation born in an independent Ukraine. Member Sam Kysly has described their experimental work as

that of "art hooligans," disruptors. Like the Dakh Daughters' Freak Cabaret, the Hooligans' performances are hybrids attempting to transcend
linguistic boundaries, connecting with their audiences through movement, song, dance, and emotion. In the past, the group created productions on topical issues such as the legacy of Chornobyl, on vulnerability
and violence, issues of masculinity and identity, and the experience of
refugees. They also produced a film, *Hooligan: In the Field* (2020)[45] about
creative life under the COVID-19 lockdown, At the beginning of 2022,
the Hooligan Art Community was preparing a show as part of the British
Council's Ukraine/UK season when the war erupted. Some of the young
performers became refugees, others remained by choice, while still others, as young men eligible for military service, were restricted from leaving the country. Although under rocket fire, those remaining began to
work on a show in a bunker in Kyiv. Recording short films of themselves
performing songs, satirical pieces, and sketches, they exchanged these
with those colleagues who were abroad. Working together virtually, they
created a new show, *Bunker Cabaret.* As their website states,

> The war tried to stop our work together but we have fought to sustain it.
> Making new work together is a lifeline for us; an opportunity to energize
> our work, take agency and support Ukraine the way we know how. This is
> the beginning a new chapter for our company and our lives.[46]

In a lengthy interview with Dominic Cavendish, theatre critic for the
Daily Telegraph in the UK, Hooligan member Sam Kysly confessed that

> making art was the only thing that saved me during this war. Because in the
> beginning I was so terrified and in shock. When the war started, I thought:
> I will never go on the stage, dance or sing or laugh. My feelings were com-
> pleted paralysed by this experience. There were moments when we started
> to work on this in a bunker in May…I thought: finally I can feel something,
> finally I can make art. I found that this process helped my soul to survive
> and helped my feelings come back to life.[47]

Eventually brought safely together, the Hooligan team performed *Bunker Cabaret* in Berlin in early February 2023 and, on the first anniversary
of the war, in the experimental space beneath Somerset House in central London. The Courtauld Institute's website describes *Bunker Cabaret*
"a powerful exploration of love versus totalitarianism and the personal
conflicts of making art in a time of war. By turns ironic, raw, funny, and
devastating, the performance starkly reveals the performer's individual
experiences of the war while communicating a shared humanity."[48]

The wild and whirling antics of cabaret return us to those hard questions: What is the role of art in times of war? What is the artist's responsibility in such circumstances? How can theatre embrace war's terrible spectrum, from barbarism to moments of great humanity and tenderness? Or, as Ukrainian scholar Nataliya Torkut has more specifically posed the question: "So is there a place for Shakespeare in a life that resembles a permanent prolonged Armageddon? Can we hear his voice when the wailing of sirens and the sounds of shelling merge into a violent and sinister apocalyptic motif?" Her answer is that, indeed, yes. Shakespeare's response to "the time is out of joint" is "to preserve the 'human in man.'" Like Kenneth Burke's proposed second way of dealing with war, Shakespeare offers up the complexity of the human – or, to use Hamlet's terms, it embraces both Hyperion *and* the satyr. With its galvanizing mix of the lyrical and the aggressive, the ugly and the beautiful, the derisive and the touching, the intellectual and the irrational, with its consistent and irreverent crossing of cultural and generic boundaries, cabaret resembles Hamlet's antic disposition. It engages in an oblique fashion with the question, "*Who are you as a human being?*" Indeed, that question is truly at the basis of everything, including the Dakh Daughters' most recent work, *Danse macabre,* created in 2022. Not inspired by Shakespeare but, going further back in time, to the medieval tradition of the Dance of Death, this project reaches for a language of performance that can withstand and express the ravages of war, the loss, grief, horror but also the beauty and love.[49]

12
Afterword: Shakespeare at War Today

A sense of déja vu, disbelief, and dread engulfed many people around the world on the morning of 22 February 2024. For scholars of Ukrainian history, President Putin's declaration, that Ukraine, and its language and culture, do not exist, chillingly echoed the words of nineteenth century tsarist Minister Pyotr Valuev's assertion that no Ukrainian language ever existed, does exist, or ever could exist. Since the war began, Russian missiles and drones have targeted the core of identity: heritage, language, and cultural memory. Theatres, museums, churches, schools, archives, and even a publishing house have been destroyed. Under the guise of protecting art objects, soldiers have removed and appropriated historical artifacts and paintings. As Charlotte Higgins of *The Guardian* has perspicaciously observed, "Russia's aggression is an event of shocking magnitude in every individual life in Ukraine, and in lives elsewhere, too. The war is not only happening on the frontline but in homes and hearts."[1]

Performers, writers, poets, and artists, including one of its most famous poets and also a rock star, Serhii Zhadan, joined the army. Others have become part of a network of volunteers assisting with humanitarian efforts by helping to raise funds, providing food and temporary shelter, assisting refugees, and forwarding medications and other products to the front. Some theatres, like the Les Kurbas Lviv Academic Theatre, have been utterly transformed by the requirements of the war. The boards where actors used to tread became a place of refuge, serving nearly a thousand people who have been able to rest, sleep, eat, and obtain clothing there, all free of charge.[2]

The barbarous and unprovoked war has, however, led to some surprising and ironic consequences, one of which is the widespread efflorescence of Ukrainian arts, culture, and scholarship. The attempt to eradicate Ukrainian culture, language, and identity has led to its opposite. Such fertile creativity in the midst of war, devastation, and uncertainty cannot help but recall the 1920s, when, despite similar challenges, Les Kurbas first brought Shakespeare to the Ukrainian stage. Remarkably, in today's chaotic and uncertain circumstances, Shakespeare continues to matter. The previous chapters have shown only a few examples of the way in which Shakespeare has become deeply embedded in Ukrainian cultural life. During the past century and a half, Shakespeare has taken on a multitude of roles: as mirror, prism, cultural mediator, inspirer of cross-cultural communication, source of solace, and as a megaphone, distinctly proclaiming Ukrainians' cultural values to the West, especially in times when these views could not otherwise be openly expressed. As Ukrainian scholar Nataliya Torkut has emphasized, Shakespeare has also acted as a "provocateur" who continues to stimulate new discourses, ideas, works, and thoughts.[3] His generative influence certainly remains true even, or especially, in the current circumstances of the war in Ukraine.

Beyond signalling Ukrainians' existence and resilience, creativity has been essential to life as a coping mechanism, as therapy, distraction, and as a connecting and humanizing activity. The production of *Hamlet* directed by Rostyslav Derzhypilsky in the basement of the Ivano-Frankivsk Drama Theatre (mentioned in Chapter One) and first produced in the days after the war began is but one small example of the many productions that have taken place since 2022. Indeed, theatrical performances in shelters began to be created throughout Ukraine. In 2023 alone, *Richard III, The Two Gentlemen of Verona, King Lear, Romeo and Juliet*, as well as *Hamlet*, were all performed. Drawing attention to the improbability of wartime creativity, the Frankivsk Theatre's website announced its eighty-fifth season with the following: "We didn't know it was impossible. That's why we did it."[4]

One of the many notable live productions was *King Lear*, adapted and directed by Vyacheslav Yehorov, with Theatre Studio of IDP's (Internationally Displaced Persons) Uzhik, and first performed in Uzhorod in the early days of the war with a cast entirely made up of amateur actors, all refugees. Fleeing to this town in Western Ukraine to escape the war in the East, they discovered a mirror of their loss, displacement, and anguish in Shakespeare's tragedy. But the play also spoke powerfully to them about the ultimate importance of love, the overarching theme of the whole production. The company's story of refugees brought together through Shakespeare inspired a documentary, *King Lear: How We Looked for Love During the War*, directed by Dmytro Hreshko, and premiered at the SEEfest festival in San Francisco in 2023. In June 2024, the stage production travelled to Stratford-upon-Avon where it was performed at The Other Place; it has also been announced for the Royal Shakespeare Company's 2024–5 season.[5]

Figure 12.1. Oleksiy Hnatkovsky as Hamlet in Yuri Andrukhovych's translation of *Hamlet*. Performed at the Ivano-Frankivsk National Academic Drama Theater, directed by Rostyslav Derzhypilsky, 2022.

Source: Photo by Valentyn Kuzan. Courtesy of the Ivano-Frankivsk Drama Theatre.

Figure 12.2. Lear and the Fool, Uzhorod *King Lear*, adapted and directed by Vyacheslav Yehorov, with Theatre Studio of IDP's Uzhik, 2024.

Source: Photo by Pamela Rath ©RSC.

Figure 12.3. Titania (Daria Hrachova) from *A Midsummer Night's Dream*, directed by Andriy Bilous, Molodyi Theatre, Kyiv, 2024.

Source: Photo by Sofiia Sanina. Courtesy of the Kyiv National Academic Molodyi Theatre.

Another prominent Ukrainian company that first performed at home (at the First Ukrainian Shakespeare Festival) and then abroad is The Kyiv National Academic Molodyi Theatre (its name a homage to Kurbas's first company). *A Midsummer Night's Dream*, directed by Andriy Bilous, travelled to the 2023 York International Shakespeare Festival, where it was acknowledged as a highlight of the whole program. Performed entirely in Ukrainian before a British audience, the company asserted the existence of their language and culture and showed how Shakespeare could be a bridge to cultural understanding and a sharing of values. In August 2024, their new production, *Comedy of Errors* with its theme of shipwreck, loss, and rediscovery, was performed at the Verona Shakespeare Fringe Festival.

It is in this context of cultural activity as a necessity, and as visible, celebratory display of identity that the First Ukrainian Shakespeare Festival took place in Ivano-Frankivsk from 17–22 June 2024. In an interview just a few months earlier, the festival's catalyst, the ever energetic Rostyslav Derzhypilsky, explained that the war offered the "perfect moment" for such an event to create international platforms to strengthen and amplify Ukrainian voices. He was also inspired by the sold-out performances of

Figure 12.4. Web poster, first Ukrainian Shakespeare Festival, 2024.

Source: Design by studio "the91 büro." Courtesy of the Ivano-Frankivsk Drama Theatre.

his production of *Romeo and Juliet*. Recalling Shakespeare's past connections with Ukraine in times of struggle, he specifically evoked Les Kurbas's 1920 *Macbeth* and Yosyp Hirniak's 1943 *Hamlet*. In each case, he noted, Shakespeare was part of Ukraine's struggle to affirm its desire "to be."[6] His humanizing works offer a counter to the dehumanization of war.

Shakespeare productions, festivals, and related events all carry the weight of the times but also the desire to strengthen, forge, and renew international connections. Theatre scholar Maya Harbuziuk explained that the whole process "is about the return of Ukrainian theatre to the European cultural space" from which it emerged "more than four centuries ago and [to which it] is genetically and mentally connected."[7] More than just ideological weapons, cultural events also provide spiritual resources: they unify, fortify, as well as mobilize. As director and founder of the ProEnglish Theatre in Kyiv, Alex Borovensky has pointed out, "We saw the tanks" and then had "this urgent understanding: create art or die."[8]

Those who have sought refuge in other countries have also felt the call to create and tell the story of Ukraine. In Canada, at the Langham Court

Theatre in Victoria, B.C., Diana Budiachenko, originally from Odesa, co-directed *A Dictionary of Emotions in War Time*, a co-production of Help Ukraine Vancouver Island Society and Langham Court. The production presented the stark details of the Russian invasion, "educating audiences in Victoria about the atrocities of war."[9] *First Métis Man of Odesa*, co-written and acted by its creators, playwright Métis Matthew MacKenzie and Ukrainian actress Mariya Khomutova, now settled in Toronto, tells the story of their real-life romance set against the background of the war and their need and responsibility to share the story of Ukraine with the world. For refugee Anastasiia Haiduchenko, a member of the Artis troupe in Calgary, theatre "is the way I heal my soul."[10]

Poland, where many Ukrainian refugees have fled, has also been an active centre of creative endeavours aimed at putting a spotlight on Ukraine's plight. *Hamlet Syndrome*, an award winning documentary film created by Elwira Niewiera and Piotr Rosołowski, follows a group of young Ukrainians preparing to stage an adapted *Hamlet*; in articulating their wartime experiences and traumas, they discover thematic mirrors in Shakespeare's play. *History of Ukraine*, a "performative documentary," created by three Ukrainian women (Daria Bohdan, Vasylyna Martseniuk, and Sofia Onyshchenko) in Poland, uses their personal experiences of the war to explore themes of exile and war, creativity, resilience, and self-expression. In a play whose text changes with the circumstances of the war, co-creator Sofia Onyshchenko explained that she conceives of performance as a kind of megaphone: "I want Ukraine to be heard.…In our performance, we are the voice of millions of Ukrainians." Releasing their deep feelings in front of the audience, the actor-writers are sharing, not analysing: "We are not yet at the stage of reflecting on the trauma. We are at the stage of bleeding wounds that cannot begin to heal because Russian troops are in my home." For Onyshchenko, performing is not escape but "a return to reality…remembering that there is war, that this is really happening, is necessary. Forgetting and getting used to it is a crime for me."[11] Despite the continuing trauma, Onyshchenko insists that they do not perform or view themselves as victims: "we are warriors and creators."

History of Ukraine is but one example of a flourishing theatre scene that has its roots in Ukraine. Since 2022, a dizzying number of events have taken place, including various festivals. The 24th International Theatre Festival Melpomene of Tauria: Voices of Kherson Region (June 2024) involved more than thirty theatres from Ukraine, Poland, Romania, Portugal, and Georgia. The first Ukrainian fringe festival, "Steel Standing," a ten-day event organized by Alex Borovensky, opened in August 2024 to coincide with celebrations of Ukrainian Independence Day. Ambitiously intended that the festival become "Edinburgh number 2," Borovensky has stressed the importance of humour: "[I]f we were to take war seriously, we would die. We laugh in the face of war, and this is what I believe Ukrainians can give to the world. A sense of humour and, of course, the president is a comedian."[12] The "Golden Lion" Theatre Festival in Lviv, now into its 35th edition in October 2024 took as its theme "Theatre is the language of identity."

Theatre and film are not the only art forms that are flourishing: poetry, art and photo exhibitions, classical music recitals, chamber opera performances, dance, staged readings, all these have multiplied. Children's theatre has a particularly important function in helping to alleviate the trauma of war. So, for example, The Academic State Puppet Theatre in Kharkiv has been performing for children and their families in metro stations, spaces where musicians and poets have also shared their works with those seeking shelter.

Ukrainian performers and artists have travelled the world in their role as unofficial cultural ambassadors, displaying and sharing Ukraine's rich culture and heritage that, until recently, have been marginalized by a focus on Russia. Art exhibitions have taken place in Madrid, Vienna, New York, and at the Royal Academy in London. Exhibiting Ukrainian avant-garde art of the 1900–30s, these shows have challenged the old stereotype of Ukrainians as limited to folk arts and have helped in the process of decolonizing artists that had been mislabeled as Russian. At the Venice Biennale in 2024, Ukraine presented *Repeat After Me,* a documentary film of ordinary Ukrainians each of whom imitate the sounds of war, from drones to missiles, then encourage viewers to repeat them so that they can remember and recognize how war sounds. At the Vienna Contemporary 2024, the works of Ukrainian artist Veronika Harchenko looked back on the "black void" of the USSR: that is, on the "distorted" and "romanticized" memory' of the Soviet period in order to begin to understand the "colonial trauma" of its former nations and to bring to the world's attention the erasure of identity that had taken place when "Soviet" was equated with "Russian." The Kharkiv National Opera Theatre successfully performed in Baltic and Central European countries for several months. The National Ballet of Ukraine has gone on a multi-city tour of the USA, beginning in Washington's Kennedy Centre for the Performing Arts, while The Kyiv National Academic Operetta Theatre has performed Ukrainian and zarzuela music in Madrid, leading Ukraine's ambassador to Spain to assert that music is not only "a powerful tool that strengthens the spirit, inspires and nourishes hope," but it also demonstrates that Ukrainian "cultural heritage is an essential part of the vibrant and diverse map of world culture."[13]

Figure 12.5. National Ballet of Ukraine.

Source: Photo by Inara Prusakova/Shutterstock.com.

Through shared performance, exhibition, and cooperation, Ukraine's artists and performers have engaged in creating a vibrant cultural front to display Ukraine's rich cultural heritage, to show that Ukraine exists, and also, as importantly, to insist that it is part of world culture. And the world is discovering Ukraine. Google Arts & Culture has launched a new section, "Ukraine is Here," dedicated to Ukrainian art with images, stories, 3D models of museums and landmarks, a 360-degree video of a theatrical performance, and virtual galleries. Informing, preserving, and promoting Ukrainian culture but also maintaining and celebrating Ukrainian identity, these initiatives also open it up to the world for exploration.

In theatre, education, and scholarship, Shakespeare has continued to be a significant force. The Shakespeare Centre in Zaporizhzhia headed by Nataliya Torkut has maintained classes in hallways, basements, and bunkers, as well as online. As Torkut has asserted, "The public resonance that Shakespearean performances evoke in times of war also testifies to their potent art's therapeutic potential."[14] "Shakespeare Days" – an annual month-long Shakespeare-themed series of activities and events, not only took place despite the war but grew in size, engaging students from across eleven regions of the country and an equal number of universities, colleges, and schools. Concerts, public lectures, panel discussions, round-tables, and workshops all continued, unabated. Ukrainian Shakespeare scholars have continued to participate in international conferences and to contribute to scholarly journals. Torkut fervently believes in the power of Shakespeare and, more generally culture, to help Ukraine survive the war. As she has claimed, "It is the essence of our human nature that we can't live without beauty, without something that is much more important than our everyday situation."[15] These beliefs have been translated into active service. Among their many projects is a collaboration with Flute Theatre (Kelly Hunter, artistic director) using Shakespeare as therapy to help support Ukrainian refugees with autistic children. Other projects have focused on working with mental health professionals using theatre to assist those with war-related trauma.

Shakespeare has helped strengthen ties with the West, particularly through the active network of Shakespearean associations and organizations, as well as through collaborations with individual scholars. The solidarity of Shakespeareans with Ukrainians during this difficult time was notably marked by a very special event on 23 April 2023. Nataliya Torkut, along with her colleague Maya Harbuziuk, Dean of the Faculty of Culture and Arts at the Ivan Franko National University in Lviv, were the special guests representing Ukraine in the parade at the annual commemorations in Stratford-upon-Avon marking Shakespeare's birthday. Torkut received a special honour: she was invited to offer the toast "To the Immortal Memory of William Shakespeare" at the official lunch on Shakespeare's 459th birthday. Her moving speech is reprinted here with her permission. Written from the perspective of a woman experiencing the unexpected horrors of war yet again visited on Ukraine, Torkut's toast fittingly – and best – sums up the significance of Shakespeare to Ukraine today.

Dear Ladies and Gentlemen, Dear Friends!

I must begin by thanking those who have made it possible for me, almost incredibly, to come from the midst of a cruel war to this peaceful and joyous celebration. So I thank the kind Pragnell family who have enabled me to be here; and I thank the University of Birmingham, especially its Shakespeare Institute, who have sponsored my visa.

I have the honour to represent here my native country, Ukraine, which is currently experiencing the most dramatic period of its centuries-long history, and whose sacrificial heroism will determine what the future of the world will look like. It is there, so far away from this elegant marquee, in the half-ruined but still defiant Ukrainian cities, and in the wiped-out Ukrainian villages that have been surprised, like Macduff's castle, by a tyrant, that the question of whether our civilisation is to be or not to be is being decided right now, at this very moment.

On behalf of my country, I am here to thank, above all the other inhabitants of this blessed town, past and present, William Shakespeare. By appealing to our emotions and aesthetic sensations, our critical thinking and the subconscious, Shakespeare's poetic genius is today not only transmitting eternal values but also inspiring their defence. The generous plurality and freedom of expression supremely exemplified in the contents of the First Folio, 400 years old this year, are under threat in 2023 as never before. Today, Ukraine is fighting not only for its own future and independence: we are fighting for the free civilization which Shakespeare has helped shape. We are fighting for life and love, freedom and dignity, honour and goodness, for the right to be.

Who am I? I am a mother, whose son, like thousands of other Ukrainian people, is at the frontline today. He is fighting for our freedom and for yours too. I am a grandmother whose grandchildren are forced to hide from Russian cruise missiles in the basement of the kindergarten and the school bomb shelter several times a day. I am a university professor whose online lectures are interrupted daily by air raid warnings and whose students can tell by ear what exactly has come flying from the northern neighbour: S-300 missiles, Shaheds, missiles of the "Calibre" type, or Kinzhals.

I am the head of the Ukrainian Shakespeare Centre, which has kept on working throughout the war – staging performances, teaching students, and organizing symposia, even when these have had to take place by hand-held torchlight in bomb shelters. Our members know that Shakespeare has always been part of our country's long history of resistance to oppression. Ukrainian translations of Shakespeare were banned under the tsars; our great modernist director of Shakespeare, Les Kurbas, was shot under the Soviets; our great poet Dmytro Palamarchuk completed his Ukrainian rendition of the Sonnets in one of Stalin's labour camps. But Ukrainians have defiantly performed *Hamlet* in their own language from the 19th century to the 21st, and despite the opposition of the Kremlin we published a Ukrainian translation of the entire Complete Works even in 1986. The current war has only made that Shakespearean resistance more determined. The underground Shakespearean theatre in Ivano-Frankivsk is now an air-raid shelter, but it is still performing. The Shakespearean directors Oleksiy Kravchuk and Ihor Zadnipriany, along with Andriy Petruk, the first Ukrainian actor to play Florizel, are now in uniform at the front, to name only three. But in spring 2023 their compatriots are attending productions of *Richard III*, *The Two Gentlemen of Verona*, *Hamlet*, *King Lear* and *Romeo and Juliet*, and our students are as passionate about their great English colleague as always.

On behalf of my people, I thank the Government of the United Kingdom for its powerful support. I thank Stratford Town Hall for flying my country's flag.

I thank the RSC for staging a concert in support of my country; and I thank those here who have given shelter to our refugees, and donations towards our cause. I thank all of you, dear friends, for your sincere prayers and ceaseless help. As Le Beau says in *As You Like It*, "Hereafter in a better world than this, I shall desire more love and knowledge of you." But for now, before I return to the war, I thank above all the man of Stratford whom I regard as our greatest shared asset and our greatest ally. If you will raise your glasses with me, I give you the toast: To the Immortal Memory of William Shakespeare.

Nataliya Torkut

Notes

1 Irena R. Makaryk, "Soviet Views of Shakespeare's Comedies," *Shakespeare Studies* (1982): 281–314.
2 Irena R. Makaryk, "Calibans All: Shakespeare at the Intersection of Colonialisms," in *Multicultural Shakespeare: Translation, Appropriation, Performance* 1 (2004): 105–16. Reprinted here with the permission of Wydawnictwo Uniwersytetu Łódzkiego.
3 Irena R. Makaryk, "'North by North West': Shevchenko and Shakespeare," *Slavic Drama: A Question of Innovation, Proceedings,* eds. Andrew Donskov and Richard Sokoloski (Ottawa: University of Ottawa Press, 1991). Reprinted with the permission of the University of Ottawa Press.
4 Irena R. Makaryk, "Ophelia as Poet: Lesya Ukrainka and the Woman as Artist," *Canadian Review of Comparative Literature / Revue Canadienne de Littérature Comparée* (1993): 338–54. Reprinted with the permission of its Editor.
5 Irena R. Makaryk, "Periphery against Centre: *Hamlet* in Early Soviet Ukrainian Poetry," in *Living Record: Essays in Memory of Constantine Bida,* ed. Irena R. Makaryk (Ottawa: University of Ottawa Press, 1991), 281–93. Reprinted with the permission of the University of Ottawa Press.
6 Irena R. Makaryk, *Shakespeare in the Undiscovered Bourn: Les' Kurbas, Ukrainian Modernism and Early Soviet Cultural Politics* (Toronto: University of Toronto Press, 2004).
7 Irena R. Makaryk, "Shakespeare Right and Wrong," *Theatre Journal* 50, no. 2 (1998): 153–63; and Irena R. Makaryk, "The Perfect Production: Les Kurbas's Analysis of the Early Soviet Audience," *Gramma: Journal of Theory and Criticism* 15 (2007),: 89–109. Reprinted with the generous permission of both Presses.
8 Irena R. Makaryk, "Wartime Shakespeare," in *Shakespeare in the Worlds of Communism and Socialism,* ed. Irena R. Makaryk and Joseph G. Price (Toronto: University of Toronto Press, 2006), 136–52.

9 Irena R. Makaryk, "Shakespeare Inside Out: *Hamlet* as Intertext in the USSR 1934–43," in *Shakespeare in Cold War Europe: Conflict, Commemoration, Celebration,* eds. Erica Sheen and Isabel Karremann (Palgrave Macmillan, 2016), 116–34. Reprinted with permission from Springer Nature BV.

10 Chapter Nine incorporates sections from Irena R. Makaryk, "Stalin and Shakespeare," in *International Shakespeare Yearbook* 18, eds. Natalia Khomenko, Tom Bishop, and Alexa Alice Joubin (Cambridge University Press, 2021): 43–60. Special issue Soviet and Post-Soviet Shakespeare. Reprinted by permission of Taylor and Francis Group.

11 Irena R. Makaryk, "Divergence and Convergence: The 'Universal' versus the National Bard," in *Memorialising Shakespeare. Commemoration and Collective Identity,* eds. Monika Smialkowska and Edmund G.C. King (Palgrave Shakespeare Studies, 2022), 117–47. Reprinted with permission from Springer Nature BV.

12 Irena R. Makaryk, "Antic Dispositions: Shakespeare, War and Cabaret," a conference paper delivered in Stratford-upon-Avon at the International Shakespeare Conference in 2018, was published in *Shakespeare Survey* 27, Special issue Shakespeare and War (Cambridge University Press, 2019), 86–97, edited by Emma Smith. Reprinted here by permission of the Editor and Cambridge University Press.

1. Introduction

1 The President's speech was widely reported by the global media. His Address to the UK Parliament may be found on YouTube: "Zelensky Answers Hamlet," 12 March 2022, https://www.youtube.com/watch?v=DO9WUcyozRQ. The Address was also reprinted in Volodymyr Zelensky, *A Message from Ukraine. Speeches, 2019–2022* (New York, Crown, 2022), 65–9. The *Hamlet* reference comes on page 69.

2 Michael Dobson, "Elsinore's Star Bullshitter, *London Review of Books,* vol. 40, no. 17, 13 September 2018, https://www.lrb.co.uk/the-paper/v40/n17/michael-dobson/elsinore-s-star-bullshitter.

3 Annie Brisset, *A Sociocritique of Translation: Theatre and Alterity in Quebec (1966–1988),* trans. by Roger Gannon and Rosalind Gill (Toronto: University of Toronto Press, 1996), 5.

4 For an excellent concise history of Ukraine, see Serhii Plokhy, *The Gates of Europe: A History of Ukraine* (New York: Basic Books, 2015) and his companion volume, *The Frontline: Essays on Ukraine's Past and Present* (Cambridge: Harvard Series in Ukrainian Studies, 2023). Also see Orest Subtelny, *Ukraine, a History* (Edmonton: University of Alberta Press, 2000) and the many publications of Paul Magocsi, including *Ukraine: An Illustrated History* (Seattle: University of Washington Press, 2007). For a discussion of

literature, culture, and discourses of imperialism and postcolonialism, see Myroslav Shkandrij, *Russia and Ukraine: Literature and the Discourse of Empire from Napoleonic to Postcolonial Times* (Montreal: McGill-Queen's University Press, 2001). Also see the magisterial multivolume work of Mykhailo Hrushevsky, *History of Ukraine-Rus'* (Edmonton: Canadian Institute of Ukrainian Studies, 1997–2021).

5 For a discussion of the Hetmanate see Zenon Kohut, *Russian Centralism and Ukrainian Autonomy: Imperial Absorption of the Hetmanate, 1760s–1830s* (Cambridge: Harvard Ukrainian Research Institute, 1988). For a more recent view, see Victor Ostapchuk, "Cossack Ukraine in and out of Ottoman Orbit, 1648–1681" in *The European Tributary States of the Ottoman Empire in the Sixteenth and Seventeenth Centuries*, Series The Ottoman Empire and its Heritage, Volume: 53, eds. Gábor Kármán and Lovro Kunčević (Leiden: Brill, 2013), 123–52.

6 Valerian Revutsky, "The Act of Ems (18 A76) and Its Effect on Ukrainian Theatre," *Nationalities Papers* (Charleston) 5.1 (1977): 67–77. For an analysis from the Russian perspective and for the complete text of the Valuev Circular and the Ems Ukaz, see A.I. Miller, *The Ukrainian Question: The Russian Empire and Nationalism in the Nineteenth Century* (Budapest, New York: Central European University Press, 2003), Appendix I, "The Circular of the Minister of the Interior P.A. Valuev to the Kiev, Moscow and Petersburg Censorship Committees, 18 July 1863," and Appendix 2. "The conclusions of the Special Council regarding measures to curb Ukrainophile propaganda, after corrections in accordance with remarks made by Alexander II on 18 May in the town of Ems." Miller's book is available as an online ACLS Humanities Book: https://www.fulcrum.org /concern/monographs/7p88ch04n.

7 I explore the consequences of these devastating prohibitions and attempts at erasing Ukrainian culture in the first chapter of my *Shakespeare in the Undiscovered Bourn: Les' Kurbas, Ukrainian Modernism, and Early Soviet Cultural Politics* (Toronto: University of Toronto Press, 2004).

8 Revutsky, "The Act of Ems," 72.

9 So according to Tobilevych's wife, Sofiia, in her book Sofiia Tobilevych, *Zhyttia Ivana Tobilevycha (Karpenka-Karoho)* (Kharkiv: Mystetstvo, 1945) cited in multiple sources, for example, by Oleksa Novyts'kyi with the participation of Herbert Marshall, in "Taras Shevchenko i Aira Oldridzh," in Herbert Marshall and Mildred Stock, *Aira Oldridzh. Nehretians'kyi trahik*, trans. Oleksa Novyts'kyi and Valentyn Shyhans'kyi (Kyiv: Mystetstvo, 1966), 169–219 (200). The same claim appears in most Soviet studies of Tobilevych. See, for examples, L. Stetsenko, *I. Karpenko-Karyi. (I.K. Tobilevych) Zhyttia i tvorcha diial'nist'* [I. Karpenko-Karyi (I.K. Tobilevych) Life and Creative Activities] (Kyiv: Derzhavne vydavnytstvo obrazotvorchoho mystetstva i muzychnoi literatury,

1957), 196; Ivan Pil'huk, *Ivan Karpenko-Karyi (Tobilevych)* (Kyiv: Molod',
1976), 26. The estimated number of *versts* Tobilevych travelled vary in these
accounts, from forty-nine to sixty. Sofiia recalled that Tobilevych had told her
that, after walking all night, he arrived at dawn in Yelysavethrad (since 2016,
Kropyvnytskyi) and waited all day for the theatre to open in the evening.
Astonished and moved by Aldridge's passionate Othello and by the perfidy of
Iago, Tobilevych then walked the same long route back home to his home in
Bobrynets.' A year-by-year detailed chronology of Tobilevych's life and work
may be found in O.S. Tsyban'iova's *Litopys zhyttia i tvorchosti I. Karpenka-Karoho
(I.K. Tobilevycha)* [Chronicle of the Life and Creative Work of I. Karpenko-
Karyi (I.K.Tobilevych] (Kyiv: Dnipro, 1967); the Aldridge episode is recorded
on page 6 alongside the only other significant event of 1861, the death of
Taras Shevchenko. Notably, Tobilevych derived the second half of his stage
name (Karyi) from a favourite character (Hnat Karyi) in Shevchenko's play,
Nazar Stodolia that Tobilevych had played when still a young amateur (the first
half of his stage name, Karpenko, was a nod to his father's name, Karpo). See
I. Skrypnyk, *Ivan Karpenko-Karyi (Ivan Karpovych Tobilevych) Literaturnyi portret*
[Ivan Karpenko-Karyi (Ivan Karpovych Tobilevych) A Literary Portrait] (Kyiv:
Khudozhnia literatura, 1960), 6.

10 The most extensive study of Ira Aldridge has been made by Bernth Lindfors
in his multivolume examination of the details of Aldridge's tours. Material
on Aldridge's friendship with Taras Shevchenko and the actor's subsequent
tour of Ukrainian cities, including his influence on Tobilevych, appears
in Bernth Lindfors, *Ira Aldridge. The Last Years, 1855–1867* (Rochester:
University of Rochester Press, 2015). Lindfors, who does not read
Ukrainian, is dependent upon the information of Iryna Vanina, *Ukrains'ka
Shekspiriana* (Kyiv: Mystetstvo, 1964).

11 The detailed circumstances surrounding the first productions of
Shakespeare in this volatile political and cultural period of the early
twentieth century is the subject of my 2004 book, Irena R. Makaryk,
*Shakespeare in the Undiscovered Bourn: Les' Kurbas, Ukrainian Modernism, and
Early Soviet Politics* (Toronto: University of Toronto Press, 2004). See chapter
four for a discussion of Panas Saksahans'kyi's production of *Othello*.

12 See the entry for "|Mykola Storozhenko," *Entsyklopediia ukrainoznavstva*, ed.
Volodymyr Kubiyovych, vol. 8 (Naukove tovarystvo im. Shevchenka: Paris,
New York, 1976), 3065–6; *Internet Encyclopedia of Ukraine*: https://www
.encyclopediaofukraine.com/display.asp?linkpath=pages%5CS%5CT%5
CStorozhenkoMykolaI.htm; also see "Nikolai Storozhenko" in Wikipedia:
https://en.wikipedia.org/wiki/Nikolay_I._Storozhenko.

13 These restrictions, restored in 1910 by Interior Minister Piotr Stolypin, were
never entirely lifted but simply became null and void following the February
Revolution of 1917–8.

14 Kyiv, a centre of modernist experimentation in all the arts, is the focus
of Irena R. Makaryk and Virlana Tkacz's *Modernism in Kyiv: Jubilant
Experimentation* (Toronto: University of Toronto Press, 2000).

15 Mykola Khvyl'ovyi, "On Copernicus of Frauenberg or The ABC of the
Asiatic Renaissance in Art (A Second Letter to Literary Youth)," in *Quo
vadis?* 1925. Rpt. in Myroslav Shkandrij, *The Cultural Renaissance in Ukraine,
Polemical Pamphlets, 1925–26* (Edmonton: Canadian Institute of Ukrainian
Studies, 1986), 39–93 (75).

16 A historical timeline for major changes of government and key events
during this very complex period may be found in Makaryk and Tkacz,
Modernism in Kyiv, Appendix 2, 584–7.

17 Les' Kurbas cited in an interview (by S. Bondarchuk?), "Do postanovky
Makbeta v 4 maisterni M.O.B.," *Bil'shovyk* (Kyiv) 3 (971) (1 April 1924): 6.

18 Ola Hnatiuk, *Courage and Fear*, trans. Ewa Siwak (Boston: Harvard Ukrainian
Research Institute, 2019), translated from Polish.

19 See https://www.artsteps.com/view/657d8dcb3e7698b59c6de2a7

20 Peter Brook brought a production of *Hamlet* starring a young Paul Scofield
to Moscow shortly after Stalin's death. Much discussed at the time, it may
have influenced Nord. Soviet spectators could see one of thirteen live
performances in Moscow or they could view the production on television.
Many were struck by the youth of the Danish Prince in contrast to the
considerably older Evgenii Samoilov who was playing the same role in
Nikolai Okhlopkov's Soviet version. The extreme simplicity of the staging
was also remarked upon. The austerity of the production also chimed
with Les' Kurbas's experiments in the 1920s. For a nuanced analysis of
Brook's production and its Cold War contexts, see Sarah Davies, "From
Iron Curtain to Velvet Curtain? Peter Brook's Hamlet and the Origins
of British–Soviet Cultural Relations during the Cold War," *Contemporary
European History* 27, 4 (2018), 601–26, doi https://doi.org/10.1017
/S0960777318000395.

21 A thoughtful review of this production and of early post-independence
Ukrainian produtions is Bohdan Korneliuk and Daria Moskvitina's
"Cabbages and Kings: Posthumanistic Shakespeare on the Contemporary
Ukrainian Stage," *Multicultural Shakespeare: Translation, Appropriation and
Performance* vol. 24 (39), 2021: 213–24 (215).

22 https://www.proenglishtheatre.com/.

23 Video of Rostyslav Derzhypilsky recorded on 7 March 2024: https://www
.facebook.com/dramteatr.if/videos/287142330916043/.

24 https://ifshakespeare.in.ua/en.

25 "In Ivano-Frankivsk, the Shakespeare Festival has begun," The Ministry of
Culture and Information Policy of Ukraine (MCIP), https://mcip.gov.ua
/en/news/in-ivano-frankivsk-the-shakespeare-festival-has-begun/.

26 Professor of Shakespeare at the University of Worcester, Nicoleta Cinpoeş
   was an early proponent of the Festival. See https://www.worcester.ac.uk
   /about/news/2023-academic-in-bid-to-help-ukraine-preserve-its-heritage
   and also Andy Giddings, "Academic Watched Shakespeare in Ukrainian
   Bomb Shelters," *BBC News*, West Midlands, 20 September 2023, https://
   www.bbc.com/news/uk-england-hereford-worcester-66847690.
27 Plokhy, *The Gates of Europe*, 364.

2. Calibans All: Shakespeare at the Intersection of Colonialisms

1 Panteleimon Kulish, *Tvory* [Works], Vol. 6 (L'viv: Prosvita, 1910), 457–8;
  my translation. Kulish's enormous oeuvre is currently the focus of a major
  republication project under the "Krytyka" label and under the general
  editorship of George Grabowicz. The first volume of his translations
  (*Othello, Troilus and Cressida,* and *Comedy of Errors*) was published in an
  impressive format in Kyiv in 2020.
2 Herbert Marshall and Mildred Stock, *Ira Aldridge: The Negro Tragedian*
  (New York: Macmillan, 1958), were among the very first scholars to draw
  significant attention to Aldridge's life and career. Scholarly and popular
  interest in Ira Aldridge has been growing since the turn of this century
  and includes Krystyna Kujawińska-Courtney and Maria Łukowska's eds., *Ira
  Aldridge (1807–1867): The Great Shakespearean Tragedian on the Bicentennial
  Anniversary of his Birth* (Frankfurt, Berlin, Brussels, New York: Peter
  Lang, 2009); and the popular biography by Martin Hoyles, *Ira Aldridge:
  Celebrated 19th Century Actor* (UK: Hansib Publications, 2008). Broader
  awareness of Aldridge as the "African Roscius" was considerably enhanced
  by *Red Velvet* a play by Lolita Chakrabarti, first produced in London and,
  subsequently, at various theatres in the USA. In 2014, Yara Arts Group,
  a resident company at the LaMama Theatre in New York led by director,
  poet, translator, and theatre historian Virlana Tkacz, created *Dark Night,
  Bright Stars,* based on Aldridge's encounter with Taras Shevchenko. The
  scholar who has made the greatest contribution to Aldridge studies is
  Bernth Lindfors. In addition to various articles and an edited book, he
  has produced four meticulously researched volumes on the life and career
  of Aldridge: Bernth Lindfors, *Ira Aldridge: The Early Years, 1807–1833*
  (Rochester: Rochester University Press, 2011); Bernth Lindfors, *Ira
  Aldridge: The Vagabond Years, 1833–1852* (Rochester: Rochester University
  Press, 2011); Bernth Lindfors, *Ira Aldridge: Performing Shakespeare in Europe,
  1852–1855* (Rochester: Rochester University Press, 2013); and Bernth
  Lindfors, *Ira Aldridge: The Last Years, 1855–1867* (Rochester: Rochester
  University Press, 2015).

3 For an overview, see Irena R. Makaryk, "Russia and the Former Soviet Union," in *The Oxford Companion to Shakespeare*, eds. Michael Dobson, Stanley Wells, Will Sharpe, and Erin Sullivan (2nd ed., Oxford University Press, 2015).

4 Cited in Marshall and Stock *Ira Aldridge*, 224. Marshall and Stock published a fairly exhaustive list of responses to Aldridge in their biography of the actor. The Ukrainian translation of this book, however, also includes a separate chapter on Shevchenko and Aldridge authored by Oleksa Novyts'kyi "with the participation of Herbert Marshall." This extensive chapter, "Taras Shevchenko i Aira Oldridzh" (169–219) includes material not found in the original English biography of the Black actor. Herbert Marshall and Mildred Stock, *Aira Oldridzh, Nehretians'kyi trahik* [Ira Aldridge. The Negro Tragedian], 1958, trans. Oleksa Novyts'kyi and Valentyn Shyhans'kyi (Kyiv: Mystetstvo, 1966). Unless otherwise specified, the notes reference the original English text.

5 In his early touring days of Europe, Aldridge brought with him a small group of British actors but, having found himself the key attraction and considering the expense involved, he began acting with local professional troupes whose actors spoke in their own language. Since this experiment worked well, he then dismissed the British actors and from that point continued to act in English while local actors performed in their own native language. Lindfors, *Last Years*, 2.

6 Cited in English in Marshall and Stock, *Ira Aldridge*, 229-30.

7 Lindfors, *Last Years*, 115. Lindfors's source for these comments is an anonymous article published in *Teatral'naia Nedelia* 22, no. 46 (1940): 17. The comments about this nameless Englishman may be a fabrication, bearing in mind that the article was published in the Soviet period before the USSR became an ally of Britain in the fight against Hitler.

8 Cited in Marshall and Stock, *Ira Aldridge*, 221-22.

9 Marshall and Stock, *Ira Aldridge*, 320.

10 Hugh Quarshie, *Second Thoughts about Othello*, International Shakespeare Association Occasional Paper, No. 7 (Chipping Camden: Clouds Hill Printers for the International Shakespeare Association, 1999).

11 Cited in Marshall and Stock, *Ira Aldridge*, 234.

12 Errol Hill, *Shakespeare in Sable: A History of Black Shakespearean Actors* (Amherst, Mass.: University of Massachusetts Press, 1984), 41.

13 Cited in Marshall and Stock, *Ira Aldridge*, 232.

14 Mikhail M. Morozov., ed., "Aira Oldridzh" [Ira Aldridge], in *Shekspir na stsene: mastra teatra v obrazakh Shekspira* [Shakespeare on Stage: Masters of Theatre in Shakespeare's Images] (Moscow-Leningrad: Vserossiiskoe teatral'noe obshchestvo, 1939), 56.

15 Ira Aldridge, Letter, London, 29 May 1855. Cited in Lindfors, *Last Years*, 7.

16 M.P. Alekseev, ed., *Shekspir i ruskaia kul'tura* [Shakespeare and Russian Culture] (Moscow-Leningrad, Nauka, 1965), 542.

17 See Lindfors, *Last Years* for contemporary responses to all of Aldridge's performances.

18 T. Gautier, *Voyage en Russie*, Vol. 12 (Paris: Charpentier and Fasquelle, 1895), 254–6.

19 Marshall and Stock, *Ira Aldridge*, 224.

20 Shevchenko's various requests are found in F.M. Bilets'kyi, "T.H. Shevchenko pro Vil'iama Shekspira" [T.H. Shevchenko about William Shakespeare], *Inozemna filolohiia* 1964, No. 1: 39–40.

21 Bilets'kyi, "T.H. Shevchenko," 42.

22 George Grabowicz, *The Poet as Mythmaker; A Study of Symbolic Meaning in Taras Shevchenko* (Cambridge: Harvard University Press, 1982), 145.

23 Cited in A. Borshchagovskii, "Teatral'ni ideï Shevchenka" [Shevchenko's Ideas about Theatre], *Teatr* (Moscow, 1939), No. 2–3: 11–14 (11).

24 M. Savychev in *Spohady pro Shevchenka* [Reminiscences about Shevchenko] (Kyiv: Khudozhnia literatura, 1958), 395.

25 O. Novyts'kyi (with the participation of Herbert Marshall), "Taras Shevchenko i Aira Aldridge," in Marshall and Stock, *Aira Oldridzh*, 169–219 (200).

26 Cited in Marshall and Stock, *Ira Aldridge*, 242.

27 Similarly, Zvantsov characterized Aldridge as possessing both a "leonine and at the same time childlike nature" (cited in Marshall and Stock, *Ira Aldridge*, 232). Panaev, who highly praised Aldridge's *Othello*, drew attention to his childlike innocence which, he claimed, nonetheless somehow revealed the tiger underneath. Panaev also begins his review in *Sovremennik* with the racist comment that Aldridge is more like a Moor than a Black since his lips are not quite so thick (cited in Morozov, "Aira Oldridzh," 56).

28 Kulish's translations of *Othello*, *Troilus and Cressida*, and *The Comedy of Errors*, all published in 1882, were followed by *Hamlet* in 1889; *Coriolanus*, *Macbeth*, *The Taming of the Shrew*, *Julius Caesar* in 1900; *Antony and Cleopatra*, *Much Ado about Nothing*, *Romeo and Juliet* in 1901; and *King Lear* and *Measure for Measure* in 1902.

29 O. Novyts'kyi (with the participation of Herbert Marshall), "Taras Shevchenko i Aira Oldridzh," in Marshall and Stock, *Aira Oldridzh*, 200..

30 Diana Taylor, *The Archive and the Repertoire* (Durham, NC: Duke University Press, 2003), 2.

31 Taylor, *The Archive*, 19–20.

32 Lindfors, *Last Years*, 169.

33 Aldridge was buried in Łódź in the graveyard of the Evangelical Church. Damaged during the Second World war, his gravestone was restored in 2024. See the online Ira Aldridge exhibition, Shakespeare Birthplace Trust, for an image of the monument, as well as playbills advertising his performances: https://collections.shakespeare.org.uk/exhibition/exhibition/ira-aldridge -in-the-collections.

3. "North by North West": Shevchenko and Shakespeare

1 The critical response to Shevchenko's dramas is summed up by V.Ie.
   Shubravs'kyi, "Dramaturhiia," in Ie.P. Kyryliuk, ed., *Shevchenkoznavstvo:
   pidsumky i problemy* [Shevchenkiana: Summations and Problematics]
   (Kyiv: Naukova dumka, 1975), 483–96. While emphasizing the negative
   criticism offered by scholars and reviewers, Shubravs'kyi also observes
   that Shevchenko's *Nazar Stodolia* has been consistently successful on stage.
   Further attesting to this success is L. Baraban, "Dramaturhiia Shevchenka
   v deiakykh perekladakh ta stsenichnii interpretatsiï kraïn sotsialistychnoï
   spivdruzhnosti (Bolhariia i Chekhoslovachchyna)" [Shevchenko's
   Dramaturgy in Some Translations and Stage Interpretations of Socialist
   Friendly Countries (Bulgaria and Czechoslovakia)], in *Zbirnyk prats' 26
   Naukovoiï shevchenkivs'koiï konferentsiï* [Anthology of Works, 26th Scholarly
   Shevchenko Conference] (Kyiv: Naukova dumka, 1985), 269–80. *Nazar
   Stodolia* has also been filmed twice (1937, 1955).
2 Panteleimon Kulish, *Tvory* [Works], vol. 6 (Lviv, 1910) 377. Also cf. *Spohady
   pro Shevchenka* [Reminiscences about Shevchenko] (Kyiv: Khudozhnia
   literatura, 1958), 138.
3 V.Ie. Shubravs'kyi, *Dramaturhiia T.H. Shevchenka*, 2nd ed. (Kyiv: Khudozhnia
   literatura, 1961), 40–4, looks at the problems of dating and of determining
   the number of plays Shevchenko wrote. In a later article on the same topic,
   printed in *Shevchenkoznavstvo*, Shubravs'kyi changed his mind and suggested
   that *Nevesta* is yet a third, separate play (see 495–6). Although the evidence
   he offers does not seem to be persuasive, it cannot be entirely discounted,
   since the play has disappeared and scholars are dependent upon second-
   and third-hand accounts of it. For an alternative view, see Valerian Revutsky,
   "Shevchenko and the Theatre," in *Taras Shevchenko 1814–1861: A Symposium*,
   eds. Volodymyr Miiakovs'kyi and George Y. Shevelov (The Hague: Mouton,
   1962), 148–50.
4 The only scholar to mention such a reference is Shubravs'kyi, *Dramaturhiia
   T.H. Shevchenka*, 43–4.
5 For a detailed study of Aldridge's tour, see Herbert Marshall and Mildred
   Stock, *Ira Aldridge: The Negro Tragedian* (Carbondale and Edwardsville:
   Southern Illinois University Press, 1958) and, more recently, Bernth
   Lindfors, *Ira Aldridge, The Last Years, 1855–1867* (Rochester: University of
   Rochester Press, 2015).
6 Quoted in *Spohady pro Shevchenka*, 457–8 (my translation).
7 Much has been written about Shevchenko's friendship with Shchepkin and
   his general acquaintance with the actors and the theatrical repertory of
   his day. See for example A. Borshchagovskii, "Teatral'nie ideï Shevchenka"
   [Shevchenko's Theatrical Ideas], *Teatr* (Moscow) 2–3 (1939): 11–14.

8 P.R. Zaborov, "Ot klassitsizma k romantizmu" [From Classicism to Romanticism], in *Shekspir i russkaia kul'tura* [Shakespeare and Russian Culture], ed. M.P. Alekseev (Moscow and Leningrad: Nauka, 1965), 121.

9 P. Rulin, "Dramatychni sproby Shevchenka" [Shevchenko's Dramatic Experiments], in *Taras Shevchenko*, eds. Ie. Hryhoriuk and P. Fylypovych (Kyiv, 1921), 97–106.

10 O. Kysil', *Ukraïns'kyi teatr* [Ukrainian Theatre] (Kyiv, 1925; rpt. Mystetstvo, 1968), 151.

11 Revutsky, "Shevchenko and the Theatre," 136–52.

12 I. Pil'huk, "Vid *Natalky Poltavky* do *Nazara Stodolia*" [From *Natalka Poltavka* to *Nazar Stodolia*], *Literaturna krytyka* [Literary Criticism] 4 (1937): 21–36.

13 A. Pypin, "Russkie sochineniia Shevchenka" [Shevchenko's Russian Works], *Vestnik Evropy* [Europe's Herald] 3 (1888): 246–86. Quoted by Shubravs'kyi, *Shevchenkoznavstvo*, 487.

14 S.M. Shakhovs'kyi, "Shevchenko-dramaturh" [Shevchenko-Dramatist], *Ucheni zapysky Kharkivs'koho universytetu* [Kharkiv University Scientific Notes] 17 (1939): 38. Quoted by Shubravs'kyi, *Shevchenkoznavstvo*, 490.

15 James L. Smith, *Melodrama* (London: Methuen, 1973), 7.

16 Peter Brooks, *The Melodramatic Imagination: Balzac, Henry James, Melodrama, and the Mode of Excess* (New Haven & London: Yale University Press, 1976). Chapter two is entitled "Aesthetics of Astonishment."

17 Brooks, *The Melodramatic Imagination*, 20.

18 Northrop Frye's analysis of comedy and the new society formulated at its conclusion first appears in his seminal work, Northrop Frye, *The Anatomy of Criticism* (Princeton University Press, 1957).

19 Brooks, *The Melodramatic Imagination*, 32.

20 Brooks, *The Melodramatic Imagination*, 42.

21 "*Prychynna*" [The Bewitched] in Taras Shevchenko, in *Taras Shevchenko: Selected Works: Poetry and Prose*, trans. Irina Zeleznova (Moscow: Progress, 1979). Among the more recent translations is the useful bilingual (Ukrainian-English) translation by Michael Naydan, *The Essential Poetry of Taras Shevchenko* (Lviv: Piramida, 2014). He translates *Prychynna* as "The Moonstruck Girl."

22 In Shevchenko, *Taras Shevchenko: Selected Works*, 498 (translated by Irina Zeleznova).

23 Ie.S. Shabliovs'kyi, "Shevchenko i vyzvol'nyi rukh 40–60x rokiv XIX st. v Rosiï i na Ukraïni" [Shevchenko and the Liberation Movement in the 1840s–60s in Russia and in Ukraine], in Shubravs'kyi, *Shevchenkoznavstvo*, 314.

24 For example, Iryna Vanina, *Ukraïns'ka Shekspiriana: do istoriï vtilennia p'es Shekspira na ukraïns'kii stseni* [Ukrainian Shakespeareana: Towards a History of Shakespeare on the Ukrainian Stage] (Kyiv: Mystetstvo, 1964), 21.

25 Ducis himself did not know a word of English. See C.M. Haines, *Shakespeare in France. Criticism: From Voltaire to Hugo* (London: Oxford University Press for the Shakespeare Association, 1925), 733.

26 Zaborov, "Ot klassitsizma k romantizmu," 122.

27 Iu.D. Levin, "Russkii romantizm" [Russian Romanticism], in Alekseev, 303.

28 J.-F. Ducis, "Hamlet," in *Œuvres* de J.-F. Ducis, vol. 1 (Paris: Bibliothèque Choisie, 1829) 5–78. Hamlet's concluding remarks are: « Reservé pour souffrir, / Je saurai vivre encore; je fais plus que mourir » (75).

29 Frank Rahill, *The World of Melodrama* (University Park and London: Pennsylvania State University Press, 1967), 40.

30 In Taras Shevchenko, "Progul'ka s udol'stviem i ne bez morali" [A Pleasurable Walk and Not Without a Moral in Taras Shevchenko, *Zibrannia tvoriv u shesty tomakh* [Collected Works in Six Volumes], vol. 4. (Kyïv: Naukova duma, 2003).

31 Zaborov, "Ot klassitsizma k romantizmu," 91.

32 Levin, "Russkii romantizm," 279–80.

33 Encouragement to study Shakespeare came from various quarters, including Kulish and, of course Karl Bryulov, who possessed a magnificent library. For Kulish's advice on using Shakespeare as a literary model, see P.M. Fedchenko, "Shevchenko, Kulish i Kostomarov u Kyrylo-Mefodiïvs'komu tovarystvi" [Shevchenko, Kulish and Kostomarov in the Cyril-Methodius Brotherhood], *Radians'ke literaturoznavstvo* [Soviet Literary Studies] 7 (1989): 29–36.

34 On Shevchenko's knowledge of world literature, see, for example, S. Savchenko, "Shevchenko i svitova literatura" [Shevchenko and World Literature], *Radians'ka literatura* [Soviet Literature] (Kyiv) 7 (1939): 116–28. Specifically on Shakespeare, see F.M. Bilets'kyi, "T.H. Shevchenko pro Vil'iama Shekspira" [T.H. Shevchenko about William Shakespeare] *Inozemna filolohiia* [Foreign Philology] 1.1 (1964): 38–47.

35 In Bernard F. Dukore, *Dramatic Theory and Criticism* (New York: Holt, Rinehart and Winston, 1974), 459.

36 In Dukore, *Dramatic Theory,* 444–5.

37 In Dukore, *Dramatic Theory,* 444–5.

38 George G. Grabowicz, *The Poet as Mythmaker: A Study of Symbolic Meaning in Taras Shevchenko* (Cambridge, Mass.: Harvard Ukrainian Research Institute, 1982), 39.

39 The emphasis on an heroic (as opposed to a merely ethnographic) past was, however, new to the Ukrainian theatrical repertory. See P.G. Prykhod'ko, *Shevchenko i ukraïns'kyi romantyzm 30–50 rr. XIX st.* [Shevchenko and Ukrainian Romanticism in the 30–50s of the 19th Century] (Kyïv: Akademiia Nauk, 1963), 222.

40 Brooks, *The Melodramatic Imagination,* 16.

41 See Lisa Efimov Schneider, "An Examination of Shevchenko's Romanticism," in *Shevchenko and the Critics 1861–1980*, ed. G.S.N. Luckyj (Toronto: University of Toronto Press, 1980), 430–53. Schneider contrasts Shevchenko's concept of Romanticism with that of Western European writers and argues that one of the essential features is that "Shevchenko represents a literary voice fighting for its right to speak in a largely unreceptive environment" (434).

42 Shevchenko's famous reply to Belinsky appears in his *Haidamaky*, written about the same time that Shevchenko was working on his plays. For a study of the relationship between the two, see Victor Swoboda, "Shevchenko and Belinsky," *Slavonic & East European Review* 40.94 (1961): 168–83.

43 George S.N. Luckyj, *Young Ukraine: the Brotherhood of Sts. Cyril and Methodius* (Ottawa: University of Ottawa Press, 1991), 108.

4. Ophelia as Poet: Lesya Ukrainka and the Woman as Artist

1 For example, the tsarist circulars and ukases (1863, 1876, and 1881) prohibited the performance of all Ukrainian works, including foreign plays in Ukrainian translations. As Roman Solchanyk points out, the most draconian of these was the Ems Ukase of 1876 which was "introduced secretly through the censorship committees of the government bureaucracy" (1977, 225). Contemporary attempts to inform the European world of its severe measures are discussed by Roman Solchanyk, *"Lex Jusephovicia* 1876," *Suchasnist'* 16.5 (May 1976): 36–68; and Roman Solchanyk, "Mykhailo Drahomanov and the Ems Ukase: A Note on the Ukrainian Question at the 1878 International Literary Congress in Paris," *Harvard Ukrainian Studies* 1.2 (1977): 225–9. The specific consequences for Ukrainian theatre are studied by Valerian Revutsky who writes of a "state of fear" in Kyiv, and of a total paralysis of the arts. The harsh censorship lasted nearly ten years and affected not only the language but also the contents and genre of plays permitted. The Ukase was, for all intents and purposes, still in practical use until the Soviet period, since Ukrainian plays needed to be granted a license for performance. Many were not. Valerian Revutsky, "The Act of Ems (1876) and Its Effect on Ukrainian Theatre," *Nationalities Papers* 5.1 (1977): 67–77.

2 Except where noted, the translations in this chapter are the author's. They are meant to be serviceable rather than poetic renderings of Ukrainka's works. For more poetic (but, for my purposes, less accurate) translations of "Avenging Angel" and "The Forgotten Shadow," see Lesya Ukrainka, *Spirit of Flame: A Collection of the Works of Lesya Ukraïnka*, trans. Percival Cundy (Westport, Conn.: Greenwood P, 1971). For "Adagio Penseroso," see Lesya Ukrainka, *Hope: Selected Poetry*, trans. Gladys Evans (Kyiv: Dnipro, 1975).

As far as I am aware, there are no English translations of "Sappho," "A
Woman's Portrait," and "To Be or Not to Be?"

3 Lesia Ukraïnka, "Sapfo," in *Tvory v desiaty tomakh* [Works in Ten Volumes]
(Kyiv: Khudozhnia literatura, 1963–65), 10 Vols, 46.

4 Elaine Showalter, "Representing Ophelia: Women, Madness, and the
Responsibilities of Feminist Criticism," in *Shakespeare and the Question of
Theory*, eds. Patricia Parker and Geoffrey Hartman (New York and London:
Methuen, 1985), 77–94 (83).

5 Nina Auerbach, *Romantic Imprisonment: Women and Other Glorified Outcasts*
(New York: Columbia University Press, 1986), 282.

6 Untitled excerpt, [Сапфо] in *Lesia Ukrainka. Zibrannia tvoriv u dvanadtsiaty
tomakh* [Lesya Ukrainka. Collected Works in Twelve Volumes], ed. B.A.
Derkach (Kyiv: Naukova Dumka, 1977), 385–9.

7 Simone de Beauvoir, *Le deuxième sexe* [The Second Sex], first published in
two volumes as essays, then as a book (Paris: Gallimard, 1949).

8 The idea of the woman's surrender of self, conceived as a life without a
story, receives a thorough theoretical treatment in the now classic study,
Sandra Gilbert and Susan Gubar, *The Madwoman in the Attic: The Woman
Writer and the Nineteenth-Century Literary Imagination* (New Haven: Yale
University Press, 1979), 24–6. Gubar and Gilbert observe that part of the
task of the "angel woman" is to minister to the dying; she herself is already
dead because a life without a story is a life of death. Gubar and Gilbert's
analysis is also valuable for an understanding of "The Forgotten Shadow,"
discussed later in this chapter.

9 Ukraïnka, *Tvory*, Vol. I, 370–1.

10 Gilbert and Gubar, *The Madwoman*, 25.

11 Ukraïnka, *Tvory*, Vol. 1, 224–5.

12 Shoshana Felman, "Women and Madness: The Critical Fallacy," *Diacritics* 5.4
(Winter 1975): 2–10 (2).

13 Ukraïnka, *Tvory*, Vol. I, 174–5.

14 Gilbert and Gubar, *The Madwoman*, 77.

15 See, for example, "The Weapon of the Word" (48), "Moods" (52), "The
Power of Song" (54), and the cycle "Seven Strings" (56), among many
others in English translation in Ukrainka, *Spirit of Flame*.

16 There are interesting parallels between Ukraïnka's drama and the American
writer Charlotte Perkins Gilman's *The Yellow Wallpaper*, first published in January
1892 in *The New England Magazine*, Charlotte Perkins Gilman, *The Yellow Wall-
Paper, and Other Stories*. (New York: Oxford University Press, 1995); however, I
have not found any evidence that Ukraïnka was aware of Gilman's work.

17 The conflated reference to Ophelia-Lady Macbeth occurs in only one extant
printed version of *The Azure Rose* in the five-volume edition of Ukraïnka's
work (Kyiv: Khudozhnia literatura, 1951–56, Vol. II, 11). Unfortunately,

the bibliographical notes are obscure; without consulting the archives in
Kyiv, it is impossible to say to which version of the text the Ophelia-Lady
Macbeth references belong. We do know that the manuscript underwent
many revisions and that additional and extensive changes in blue ink were
also made by her colleague, dramatist Mykhailo Staryts'kyi. None of the
published versions of the play indicate whose changes these are, although
it is probably safe to assume that these particular ones are Ukrainka's. The
yoking of these two Shakespearean figures is of a piece with her interests
and concerns, as this chapter argues.

18 Elaine Showalter, *The Female Malady: Women, Madness, and English Culture,
    1930–1980* (New York: Pantheon Books, 1985), 86–7; Bridget Gellert Lyons,
    "The Iconography of Ophelia," *English Literary History* 44 (1977): 60–1.

19 David Leverenz, "The Woman in Hamlet: An Interpersonal View," in
    Representing Shakespeare: New Psychoanalytic Essays, eds. Murray M. Schwartz
    and Coppélia Kahn (Baltimore and London: The Johns Hopkins UP, 1980),
    110–28 (119).

20 Maurice Charney and Hanna Charney. "The Language of Madwomen in
    Shakespeare and in His Fellow Dramatists," *Signs* 3 (1977): 451–60 (451).

21 For an examination of the Strindbergian themes in this play, especially of
    the vampire motif, see Irena R. Makaryk, "Lesia Ukrainka's *Blakytna troianda*:
    Apropos the Theme of Psychic Murder," *Studia Ucrainica* 2 (1984): 25–32.
    More recently, the Ukrainian philosopher and writer Oksana Zabuzhko has
    made Ukrainka's oeuvre the focus of an impressive book, Oksana Zabuzhko,
    Notre Dame d'Ukraine: Ukraïnka v konflikti mifolohiy [Notre Dame of Ukraine:
    Ukrainka in the Conflict of Mythologies] (Kyiv: Fakt, 2007).

22 I am indebted to Roman Weretelnyk, who discussed some of these ideas
    with me when he worked on his doctoral dissertation under my direction:
    Roman Weretelnyk, "A Feminist Reading of Lesia Ukrainka's Dramas," PhD
    Diss. (University of Ottawa, 1985).

23 As Felman points out, the critical tendency in European, especially French
    feminist, theory has been to "glamorize" madness as political protest, and
    social and cultural contestation (Felman 2). Elaine Showalter's *The Female
    Malady* argues that madness may be viewed as both mental pathology and
    as a mode of protest, particularly for women deprived of the possibility
    of intellectual and social outlets that stymied expressive opinions. On the
    connections among hysteria, the telling of stories, and femininity, see Mary
    Jacobus, *Reading Woman: Essays in Feminist Criticism* (New York: Columbia
    University Press, 1986). Jacobus notes that hysteria is inseparable from
    femininity; it is the "translation of psychic metaphors into the language
    of the body" (199). *Pace* Freud, she argues that the "hysterical language
    attempts to recover a lost, literal dimension of language" (209). Also on
    similar themes, see Maggie Humm, *Feminist Criticism: Women as Contemporary*

Critics (Brighton: Harvester, 1986), especially chapter three, "Language and Psychoanalysis." Other important theorists and writers who have worked on this and contiguous domains include Hélène Cixous, Julia Kristeva, and Luce Irigaray.

24 Leverenz, "The Woman in Hamlet," 111.
25 Showalter, *Female Malady*, 91.
26 Ukraïnka, *Tvory*, Vol. I, 184–5.
27 This particular theme is prominently featured in her play *In the Wilderness* (*У пущі*, 1907) which contains some verbal echoes from this poem.
28 Ukraïnka, *Tvory* I, 248.
29 Ukrainka, *Spirit*, 232.
30 Ukrainka, *Spirit*, 239.
31 Ukrainka, *Spirit*, 239.
32 Mavky, or forest nymphs, are traditionally associated with vampires in Ukrainian folklore. Ukraïnka avoids overt reference to this belief and makes her Mavka a sympathetic and positive creature. However, like Lyubov (also referred to as a vampire in *The Azure Rose*), Mavka seems to take on some subtle vampire-like characteristics when, at the end, she saps her lover of his artistic talents, and, secondarily, of his physical strength. This psychic exchange appears to have more to do with the spiritual superiority of Ukrainka's female characters than with folkloric belief.
33 Ukraïnka, *Tvory*, Vol. V, 289–90.
34 For an overview in English of Lesya Ukrainka's life, see Constantine Bida, "Life and Work" in Constantine Bida, *Lesya Ukrainka*, trans. Vera Rich (Toronto: University of Toronto Press, 1968), 3–84.
35 See Lesia Ukraïnka, *Pro literaturu. Poeziï, statti, krytychni ohliady, lysty* [Lesya Ukrainka. About Literature. Poetry, Articles, Critical Views, Letters], ed. O.K. Babyshkin (Kyiv: Khudozhna literatura, 1955).

5. Periphery Against Centre: *Hamlet* in Early Soviet Ukrainian Poetry

1 Constantine Bida, "Shakespeare's Entrance into the Slavic World," *Proceedings of the IIIrd Congress of the International Comparative Literature Association* (The Hague: Mouton and Co., 1962), 340.
2 Itamar Even-Zohar, "Polysystem Theory," *Poetics Today 1*, no. 1–2 (1979): 287–310. The periphery as the zone of transformation or renewal is an idea earlier explored by such scholars as Viktor Shklovskii, Mikhail Bakhtin, and Claudio Guillén.
3 Jean E. Howard and Marion F. O'Connor, "Introduction," in *Shakespeare Reproduced; The Text in History and Ideology*, eds. Jean E. Howard and Marion F. O'Connor (New York and London: Methuen, 1987), 7–8.

4 Even-Zohar, "Polysystem Theory," 303.

5 Bohdan Rubchak, "Images of Center and Periphery in the Poetry of Taras Sevčenko," *The Annals of the Ukrainian Academy of Arts and Sciences in the U.S.,* 16, no. 41–2 (1984–1985): 85–6.

6 I use "canonicity" in Even-Zohar's sense of the term.

7 George S. N, Luckyj, "Ukrainian Literature: The Last Twenty-five Years," *Books Abroad* 30 (1956):133.

8 George S.N. Luckyj, *Literary Politics in the Soviet Ukraine 1917–1934* (New York: Columbia University Press, 1956), 25. Luckyj's was the first book to deal with the Literary Discussion. Since then, Myroslav Shkandrij has made an invaluable study of this crucial period, particularly in his Myroslav Shkandrij, *Modernists, Marxists, and the Nation: The Ukrainian Literary Discussion of the 1920s* (Edmonton: Canadian Institute of Ukrainian Studies Press, 1993).

9 Oleh S. Ilnytzkyj, "Futurist Polemics with Xvyl'ovyj During the Prolitfront Period," *The Annals of the Ukrainian Academy of Arts and Sciences in the U.S.,* 16, no. 41–42 (1984–1985): 232.

10 Maksym Ryl's'kyi, "Epokhy de b dusheiu vidpochyt" [Eras Where the Soul Might Rest], in *Tvory* [Works] (Kyiv: Derzhavne vydavnytsvo khudozhn'oï literatury, 1960), 246. Unless otherwise noted, all translations are mine.

11 Luckyj, "Ukrainian Literature," 134.

12 E. F. Hirchak, *Na dva fronta v bor'be s natsionalizmom* [On Two Fronts in the Struggle with Nationalism] (Moscow-Leningrad: Gosizdat, 1930), 55–6. Quoted in Luckyj, *Literary Politics,* 99.

13 Mykola Khvyl'ovyi, "Apolohety pysaryzmu" [Apologists of Scribalism], in *Rostriliane vidrodzhennia: Antolohiia 1917–1933* [The Executed Renaissance. An Anthology 1917–1933], ed. Iurii Lavrinenko (Paris: Instytut Literatski, 1959), 827–8.

14 Khvyl'ovyi, "Apolohety pysaryzmu," 828.

15 Khvyl'ovyi, "Apolohety pysaryzmu," 828.

16 Mykola Khvyl'ovyi, *Dumky proty techii* [Thoughts Against the Current], in Lavrinenko, *Rostriliane,* 812–3.

17 Les' Kurbas, *Robitnycha hazeta,* 23 September 1917. Quoted in Luckyj, *Literary Politics,* 26.

18 Orest Subtelny, *Ukraine: A History* (Toronto: University of Toronto Press, 1988), 392. A similar point has been made by Oleh Ilnytzkyj about the Ukrainian Futurists, who believed that national orientation was, by definition, reactionary and that the "orientation of *Ukrainian* culture had to be international." See Ilnytzkyj, "Futurist Polemics," 233.

19 Bohdan Ryl's'kyi, "Mandrivka v molodist' bat'ka" [A Journey into My Father's Youth], *Literaturna Ukraina,* January 17, 1969, 105.

20 Luckyj, "Ukrainian Literature," 136.

21 Luckyj, *Literary Politics*, 124.

22 Harri Jünger, ed., *The Literatures of the Soviet Peoples* (New York: Frederick Ungar, 1970), 380.

23 Maksym Ryl's'kyi, "Shekspir," in *Tvory*, 1, 173.

24 O. Belets'kyi, "Tvorchist' Maksyma Ryl's'koho" [The Creative Works of Maksym Ryl's'kyi], in *Tvory*, 1, 19.

25 Irena Makaryk and Virlana Tkacz, eds., *Modernism in Kyiv: Jubilant Experimentation* (Toronto: University of Toronto Press, 2010).

26 M.S. Shapovalova, *Shekspir v ukrains'kii literaturi* [Shakespeare in Ukrainian Literature] (Lviv: Vyshcha shkola, 1976), 172.

27 Maksym Ryl's'kyi, "*Hamlet* u vykonanni Serhiia Balashova" [Shakespeare in the Interpretation of Serhii Balahsov], in *Tvory*, 10, 409.

28 Quoted in Shapovalova, *Shekspir*, 172.

29 Bilets'kyi, "Tvorchist' Maksyma Ryl's'koho," 14.

30 Maksym Ryl's'kyi, "Falstaf," in *Tvory*, 1, 233.

31 Shapovalova, *Shekspir*, 175.

32 Maksym Ryl's'kyi, *Homin i vidhomin* [Echo and Reverberation] (Kyiv: Derzhvydav, 1929), 19.

33 Jünger, *The Literatures*, 127.

34 L. Novychenko, "Na mahistraliakh chasu" [On the Highways of Time], in Mykola Bazhan, *Poezii ta poemy* [Poetry and Poems], 1 (Kyiv: Dnipro, 1965), 14.

35 Lazar Smul'son, *Etudy pro ukrains'ku radians'ku poeziiu* [Studies of Soviet Ukrainian Poetry] (Kyiv: Derzhavne literaturne vydavnytsvo, 1940), 84.

36 O. Levada, "Notatky pro tvorchist' Mykoly Bazhana" [Notes About the Creative Works of Mykola Bazhan], *Radians'ka literatura* [Soviet Literature], no. 7 (1933): 206. Quoted in Luckyj, *Literary Politics*, 123.

37 A. Chepurniuk, "Poeziia vyshukanykh katastrof idealistychnoï filosofiï" [The Poetry of the Refined Catastrophies of Idealistic Philosophy], *Chervonyi shliakh* [Red Path] no. 1 (1934): 186. Quoted in Luckyj, *Literary Politics*, 123–4.

38 Shapovalova, *Shekspir*, 192.

39 Subtelny, *Ukraine*, 422.

40 Iurii Ivanovich Surovtsev, *Poeziia Mikoly Bazhana* [The Poetry of Mykola Bazhan] (Moscow: Sovetskii pisatel', 1970), 177.

41 Nataliya Torkut and Yurii Cherniak, "Ukrainian Hamlet and 'Hamletizing' Ukraine: 'Will You Play Upon This Pipe?'" *Renesansni studiï* [Renaissance Studies] (Zaporizhzhia, 2014), vol. 22: 98–115 (101).

42 Torkut and Cherniak, "Ukrainian Hamlet," 101.

43 Mykola Bazhan, "The Death of Hamlet" in Bazhan, *Poezii ta poemy*, 1, 130.

44 Surovtsev, *Poeziia Mikoly Bazhana*, 177.

45 Ie. S. Shabliovs'kyi, ed., *Istoriia ukraïns'koi literatury*, 2 (Kyiv: Naukova Dumka, 1957), 655.

46 Subtelny, *Ukraine*, 417–8.

47 Khvyl'ovyi, *Kamo hriadeshy*, 36–7.

48 Khvyl'ovyi, *Kamo hriadeshi*, 37–8.

49 See, for example, S.I. Rodzevych, "Vil'iam Shekspir," in *Vil'iam Shekspir; Zbirka stattei* [William Shakespeare; A Collection of Articles], ed. and introduction byO. Bilets'kyi (Kharkiv: Mystetsvo, 1939), 15.

50 O.I. Bilets'kyi, "Introduction," in *Vil'iam Shekspir*, 8–9.

51 A.A. Smirnov, *Shakespeare: A Marxist Interpretation*, trans. Sonia Volochova et al. (New York: The Critics' Group. 1936), 27.

52 O.M. Borshchahovs'kyi, "Shekspir i ukraïns'kyi teatr"[Shakespeare and Ukrainian Theatre], in O.I. Bilets'kyi, *Vil'iam Shekspir*, 142.

53 See Irene R. Makaryk, *Comic Justice in Shakespeare's Comedies* (Salzburg: University of Salzburg Studies in English Literature 91, 1980).

54 Frederick Ahl, "Ars Est Caelare Artem (Art in Puns and Anagrams Engraved)," in *On Puns: The Foundation of Letters*, ed. Jonathan Culler (Oxford: Basil Blackwell, 1988), 32–3.

55 Iurii Klen, *Spohady pro neokliasykiv* (Munich: Ukrains'ka vydavnycha spilka, 1947), 22.

56 Joseph Stalin, Letter to Lazar Kaganovich, April 26, 1926, quoted in Luckyj, *Literary Politics*, 68.

57 Ievhen Pluzhnyk, *Vybrani poeziï* [Selected Poetry] (Kyiv: Radians'kyi pys'mennyk, 1966), 210.

58 Volodymyr Derzhavyn, "Liryka Ievhena Pluzhnyka" [Yevhen Pluzhnyk's Lyric Poetry], in Ievhen Pluzhnyk, *Try zbirky* [Three Collections] (Munich: Instytut literatury im. Mykhaila Oresta, 1979), 232.

59 For a detailed study of early Soviet prose models of the new Soviet man, see Myroslav Shkandrij, "Fiction by Formula: The Worker in Soviet Ukrainian Prose," *Journal of Ukrainian Studies* 7, no. 2 (1982): 47–60, For source material, see *Pervyi vsesoiuznyi s'iezd sovetskikh pisatelei 1934* [The First All-Union Congress of Soviet Writers 1934] (Moscow: Gosudarstvennoe izdatel'stvo, khudozhestvennaia literatura, 1934).

60 Shkandrij, "Fiction by Formula," 49.

61 Shkandrij, "Fiction by Formula", 51.

62 Shkandrij, "Fiction by Formula," 53.

63 Shkandrij, "Fiction by Formula," 48.

64 Shkandrij, "Fiction by Formula," 53.

65 Shkandrij, "Fiction by Formula," 56.

66 Constantine Bida, "'Shakespeare and National Traits in Literatures (The Problem of Interpretation),' "" in Proc*eedings of the IVth International Cof the International Comparative Literature Association* (The Hague and Paris, Mouton, 1966), p. 279.

67 Bida, "Shakespeare and National Traits," 280.

68 Bida, "Shakespeare and National Traits," 279.

69 V.I. Lenin, *Sochineniia* [Essays] 8, 3rd ed. (Moscow: Gosudarstvennoe izdatel'stvo Partizdat, 1930–1935), 389.

70 Lina Kostenko, "Dz'obata khata dobuvae den'" [The Peaked House Gets
   the Day], in Lina Kostenko, *Nepovtornist* [The Unrepeatable] (Kyiv: Molod',
   1980), 173.

6. Shakespeare Right or Wrong?

1 Harold Hobson, Jane Howell, Irving Wardle, John Calder, "A Discussion
   with Edward Bond," *Gambit* 17.5 (1970): 24.
2 Kh. Tokar, "'Desiat' let 'Bereziliia'" [*sic.*, Ten Years of the Berezil], *Teatr i
   dramaturgiia* [Theatre and Dramaturgy] (Moscow) 4 (1933): 61.
3 Introducing Shakespeare into Ukraine after a century of tsarist prohibitions,
   Kurbas prepared four plays (*Romeo and Juliet, Macbeth, Othello, King Lear*)
   and did preliminary work on five others (*Hamlet, A Midsummer Night's Dream,
   Twelfth Night, Timon of Athens, Antony and Cleopatra*), intending, eventually, to
   produce the whole Shakespearean canon.
4 Les' Kurbas, "Nastanova do trahediï Makbet," [An Approach to the Tragedy
   of *Macbeth*] 1920. Rpt. in *Berezil': Les' Kurbas iz tvorchoi spadshchyny* [Berezil:
   Les' Kurbas: from his Creative Legacy], ed. M.H. Labins'kyi (Kyiv: Dnipro,
   1988), 226.
5 [Anon.] "Do postanovky 'Makbeta' v 4 maisterni M.O.B. (rozmova z
   Kurbasom)" [About the Production of *Macbeth* by the Fourth Studio of the
   B[erezil] A[rtistic] A[ssociation] (a Conversation with Kurbas)], *Bil'shovyk*
   (Kyiv) 1 April 1924: n.p. All translations are the author's.
6 Endre Bojtar, *East European Avant-Garde Literature*, trans. Pál Várnai
   (Budapest: Akademiai Kiado, 1992), 37–8.
7 Vasyl' Vasyl'ko, *Shchodennyk* [Unpublished Diary], vol. 5, 1 January 1923 to
   14 May 1924, MS10369, State Museum of Theatre, Music and Film Arts of
   Ukraine (Kyiv).
8 Numerous reviews and memoirs attest to this view. A representative view
   is Ia[kiv] S[avchenko]'s "Shakespir dybom" [Shakespeare Upside Down],
   Bil'shovyk (Kyiv), No. 76 (974) 4 April 1924: 6.
9 For a detailed study of this remarkable production, see Irena R.
   Makaryk, *Shakespeare in the Undiscovered Bourn: Les Kurbas, Ukrainian
   Modernism, and Early Soviet Cultural Politics* (Toronto: University of
   Toronto Press, 2004).
10 Although various scholars cite the opening of the play as 1 April 1924,
   in fact, according to Vasyl' Vasyl'ko's diary, it did not open until 2 April
   because the costumes were not ready. On 2 April, even as the performance
   was proceeding, the costumes were still being completed.
11 Benjamin Bennett, *Theatre as Problem: Modern Drama and Its Place in Literature*
   (Ithaca: Cornell University Press, 1990), 33. On Kurbas as Expressionist, see
   Romana Bahrij Pikulyk, "The Expressionist Experiment in Berezil': Kurbas
   and Kulish," *Canadian Slavonic Papers* 14.2 (1972): 324–43.

12 Vasyl' Desniak, "Berezil'" *Hlobus* [The Globe] (Kyiv) 5 (1925): 116.

13 Meller is the father of Constructivism on the Ukrainian stage and was
responsible for some of Kurbas's most inventive, original stage designs. He
turned to stage design after his paintings were destroyed during World War I;
his theatrical *début* took place in 1918. See V. Kucherenko, *Vadym Meller,
1884–1962* (Kyiv: Mystetstvo, 1975) for a beautiful catalogue of his surviving
works.

14 Virlana Tkacz argues that these may have been influenced by silent movies.
See Virlana Tkacz, "Les Kurbas's Use of Film Language in His Stage
Productions of *Jimmie Higgins* and *Macbeth*," *Canadian Slavonic Papers* 36.1
(March, 1990): 59–76. Also see Irena R. Makaryk, "Dissecting Time/Space:
The Scottish Play and the New Technology of Film," in Irena Makaryk and
Virlana Tkacz, *Modernism in Kyiv: Jubilant Experimentation* (Toronto: University
of Toronto Press, 2010), 443–77. On a related topic, see Iona Shevchenko,
Suchasnyi ukrains'kyi teatr [The Contemporary Ukrainian Theatre] (Kharkiv:
Derzhavne vydavnytstvo Ukraïny, 1929), 83; he argues that the notion of
peretvorennia is linked to methods of cinematographic montage. He cites
Eisenstein and his notion of "an attraction" in this relation.

15 See the description of Khanan Shmain, "Rezhyser, pedahoh, uchenyi"
[Director, Pedagogue, Scholar], in *Les' Kurbas: spohady suchasnykiv* [Les'
Kurbas: Reminiscences by His Contemporaries] ed. Vasyl' Vasyl'ko (Kyiv:
Mystetstvo, 1969), 137–42.

16 Iosyp Hirniak, *Spomyny* [Memoirs] (New York: Suchasnist', 1982), 196–7.

17 Hirniak noted that the work of Viktor Shklovsky was widely read by the
members of Berezil'. Interview with Hirniak 10 August 1982 (New York),
cited by Virlana Tkacz, "Les Kurbas and the Creation of a Ukrainian Avant-
Garde Theatre," M.A. thesis, (Columbia University, 1983), 65. Kurbas's
practical use of "estrangement" techniques occurs first in this production
of *Macbeth*, and, as Tkacz notes, predates Brecht's use by at almost ten years
(Tkacz, M.A. thesis, 68).

18 Konstantin Rudnitsky, *Russian and Soviet Theatre: Tradition and the Avant-
Garde*, trans. Roxane Permar (New York: Thames and Hudson), 112.

19 Iryna Steshenko, "Pro navchytelia moho i druha" [About My Mentor
and Friend], in *Les' Kurbas: spohady suchasnykiv*, ed. Vasyl' Vasyl'ko (Kyiv:
Mystetstvo, 1969), 170.

20 Iryna Avdieva, "Pro naikrashchu liudyny, iaku ia znala v iunats'ki roky,"
[About the Best Person that I Ever Knew in My Youth], in *Les' Kurbas:
spohady suchasnykiv*, ed. Vasyl' Vasyl'ko (Kyiv: Mystetstvo, 1969), 153.

21 Polina Samiilenko, *Nezabutni dni horin'* [Unforgettable Blazing Days] (Kyiv:
Mystetstvo, 1970), 64.

22 Natalia Kuziakina, "Ledi Makbet ta inshi" [Lady Macbeth and Others],
Vitchyzna (Kyiv) 3 (1969): 193.

23 So, at least, my examination of the photos in the archival collection of the
Ukrainian State Museum of Theatre, Music, and Cinema Arts seemed
to me. In one, Hakkebush faces the viewer in a close-up which shows
her heavily made up eyes and her whole face shrinking in terror from
something. In the second photo, looking beautiful and innocent, she
carries a light in front of her in her outstretched hand. This is the only
photo extant which I have examined which shows her in an upright posture,
her head back, her long hair streaming behind her. In other photos from
the earlier parts of the play, she is never upright, always stylized in her
movements, and usually hunched over, whether reading the letter from
Macbeth, walking with him, or responding to his rage (probably after the
murder of Duncan). In the sleepwalking photos, she is also shown sitting or,
more accurately, reclining. Had I not known that these were photos taken
of Lady Macbeth, I would certainly have thought that they were photos of
Ophelia. The stage imagery of femininity – the white colour of her shift, the
loose hair, and the feminine and less stylized gestures – suggest this.

24 On the three Lady Macbeths of the Soviet Ukrainian stage, all played by
Lyubov Hakkebush, see Iurii Smolych, *Pro teatr* [About Theatre] (Kyiv:
Mystetstvo, 1977), 155-56, and Natalia Kuziakina, "Ledi Makbet ta inshi"
[Lady Macbeth and Others], *Vitchyzna* (Kyiv) 3 (1969): 190–8.

25 I. Turkel'taub, "Hastroli M. 'Berezil' Ledi Makbet" [The Tours of the
Berezil. Lady Macbeth], *Kul'tura i mystetstvo*, Visti VUTsVK 121 (Kharkiv) 30
May 1924: 4.

26 Natalia Pylypenko, *Zhyttia v teatri* [Life in the Theatre] (New York: n.p.,
1968), 15.

27 So, according to Valentyna Zabolotna, a theatrical historian and great-
granddaughter of Amvrosii Buchma, who played the Fool in this
production. See V. Zabolotna, *Aktors'ke mystetstvo Ukrainy (1922–1927)* [The
Actor's Art in Ukraine] (Kyiv: Institut teatral'noho mystetstva im. K. Karoho,
1992), 53. Similar views were voiced in conversation with me in Kyiv on 12
September 1995.

28 The description of the intermedia, and of all of Kurbas's productions
described here, is a composite derived from many sources including
Hirniak, *Spomyny*; Zabolotna, *Aktors'ke mystetstvo*; Iurii Kosach, *Dushi liuds'koi
charodii* [Enchanter of the Human Soul] (Kyiv: Veselka, 1973), 103; Ivan
Kryha, "Samobutnii pedahoh" [The Original Pedagogue], in *Les' Kurbas:
spohady suchasnykiv*, ed. Vasyl' Vasyl'ko (Kyiv: Mystetstvo, 1969) 190–3;
Kuziakina, "Ledi Makbet ta inshi'"; and Natalia Kuziakina "*Makbet* Shekspira
v postanovkakh Lesia Kurbasa" [Les' Kurbas's productions of Shakespeare's
Macbeth], *P'esa i spektakl'* [The Play and the Performance], ed. A.Z. Iufit
(Leningrad: Gosudarstvennyi Institut teatra, muzyki i kinematografii, 1978),
50–66; and Savchenko, "Shekspir dybom" [Shakespeare Upside Down],

each of whom recalls or writes about different elements of the production. The fact that both celebrators and detractors mention the final sequence, the crowning scene, is a good indication of its potency.

29 For example, Mykhailo Mohylians'kyi, "*Makbet* u Berezoli" [*Macbeth* at the Berezil] *Chervonyi shliakh* (Kharkiv), no. 4–5 (April–May 1924): 282 and Al. G-tov, "Kul'tura i iskusstvo *Makbeta* u Kurbasa" [Culture and Art in Kurbas's *Macbeth*], *Khar'kovskii proletarii* (Kharkiv), no. 37 (30 May 1924): 6.

30 Valerian Revutsky, in correspondence with me, letter dated 3 December 1992. The interpretation of the production as scandal is best indicated by I[akiv] S[avchenko]'s review, "Shakespir dybom."

31 Beginning with her Master's thesis, Virlana Tkacz has been both the first and one of the most astute analysists of Kurbas's experimental productions and his drive toward creating a conceptual theatre. She has explored Kurbas's work more thoroughly in our co-edited and co-written volume, Makaryk and Tkacz, *Modernism in Kyiv*; see her chapters 10 and 14, "Towards a New Vision of Theatre: Les Kurbas's Work at the Young Theatre in Kyiv" (278–309) and "Les Kurbas's Early Work at the Berezil: From Bodies in Motion to Performing the Invisible" (362–85).

32 Hirniak, *Spomyny*, 193, 197.

33 For attacks on Kurbas, see the printed speeches from the Theatrical Discussions of 1927 and 1929 in Valerian Revutsky, ed., *Les' Kurbas u teatral'nii dial'nosti, v otsinkakh suchasnykiv* [Les' Kurbas's theatrical activities in the assessments of his contemporaries] (Baltimore: Smoloskyp, 1989), 606. In one of the many defenses of Kurbas, Mykhailo Mohylians'kyi, "'Makbet' u Berezoli," makes the sensible point that every production, including that of Shakespeare's company, in some way modifies the original play. Mohylians'kyi argues that it is pointless to stand on principle; rather, the attackers should simply respond to the "spring delight" of this "great artistic achievement" (6).

34 Savchenko, "Shekspir dybom" [Shakespeare Upside Down], 6.

35 Hnat Iura, "Natsionalistychna estetyka Kurbasa" [Kurbas's Nationalistic Aesthetic], *Za markso-lenins'ku krytyku* (Kyiv) 12 (December 1934): 48–61. This vicious attack appeared the same month in which Kurbas was arrested; however, it may have been written by someone else but conveniently attributed to Iura, who had often been unfavourably compared with Kurbas in the 1920s.

36 This is a point many scholars of Slavic drama have made; for example, Lars Kleberg, *Theatre as Action: Soviet Russian Avant-Garde Aesthetics*, trans. Charles Rougle (Houndsmills: Macmillan, 1990), 4.

37 M. Semenko, "Mystetstvo iak kul't" [Art as Cult], *Chervonyi shliakh* 3 (1924): 222–9, cited in Oleh Ilnytzkyj, "Ukrainian Futurism, 1914–1930: History, Theory and Practice," Ph.D. diss. (Harvard University, 1983), 337.

38 Kurbas, "Z pryvodu symptomiv reaktsii" [Apropos Symptoms of the Reaction], 1925. Rpt. in *Berezil': Les' Kurbas iz tvorchoï spadshchyny* [Berezil: Les' Kurbas: from his Creative Legacy], ed. M.H. Labins'kyi (Kyiv: Dnipro, 1988), 244.

39 Bennett, *Theatre as Problem*, 26–7.

40 Kleberg, *Theatre as Action*, 64.

41 See Bennett, *Theatre as Problem*, 60–83, for a discussion of ceremony. The notion of theatre as church occurs frequently in the writings of Kurbas.

42 Astradur Eysteinsson, *The Concept of Modernism* (Ithaca: Cornell University Press, 1990), 228.

43 Zabolotna, *Aktors'ke mystetstvo*, 53.

44 Zabolotna, *Aktors'ke mystetstvo*, 53–4.

7. The Perfect Production: Les Kurbas's Analysis of the Early Soviet Audience

1 The Soviet period was initiated in 1922 with the creation of the Union of Soviet Socialist Republics (USSR) and was dissolved in 1991. Initially, it consisted of Russia, Ukraine, Belarus, and Transcaucasia (Georgia, Armenia, and Azerbaijan) but gradually encompassed fifteen republics. The USSR was often incorrectly used as a synonym for Russia, which was the largest and dominant constituent state of the federation.

2 Willmar Sauter, "Who Reacts When, How and Upon What: From Audience Surveys to the Theatrical Event," *Contemporary Theatre Review* 12 (2002): 115–29 (116).

3 For a detailed look at these debates, see Irena R. Makaryk, *Shakespeare in the Undiscovered Bourn: Les Kurbas, Ukrainian Modernism, and Early Soviet Cultural Politics* (Toronto: University of Toronto Press, 2004), *passim*, ch. 4, 144–64.

4 For Kurbas's ambitious plan to stage the full canon of Shakespeare's plays and the politics of the time that prevented its fulfillment, see Makaryk, *Shakespeare in the Undiscovered Bourn.*

5 Les' Kurbas, "Suspil'ne pryznachennia mystets'koho tvoru i etapy rozvytku suchasnykh teatriv. Molodyi teatr" [The Social Purpose of the Artistic Work and the Stages of its Development in Contemporary Theatres. The Young Theatre], in *Berezil': Les' Kurbas iz tvorchoï spadshchyny* [Berezil: From the Creative Legacy of Les Kurbas], ed. M.H. Labins'kyi (Kyiv: Dnipro, 1988), 91.

6 Les' Kurbas, "Rezhysers'kyi shchhodennyk, iz staroho zshytka" [Director's Diary, from an Old Notebook] (1920), Bila Tserkva 16/08, 1922, Instytut mystetstva, folkloru i etnohrafii im. M. Ryl's'koho, Akademiia Nauk Ukrainy, f. 42/49, 11.

7 Les' Kurbas, "Pro vykhovannia samostiinoho, dumaiuchoho, tvorchoho aktyvnoho rezhysera" [About the Education of an Independent,

Thoughtful, and Creative Stage Director], dated January 17, 1926, reprinted in Labins'kyi, 69.

8 Sauter, "Who Reacts," 127–8. Sauter does not provide a source for this information.

9 Exhibition organized by Pierre Théberge, then director of the National Gallery of Canada. The exhibition catalogue of the same name examines some of the connections between Harlequin and "the thrice-great" Hermes. Jean Clair, ed., *The Great Parade: Portrait of the Artist as Clown* (New Haven and London: Yale University Press, 2004), 336.

10 For example, see Kurbas's, "Director's Diary."

11 "Berezil" is the archaic Ukrainian term for "March," the first month of spring and the beginning of the year in the old calendar. It suggests youth, energy, revolution. In choosing this name, Kurbas was inspired by a poem by the Norwegian writer Bjørnstjerne Bjørnsone.

12 Iryna Avdievna, "Pro naikrashchu liudynu, iaku ia znala v iunatski roky" [About the Best Person I Ever Knew in My Youth], in *Les' Kurbas: spohady suchasnykiv* [Les' Kurbas: Reminiscences by His Contemporaries] (Kyiv: Mystetstvo, 1969), ed. Vasyl' Vasyl'ko (Kyiv: Mystetstvo, 1969), 147–57 (150).

13 Vasyl' Desniak, "Berezil," *Hlobus* 5 (Kyiv, 1925): 116–7. Also see "B.," "Raionnyi teatr-maisternia 'Berezil' v Mokrii Kalyhirtsi" [Regional Theatre-Workshop of the Berezil in Mokra Kalyhirka] *Hlobus* 7 (1925): 165. The unidentified author mentions three branches of the Berezil: dramatic, vocal music, and instrumental music sections, as well as a Jewish section and a children's theatre. The model explicitly followed was that of the touring group Berezil created in Bila Tserkva and was composed of "ideologically sure co-workers of poor and working class origins."

14 For a detailed reconstruction, see Makaryk, *Shakespeare in the Undiscovered Bourn*, ch. 2. The full questionnaire was first reproduced and briefly discussed by actor-director Vasyl' Vasy'lko in the appendix to his diary. A member of the director's lab, Vasyl'ko also appears to have been responsible for tabulating the results or at least for publishing them. Vasyl' Vasyl'ko, "Pidsumky" [Summary]. See Vasyl' Vasyl'ko, *Shchodennyk* [Unpublished Diary], vol. 5, 1 January 1923 to 14 May 1924, MS10369, 85-6, Ukrainian State Museum of Theatre, Music, and Cinema Arts (Kyiv).

15 Dean Keith Simonton, "Qualitative and Quantitative Analyses of Historical Data," *Annual Review of Psychology* 54 (2003): 619–20 (619).

16 Gary Thurston, "Theatre and Acculturation in Russia from Peasant Emancipation to the First World War," *Journal of Popular Culture* 18.2 (Fall 1984): 3–16 (10). The questions posed were: Did the audience understand the plays? Were they satisfied with the entertainment? What did they understand to be the moral significance of the show?

17 Gary Thurston, *The Popular Theatre Movement in Russia, 1862–1919* (Evanston, Ill.: Northwestern University Press, 1998), 136.

18 As a citizen of the Austro-Hungarian empire, Kurbas would also have had access to information about questionnaires in journals or from other sources, but, so far, an exploration of both German and Polish sources has not yielded any results.

19 Lars Kleberg, "The Nature of the Soviet Audience," in *Russian Theatre in the Age of Modernism*, eds. Robert Russell and Andrew Barratt (Basingstoke: Macmillan, 1990), 172–95 (191, note 15).

20 Lars Kleberg has shown that audience research seems to have been more firmly established in children's and youth theatre and speculates that it was probably only later transferred to adult theatre. The methods employed were mostly observation but simple questionnaires were also sometimes distributed to teachers or parents. It was an informal and loosely-constructed practice whose aim was to ensure that the entertainment provided was not just satisfying to its young audience but also morally and ethically educative. In that sense, the aims of the surveys of both the Nevsky Society and the children's theatres appear to have served similar functions. (See Kleberg, "Nature," 181, 184).

21 Vsevolod Meyerhold was in Kyiv in 1923, where a famous "face-off" occurred: three productions by Meyerhold and three by Kurbas. The partisan Kyivan press pronounced Kurbas the winner. Meyerhold, impressed with Kurbas's *Jimmie Higgins*, invited him to bring the show to Moscow. For press coverage, see Em. Boim, "Kurbas–Meierkhol'd" [Kurbas – Meyerhold], *Teatral'naia gazeta* [Theatrical Newspaper] (Kharkiv) 18 (20–6 Oct 1924): 2; Panfuturyst-ekstruktor [pseud.. Mykola Bazhan], "Les' Kurbas i Vsevolod Meierkhol'd" [Les' Kurbas and Vsevolod Meyerhold], *Bil'shovyk* (Kyiv) 138 (740) (23 June 1923): 2–3., and "Ia. F.," "Kurbas i Meierkhol'd (Lyst z Kyiva)" [Kurbas and Meyerhold (A Letter from Kyiv)], *Visti VUTsVK* (Kharkiv) 137 (24 June 1923): 3, Kurbas papers, Instytut mystetstva, folkloru i etnografii im. M. Ryl's'koho [The Ryl's'kyi Institute of Art, Folklore and Ethnography], Academy of Sciences of Ukraine, f. 42/53. "Ia. F" commented: "Meyerhold has heroes; Kurbas has masses … their movements are organized into harmonious music-like waves … not a photographic but a deeply artistic impression of the struggle of the proletariat." (3).

22 See Lars Kleberg, "The Audience as Myth and Reality," in *Theatre as Action: Soviet Russian Avant-Garde Aesthetics*, trans. Charles Rougle (Houndmills: Macmillan, 1990), ch. 9, 93–102. In his article, "The Nature of the Soviet Audience," 192, note 28, Kleberg observes that, in 1925, Meyerhold's theatre also used "objective" research questions for evaluating guest performances in towns outside of Moscow.

23 M. Zagorskii, M., "Kak reagiruet zritel'" [How the Spectator Reacts], *Lef* 2
   (6) (1924): 141–51.

24 Zagorsky, "Kak reagiruet zritel'," 151.

25 Parenthetically, we may note the continuing problem of terminology: the
   collective noun "audience" implies homogeneity and connotes a passive
   listening mode; the alternative term "spectators" is equally unsatisfactory in
   focusing on the act of looking, again, with a passive connotation.

26 Zagorsky, "Kak reagiruet zritel'," 141–2.

27 Makaryk, *Shakespeare in the Undiscovered Bourn.*

28 Yurii Boboshko, *Rezhyser Les' Kurbas* [The Director Les' Kurbas] [Kyiv:
   Mystetstvo, 1987], 63.

29 Yana Leonenko points out that Les' Kurbas was the first director in Ukraine
   to emphasize the rhythmic arc of theatrical productions. Over the years,
   various composers worked on the scores for his productions. Among them
   was Anatoly (Anatolii) Buts'kyi (a.k.a. "Butskoi") who lectured the Berezil
   actors on the contemporary music scene, and actively published, and
   composed atonal music. See Yana Leonenko, "Music in the Theatre of Les
   Kurbas." in *Modernism in Kyiv: Jubilant Experimentation,* eds. Irena R. Makaryk
   and Virlana Tkacz (Toronto: University of Toronto Press, 2010), 343–58.

30 Bronislava Nijinska, the choreographer, dancer, and sister of Vaclav Nijinsky,
   founded a School of Movement (École de Mouvement) in 1919 in Kyiv
   where she created the first non-representational dances and also taught
   movement to Kurbas's actors. See Maria Ratanova, "The Choreographic
   Avant-garde in Kyiv, 1916–1921: Bronislava Nijinska and Her École de
   Mouvement," in Makaryk and Tkacz, *Modernism in Kyiv,* 311–20. The most
   recent work on Nijinska is the massive biography by Lynn Garafola, *La
   Nijinska: Choreographer of the Modern* (Oxford University Press, 2022).

31 O. Kysil', "Novyi ukraïns'kyi teatr" [The New Ukrainian Theatre], *Zhyttia i
   revolutsiia* [Life and Revolution] (Kyiv) 4 (1925): 40–4 (44).

32 Iurii Smolych, "Pro vyvchannia hliadacha" [About the Education of the
   Spectator], *Nove mystetstvo* [New Art] (Kharkiv) 12 (23 March 1926): 4–5.
   In another article, Smolych urged the Berezil to commit their theory to
   paper because of the dearth of work on the sociology and theory of theatre.
   Iurii Smolych, "Teatral'na nauka" [Theatrical Education], *Kul'tura i pobut*
   [Culture and Daily Life] (Kharkiv) 1–2 (1925): 2–3.

33 M. Kruchynin, "Pidsumky pershoï Vseukrains'koï teatral'noï narady"
   [Summary of the First All-Ukrainian Theatre Conference], *Nove mystetstvo*
   (Kharkiv) 12 (23 March 1926): 1–2. (1).

34 In the 1923–4 season, 43,436 spectators attended ninety-four performances
   of eight plays; of these, 30 per cent were workers, 15 per cent peasants, 17
   per cent students, 30 per cent workers-*intelligentsia,* and 8 per cent military
   personnel. In the 1924–5 season, the numbers rose by over twelve thousand:

55,552 had seen their productions. Of these, 42 per cent were workers, 22 per cent peasants, 36 per cent workers-*intelligentsia* who attended sixty-eight performances of six plays (Vasyl'ko, "Pidsumky"). Vasyl'ko's figures were cited by D. Usenko who, analysing this information, argued that the Berezil had entered a new creative phase and that it had successfully attracted a large and mixed audience. D. Usenko, "Hliadach prybuvae' ('Berezil' sezon 24–25 r.)" [The Spectators Are Coming. (Berezil' season 1924–25)] *Kul'tura i pobut* 29 (2 August, 1925): n.p., Kurbas papers, Instytut mystetstva, folkloru i etnografii im. M. Ryl's'koho, Academy of Sciences of Ukraine, f. 42/52.

35 Such a division of audience response was also felt by actors like Iryna Avdieva, who commented about the divide separating those who supported the new theatre from those who still preferred theatre of the old ethnographic variety (Avdieva, "Pro naikrashchu liudynu," 150).

36 Les' Kurbas, "Berezil' i teperishni ioho dosiahnennia shcho do teatral'noï formy" [The Berezil and its Current Achievements in Terms of Theatrical Form], *Hlobus* (Kyiv) 5 (1925): 118–20 (118). Also see P. Bereza-Kudryts'kyi', "Berezil' v sezoni 1924/25 roku i ioho blyzhchi perspektyvy" [The Berezil in the 1924/25 Season and its Immediate Prospects], *Zhyttia i revoliutsiia* (Kyiv) 3 (1925): 89–90.

37 Kurbas produced three films: *Arsenal, Vendetta,* and *Macdonald,* They were all destroyed, probably after Kurbas was removed from his post as artistic director of the Berezil and then shot in the far north in 1937. For a discussion of Kurbas's film work, see Irena R. Makaryk, "Dissecting Time/ Space: The Scottish Play and the New Technology of Film," in Makaryk and Tkacz, *Modernism in Kyiv,* 443–77.

38 The Theses had been confirmed by the Central Committee of the Party on 29 December 1926 and published in the Ukrainian press in early January 1927. "Tezy pro teatral'nu krytyku" [Theses About Theatrical Criticism], *Nove mystetstvo* (Kharkiv) 3 (18 Jan. 1927): 10–11, continued in 4 (25 Jan. 1927): 14–15.

39 Central Committee of the Party,"Tezy."

40 Ivan Piskun, *Ukrains'kyi radians'kyi teatr* [Soviet Ukrainian Theatre] (Kyiv: Derzhavne vydavnytstvo obrazotvorchoho mystetstva i muzychnoi literatury, 1957), 9.

41 On the literary debates see Myroslav Shkandrij, *Modernists, Marxists, and the Nation: The Ukrainian Literary Discussion of the 1920s* (Edmonton: Canadian Institute of Ukrainian Studies, 1992).

8. In a Crooked Mirror: *Hamlet* as Intertext in the USSR 1934–1943

1 Sheila Fitzpatrick, *The Cultural Front: Power and Culture in Revolutionary Russia* (Ithaca: Cornell University Press, 1992), 2.

2 For a detailed study of the place of Shakespeare in the early Soviet cultural debates see Irena R. Makaryk, *Shakespeare in the Undiscovered Bourn: Les Kurbas, Ukrainian Modernism, and Early Soviet Cultural Politics* (Toronto: University of Toronto Press, 2004).

3 Katerina Clark, *Moscow, the Fourth Rome. Stalinism, Cosmopolitanism, and the Evolution of Soviet Culture, 1931–1941* (Cambridge, MA: Harvard University Press, 2011), 11.

4 Analyses of dissident Shakespeare may be found in Dennis Kennedy, ed., *Foreign Shakespeare* (Cambridge University Press, 1993); Michael Hattaway, Boika Sokolova, and Derek Roper, eds., *Shakespeare in the New Europe* (Sheffield: Sheffield Academic Press, 1994); Makaryk, *Shakespeare in the Undiscovered Bourn*; Irena R. Makaryk and Joseph G. Price, eds., *Shakespeare in the Worlds of Communism and Socialism* (Toronto: University of Toronto Press, 2006); and Irena R. Makaryk and Marissa McHugh, eds., *Shakespeare and the Second World War* (Toronto: University of Toronto Press, 2012).

5 D.T. Vakulenko, "Vstup" [Introduction], *Oleksandr Korniychuk. Dramatychni tvory* [Oleksandr Korniychuk. Dramatic Works] (Kyiv: Naukova Dumka, 1990), 5–34 (8).

6 Vakulenko, "Vstup," 9.

7 Régine Robin, *Socialist Realism: An Impossible Aesthetic*, trans. Catherine Porter (Stanford: Stanford University Press, 1992), xxiii, 70.

8 For example, Susan Bennett, *Performing Nostalgia: Shifting Shakespeare and the Contemporary Past* (London and New York: Routledge, 1996), 20.

9 Katerina Clark and Evgeny Dobrenko, "Note on the Documents," in Katerina Clark, Evgeny Dobrenko, Andrei Artizov, Oleg Naumov, *Soviet Culture and Power: A History in Documents, 1917–1953*, trans. Marian Schwartz (New Haven: Yale University Press, 2007), xi.

10 Sarah Davies and James Harris, "Joseph Stalin: Power and Ideas," in *Stalin: A New History*, eds. Sarah Davies and James Harris (Cambridge: Cambridge University Press, 2005), 1–17 (9).

11 These are, respectively, the titles of first and seventh chapter of Geoffrey Roberts, *Stalin's Library: A Dictator and His Books* (New Haven and London: Yale University Press, 2022).

12 Laurence Senelick and Sergei Ostrovsky, eds., *The Soviet Theater. A Documentary History* (New Haven: Yale University Press, 2014), 9.

13 Simon Sebag Montefiore, *Stalin. The Court of the Red Tsar* (London: Weidenfeld and Nicolson, 2003; rpt. Phoenix, 2004), 138.

14 The Great Terror or the Great Purges of the 1930s was a period in which millions were killed or incarcerated. While some scholars attribute this terrible period to the USSR's fear of being surrounded by capitalist countries, others attributed it to Stalin's paranoia. The "great mass of purge victims" were ordinary people. See David W. Lovell. "Piercing together the past:

the Comintern, the CPA, and the Archives," in *Our Unswerving Loyalty*, eds. David W. Lovell and Windle (Canberra: ANU Press, 2008), 4, as well as Stalin's important speech on the "Defects in Party Work and Measures for Liquidating Trotskyite and Other Double Dealers" in which he elaborates his view of "capitalist encirclement" and the idea that bourgeois countries were sending "more wreckers, spies, diversionists, and killers than to the rear of any bourgeois state," in "Report to the Plenum of the Central Committee of the RKP(b)," March 3, 1937 (parts 1–3 of 5) (Moscow: Cooperative Publishing Society of Foreign Workers in the USSR, 1937), accessed through Marxists Internet Archive (2005), https://www.marxists.org/.

15 Katerina Clark and Evgeny Dobrenko, "Introduction: The Bolshevization of Culture of 1917–1932," in Clark, Dobrenko, Artizov, and Naumov, *Soviet Culture and Power* 3–6 (5).

16 RGASPI f. 558, op. 11, d.1116, l.32 (26 October 1932). Quoted in David Priestland, "Stalin as Bolshevik Romantic: Ideology and Mobilisation, 1917–1939," in *Stalin: A New History*, eds. Sarah Davies and James Harris (Cambridge University Press, 2005), 181–201 (194).

17 Erik van Ree, *The Political Thought of Joseph Stalin. A Study in Twentieth-century Revolutionary Patriotism* (New York: Routledge, 2002), 174.

18 Ree, *Political Thought*, 174.

19 Biographies of Stalin are legion, among them, Joseph Iremaschwili, *Stalin und die Tragödie Georgiens* (Berlin: Verfasser, 1932); Leon Trotsky, *Stalin: An Appraisal of the Man and His Influence*, 1941, ed. trans. Charles Malamuth (New York: Stein and Day, 1967); Isaac Deutscher, *Stalin: A Biography* (Oxford: Oxford University Press, 1949); Robert Tucker, *Stalin as Revolutionary: A Study in History and Personality 1879–1929* (New York: Norton, 1973); Roy Medvedev and Zhores Medvedev, *The Unknown Stalin: His Life, Death and Legacy*, trans. Ellen Dahrendorf (Woodstock, N.Y.: Overlook Press, 2004); Robert Service, *Stalin: A Biography* (London: Pan Books, 2004); Stephen Kotkin, *Stalin: Volume 1. Paradoxes of Power 1878–1928* (New York: Penguin, 2014) and Stephen Kotkin, *Stalin: Volume 2., Waiting for Hitler* (New York: Penguin, 2017); and Christopher Read, *Stalin: From the Caucasus to the Kremlin* (New York: Routledge, 2017), https://www.taylorfrancis.com/books/9781315527642; as well as the excellent Davies and Harris, *Stalin: A New History*.

20 For a discussion of Stalin's knowledge (or lack of knowledge) of Shakespeare, see Irena R. Makaryk, "Shakespeare and Stalin," in *The Shakespeare International Yearbook. 18. Special Section, Soviet Shakespeare*, eds. Tom Bishop, Alexa Alice Joubin, and Natalia Khomenko (New York and London: Routledge, 2021), 43–60.

21 Uncorrected transcript of I.V. Stalin's speech at the session of the TsK VKP(b). RGASPI, f. 77, op.I, d. 907, ll. 72–82. 9 September 1940; in Clark and Dobrenko, "Note," 300–1.

22 Document 175, Authorized transcript of the conversation between I.V. Stalin, A.A. Zhdanov, V.M. Molotov, S.M. Eisenstein, and N.K. Cherkasov, concerning *Ivan the Terrible*, 26 February 1947, in Clark and Dobrenko, "Note," 441.

23 RGASPI f. 558, op. 11, d. 1116, l.27 (20 October 1932). Quoted in Priestland, "Stalin as Bolshevik Romantic," 194.

24 Maxim Gorky (Gor'kii), "O p'esakh" [About Plays], in *M. Gor'kii o literature* [Gorky About Literature], ed. L. Levina (Moscow: Gosudarstevnnoe idzdate'lstvo khudozhetvennoi literatury, 1961), 377. All translations are the author's.

25 Gorky, "O p'esakh," 377.

26 Gorky, "O p'esakh," 382.

27 Cited in Robin, *Socialist Realism*, 61.

28 Clark, *Moscow*, 114.

29 Davies and Harris, *Stalin's World*, 252.

30 Davies and Harris, *Stalin's World*, 252.

31 Clark, *Moscow*, 81.

32 Roman Samarin, "Preface," in *Shakespeare in the Soviet Union; A Collection of Articles*, eds. Roman Samarin and Alexander Nikolyukin, trans. Avril Pyman (Moscow: Progress Publishers, 1966), 7–14 (7).

33 P.A. Markov, *The Soviet Theatre* (New York: Benjamin Blom, 1972), 21–2.

34 Joseph MacLeod, *The New Soviet Theatre* (London: George Allen and Unwin, 1943), 218.

35 As many scholars have pointed out, including Eleanor Rowe, *Hamlet: A Window on Russia* (New York: New York UP, 1976), viii; Peter Holland, "'More a Russian than a Dane': The Usefulness of *Hamlet* in Russia," in *Translating Life: Studies in Transpositional Aesthetics*, ed. Shirley Chew and Alistair Stead (Liverpool: Liverpool University Press, 1999), 315–38 (336); Alexei Semenenko, *Hamlet the Sign: Russian Translations of Hamlet and the Literary Canon Formation* (Stockholm: Stockholm University, 2007), 11–13.

36 As explored in Ivan Turgenev's short story, "The Hamlet of Shchigri District," which appeared in his collection *A Sportsman's Sketches* (1852), and in his essay, "Hamlet and Don Quixote" (1861). The story was published in English in Ivan Turgenev, *The Novels of Ivan Turgenev*, Vol. IX, trans. Constance Garnett (New York: AMS Press, 1970). The essay, translated by Robert Nichols (London: Henderson's, 1930), was reprinted in the Folcroft Library Editions, 1972.

37 Rowe, *Hamlet: A Window on Russia*, 127.

38 Graham Holderness, "'I Covet Your Skull': Death and Desire in *Hamlet*," in *Shakespeare Survey: Theatres for Shakespeare* 60 (2007): 223–36 (224), University of Hertfordshire Research Archive, 4 Mar. 2008. Accessed 2 December 2011.

39 Marvin Carlson, *The Haunted Stage: The Theatre as Memory Machine* (Ann Arbor: University of Michigan Press, 2001), 78–9.

40 For discussions of the skull as prop throughout the ages see Holderness, "I Covet Your Skull"; Andrew Softer, "The Skull on the Renaissance Stage: Imagination and the Erotic Life of Props," *English Literary Renaissance* 28.1 (1998): 47–74 (1998); Alan R. Young, "Eighteenth- and Nineteenth-Century Visual Representations of the Graveyard Scene in Hamlet," in *Stage Directions in Hamlet: New Essays and New Directions*, ed. Hardin L. Aasand (Madison: Fairleigh Dickinson UP, 2003), 189–213; Elizabeth Williamson, "Yorick's Afterlives: Skull Properties in Performance," *Borrowers and Lenders: The Journal of Shakespeare and Appropriation* (April 2011), vol. 6, issue 1, accessed 2 December 2011; the André Tchaikowsky Website at http://andretchaikowsky.com/. The late pianist gifted his skull to the Royal Shakespeare Company for its use in performance.

41 Diana Taylor, *The Archive and the Repertoire: Performing Cultural Memory in the Americas* (Durham and London: Duke University Press, 2003), 20.

42 Taylor, *Archive and the Repertoire*, 28–30.

43 *Platon Krechet* premiered on 20 December 1934 at the Ivan Franko Theatre (Kyiv) and was directed by Kost' Koshevs'kyi.

44 D.T. Vakulenko, "Oleksandr Korniychuk" in *Istoriya ukraïn'skoï literatury v dvokh tomakh. Radians'ka literatura* [The History of Ukrainian Literature in Two Volumes. Soviet Literature], 2 Vols., eds. I.O. Dzeverin et al. (Kyiv: Naukova Dumka, 1988), Vol.2, 533–45 (533).

45 Harold B. Segel, "Drama of Struggle: The Wartime Stage Repertoire," in *Culture and Entertainment in Wartime Russia*, ed. Richard Stites (Bloomington and Indianapolis: Indiana University Press, 1995), 108–25 (123).

46 I. Duz', *Oleksandr Korniichuk. Literaturnyi portret* [Oleksandr Korniichuk. A Literary Portrait] (Kyiv: Khudozhnia literatura, 1963). Biographical details about Korniichuk may also be found in Rostyslav Kolomiiets', *Frankivtsi. Teatr i chas. Mytets' i vlada. Dusha i stsena* [The Franko Theatre Artists. Theatre and Time. The Artist and Power. The Soul and the Stage] (Kyiv: Vidrodzhennia, 1995), 77–85; Vakulenko, "Oleksandr Korniichuk," 533–45; and S.M. Tsalyk and P.O. Selihey, "Oleksandr Korniichuk: Taiemnytsi chervonoho Shekspira" [Oleksandr Korniychuk: Secrets of the Red Shakespeare], in *Tayemnytsi pys'mennyts'kykh shukhliad: detektyvna istoriia ukraïns'koï literatury* [Secrets of Writers' Drawers; A Detective History of Ukrainian Literature] (Kyiv: Nash Chas, 2011), 116–39.

47 Tsalyk and Selihey, "Oleksandr Korniichuk," 117.

48 Pierre Bourdieu, *The Field of Cultural Production: Essays on Art and Literature*, ed. Ed. R. Johnson (New York: Columbia University Press, 1993), 176.

49 "Korniichuk, Oleksandr Ievdokhmovych," *Wikipedia: The Free Encyclopedia* (Ukrainian Version). Wikimedia Foundation, Inc. n.d., accessed 2 December 2011.

50 Vakulenko, "Oleksandr Korniichuk," 538.

51 Kolomiiets', *Frankivtsi. Teatr*, 78.

52 Bourdieu, *Field*, 93.

53 Régine Robin, in Robin, *Socialist Realism*, makes the important point that "[i]n Soviet society, the literary institution does not occupy the same place in the social ensemble that it holds in Western societies. It plays a role of the first order in the formation of the social imaginary, in the constitution of a collective memory, in the elaboration of a reading of the past, and in the internalization of the dominant system of values. What counts is less its literariness than its conformity to a minimal model that allows a consensus to evolve in the framework of the same fundamental values" (295).

54 In addition to the USSR, the play was also staged in Bulgaria, Romania, Czechoslovakia, Poland, China, and Korea. See Duz', *Oleksandr Korniichuk*, 46.

55 Vakulenko, "Oleksandr Korniichuk," 536.

56 Kolomiiets', *Frankivtsi. Teatr*, 79.

57 Korniichuk, 72. Citations from this play come from the 1935 text, a translation into Russian authorized by the author himself (as noted on the title page). Despite extensive efforts (including the assistance of the University of Ottawa Interlibrary Loan staff), I have been unable to locate a copy of the Ukrainian original. The play was subsequently republished in 1947, 1965, and 1990; in these later versions, Platon's speech disappears and his ambition is scaled down. He now aims to lengthen life rather than to challenge death. Oleksandr Korniychuk, *Platon Krechet. Vybrane* [Platon Krechet. Selected [Works]] (Kyiv: Radians'kyi pys'mennyk, 1947); Oleksandr Korniichuk, *P'iesy* [Plays] (Kyiv: Dnipro, 1965); and *Dramatychni tvory* [Dramatic Works] (Kyiv: Naukova Dumka, 1990).

58 Korniichuk, 1935, 32.

59 Korniichuk, 1935, 51.

60 Hester Lees-Jeffries, *Shakespeare and Memory* (Oxford University Press, 2013), 104.

61 Kolomiiets', *Frankivtsi. Teatr*, 79.

62 Andrei Zhdanov's and Gorky's formulas for socialist realism. See Robin, *Socialist Realism* for a book length analysis of the aesthetics of socialist realism.

63 Notably, Korniychuk's work responded to the then current slogan, "Bol'she shekspirizirovat!" (roughly, "More Shakespeare-ization"), a call to create great world literature. As Katerina Clark has pointed out, in Clark, *Moscow*, 1935 could be considered "the year of Shakespeare" (234) not only because of the many productions at that time but also because of the many debates about Shakespeare, including his function as writer and his relationship to his audience (e.g., was he a bard of the people or a writer for the higher social classes?)

64 Valentyna Kharkhun, "Poetyka dramy Oleksandra Korniichuka *Platon Krechet* sotsrealistychna proektsiia" [The Poetics of Oleksander Korniychuk's *Platon Krechet*, a Socialist Realist Projection] *Naukovyi visnyk Izmail's'koho derzhavnoho humanitarnoho universytetu* [Scholarly Bulletin of the Izmail State Humanities University] 24 (2008): 96–101(97). For a full-length study of the positive hero, see Rufus Mathewson Jr., *The Positive Hero in Russian Literature* (Stanford, California: Stanford University Press, 1975).

65 Robin, *Socialist Realism*, xx, 70.

66 Kolomiiets', *Frankivtsi. Teatr*, 79.

67 Tsalyk and Selihey, "Oleksandr Korniychuk," 120.

68 Tsalyk and Selihey, "Oleksandr Korniychuk," 120.

69 Hnat Iura, "Nashe sorokorichchia" [Our Fortieth] (1960) in Hnat Iura, *Zhyttia i stsena* [Life and Stage] (Kyiv: Mystetstvo, 1965), 47–55 (51).

70 Hnat Iura, "Nash obovyazok pered kraïnoiu" [Our Responsibility to Our Country] (1942), *Zhyttia i stsena*, 63–74 (74).

71 Iura, "Nashe sorokorichchia," 50.

72 MacLeod, *The New Soviet Theatre*, 184.

73 Vakulenko, "Vstup," 70. I am grateful to Professor Maria Ignatieva, Ohio State University, for mentioning to me that *Platon Krechet* was one of the required texts she had had to read as a student in the Russian SSR. In addition to the mandatory reading of his plays, the state ensured that people saw them performed. Thus, for example, Nikita Khrushchev brought in busloads of peasants from the collective farms to the theatre in order to experience Korniychuk's plays.

74 Vakulenko, "Oleksandr Korniychuk," 534, 537.

75 Kolomiiets', *Frankivtsi. Teatr*, 79.

76 Vladimir Torin, "Alexander Korneichuk," *Soviet Literature. International Literature* 4.5 (1939): 122–43 (123).

77 1941; cited in Vakulenko, "Vstup," 17.

78 The film was released in the UK as *Guerillas of the Don* (directed by Ihor Savchenko, 1942). The play, translated by Gerard Shelley and adapted by Tyrone Guthrie as *Guerillas of the Ukrainian Steppes*, was published in *Four Soviet War Plays* (London, New York: Hutchinson, 1944).

79 Korniichuk, *Partyzany v stepakh Ukrainy* [Partisans in the Steppes of Ukraine], in *Vybrane* [Selected Works], (Kyiv: Radians'kyi pys'mennyk, 1947), 291–330 (306).

80 Korniichuk, *Partyzany*, 308.

81 Korniichuk, *Partyzany*, 301.

82 Korniichuk, *Partyzany*, 320–1.

83 Korniichuk, *Partyzany*, 303.

84 Korniichuk, *Partyzany*, 303.

85 Valentyna Kharkhun, "Modyfikatsiï estetyky sotsrealizmu v umovakh 'zahrozhenoï' kul'tury" [Modifications to Socialist Realist Aesthetics in the Context of Culture 'Under Threat'], Lecture, Ukrainian Studies Program at the Harriman Institute, Columbia University, New York, 20 March 2012.

86 Kharkhun, Lecture.

87 Valerii Haidabura's examination of theatrical archives does not reveal a single production of *Partisans* on the stages of Ukraine during the war; however, it was performed throughout the Russian SSR and later in the Far East, when the company was later evacuated from Moscow. Valerii Haidabura, *Teatr, zakhovanyy v arkhivakh. Stsenichne mystetstvo v Ukraïni period nimets'ko-fashysts'koï okupatsiï (1941–1944). Istoriia, politika, dokumenty, ideï, khudozhni realiï, liuds'ki doli* [Theatre Hidden in the Archives. Theatre Art in Ukraine During the German-Fascist occupation (1941–4). History, politics, documents, ideas, artistic realities, people's fates] (Kyiv: Mystetstvo, 1998).

88 J.L. Austin, *How to Do Things With Words* (Oxford: Clarendon Press, 1962), 5–6.

89 As Vojtech Mastny points out, the heroic myth of Soviet "dedication, discipline, and conspiratorial prowess" was untrue; Communist strength was not only "uneven" geographically but even "downright embarassing"; the appeal of communist ideology "showed almost an inverse ratio to proximity" to Russia. Vojtech Mastny, *Russia's Road to the Cold War: Diplomacy, Warfare, and the Politics of Communism, 1941–1945* (New York: Columbia UP, 1979), 86.

90 Catherine Merridale, *Ivan's War: The Red Army 1939–1945* (London: Faber and Faber, 2006), 9. The situation remains unchanged. Already in 2009, then Russian President Medvedev announcing a new body, mostly comprised of intelligence services, to combat "falsification of history" and the work of foreign "revisionists." Professional historians were not invited to participate in the commission. Luke Harding, "The War? Nothing to Do With Stalin, Says Russia's President, Dmitry Medvedev," *The Guardian*, Guardian News and Media Ltd, 30 August 2009, accessed 2 December 2011.

91 Jay Winter and Emmanuel Sivan, "Setting the Framework," in *War and Remembrance in the Twentieth Century*, ed. Jay Winter and Emmanuel Sivan (Cambridge: Cambridge University Press, 2000), 6–39 (13).

92 Alon Confino, "Collective Memory and Cultural History: Problems of Method," *The American Historical Review* 102.5 (December 1997): 1386–403 (1390).

93 On the war as altering earlier myths about "the Marxist eschatological metanarrative" and re-articulating "political and ethno-national identities within the Soviet polity," see Amir Weiner, "The Making of a Dominant Myth: The Second World War and the Construction of Political Identities within the Soviet Polity," *Russian Review* 55.4 (1996): 638–60 (638–39).

94 Kharkhun, Lecture.

95 Iu. Dmitriieva, Y. and K.L. Rudnitskii, eds., *Istoriia russkogo sovetskogo dramaticheskogo teatra: 1916–1945* [History of the Soviet Russian Drama Theatre: 1916–1945] (Moscow: Prosveshcheniie, 1984), 297.

96 According to Valentyna Kharkhun, Stalin wrote a letter to Korniichuk when the writer had submitted his play to the Central Committee and suggested various editorial changes, a fact which suggests how important this play was to the Party. The play was subsequently published in the millions of copies.

97 G.A. Khaichenko, G.A., *Stranitsy istorii sovetskogo teatra* [Pages from the History of Soviet Theatre] (Moscow: Iskusstvo, 1965), 122.

98 Nikolai A. Gorchakov, *The Theatre in Soviet Russia,* trans. Edgar Lehrman (1943; New York: Columbia University Press, 1957), 372.

99 Oleksandr Korniichuk, *Front* [Front], in *Vybrane* [Selected Works] (Kyiv: Radians'kyi pys'mennyk, 1947), 331–85 (377).

100 Historians Richard Stites and Argyrios Pisiotis argue that the repetitive call for revenge led to the atrocities committed by the Soviets, which are still much less well known today than those of the Nazis. Richard Stites, "Introduction," in *Culture and Entertainment in Wartime Russia,* ed. Richard Stites (Bloomington and Indianapolis: Indiana University Press, 1995), 1–8 (3). Argyrios K. Pisiotis, "Images of Hate in the Art of War," in Stites, *Culture and Entertainment,* 141–56 (141).

101 Irina Vishnevskaia, *Istoriia sovetskogo dramaticheskogo teatra v shesti tomakh* [History of the Soviet Drama Theatre in Six Volumes], 6 vols. (Moscow: Nauka, 1969), vol. 5, 198.

102 Confino, "Collective Memory," 1390.

103 Rowe, *Hamlet: A Window on Russia,* viii.

104 Bennett, *Performing Nostalgia,* 12.

105 Bennett, *Performing Nostalgia,* 12.

106 Boris Pasternak, "Translating Shakespeare," trans. Manya Harari, in *I Remember: Sketch for an Autobiography,* trans. David Magarshack (New York: Pantheon, 1959), 123–52 (131).

107 Stefaniia Andrusiv, "Strakh pered movoiu iak psykhokompleks suchasnoho ukraïntsia." *Suchasnist'* (Kyiv and Munich) nos. 7–8 (July/August., 1995): 148–9.

108 Davies and Harris, *Stalin's World,* 2.

109 Davies and Harris, *Stalin's World,* 232.

110 Davies and Harris, *Stalin's World,* 13.

111 Michelle Assay, "What Did Hamlet (Not) Do to Offend Stalin," *Actes des congrès de la Société française Shakespeare, Shakespeare après Shakespeare,* 35 (2017). https://doi.org/10.4000/shakespeare.3840

112 Megan Ford, "Moscow Lashes Out Against Stalin Film," *The National Interest* (6 March 2018), http://nationalinterest.org/feature/moscow-lashes-out -against-stalin-film-24775.

113 This was in retaliation for the UK government's expulsion of Russian diplomats and its assertion that Russia was to blame for the poisoning of former double agent Sergei Skripal and his daughter Yulia on British soil.

9. *Hamlet,* 1943

1 Yosyp Hirniak, "The Birth and Death of the Modern Ukrainian Theatre," in Marthe Bradshaw, ed., *Soviet Theatre 1917–1941* (N.Y.: Research Program on the USSR, 1954), Yosyp Hirniak refers to the Ukrainian theatre as not only entertainment, but "also very often the leader and even the defender of the political rights of the Ukrainian people" (250). That his production was considered a subversive and nationalistic act may also be seen in the complete silence about Hirniak and his productions in Soviet stage histories. For example, in Iryna Vanina, *Shekspir na ukraïns'kii stseni* (Kyiv: Derzhavne vydavnytstvo obrazotvorchoho mystetstva i muzychnoï literatury URSR, 1958), the author asserts that the first Hamlet was a Soviet Ukrainian one, in 1956. The Soviet Ukrainian period of drama, covered in volume two of the history of the Ukrainian theatre, M.T. Ryl's'kyi, ed., *Ukraïns'kyi dramatychnyi teatr* (Kyiv: Akademiia Nauk URSR, 1959), makes no reference to the wartime theatre in Western Ukraine.

2 Halychyna is surprisingly referred to as a piedmont in the souvenir book of the production. See Ostap Tarnavs'kyi, ed., *Hamlet Viliama Shekspira* (Lviv: Zkw Druckereibetrieb, 1943), 11.

3 Valerii Haidabura, *Teatr, zakhovanyi v arkhivakh* [Theatre Hidden in the Archives] (Kyiv: Mystetstvo, 1998), 66.

4 Richard Stites, "Introduction," in *Culture and Entertainment in Wartime Russia,* ed. Stites (Bloomington and Indianapolis: Indiana University Press, 1995), 3–8 (3). Jan Gross, *Revolution from Abroad: The Soviet Conquest of Poland's Western Ukraine and Western Belorussia* (Princeton University Press, 1988) offers the most complete study of the atrocities of this period. As both Stites and Gross observe, while German atrocities of the war are well-publicized, those committed by the Russians against their "own" peoples are only slowly emerging from deliberate obscurity.

5 Orest Subtelny, *Ukraine: A History* (Toronto: University of Toronto Press, 1988), 476.

6 Yury Boshyk, ed., *Ukraine During World War II: History and Its Aftermath* (Edmonton: Canadian Institute of Ukrainian Studies. 1986), 257.

7 Volodymyr Kosyk, *Ukraine During World War II: 1938–1945,* trans. Roman Osadchuk (Kyiv, Paris, New York, Toronto: Council for Defense and Relief of Ukraine – UCCA, Prometheus Foundation, and Ukrainica Research Institute, 1992), 424.

8 The Lviv Opera Theatre (LOT) encompassed four sections: opera, operetta, ballet, and drama. Nearly six hundred people were employed by LOT during the German occupation (1941–4), producing eighteen operas and operettas, five ballets, and twenty-four plays in three years. *Hamlet* was directed by Iosyp Hirniak and starred Volodymyr Blavats'kyi as

Hamlet, Bohdan Pazdriy as Claudius, Vera Levyts'ka as Gertrude, and Eliza Shasharovs'ka as Ophelia. Music by Mykola Lysenko and Lev Turkevych. Set and costume design by Myroslav Hryhoriïv.

9 Mykhailo Ivasivka, "Ukrains'kyi Opernyi Teatr u L'vovi," in *Nash teatr: knyha diiachiv ukraïns'koho teatral'noho mystetstva, 1915–1975*, vol. 1. [Our Theatre: A Book of Ukrainian Theatre Artists] ed. Hryhor Luzhnyts'kyi (New York, Paris, Sydney, Toronto: Association of Ukrainian Theatre Artists, 1975), 321–54 (326). Dramatic performances were intended for Ukrainian audiences, while the German occupational forces saw ballet, opera, and operetta. The week was divided between "German days" (Friday to Sunday) and "Ukrainian days" (Tuesday to Thursday). It is not clear how many Nazis attended dramatic performances. Each play text and prompt book had to be submitted to them for inspection and approval. See Bogusław Drewniak, *Das Theater in NS-Staat: Szenarium deutscher Zeitgeschichte 1933–1946* (Dusseldorf: Droste Verlag, 1993), 133.

10 Drewniak, *Das Theater*, 133–4.

11 Werner Habicht, "Shakespeare and Theatre Politics in the Third Reich," in *The Play Out of Context*, eds. H. Sčolnicov and P. Holland (Cambridge: Cambridge UP, 1989), 110–1.

12 Drewniak, *Das Theater*, 133; Habicht, "Shakespeare and Theatre."

13 *Wille und Macht* (1 February 1940). See especially 3, 10, 5, 10.

14 Drewniak, *Das Theater*, 247.

15 Jutta Wardetzky, *Theaterpolitik im faschistischen Deutschland. Studien und Dokumente* (Berlin: Henschelverlag Kunst und Gesellschaft, 1983), 81.

16 Habicht, "Shakespeare and Theatre," 117; Gross, *Revolution from Abroad*, 52.

17 Drewniak, *Das Theater*, 107.

18 Ie. Blakytnyi, "Na emigratsiï (1942–1947)" [In Emigration], in *V maskakh epokhy*, eds. V. Khmuryi, Iu. Dyvnych, Ie. Blakytnyi, (Vydavnytstvo Ukraïna, 1948), 59.

19 So, according to the letters of Iosyp Hirniak. See his selected correspondence, Mariia Revakovych, ed., *Svito-vyd* (Kyiv-New York) IV (21) (October–December 1995), 68–69 on Blavats'kyi and *Hamlet*.

20 Bohdan Melians'kyi, "Z taemnykh hlybyn aktors'koï tvorchosti: rozmova z dir. V. Blavats'kym pro ioho pratsiu nad roleiu Hamleta" [From the Secret Depths of the Actor's Creativity: A Conversation with director V. Blavats'kyi About His Work on the Role of Hamlet], *L'vivs'ki visti* (L'viv) no. 1194 (1708), 30 October 1943: 3.

21 Valerian Revuts'kyi, *Neskoreni berezil'tsi: Iosyp Hirniak i Olimpia Dobrovol's'ka* [Unvanquished Members of Berezil: Yosoyp Hirniak and Olimpia Dobrovols'ka] (New York: Ukrainian Writers' Association in Exile, "Slovo," 1985), 160.

22 Revuts'kyi, *Neskoreni berezil'tsi*, 159–60.

23 Stites, *Culture and Entertainment*, 5.

24 Stites, *Culture and Entertainment*, 4.

25 Hirniak, "Birth and Death," 251.

26 The revival of nationalism in Russia was permitted at a very early stage. As Harold B. Segel, *Twentieth-Century Russian Drama: From Gorky to the Present* (New York: Columbia UP, 1979), 302, observes, "The more imminent war appeared to the Soviet Union in the late 1930s the more intensified became the spirit of Russian nationalism (as opposed to an official 'Party line.'" Ironically, "bourgeois" and "reactionary" heroes (such as General Kutuzov and tsar Peter) were held up for heroic emulation. See, for example, Konstantin Simonov's play *Russkie liudi* [Russian People] (1942), Alexei Tolstoi's two plays about Ivan the Terrible, especially *Trudnye gody* [Difficult Years] (1943), and Vladimir Soloviov's *Field-Marshal Kutuzov* (1940). At the same time as Russian nationalism was permitted, Ukrainian nationalism was castigated. Oleksandr Korniychuk contributed to the first issue of the propaganda newspaper launched on 31 July 1941, in which he laid the blame for the wartime destruction of Ukraine on Ukrainian nationalists. See Kosyk, *Ukraine During World War II*, 147. It should be noted that the Soviets permitted German nationalism under specific, controlled circumstances. The National Committee for a Free Germany was created by the Soviets in 1943 with the help of German prisoners of war and Soviet sympathizers. See Vojtech Mastny, *Russia's Road to the Cold War: Diplomacy, Warfare, and the Politics of Communism, 1941–1945* (New York: Columbia University Press, 1979), 80.

27 Subtelny, *Ukraine: A History*, 477.

28 Before the implicit ban, a Russian production of *Hamlet*, directed by Sergei Radlov, was staged in the Theatre of the Red Army in Kyiv in 1941. It was generally panned by the critics, who referred to it as too "romantic" and "declamatory," as well as insufficiently revelatory of Hamlet as a "fighter" for great human ideals. See, for example, G. Davydov, "*Hamlet*: prem'era v Kievskom teatre Krasnoi Armii" [The Premiere of *Hamlet* in the Kyiv Theatre of the Red Army], *Sovetskaia Ukraina* (29 April 1941), n.p.

29 As Harold Segel, *Twentieth-Century Russian Drama*, 315, notes that despite their minimal value as dramatic art, Korniichuk's plays were widely published and staged, especially in Russia, so that, for all intents and purposes, he was treated by literary scholars and by the Soviet theatregoing public as a Russian playwright. Segel's comments suggest one reason why Korniichuk's plays did not inspire Ukrainian national sentiment, although his *Bohdan Khmel'nyts'kyi* was sympathetically received in many quarters; this work played unabashedly to anti-Polish sentiment, especially in the concluding scene, in which the Polish flag was destroyed. Western Ukrainians would also have had fresh in their memories Korniichuk's arrival

in L'viv during the first communist occupation when he accompanied the first divisions of the Soviet army. Given the task of organizing theatrical life in "liberated" L'viv, he proceeded to introduce his own and other propagandistic plays into the repertoire. The surrounding towns of Stanislaviv and Drohobych were also assigned the same repertoires. After his departure, Korniichuk continued to control Lviv's theatrical life from a distance until the German invasion. See H. Luzhnyts'kyi, "Ukraïns'kyi teatr pislia vyzvol'nykh zmahan'" [Ukrainian Theatre After the Liberation Struggle], in Luzhnyts'kyi, *Nash teatr*, 50–3.

30 Donald R. Shanor, *Behind the Lines: The Private War against Soviet Censorship* (New York: St Martin's Press, 1985), 38.

31 Zbyněk Zeman, *Selling the War: Art and Propaganda in World War II* (London: Orbis Publishing, 1978), 8.

32 K.R.M. Short, ed., *Film and Radio Propaganda in World War II* (London and Canberra: Croom Helm Press, 1983), 100.

33 Short, *Film and Radio*, 111.

34 See An. Glebov, "Stalinskaia konstitutsiia i teatr" [The Stalinist Constitution and the Theatre], *Teatr* 8 (Moscow, 1937): 42.

35 Peter Kenez, "Black and White: The War on Film," in Stites, *Culture and Entertainment*, 157–75 (171).

36 Jeffrey Brooks, "Pravda Goes to War," in Stites, *Culture and Entertainment*, 9–27 (22).

37 Argyrios K. Pisiotis, "Images of Hate in the Art of War," in Stites, *Culture and Entertainment*, 141–56 (141).

38 Short, *Film and Radio*, 118; Kenez, "Black and White," 171; Jay Leyda, *Kino: A History of the Russian and Soviet Film* (London: George Allen and Unwin, 1960), 377.

39 Oleksandr Dovzhenko, *Hospody, poshly meni syly: kinopovisti, opovidannia, shchodennyk* [God, Send Me the Strength: Film Scripts, Stories, Diary] (Kharkiv: Folio, 1994), 199.

40 Dovzhenko, *Hospody, poshly meni syly*, 219.

41 Iura, Hnat, *Zhyttia i stsena* [Life and the Stage] (Kyiv: Mystetstvo, 1965), 91, 162.

42 Quoted in Richard Taylor, *Film Propaganda: Soviet Russia and Nazi Germany* (London: Croom Helm; New York: Barnes and Noble, 1979), 65. Also see Leyda, *Kino*, 170.

43 Quoted in Taylor, *Film Propaganda*, 46.

44 N. Gerken-Rusova, *Heroïchnyi teatr* [Heroic Theatre] (L'viv: Ol'ha Bachyns'ka, 1939).

45 Gerken-Rusova, *Heroïchnyi teatr*, xi. *Cf* Goebbels' call for a "heroic," "steely-romantic" and "unsentimentally direct" German theatre (cited in Habicht, "Shakespeare and Theatre," 110–11). Goebbels permitted the staging of classics for an interim period, until such time as a German heroic drama

was created. See Drewniak, chapter 10, "Theaterstücke ausländischer Autoren auf deutschen Bühnen 1933–1944" in Drewniak, *Das Theater.* For their part, the Soviets also called for a "militant" literature. See, for example, issues from 1941 of *Literatura i iskusstvo* [Literature and Art], the official mouthpiece of the Union of Soviet Writers. A lead article calls for Soviet art and literature to become "a weapon, to foster the fighting spirit of the people, to consolidate the force of patriotism, to fan the hatred for German-Fascist invaders, to call for revenge." Quoted in Gleb Struve, *Russian Literature under Lenin and Stalin 1917–1953* (Norman, Oklahoma: U of Oklahoma P, 1971), 319.

46 See, for example, R.A. Foakes, "The Reception of Hamlet," *Shakespeare Survey* 45 (1993): 1–13, who thoroughly studies the wider resonance of the Hamletism disease.

47 Cited in Eleanor Rowe, *Hamlet: A Window on Russia* (New York: N.Y. University Press, 1976), 135.

48 Melians'kyi, "Z taemnykh hlybyn," p 3.

49 V. Blavats'kyi, "Try roky L'vivs'koho opernoho teatru," *Kyiv* (Philadelphia, 1951), no. 1: 20–2.

50 Kost' Pan'kivs'kyi, *Roky nimets'koï okupatsiï* (New York: Kliuchi, 1965), 351. Cited in Ola Hnatiuk, *Courage and Fear*, trans. Ewa Siwak (Boston: Harvard Research Institute, 2019), 374. Translated from Polish by Hnatiuk's sister.

51 Anastasia Vasylyk-Furman, "Trahediia V. Shekspira 'Hamlet' u perekladi Mykhaila Rudnyts'koho" [Shakespeare's Tragedy of *Hamlet* in Mykhailo Rudnyts'kyi's Translation], in *Hamlet: Viliam Shekspir*, ed. Bohdan Kozak (Lviv: Vydavnychyi tsentr LNU im. Ivana Franka, 2008), pp. 5-18 (6). Earlier were translations by Iurii Fed'kovych, Panteleimon Kulish, Mykhailo Staryts'kyi, Iurii Klen, Leonid Hrebinka, and Viktor Ver.

52 Mykhailo Rudnyts'kyi, Letter to Volodymyr Blavats'kyi, cited in Oleh Lysiak, "Velykyi den' ukraïns'koho teatru" [A Great Day for Ukrainian Theatre], in Luzhnyts'kyi, *Nash Teatr*, 743–6 (744).

53 Ostap Tarnavs'kyi, *Literaturnyi Lviv 1939–1944. Spomyny* [Literary Lviv. Reminiscences], (L'viv: Prosvita, 1995), 159. Cited in Hnatiuk, *Courage and Fear*, 375.

54 Hnatiuk, *Courage and Fear*, 375.

55 Lysiak, "Velykyi den'." 744; Ivan Nimchuk, "Velykyi den' ukraïns'koho teatru u L'vovi" [A Great Day for Ukrainian Theatre in L'viv] *Krakivs'ki visti* [Krakow News] (Cracow) 26 September 1943.

56 Bohdan Kozak, "Palimpsest ukraïns'koho 'Hamleta': pereklad Mykhaila Rudnyts'koho i praprem'iera u L'vovi 1943 roku" [The Palimpsest of the Ukrainian Hamlet: The Translation of Mykhailo Rudynts'kyi and its Premiere in L'viv in 1943], in *Hamlet: Vil'iam Shekspir*, ed. Bohdan Kozak (Lviv: Vydavnychyi Tsentr LNU, 2008), pp, 170-188 (178).

57 In a letter to Volodymyr Blavats'kyi, Rudnyts'kyi claimed to have gone for medical treatment at the Morshyn spa (Kozak, "Palimpsest ukraïns'koho 'Hamleta,'" 179). Ola Hnatiuk extensively examines the life of Mykhailo Rudnyts'kyi, the "Galician Cosmopole," and the "sizable liberal community" of L'viv in which he participated. Rudnyts'kyi, like many others, especially his siblings, was living "on the precipice." Hnatiuk suggests that the illness which prevented him from attending the premiere was likely diplomatic (*Courage and Fear*, 306–97).

58 The complete letter is cited in Bohdan Kozak, "Palimpsest ukraïns'koho 'Hamleta'," 180.

59 Hnatiuk, *Courage and Fear*, 378–9.

60 Hnatiuk, *Courage and Fear*, 375.

61 Kozak, "Palimpsest ukraïn'skoho 'Hamleta,'" 176.

62 Nimchuk, "Velykyi den'," 26 September 1943.

63 For the specific and devastating consequences of these ukases for the Ukrainian theatre, see Valerian Revutsky, "The Act of Ems (1876) and Its Effect on Ukrainian Theatre," *Nationalities Papers* 5.1 (1977): 67–77.

64 For a brief stage history of Shakespeare in Ukraine, see Valerian Revutsky, "The First Stagings of Shakespeare in Ukraine," *Ukraïns'ka Shekspiriana na Zakhodi* [Ukrainian Shakespeareana in the West] (Edmonton, Alberta) 1 (1987): 14–19 and Valerian Revuts'kyi, "Do istorii ukraïns'koho *Hamleta*" [Towards a History of Ukrainian *Hamlet*], in *Tvory*, vol. IV, ed. E. Malaniuk (Toronto: Jurij Klen Foundation, 1960), 7–13. Iryna Vanina's officially-sanctioned accounts include *Shekspir na ukraïns'kii stseni* [Shakespeare on the Ukrainian stage] and the revised version, *Ukraïns'ka Shekspiriana* [Ukrainian Shakespeareana] (1964). An (incomplete) and heavily censored overview of *Hamlet* stagings may be found in F.S. Grim's "Russkaia i ukrainskaia gumanisticheskaia kontseptsiia tragedii Shekspira *Gamleta*" [Russian and Ukrainian Humanistic Concepts of Shakespeare's Tragedy of *Hamlet*] (Kyiv: Kievskii gosudarstvenyi pedagogicheskyi Institut im. A.M. Gorkogo, 1958). Some of the early twentieth-century Ukrainian productions included *Macbeth*, produced in 1919 (Kyiv), 1920 (Bila Tserkva, Uman), and 1924 (Kyiv); *Othello* in 1922 (Lviv) and 1926 (Katerynoslav); *The Taming of the Shrew* in 1922 (Kyiv); and *A Midsummer Night's Dream* in 1927 (Kyiv). *Hamlet* was announced by Kurbas in 1932 (with Hirniak in the lead role) and by the Zan'kovets'ka Theatre Ensemble in 1939, but in neither case (for different reasons) was it actually staged. The nineteenth century provides a sad litany of censorship decisions that refused permission to stage the various translations of *Hamlet* by Mykhailo Staryts'kyi, Osyp Fed'kovych, and Marko Krovypnyts'kyi.

65 Lysiak, "Velykyi den'," 744.

66 Ivasivka, "Ukraïns'kyi opernyi teatr u L'vovi," 326.

67 *Krakivs'ki visti* or *Krakauer Zeitung* (Cracow News) was the only remaining legal Ukrainian national press published in the *Generalgouvernment*. It had both a daily and a weekly edition; its circulation ran between eighteen thousand and twenty-six thousand.

68 As cited in Lysiak, "Velykyi den','" 744, 746.

69 V. Blavats'kyi, "Try roky L'vivs'koho opernoho teatru" [Three Years of the L'viv Opera Theatre], *Kyiv* (Philadelphia, 1951), no. 1: 20–2 (20).

70 According to the eyewitness account of Valerian Revuts'kyi, there were "a great many" Germans and Hungarians in the audience. V. Revuts'kyi, letter to me, 27 July 1994. Lysiak, "Velykyi den'" also references German and Czech notices (744, 746). I have only been able to trace one of these, a very brief notice, in the Czech paper *Lidové Listy* 5 November 1943, 3, which simply mentions that the Ukrainian première of *Hamlet* took place in Lemberg with Blavats'kyi in the lead role. My thanks to my Czech colleague, Martin Hilský, for tracking down this last reference in the National Library in Prague.

71 G. Hauswaldt, "Ukrainisches Schauspiel," *Krakauer Zeitung* (Cracow) 23 September 1943: 4.

72 A term Zeman uses throughout his book.

73 Nimchuk's delight is interestingly contextualized when one views the newspaper *L'vivs'ki visti* itself. Nimchuk's is the lead article on the page, forming a large L-shape with a drawing of Blavats'kyi's portrait in the first column. At the bottom of the page is a photo with the caption, "Harvest Festival in Stanislaviv." Below the photo is the explanation, "German guests [i.e., Nazis in uniform] speaking with Ukrainian peasants" – a reminder of where the real power lay.

74 Revuts'kyi, *Neskoreni berezil'tsi*, 87. For Hirniak's distaste for comparisons between actors of different national traditions (and particularly for Revuts'kyi's attempt at such comparisons), see his letter to Ostap Tarnavs'kyi reprinted in Revakovych, *Svito-vyd*, 68.

75 O. Tarnavs'kyi, ed., *Hamlet Viliama Shekspira* [William Shakespeare's Hamlet] (L'viv: Zkw Druckereibetrieb, 1943), 11.

76 Nimchuk, "Velykyi den'."

77 I. Nimchuk, "Vystava Hamleta u L'vovi" [The Production of *Hamlet* in L'viv] *Nashi dni* (L'viv), No. 10 (October 1943): 8–9 (8).

78 Tarnavs'kyi, *Hamlet Viliama Shekspira*, 15.

79 Nimchuk, "Vystava," 9.

80 Melians'kyi, "Z taemnykh hlybyn,"

81 Tarnavs'kyi, *Hamlet Viliama Shekspira*, 16.

82 Revuts'kyi, letter to me, 3 December 1992.

83 Revuts'kyi, letter to me, 3 December 1992.

84 The inclusion of the gravediggers' scene was another bold move. By contrast, see Anne Russell, "Garrick, Evans and the G.I. *Hamlet*: Authority and Appropriation," in *Shakespeare and the Second World War: Memory, Culture, Identity*, eds. Irena R. Makaryk and Marissa McHugh (University of Toronto Press, 2012), 233–51. Russell examines Maurice Evans' production of *Hamlet* for US troops in Hawaii in 1944. Evans cut the gravediggers scene perhaps, as Russell argues, because its scene of skulls and bones was not conducive to morale building. The whole production was "consistently uncomplex," according to Rosamond Gilder, "Matter and Art: Broadway in Review," *Theatre Arts* 30 (Fall, 1946): 76.

85 Ola Hnatiuk mentions that O. Bozhydan, who had been cast in Fortinbras and took part in rehearsals, suddenly took ill and, as a result, all of the Fortinbras' scenes were cut. Bohdan Kozak, however, studied the repertoire of the Lviv Opera Theatre and noticed that Bozhydan appeared in other plays at the very same time that he was mentioned as being ill in official publications relating to the production. This fact suggests that the Nazi censor had had a hand in trimming the play of all Fortinbras references. Kozak, "Palimpsest ukraïns'koho 'Hamleta,'" 184–5.

86 Melians'kyi, "Z taemnykh hlybyn,"

87 I. Nimchuk, "Z l'vivs'kykh teatriv" [From the L'viv Theatres], *Krakivs'ki visti* (Cracow) 19 November 1943: n.p.

88 Iosyp Hirniak's memoirs end just before his work on *Hamlet*. Hirniak, *Spomyny* [Memoirs], ed. Bohdan Boichuk (New York: Suchasnist, 1982). In various telephone conversations in 1994 with Boichuk, I discovered Hirniak's attitude to this production and the reason for his silence.

89 O.O. Kulyk, *L'vivs'kyi teatr imeni M.K. Zan'kovets'koï* [The M.K. Zan'kovets'ka Theatre of L'viv] (Kyiv: Mystetstvo, 1989), 62.

90 See Valerian Revutsky, "Theatre and Cinema," in *Ukraine: A Concise Encyclopaedia*, vol. II, ed. Volodmyr Kubijovyč (Toronto: U of Toronto P, 1971), 650.

91 Iurii Shums'kyi, *Opovidannia i statti; zustrichi, vrazhennia, obrazy* [Stories and Articles; Meetings, Impressions, Images] (Kyiv: Mystetstvo, 1964), 113.

92 On this point, see historian Catherine Merridale, *Ivan's War: The Red Army 1939–45* (London: Faber and Faber, 2005).

93 Coincidentally, as I was working on updates to this chapter, I was invited to an online roundtable discussion on 21 December 2023 commemorating the 80th anniversary of the premiere of this first Ukrainian production of *Hamlet*. Organized by Nataliya Torkut, Director of the Shakespeare Centre in Zaporizhzhia, Ukraine, the discussions concluded with the launch of a new virtual theatre museum focusing on this significant production, and making primary evidence, previously available only at the archives, now available to all interested researchers: https://www.artsteps.com/view/657d 8dcb3e7698b59c6de2a7.

10. Commemoration as Amplification:
The "Universal" versus the National Bard

1 Ton Hoenselaars and Clara Calvo, "Introduction: Shakespeare and the Cultures of Commemoration," *Critical Survey*, 22.2 (2010): 1–10 (1).

2 Marijan Dović and Jón Karl Helgason, *National Poets, Cultural Saints: Canonization and Commemorative Cults of Writers in Europe*, National Cultivation of Culture, 12 (Leiden and Boston: Brill, 2017), 203.

3 For details about the Old English Court Museum, see "The Old English Court Museum," accessed 14 October 2017, http://www.russianmuseums .info/M425.

4 See "Monument to Shakespeare to Be Unveiled in Moscow Near the Old English Court Museum in Downtown Moscow by the End of 2019," *TASS*, 12 October 2017, accessed 17 October 2017, http://tass.com/society/970275.

5 Elena Teslova, "Russia Says Will Buffer Blow to UK Ties of Skripal Case," *Andalon Agency*, 23 March 2018, accessed 23 March 2018, https://aa.com.tr /en/europe/russia-says-will-buffer-blow-to-uk-ties-of-skripal-case/1097421.

6 Sheila Fitzpatrick, *The Cultural Front: Power and Culture in Revolutionary Russia* (Ithaca: Cornell University Press, 1992), 2.

7 For the list of candidates for whom such monuments would be created, see "Spisok lits koim predlozheno postavit' monumenty v g[orode] Moskve i drugikh gorodakh RSFSR" [List of Persons for Whom it is Suggested that Monuments Be Erected in the City of Moscow and Other Cities of the RSFSR], *Iskusstvo* [Art], 2 (1918): 4, cited in Christina Lodder, *Russian Constructivism* (New Haven: Yale University Press, 1983), 53.

8 Thus, the 1918 monument to Shevchenko bore the inscription "Krestianinu-poetu" [To the Peasant Poet]. See Yar Slavutych, "Taras Shevchenko in Literary Criticism," *Proceedings of the Fourth Congress of the International Comparative Literature Association*, Fribourg, 1964, 2 vols, ed. by François Jost (The Hague: Mouton and Co., 1966), I, 317–20 (318).

9 Catherine Wanner, *Burden of Dreams: History and Identity in Post-Soviet Ukraine* (University Park: Pennsylvania State University Press, 1998), 175.

10 The website for the competition is no longer functional, http://www .shakespeare.moscowarch.ru.%20/, and the Archcouncil of Moscow's website no longer includes this project under its current competitions. See, accessed 14 June 2019, https://archsovet.msk.ru/en/competitions.

11 Wanner, *Burden of Dreams*, 173 has described the USSR by the suggestive phrase "Empire of Signs."

12 *The World of Shevchenko*, accessed 4 October 2017, http://shevchenko .inter.ua/.

13 Anna Makolkin, *Name, Hero, Icon: Semiotics of Nationalism through Heroic Biography* (Berlin and New York: Mouton de Gruyter, 1992), 1.

14 For a Soviet view of Shevchenko's admiration for Shakespeare, see F.M. Bilets'kyi, "T.H. Shevchenko pro Vil'iama Shekspira" [T.H. Shevchenko About William Shakespeare], *Inozemna filolohiia* [Foreign Philology], 1.1 (1964): 38–47.

15 Serhy Yekelchyk, "Creating a Sacred Place: The Ukrainophiles and Shevchenko's Tomb in Kaniv (1861–ca. 1900)," *Journal of Ukrainian Studies*, 20.1–2 (1995): 15–33 (20).

16 Severe restrictions on the Ukrainian language and its public usage stemmed from the 1876 Ems Ukase. For details see Roman Solchanyk, "Mykhailo Drahomanov and the Ems Ukase: A Note on the Ukrainian Question at the 1878 International Literary Congress in Paris," *Harvard Ukrainian Studies*, 1.2 (1977): 225–9.

17 Uilleam Blacker, "Martyrdom, Spectacle, and Public Space in Ukraine," *Journal of Soviet and Post-Soviet Politics*, 1.2 (2015): 257–92 (264).

18 They were right to fear this possibility. As Blacker. "Martyrdom," 264 points out, in 1891, "the first Ukrainian organization in the Russian Empire to openly campaign for Ukrainian independence, the Brotherhood of Taras, was founded at the site by a group of students."

19 Lenin, cited in N. Nanaikina, ed., *Shevchenkivs'kyi kalendar shchotyzhnevyk na 1964 rik* [The Shevchenko Weekly Calendar for 1964] (Kyiv: Redaktsiia ukrains'kykh kalendariv, 1964), 24. This calendar of events in the life and afterlife of Shevchenko provides a fascinating source of both historical and (unacknowledged) apocryphal material.

20 Makolkin, 159.

21 On the importance of the positive hero in Soviet culture, see "Current Tasks of the Party's Ideological Work. Report by Comrade L.F. Ilyichev, Secretary of the CPSU Central Committee, 18 June 1963. Plenary Session of the CPSU Central Committee," in the collection of documents *Khrushchev and the Arts: The Politics of Soviet Culture, 1962–1964*, eds. Priscilla Johnson and Leopold Labedz (Cambridge, MA: MIT Press, 1965), 227–36.

22 Dović and Helgason, *National Poets*, 6.

23 Miklós Szenczi, "Shakespeare in Recent Soviet Criticism," *Angol Filológiai Tanulmáyok / Hungarian Studies in English*, 2 (1965): 37–46 (37).

24 On Kurbas's Shakespeare productions, see Irena R. Makaryk, *Shakespeare in the Undiscovered Bourn: Les Kurbas, Ukrainian Modernism, and Early Soviet Cultural Politics* (Toronto: University of Toronto Press, 2004).

25 Cited in Nanaikina, *Shevchenkivs'kyi kalendar*, 8. Unless otherwise stated, all translations from the Russian and Ukrainian are the author's.

26 P. Odarchenko, "The Struggle for Shevchenko: Shevchenko in Soviet Interpretation," *The Annals of the Ukrainian Academic of Arts and Sciences in the USA*, 3.3 (1954): 824–37 (827).

27 I am grateful to Virlana Tkacz, artistic director of the Yara Arts Group, for this information about the Kharkiv monument.

28 See Makaryk, *Shakespeare in the Undiscovered Bourn*, 192–9.

29 Roman Cherkashyn, "My – Berezil'tsi" [We – Berezil Members], *Suchasnist'* [Contemporaneity], 6 (June 1996): 159–87 (163).

30 Anastasia Felcher, "Public Festivities and the Making of a National Poet: A Case Study of Alexander Pushkin's Biography in 1899 and 1937," *European Review of History – Revue européenne d'histoire* 19.5 (October 2012): 767–88 (781). On the Pushkin Jubilee and its significance see Jonathan Brooks Platt, *Greetings, Pushkin! Stalinist Cultural Politics and the National Bard* (Pittsburgh: University of Pittsburgh Press, 2016). On Soviet celebrations see Karen Petrone, *Life Has Become More Joyous, Comrades: Celebrations in the Time of Stalin* (Bloomington: Indiana University Press, 2000).

31 Alexey Bartoshevitch, "The Forest of Arden in Stalin's Russia: Shakespeare's Comedies in the Soviet Theatre of the Thirties," in *Shakespeare in the Worlds of Communism and Socialism*, eds. Irena R. Makaryk and Joseph G. Price (Toronto: University of Toronto Press, 2006), 104–13 (106).

32 See Felcher, "Public Festivities," 781.

33 David McDonald, "Nationhood and Its Discontents: Ukrainian Intellectual History at Empire's End," *Journal of Ukrainian Studies* 23.2 (Winter 1998): 105–16 (112).

34 Rolf Malte, *Soviet Mass Festivals, 1917–1991*, trans. Cynthia Klohr (Pittsburgh: University of Pittsburgh Press, 2006), 59.

35 Serhy Yekelchyk, *Stalin's Empire of Memory: Russian-Ukrainian Relations in the Soviet Historical Imagination* (Toronto: University of Toronto Press, 2004), 4.

36 See Yekelchyk, *Stalin's Empire*, 11.

37 Karen Petrone, *Life Has Become More Joyous, Comrades: Celebrations in the Time of Stalin* (Bloomington: Indiana University Press, 2000), 130.

38 Petrone, *Life Has Become*, 131.

39 Cited in Nanaikina, *Shevchenkivs'kyi kalendar*, 23.

40 Yekelchyk, *Stalin's Empire*, 23–4.

41 Dović and Helgason, *National Poets*, 93.

42 See Dović and Helgason, *National Poets*, 89.

43 Nanaikina, *Shevchenkivs'kyi kalendar*, 3–4.

44 On this point see Bohdan Rubchak, "Introduction," in *Shevchenko and the Critics, 1861–1980*, ed. by George S.N. Luckyj (Toronto: University of Toronto Press, 1980), 3–54.

45 See Blacker, "Martyrdom," 265.

46 Quoted in Régine Robin, *Socialist Realism: An Impossible Aesthetic* (1986), trans. Catherine Porter (Stanford: Stanford University Press, 1992), 61.

47 Dović and Helgason, *National Poets*, 67.

48 Szenczi, "Shakespeare in Recent Soviet Criticism," 38.

49 Cited in Yekelchyk, *Stalin's Empire*, 70.

50 George Gibian, "Shakespeare in Soviet Russia," *Russian Review* 11 (1952): 24–34 (33–4).

51 V. Kemenov, "Shekspir v obiatiiyakh sotsiologa" [Shakespeare in the Embrace of the Sociologist], *Literaturny kritik* [Literary Critic] 1 (1936), 224, cited in Aydin Dzhebrailov, "The King is Dead. Long Live the King! Post-Revolutionary and Stalinist Shakespeare," trans. Cathy Porter, *History Workshop Journal* 32 (Autumn 1991): 1–18 (10).

52 Ann Rigney and Joep Leerssen, "Introduction: Fanning out from Shakespeare," *Commemorating Writers in Nineteenth-Century Europe*, ed. Ann Rigney and Joep Leerssen (Basingstoke: Palgrave Macmillan), 1–23 (10).

53 On the development of Soviet rituals of celebration and remembrance see Rolf Malte, *Soviet Mass Festivals*; Christel Lane, *The Rites of Rulers. Ritual in Industrial Society: The Soviet Case* (Cambridge: Cambridge University Press, 1981); and Thomas Seifrid, *Staging the Absolute: Ritual in Russia's Modern Era* (Toronto: University of Toronto Press, 2023).

54 Mikhail Morozov, "Falsifikatory Shekspira" [Falsifiers of Shakespeare], *Teatr* 1 (January 1949): 53–6.

55 Yekelchyk, *Stalin's Empire*, 108.

56 Cited in Odarchenko, "The Struggle," 834.

57 Dović and Helgason, *National Poets*, 68–9.

58 Kirk Savage, "Between Diaspora and Empire: The Shevchenko Monument in Washington, D.C.," in *Transnational American Memories*, ed. Udo J. Hebel (Berlin and New York: de Gruyter, 2009), 338.

59 On the Cold War and the subsequent "Thaw," see Yale Richmond, *Cultural Exchange and the Cold War: Raising the Iron Curtain* (University Park: Pennsylvania State University Press, 2003).

60 This summary of the new principles that governed Soviet rituals post 1964 comes from Lane, *The Rites of Rulers*, 47.

61 See Irena R. Makaryk, "'Here is My Space': The 1964 Shakespeare Celebrations in the USSR," in *Celebrating Shakespeare in Cold War Europe*, ed. Erica Sheen and Isabel Karremann (London: Palgrave Macmillan, 2016), 51–62.

62 Denis Kozlov, "Introduction," in *The Thaw: Soviet Society and Culture in the 1950s and 1960s*, eds. by Denis Kozlov and Eleonory Gilburd (Toronto: University of Toronto Press, 2013), 3–17 (13).

63 Lane, *The Rites of Rulers*, 229.

64 Alexander Anikst, "Shakespeare – A Writer of the People," in *Shakespeare in the Soviet Union: A Collection of Articles*, ed. Roman Samarin, trans. Avril Pyman (Moscow: Progress, 1966), 113–39 (113).

65 M. Odynets', "Shevchenkovskie dni na Ukraine" [Shevchenko Days in Ukraine], *Pravda*, 8 March 1964: 1.

66 Savage, "Between Diaspora and Empire," 334.

67 Savage, "Between Diaspora and Empire," 334.

68 See Marta Tarnawsky, *Ukrainian Literature in English. An Annotated Bibliography*, accessed 7 October 2017, http://sites.utoronto.ca/elul/English/ULE/.

69 "Slovo o Velikom Kobzare" [About the Great Bard], *Pravda*, 28 May 1964): 4.

70 "Sovietskie liudi chestvuiut Shekspira" [Soviet People Honour Shakespeare], *Pravda*, 24 April 1964; 1, 6. Also see N. Anisimov, "Zhiznieutverzhdaiushchii gumanism" [Life-Affirming Humanism], *Pravda*, 23 April 1964: 4.

71 Cited in Joseph MacLeod, *The New Soviet Theatre* (London: Allen and Unwin, 1943), 41.

72 Odynets', "Shevchenkovskie dni na Ukraine," 4.

73 Yekelchyk, *Stalin's Empire*, 160.

74 Blacker, "Martyrdom," 268.

75 Savage, "Between Diaspora and Empire," 335–6.

76 Yekelchyk, *Stalin's Empire*, 11.

77 Natalia Zinets and Timothy Heritage, "National Hero Shevchenko Fails to Unite Ukrainians and Russians," *Reuters World News*, 9 March 2014, accessed 10 April 2018, https://www.reuters.com/article/us-ukraine-crisis-shevchenko/national-hero-shevchenko-fails-to-unite-ukrainians-and-russians-idUSBREA280UJ20140309.

78 Anna Makolkin, *Name, Hero, Icon: Semiotics of Nationalism Through Heroic Biography* (Berlin and New York: Mouton de Gruyter, 1992), 1.

79 Faustine Vincent and Thomas d'Istria, "The all-out Russification of Ukraine's Occupied Territories," *Le Monde*, 20 January 2024. The authors cite the destruction of Ukrainian identity, forced mobilization and increased repression, among the means Russia is using to assert control and to integrate these regions into Russia. The thousands of child abductions is yet another such act of erasing identity and culture.

80 Ruby Mellen, Zoeann Murphy, Kostiantyn Khudov, and Kasia Strek, "Ukraine's Cultural Counteroffensive: The Rush to Erase Russia's Imprint," *The Washington Post*, 11 May 2023, https://www.washingtonpost.com/world/interactive/2023/ukraine-russian-influence-destruction.

81 See "Should Something Be Done with Pushkin: A Discussion on the Fate of the Monument and Street Name Took Place in Odesa," 2 December 2023, https://mediacenter.org.ua/should-something-be-done-with-pushkin-a-discussion-on-the-fate-of-the-monument-and-street-name-took-place-in-odesa/.

82 Quoted in Mellen, Murphy, Khudov, and Strek, "Should Something Be Done."

83 "No one has done more to de-Russify Ukraine than Putin," claims Cambridge University professor Rory Finnin. The war, argues Finnin, has "pushed many to seek the complete removal of Russian culture and history." Quoted in Mellen, Murphy, Khudov and Strek, "Should Something Be Done."

84 Yuliia Boichenko "A monument to Pushkin will be demolished in the center of Odesa: the order has already been signed," 14:13, 20 September 2024.

11. Antic Dispositions: Shakespeare, War, and Cabaret

1 *Shakespeare Cabaret* was conceived by Lance Mulcahy, who also wrote the music. The production was directed by John Driver and opened at the Bijou Theater, 209 West 45th Street, in New York. See https://www.nytimes .com/1981/01/22/theater/revue-music-of-the-present-in-shakespeare-s -cabaret.html.

2 https://www.bl.uk/events/late-at-the-library-spymonkeys-shakespeare-cabaret.

3 https://www.cambridgeartstheatre.com/show/shakespeare-revue.

4 https://www.chicagoshakes.com/plays_and_events/tonight.

5 https://www.facebook.com/events/987853034692649/.

6 Kenneth Burke, "War, Response, Contradiction," in Kenneth Burke, *The Philosophy of Literary Form* [1941] (Baton Rouge: LA Louisiana State University Press, 1967), 234–57.

7 Burke, "War, Response, Contradiction," 239.

8 Burke, "War, Response, Contradiction," 239–40.

9 Lisa Appignanesi, *The Cabaret* (New Haven, CT: Yale University Press, 1984), 6.

10 The German term is "Kleinkunst"; the Russian, "Theatre of Miniatures"; the Ukrainian, "Theatre of Small Forms."

11 Harold B. Segel, *Turn-of-the-Century Cabaret: Paris, Barcelona, Berlin, Munich, Vienna, Cracow, Moscow, St. Petersburg, Zurich* (New York: Columbia University Press, 1987); Laurence Senelick, ed., *Cabaret Performance*, Volume 1: *Europe 1890–1920. Songs, Sketches, Monologues, Memoirs* (New York: PAJ Publications, 1989); Laurence Senelick, ed., *Cabaret Performance*, Volume 2: *Europe 1920–1940* (Baltimore, Maryland: Johns Hopkins, 1993).

12 Senelick, *Cabaret* 1, 9.

13 Senelick, *Cabaret* 2, xiii.

14 Appignanesi, *The Cabaret*, 40.

15 Appignanesi, *The Cabaret*, 205. Great Britain generally remained immune to the attractions of avant-garde cabaret, particularly of the more "acid" variety. Appignanesi speculates that presence of more democratic institutions in the UK tended to diffuse the sharpest of political satire (208).

16 Appignanesi, *The Cabaret*, 2.

17 On this and other Shakespeare productions in early Soviet Ukraine, including *Romeo and Juliet, Othello,* and *A Midsummer Night's Dream,* see Irena R. Makaryk, *Shakespeare in the Undiscovered Bourn: Les Kurbas, Ukrainian Modernism, and Early Soviet Cultural Politics* (Toronto: University of Toronto Press, 2004).

18 Or, rather, re-founded. It had a brief, earlier, life as *Nachtlicht* ("Nightlight," founded in 1906).

19 Appignanesi, *The Cabaret*, 52.

20 Peter Altenberg, *Bilderbögen des kleinen Lebens* (Berlin: S. Fischer, 1908). Quoted in Segel, *Turn-of-the-Century,* 198.

21 On the ferment in Kyiv's theatre scene, see Hanna Veselovska, "Kyiv's Multicultural Theatrical Life, 1917–1926," in *Modernism in Kyiv: Jubilant Experimentation*, eds. Irena R. Makaryk and Virlana Tkacz (Toronto: University of Toronto Press, 2010), 243–74. Also see Mayhill Fowler's delightful and fascinating book, *Beau Monde on Empire's Edge: State and Stage in Soviet Ukraine* (Toronto: University of Toronto Press, 2017) that examines the intertwining of politics and culture, as well as the captivating personalities of multi-ethnic Ukraine in the early Soviet period.

22 The Berezil', which takes it name for the archaic Ukrainian name for the month of March (i.e., spring, renewal, revolution, energy), was founded in 1922.

23 On the Production of *Macbeth* by the Fourth Studio of the Berezil Artistic Association, see "Do postanovky *Makbeta* v maisterni M.O.B.," *Bil'shovyk* (Kyiv) 3 (971) (1 April 1924), 6 – an unsigned article, probably written by Stepan Bondarchuk.

24 See chapter 2, "Tilting at da Vinci: Kurbas's 1924 *Macbeth*," in Makaryk, *Shakespeare in the Undiscovered Bourn*, 65–112.

25 The significance of this production was reiterated again and again by critics, actors, and scholars of the time. See for example, I[akiv] S[avchenko], "Shekspir dybom" [Shakespeare Upside-down], *Bil'shovyk* (Kyiv) 76 (974) (4 April 1924): 6, who predicted that many separate scholarly studies would, and should, be written about each scene of this production.

26 Valentyna Zabolotna, *Aktors'ke mystetstvo Ukraïny* [The Actor's Art in Ukraine] (1922–1927) (Kyiv: Institut teatral'noho mystetstva im. K. Karoho, 1992), 53. Zabolotna was Buchma's granddaughter.

27 Kurbas to his directorial lab cited in "Do postanovky *Makbeta* v maisterni M.O.B."

28 Vasyl' Vasyl'ko, "Shchodennyk" [Diary], 3 April 1924, 124. Vasyl'ko's unpublished diary is an invaluable source for a study of theatre of this period and particularly of the work of Kurbas. Vasyl' Vasyl'ko papers, Ukrainian State Museum of Theatre, Music, and Cinema Arts (Kyiv), inv. 10369.

29 Simon Barker, *War and Nation in the Theatre of Shakespeare and His Contemporaries* (Edinburgh University Press, 2007), 28.

30 See Makaryk and Tkacz, *Modernism in Kyiv* on the vast range of experiments in various disciplines, including graphic design, dance, poetry, theatre, visual art, and music.

31 Working through the KGB archives, the St. Petersburg "Memorial" group discovered that daily executions took place in the far north of Russia, not far from the White and Baltic seas, from 27 October to 4 November 1937. In 1997, the mass graves off 1,100 men and women of various nationalities were uncovered. On the list of those shot at close range was Les' Kurbas. See Iulii Shelest and Volodymyr Shcherbyna, "S'iomoho lystopada – den'

pam'iati zhertv komunistychnoho totalitaryzmu," *Vechirnii Kyïv* (Kyiv) 4
Nov 1997: 3; and Larysa Krushel'nyts'ka, "Sandormokh," *Svoboda* (New
Jersey) 30 Jan 1998: 3, 6. I am grateful to Gennady Estraikh for sending me
information about Mikhail Rodionovich Matveev, the man who, "achieving
the impossible," efficiently carried out these executions over a short period
of only five days. Matveev survived to live a long life, finally dying in the
"late Brezhnev" years. Aleksandr Cherkasov, "Zapredel. Preuspevshii v
nevozmozhnom" [Beyond Succeeding in the Impossible], *Vechernii N'iu Iork*
(New York) 9–15 November 2007, 40.

32 Maria Sonevytsky, "The Freak Cabaret on the Revolution Stage: On the
Ambivalent Politics of Femininity, Rurality, and Nationalism in Ukrainian
Popular Music," *Journal of Popular Music Studies*, vol. 28, issue 3 (September
2016): 291–314 (294). DOI: 10.1111/jpms.12174.

33 Sonevytsky, "The Freak Cabaret," 307n3.

34 A. Debritto, *Charles Bukowski, King of the Underground: From Obscurity to
Literary Icon* (Palgrave Macmillan, 2013), 6. DOI: 10.1057/9781137343550.

35 See the Dakh website at https://dakhdaughters.com A flavour of the ritualistic,
trance-like atmosphere created by the Dakh style is well described in Lyn
Gardner's review in *The Guardian* (3 February 2007) of *Prolog Macbeth*: "more
like hallucination than theatre." http://dax.com.ua/en/press/article3040.

36 http://www/go2kiev.com/view/dakh.html. To date, the Dakh Daughters
have performed in the Netherlands, Switzerland, Portugal, Slovakia,
Germany, Norway, Austria, Estonia, Belgium, Poland, France, Russia, Brazil,
and throughout Ukraine.

37 http://www.go2kiev.com/view/dakh.html.

38 https://www.youtube.com/watch?v=6wCgZh-nczY.

39 Sonevytsky, "The Freak Cabaret," 291.

40 Sonevytsky, "The Freak Cabaret," 292.

41 See "The Story of How Dakh Daughters Wrote Rozy/Donbass, Their Most
Famous Song that Became Prophetic," https://slukh.media/en/texts/rozy
-donbass-story/.

42 See https://www.unesco.org/en/articles/damaged-cultural-sites-ukraine
-verified-unesco?hub=66116. The statistics cited are from those provided on
this website on December 5, 2023.

43 Timofei Sergeitsev, "Chto Rossia dolzhna sdielat' s Ukrainoi" [What
Russia Should do With Ukraine] *RIA Novosti*, 3 April 2022, https://ria
.ru/20220403/ukraina-1781469605.html.

44 Le Bec, Marie. « Choix de la rédaction les dakh daughters, » www.
lintermede.com. Retrieved 2024-01-09. The full quotation is as follows: "Ces
poèmes ou récits chantés, scandés, rappés, interrogent toujours la lutte
universelle et intemporelle de l'Homme pour la défense de sa liberté et de
ses appartenances. Ainsi, les Dakh Daughters parviennent à élaborer une

poésie de la colère au rythme des tambours de guerre, des sanglots des violons et de l'espérance forcenée de « l'Ukraine en feu. »"

45 The twenty-minute film may be found here: https://www.voicesofukraine.net/work/hooligan-in-the-field.

46 See their website https://www.hooliganart.org/.

47 Dominic Cavendish, "Bunker Cabaret – Ukrainian theatre from the civilian frontline," 12 February 2023, https://www.criticalmuse.com/stage/bunker-cabaret-ukrainian-theatre-from-the-civilian-frontline/.

48 https://courtauld.ac.uk/whats-on/in-conversation-hooligan-art-community/.

49 Numerous excerpts from their performances, as well as interviews with the Dakh Daughter are found on YouTube. See, for example, https://www.youtube.com/watch?v=hJ5L5DKpKsU and https://www.youtube.com/watch?v=Oq1AvZkEj7M.

12. Afterword: Shakespeare at War Today

1 Charlotte Higgins, "Art Shows the Surreal Reality of Wartime Ukraine in a Way the News Never Could," *The Guardian*, 25 February 2024, https://www.theguardian.com/commentisfree/2024/feb/25/art-reality-wartime-ukraine-poem-war.

2 See Hanna Vesselovska, "Living in the War: The Ukrainian Theatre Since the Russian Invasion," *Critical Stages / Scènes critiques*, Focus: Ukraine, December 2022: Issue No 26, https://www.critical-stages.org/26/living-in-the-war-the-ukrainian-theatre-since-the-russian-invasion/.

3 Nataliya Torkut and Yurii Cherniak, "Ukrainian Hamlet and 'Hamletizing' Ukraine: 'Will You Play Upon This Pipe?'" *Renesantsnii studii* [Renaissance Studies (Zaporizhzhia, 2014)], vol. 22, 98–115.

4 http://www.dramteatr.if.ua/en/about-en/.

5 The ninety-minute film and the trailer may be found here: https://takflix.com/en/films/kinglear.

6 Rostyslav Derzhypils'kyi, 7 March 2024, https://www.facebook.com/dramteatr.if/videos/287142330916043/.

7 Maiia Harbuziuk, "Theatre as a Humanitarian Mission: Ukraine`s Experience 2022," *Critical Stages / Scènes critiques*, Focus: Ukraine. June 2022. Issue no. 25, https://www.critical-stages.org/25/theatre-as-a-%ce%b7umanitarian-mission-ukraines-experience-2022/.

8 Dominic Cavendish, "Alex Borovenskiy of ProEnglish Theatre of Ukraine, in conversation," 10 March 2023, https://www.criticalmuse.com/stage/alex-borovenskiy-of-proenglish-theatre-of-ukraine-in-conversation/.

9 Mike Devlin, "Langham Court Enters Scary Season with a Whodunit," *Times Colonist – Victoria, BC*, https://www.timescolonist.com/entertainment/langham-court-enters-scary-season-with-a-whodunit-9572950

10 Kevin Fleming, "'This is the Way I Heal My Soul': Ukrainian Theatre Troupe Express Selves Through Arts," Calgary CTV News, 8 August 2024, https://calgary.ctvnews.ca/this-is-the-way-i-heal-my-soul-ukrainian-theatre-troupe -express-selves-through-arts-1.6993789.

11 Sofiia Onyshchenko, Daria Bohdan, and Vasylyna Martseniuk, "Історія України / Historia Ukrainy / History of Ukraine" [In Conversation About Their Play], *Critical Stages*, June 2022, issue 25.

12 Dominic Cavendish, "Alex Borovenskiy of ProEnglish Theatre of Ukraine, in Conversation," 10 March 2023, https://www.criticalmuse.com/stage /alex-borovenskiy-of-proenglish-theatre-of-ukraine-in-conversation/.

13 Juan David Latorre, "Concert 'Heart to heart' offered by the Ukrainian Embassy," *The Diplomat*, 2 October 2024, https://thediplomatinspain.com /en/2024/10/02/concert-heart-to-heart-offered-by-the-ukrainian-embassy/

14 Nataliya Torkut, "Shakespeare in Ukraine," University of Birmingham, 17 August 2022, YouTube video, 52:13, https://www.youtube.com/watch?v= RWwfndo2GUg.

15 Quoted in "'Shakespeare can help us survive war': Ukrainian academic toasts bard in UK visit," *The Guardian*. 22 April 2024, https://www.theguardian .com/world/2023/apr/22/shakespeare-can-help-us-survive-war-ukrainian -academic-toasts-bard-in-uk-visit.

Index